NURSE'S
LEGAL
HANDBOOK

Springhouse Corporation
Springhouse, Pennsylvania

Developmental Editor   Regina Daley Ford
Clinical Editor   Lenora Haston, RN, MSN
Designer   Carol Cameron-Sears
Copy Supervisor   David Moreau
Director, Typography/Editorial Computer Services   David C. Kosten
Production Manager/Books   Wilbur D. Davidson

The procedures described and recommended in this publication are based on research and consultation with legal and nursing authorities. To the best of our knowledge, these procedures reflect currently accepted practice; nevertheless, they can't be considered absolute and universal recommendations, nor can they be considered legal advice. For individual application, all recommendations must be considered in light of the unique circumstances of each legal or administrative situation. The authors and the publisher disclaim responsibility for any adverse consequences due to directly or indirectly following the suggested procedures without first seeking legal advice; for any undetected errors; or for the reader's misunderstanding of the text.

Adapted from *Practices* (Nurse's Reference Library®), Copyright 1984 by Springhouse Corporation.

Library of Congress Cataloging in Publication Data
Main entry under title:

Nurse's legal handbook.
   "Adapted from Practices (Nurse's reference library),
Copyright 1984 by Springhouse Corporation"—T.p. verso.
   Includes bibliographies and indexes.
   1. Nursing—Practice.   2. Nursing ethics.
3. Nursing—Law and legislation.   I. Springhouse
Corporation.   II. Practices.   [DNLM: 1. Ethics,
Nursing.   2. Legislation, Nursing—United States.
3. Malpractice—United States—legislation.
4. Malpractice—United States—nurses' instruction.
WY 33 AA1 N7]
RT86.7.N88   1985   344.73'0414   85-12702
ISBN 0-916730-93-X   347.304414

Table of Contents

Contributors *(continued)*

Belva Chang McDavid, RN, BSN, MN, JD, Freelance Lecturer, Consultant, Wakarusa, Kan.; Staff Nurse, Veterans Administration Medical Center, Topeka, Kan.

Martha Jean Minniti, RN, BS, CCRN, President, Skilled Nursing, Inc., Springhouse, Pa.

Anne Moraca-Sawicki, RN, MSN, CNS, Clinical Nurse Specialist, Mount St. Mary's Hospital, Lewiston, N.Y.

Ellen K. Murphy, RN, MS, CNOR, JD, Assistant Professor, University of Wisconsin, Milwaukee

Lois M. Murphy, RN, MS, Nurse Consultant, Lois M. Murphy Associates, Hudson, N.H.

Claire C. Obade, RN, BA, JD, Attorney, Saul, Ewing, Remick, and Saul, Philadelphia

Deborah M. Peyton, RN, BSN, JD Law Clerk, Eugene Edgett Law Offices, Baltimore

Elizabeth Price, RN, MS, JD, Attorney Advisor, Department of Health and Human Services, Office of the General Counsel, Washington, D.C.

Jean Rabinow, BA, JD, Attorney, McMillan & Still, Trumball, Conn.

Peggy J. Reiley, RN, MS, Head Nurse, Beth Israel Hospital, Boston

Erline A. Reilly, RN, BA, JD, Attorney, Concord, N.H.

Paula Laros Rich, RN, MSN, Nurse Consultant, Professional Nursing Development, Philadelphia

Mary Margaret Rock, RN, BSN, Utilization Review Coordinator, Creighton Physicians, Inc., Omaha

Linda Faith Rosen, RN, MA, JD, Attorney, M. Mark Mendel, Ltd., Philadelphia

Thomas E. Rubbert, BSL, LLB, JD, Attorney-at-Law, Pasadena, Calif.

Harold H. Simpson II, JD, Attorney, Gill, Skokas, Simpson, Buford, & Graham, P.A., Little Rock, Ark.

Carol E. Smith, RN, PhD, Associate Professor, Graduate School of Nursing, Health Sciences Center, University of Kansas, Kansas City

Maryann R. Sparks, RN, MEd, Auditor Specialist, Republic Service Bureau, Inc., Naperville, Ill.

Virgie M. Vakil, RN, BA, JD, Attorney, Media, Pa.

Amy C. Vasquez, BA, Director of Communications, Skilled Nursing, Inc., Springhouse, Pa.

Barbara J. Virnig, RN, CHN, MSN, Community Health Nurse, Olmsted County Health Department, Rochester, Minn.

Janice W. Wise, BS, MA, JD, Assistant Director, Economic and General Welfare Program, Ohio Nurses Association, Columbus

Lynn M. Worley, RN, JD, Assistant State's Attorney, Health Division. Cook County State's Attorney's Office, Chicago

Barbara J. Youngberg, RN, BSN, MICN, MSW, JD, Medical Legal Consultant, Surgical Resource Team Member, Children's Memorial Hospital, Chicago

Clinical and Legal Consultants

Glenn M. Barnes, BSc, MHA, LLB, Barrister and Solicitor, Ottawa

Judith Renzi Brown, RN, JD, Vice President and Director of Risk Management and Loss Prevention, Assistant Counsel for Claims, Pennsylvania Medical Society Liability Insurance Company, Lemoyne, Pa.

Jeanne M. Dunn, RN, BSN, JD, Attorney, Balsama & Dunn, Media, Pa.

Claire C. Obade, RN, BA, JD, Attorney, Saul, Ewing, Remick, and Saul, Philadelphia

Jean Rabinow, BA, JD, Attorney, McMillan & Still, Trumball, Conn.

Linda Faith Rosen, RN, MA, JD, Attorney, M. Mark Mendel, Ltd., Philadelphia

Foreword

As nurses, we work long and hard to achieve greater respect for our education and for our skill as health-care providers. We can be proud of our expanded roles in all aspects of health care and of the increasingly complex and important functions we fulfill. However, the ever-broadening scope of nursing practice, which makes contemporary nursing so exciting and rewarding, has also complicated our work. Yes, nursing has emerged as a challenging profession requiring a high level of education, knowledge, skill, and decision-making capabilities. Nurses have a lot more responsibility today. But with increased clinical responsibility comes increased risk of liability. You owe it to yourself and your patients to keep abreast of changes in the laws and regulations that define your professional responsibilities. You also need to come to terms with the difficult ethical and professional dilemmas that modern society and science have created for the health team. These issues create a paradoxical situation for you: they require a lot of thought before you can be sure of your feelings about them, but often they arise in patient-care circumstances where you're required to act quickly as well as conscientiously.

Keeping up with development and application of new nursing interventions isn't enough to help you chart the career path that's best suited to your skills and values. Nor can the clinical skills you apply in your everyday work help you when you're not sure how to proceed legally, or when you feel your ethics are being compromised. THE NURSE'S LEGAL HANDBOOK has been published to give you this kind of help. Its contributors have sorted through our complicated legal system, tuned in to our lengthy and ongoing ethical debates, and selected those portions relevant to you as a nurse. They've organized this information into succinct and comprehensive chapters that present the information in a readily understandable and accessible form.

Chapters 1 through 6 of THE NURSE'S LEGAL HANDBOOK deal with the interaction between nursing and the law. Because your nursing responsibilities are expanding so rapidly, the laws defining them can't always keep up. This means you must be thoroughly familiar with the legal boundaries of nursing practice in your state, so you know when you're on solid legal ground and when you should get legal or administrative advice before proceeding. These chapters describe your legal risks and responsibilities in traditional and alternative practice settings, on and off duty. You'll find in-depth coverage of documenting and of strategies for preventing malpractice charges—even for coping with a lawsuit. You'll also find a full chapter on patients' legal rights in the hospital—a topic of great interest to nurses, who do so much to safeguard patients' rights.

Chapter 7 deals with *your* rights and options as a health-care employee. Here you'll discover vital information on employment contracts, collective bargaining, and grievance procedures. Chapter 8 deals with a topic that's vitally involved in job satisfaction but that generally isn't discussed in relation to it—the burgeoning area of health-care ethics. Besides outlining your legal responsibilities, the entries on this topic will help you clarify your own ethical stance concerning abortion, transplants, life support for brain-dead patients, no-code and slow-code orders, and occasions when you're asked to cover up a colleague's errors or incompetence.

Each chapter begins with a clear and concise introduction. Every effort has been made to relate "the law" directly to your circumstances. Here you'll find no abstract theories or vague generalizations. Instead, you'll find illustrative court cases, boxed questions and answers about legal problems, charts that describe state-by-state variations in nursing law, and many other features that make understanding nursing law easy for you.

But THE NURSE'S LEGAL HANDBOOK doesn't stop here. Following its 8 chapters, you'll find a detailed and most interesting section containing charts, lists, and other information to supplement what you've learned in THE NURSE'S LEGAL HANDBOOK's pages. You'll consult this section often for help in managing legal and professional problems on the job.

Both in content and format, THE NURSE'S LEGAL HANDBOOK is a clearly written and exhaustively detailed reference that will quickly become indispensable. This handbook is a must if you're a nurse who wants to protect her career to the fullest extent. THE NURSE'S LEGAL HANDBOOK can help you achieve true satisfaction on the job—the satisfaction of knowing that, within the limits of the law, you're reaping the full potential of your capabilities and your ambitions.

BEATRICE J. KALISCH, RN, EdD, FAAN

Overview

What is "the law"?

Basically, laws help us define our personal and professional relationships. Laws tell us what we may and may not do, alone and to and with each other. But "the law" isn't as clear-cut as this definition is. It isn't a static body of knowledge, something you can learn once that's valid forever. The law has movement and momentum; it can expand or contract. Parts of it can even die off—like the laws that prevented women from inheriting property and the laws that sanctioned slavery.

Nursing law is changing, too, as our profession matures toward the goals of increased autonomy and independent responsibility for patient care. Nursing law doesn't exist as a separate entity, apart from the general laws, rules, and regulations that society uses to govern itself. Instead, the term *nursing law* describes specific areas of federal and state constitutional, civil, criminal, and administrative law. These areas of law directly influence the professional relationships so essential to nursing practice.

Both you and your patient benefit when you practice your profession within appropriate legal limits. Your patient benefits because your care protects him from unnecessary harm. You benefit by protecting yourself from lawsuits, from damage to your professional reputation, and from possible financial hardship if you must pay damages to a patient who wins his case against you.

So nursing law isn't, as some nurses believe, an array of narrow, confusing ultimatums designed to contain and constrain the nursing profession. Instead, the effect of the law on nursing is like the many veins that run through a leaf: it provides definition, strength, and integrity.

To understand nurses' legal relationships, you need to understand the various types of laws that create rights and responsibilities for nurses.

Public law determines your relationship to the federal government and the states. It consists of constitutional law, administrative law, and criminal law. *Private law* (also called civil law) determines your relationship to other individuals. It consists of contract law and tort law.

Constitutional law is the type of public law that considers your rights and responsibilities under the federal and state constitutions, as the U.S. and state supreme courts interpret them. Patients' right to life, right to die, and right to self-determination in refusing treatment, and your rights to life, liberty, and religious freedom, are all founded in constitutional law. This is an area of intimate issues, where law and ethics are closely intertwined.

Administrative law is the type of public law that concerns the administrative agencies, boards, and commissions legislated by Congress or the state legislatures. For nurses, the most important administrative agency is the state board of nursing, created under the provisions of each state's nurse practice act. This agency has the power to regulate nursing practice and nursing education, and it's the supreme authority on nursing practice issues in the state. No other agency may legally institute a nursing policy that contradicts a state board of nursing ruling. However, if a nurse is censured in a board action, she may appeal the board's decision to a state court.

Criminal law is public law concerning each state's criminal statutes, which define criminal actions such as murder, manslaughter, criminal negligence, theft, and illegal possession of drugs. Nurses risk violating criminal laws when they become involved in such actions as removing life-support systems, carrying out no-code orders, administering high doses of pain-killing medication to terminally ill patients, or failing to nourish or medicate deformed newborns and in obviously criminal acts such as stealing medications or narcotics. Nurses also may be involved in criminal court proceedings as witnesses, if they care for victims of rape, shootings, and other violent crimes.

Contract law is private law involving agreements (contracts) between two or more parties to do something, for some type of remuneration—a "bargained-for exchange." In essence, a contract is a promissory agreement between two or more persons that creates, modifies, or destroys a legal relationship. In many situations, an oral agreement is also legally binding. Many nurses have individual oral or written contracts detailing their work schedules and job descriptions, as well as the personnel policies they're expected to follow. Similar contracts exist for unionized nurses, private-duty nurses, and others. If it can be said that job satisfaction begins with a clear understanding of your rights and responsibilities and those of your employer, then a written contract is an effective starting point on the road to that goal.

Tort law is private law concerning reparation of a wrong or injury inflicted by one person on another. This is the area of law that nurses are most familiar with. Why? Because it specifically addresses the nurse-patient relationship. Tort law is particularly concerned with the way you practice your profession and with your ability to prove that your care meets the required legal standard. Common causes of tort law action include malpractice, assault and battery, invasion of privacy, false imprisonment, and defamation.

The area of professional malpractice is very broad, encompassing any professional misconduct including negligence, betrayal of patients' trust and confidence, and other illegal or immoral actions. Of these, negligence is the most common charge against nurses. A charge of negligence against a nurse focuses on the standard of care: the patient attempts to prove that a certain standard was required in his care, that the defendant-nurse breached that standard, and that harm directly resulted. The defendant-nurse, of course, must attempt to disprove these charges. In this critical situation, the nursing process, properly documented, is every nurse's best defense.

No one has to tell you that the practice of nursing has become increasingly complex—and that nurses' risk of liability has increased proportionately. To make sure your care consistently meets appropriate legal and professional standards, you need sound knowledge of the relationship between the law and nursing practice. THE NURSE'S LEGAL HANDBOOK can answer your questions and help you provide high-quality care at minimal legal risk. With the information THE NURSE'S LEGAL HANDBOOK provides, you'll also be better prepared to identify and promote legal reforms for advancing our profession—and, by extension, your own career as a nurse.

CARMELL P. COURNOYER, RN, MA, JD

1

Legal Aspects of Nursing Practice

As a nurse, you need a thorough understanding of nursing's relationships to the law. You know that law is the body of rules and regulations that govern all of society—protecting the health, safety, and welfare of its citizens. And, of course, you also know that any departure from the law spells trouble.

The federal government and the states hold constitutional authority to enact laws. As you might expect, this means the health-care field abounds with federal and state legislation that directly shapes and influences the practice of nursing. But the laws aren't rigid and unyielding. Instead, they're dynamic, responsive—like the nursing profession they serve. As nursing changes, laws change, too. The laws must have this flexibility so that nurses can care for patients in a variety of clinical situations, while still remaining within the legal scope of nursing practice.

Why should you concern yourself with the law? Because you've worked hard to earn entry into the nursing profession. You've spent time, effort, and money to graduate from an accredited school of nursing. And you've demonstrated your nursing knowledge and skill by successfully completing your state board examination or (after 1981) the National Council Licensure Examination (NCLEX). Your nursing license was the beginning of a lifelong commitment to a challenging and rewarding career. Now, like other professionals, you want opportunities for personal advancement, increased economic benefits, and a guarantee that your profession will have the means to keep pace with the latest technologic advancements. These are worthy goals for the nursing profession. But they can only be realized if you're willing to accept the professional and legal responsibilities involved. And remember, ignorance of the law isn't a valid defense in any type of legal proceeding. As a nurse, you're expected to know and understand the laws that directly and indirectly affect your practice. Chapter 1 explores these and other timely issues. Each entry will provide you with accurate, comprehensive legal information that you need every day as you care for patients.

A history of nursing law
By the early 1900s, nursing practice had developed and matured to the point where laws and regulations became necessary to establish minimum standards for entry into the profession. (See *Landmarks in Nursing Law,* page 2.)

The first such laws were nurse registration acts. These acts were *permissive,* meaning that anyone could practice nursing but only those registered could use the initials "RN." The first nurse registration act was made law in North Carolina in March 1903. It stated that anyone who paid a fee to be listed in the state register could practice nursing. (Unregistered persons could still practice nursing, whether or not they'd completed nursing training.) By 1923, every state had some type of nurse registration law. In 1938, New York State passed the first *mandatory* nurse practice act, a law that established two levels of nursing: licensed registered

Landmarks in Nursing Law

1901: First state nurses' associations organize to work toward state laws to control nursing practice

1903: North Carolina passes the first permissive nurse practice act; New York, New Jersey, and Virginia soon follow

1938: New York passes the first mandatory nurse practice act

1952: All states, the District of Columbia, and all territories have enacted nurse practice acts

1953: American Nurses' Association (ANA) adopts a statement on principles of legislation relating to nursing practice

1955: ANA approves a definition of the practice of nursing to serve as a guide for nurses and for licensing legislation

1970: ANA amends its definition of practice to eliminate the prohibition on nursing diagnosis

1973: ANA publishes standards of nursing practice

1979: ANA further amends its definition of practice to reflect nursing's broadening scope

nurse and licensed practical nurse. This practice act mandated that *only* professionals licensed under the act could practice nursing. Other states followed with similar laws. By 1952, all the states, the District of Columbia, and all U.S. territories had enacted nurse practice acts.

Since those early years of legislative activity, numerous significant changes have occurred, including changes in the definition of nursing practice and (recently, in a few states) recognition of the nurse's modern role, which allows nurses to make nursing diagnoses. In 1970, the American Nurses' Association (ANA) amended the wording of its 1955 model definition of nursing to eliminate the prohibition on nursing diagnosis. By 1977, 24 states had enacted new or additional amendments to their nurse practice acts, generally eliminating the prohibition on nursing diagnosis. Some states also legally recognized the nurse's expanded role. In 1979, the ANA further amended its definition of nursing to encompass the broad scope of nursing in today's practice settings. To date, only New York and California have enacted adaptations of the 1979 ANA definition into law.

Other areas of nursing concern, however, have received only selective legislative attention or verbal support. Two such areas are standards of patient care and standards of nursing practice.

Standards of patient care

The purpose of all health law and regulation is to protect the public from the uninformed, the unprepared, and the unscrupulous health-care practitioner. However, some consumers and legislators—and even some health-care professionals—argue that only minimal regulation is necessary to safeguard health-care consumers. In these persons' view, the proliferation of health-care providers and subsequent regulation is a costly impediment to optimum delivery of health-care services.

The law has responded to such arguments in a limited way—for example, by establishing standards of care for patients in government-sponsored health-care programs. Medicare and Medicaid regulations, which cover elderly (and some disabled) patients in hospitals and nursing homes, specify which conditions can be treated and, in some instances, minimum treatment requirements. Patients' rights legislation protects the rights of all patients, including those in nursing homes and mental hospitals. And so-called right-to-die legislation recognizes health-care professionals' ethical as well as professional responsibilities when using life-

JCAH Accreditation

The public wants to know that the health-care institutions that treat them have high professional standards. That's where the Joint Commission on Accreditation of Hospitals (JCAH) comes in. It sets voluntary standards of operation for hospitals and other health-care institutions and accredits those which meet JCAH standards. The JCAH grants accreditation for 3 years, requiring the health-care institution to conduct its own survey, 18 months after it receives accreditation, and to report the results to the JCAH. The American College of Physicians, the American College of Surgeons, and the American Hospital Association sponsor the JCAH. Representatives from each of these organizations make up the JCAH board of commissioners.

To receive JCAH accreditation, a hospital must:
• maintain a safe, clean facility and exercise continuous infection control
• publish rules and regulations for the medical staff
• publish the procedure doctors can follow to apply for medical staff memberships
• form medical staff committees to review the quality of medical care given by its members.

The JCAH recommends (but doesn't require for accreditation) that health-care institutions do the following to maintain high-quality care:
• maintain a governing body that's responsible for all hospital functions, headed by a chief executive responsible for hospital administration
• maintain a staff of doctors
• provide supervision for nursing staff and other nursing services
• maintain a pharmacy that's staffed by a registered pharmacist
• provide diagnostic X-ray services for patients
• provide clinical laboratory services
• maintain a room suitable for surgery.

sustaining technology. These laws preserve the patient's right to choose the direction of his care in life-or-death situations.

In some states, standards for care of hospital patients have been incorporated into state law by a process that accepts or adapts the accreditation of the Joint Commission on Accreditation of Hospitals. (See *JCAH Accreditation.*) This incorporation into law has resulted in broadly applicable standards of patient care. These standards are increasingly used in preference to local standards when courts seek to determine applicable standards of care and admit expert-witness testimony in malpractice lawsuits. National patient-care standards will help develop uniform expectations of nursing care and eliminate regional differences in evaluating that care.

Nursing practice standards

Nursing practice standards are established by state boards of nursing. Some states refer to standards in their nurse practice acts. Unless they're specifically cited in nurse practice acts, professional standards aren't laws—they're guidelines for sound nursing practice. Until 1971, individual hospitals determined nursing practice standards according to local standards. But in 1973 the ANA published its nursing standards, which have since gained widespread acceptance.

Nursing standards may or may not be in written form. Nevertheless, courts decide nursing malpractice lawsuits largely on whether defendant-nurses meet applicable standards of nursing care. So, although they aren't laws themselves, standards have important legal significance for nurses.

RN and LPN/LVN practice: Legal differences

As you know, two levels of nursing practice currently exist—the registered nurse (RN) and the licensed practical/vocational nurse (LPN/LVN). RNs complete a longer and more intensive educational program for entry into practice than LPNs/LVNs do. Once licensed, the RN is responsible for developing and managing patient care. She must also make professional nursing judgments based on the nursing process—including patient assessment, nursing diagnosis, intervention, and evaluation.

Definitions of the RN's role vary somewhat among states, but her basic responsibilities include observing patients' signs and symptoms, recording her observations, carrying out doctors' orders for patient treatments, and appropriately delegating responsibilities for patient care.

The LPN/LVN is often referred to as the "bedside nurse" because her role has traditionally centered on the patient's basic physical needs for hygiene and comfort. Many state nurse practice acts define LPN/LVN practice as the performance of duties that assist the professional nurse in a team relationship. In some states, the duties of LPNs/LVNs are more clearly defined in terms of scope of practice. For example, Washington State's nurse practice act prohibits LPNs/LVNs from administering medications and injections.

Nursing practice in Canada

Canada permits licensure of registered nurses, registered nursing assistants, and—in some provinces—practical or vocational nurses. In recent years, some Canadian nursing associations have recognized clinical nurse specialists (who generally have master's or doctoral degrees in specific specialties).

In most of Canada's 10 provinces, professional nurses' associations set requirements for graduation from an approved school of nursing, for licensing, for nurses' professional behavior, and for registration fees.

The Canadian registered nurse may receive her education in a diploma school (such as a hospital school of nursing), in a community college, or in a bachelor's program. The licensing examination she must take varies by province—some use NCLEX and some compile their own (thus complicating U.S.-Canadian nurse licensure reciprocity). Requirements for becoming a registered nursing assistant usually consist of a 10-month program and, in some provinces, a licensure examination.

What's ahead for nursing?

Surveys predict many challenges for the nursing profession in the 1990s, such as deciding on requirements for entry-level education, establishing greater responsibilities for clinical nurse specialists, resolving conflicts between nursing and medicine, improving the nurse's status as an independent health-care provider, securing increased economic advantages for nurses, and retaining control of the profession. These challenges may seem diverse at first glance, but they're united by their relationship with the law and its effect on nursing practice.

Basic elements of nurse practice acts

Every nurse practice act is designed to protect the public by broadly defining the legal scope of nursing practice. Every nurse can thus be expected to care for patients within *defined practice limits;* if she gives care beyond those limits, she becomes vulnerable to charges of violating her state nurse practice act. Of course, nurse practice acts also serve to exclude untrained or unlicensed persons from practicing nursing.

Your state nurse practice act is the most important law affecting your nursing practice. (See *State Nurse Practice Acts: Qualifications for Licensure,* pages 6 to 11.) In every state and Canadian province, the nurse practice act creates a state or provincial board of nursing, authorized to formulate and enforce rules and regulations concerning the nursing profession. The board of nursing is bound by the provisions of the nurse practice act that created it. The nurse practice act is the *law;* the board of nursing can't grant exemptions to it or waive any of its provisions. Only the state or provincial legislature can change the law. For example, if the nurse practice act specifies that, to be licensed, a nurse must have graduated from an approved school of nursing, then the board of nursing must deny a license to anyone who hasn't. This holds true even for applicants who can provide evidence of equivalency and competence (*Richardson v. Brunelle,* 1979).

In many states and provinces, the board of nursing may grant exemptions and waivers to the rules and regulations it has formulated. For example, if a regulation says that all nursing faculty must have master's degrees, the board may waive this requirement temporarily for a faculty member who's in the process of obtaining one.

A state legislature can change or expand the state's nurse practice act, but it must also repeal sections that conflict with its changes. For example, if a state legislature decides to adopt the board of nursing's recommendation for a newly broadened definition of nursing, it must repeal the old definition in the state nurse practice act before it can enact the new definition into law.

A short history

In 1938, the New York State Legislature passed the first mandatory nurse practice act. This law, requiring nurses to obtain licenses to practice, raised the question, "Exactly what should a nursing license permit a nurse to do?" The answer was specified in nurse practice acts on a state-by-state basis until 1955, when the American Nurses' Association developed a model definition of nursing practice. Eventually, many states incorporated this model definition, and its 1970 amendments, into their state nurse practice acts.

Nurse practice acts define nursing practice

Nurse practice acts generally begin by defining important terms, including *the practice of registered nursing* and *the practice of licensed practical/vocational nursing.* These definitions are very important because they differentiate between RNs and LPNs/LVNs according to their specific scopes of practice and their educational requirements.

(Note: Some states have separate nurse practice acts for registered and practical/vocational nurses.)

Early nurse practice acts contained statements prohibiting nurses from performing tasks considered to be within the scope of medical practice. Nurses could not diagnose any patient problem or treat a patient without instructions from a doctor. More recently, however, interdisciplinary committees (consisting of nurses, doctors, pharmacists, dentists, and hospital representatives) have helped ease this restriction on nursing practice. After reviewing some medical procedures that nurses commonly perform, these committees have issued *joint statements* recommending that nurses be legally permitted to do these procedures in specified circumstances. (Note that such joint statements do not have the force of the law—unless state legislatures amend their nurse practice acts to include them.) Some joint statements have recommended that nurses be specifically allowed to perform venipunctures, cardiopulmonary resuscitation, and cardiac defibrillation. Still other joint statements (as well as *interpretative statements* issued by state boards of nursing and nursing organizations) recommend that nurses specifically be permitted to perform such functions as nursing assessment and nursing diagnosis. Some state legislatures have responded by incorporating these tasks and functions into nurse practice acts, thus clearly expanding the legal scope of nursing practice.

In addition to specifying the conditions for RN and LPN/LVN licensure, your nurse practice act may also specify the rules and regulations for licensure (usually termed *certification*) in special areas of nursing practice. Your nurse practice act also establishes your state nursing board's authority to administer and enforce the act's provisions and specifies the makeup of the board—the number of members as well as their educational and professional requirements. In some states, the nurse practice act requires two nursing boards—one for RNs and one for LPNs/LVNs.

State Nurse Practice Acts: Qualifications for Licensure

	Alabama Title 34	Alaska Title 8	Arizona Title 32	Arkansas Title 72	California Business and Professions Code	Colorado Chapter 12	Connecticut Title 20	
Frequency of license renewal (annual or biennial)	b	b	a	a	b	b	a	
RNs								
Good moral character	●			●				
Good physical and mental health								
High school graduation (or equivalent)	●		●	●				
Completion of basic professional nursing education program	●	●	●	●	●	●	●	
No drug/alcohol addiction						●		
Minimum age								
Fluency in English								
LPNs/LVNs								
Good moral character	●			●				
Good physical and mental health								
High school graduation (or equivalent)	●		10th grade	●	10th grade			
Completion of basic professional nursing education program	●	●	●	●	●	●	●	
No drug/alcohol addiction						●		
Minimum age				17				
Fluency in English								

To become licensed to practice nursing in your state, you not only have to pass the required examination, you have to meet certain other qualifications as well. For information on these requirements, check your state's listing below.

	Delaware Title 24	District of Columbia Title 2	Florida Chapter 464	Georgia Title 43	Hawaii Title 25	Idaho Title 54	Illinois Chapter 111	Indiana Title 25	Iowa Title 8	Kansas Title 65
	a	a	b	b	b	b	b	b	b	b
		●				●	●			●
	●		●			●				
	●		●		●	●	●	●	●	●
	●	●	●	●	●	●	●	●	●	●
		18					18			
	●		●							
		●				●	●			●
	●	●	●			●				
		10th grade	●	●	●	10th grade	●	●	●	●
	●	●	●	●	●	●	●	●	●	●
		18		18			18			
	●		●							

(continued)

State Nurse Practice Acts: Qualifications for Licensure (continued)

	Kentucky Title 26	Louisiana Title 37	Maine Title 32	Maryland Health Occupations	Massachusetts Chapter 112	Michigan Chapter 333	Minnesota Chapter 148
Frequency of license renewal (annual or biennial)	a	a	a	b	b	a	b
RNs							
Good moral character					●	●	●
Good physical and mental health	●						●
High school graduation (or equivalent)	●		●				●
Completion of basic professional nursing education program	●	●	●	●	●	●	●
No drug/alcohol addiction							
Minimum age						18	
Fluency in English						●	
LPNs/LVNs							
Good moral character					●	●	●
Good physical and mental health	●		●				●
High school graduation (or equivalent)	●		●	●			●
Completion of basic professional nursing education program	●	●	●	●	●	●	●
No drug/alcohol addiction							
Minimum age						18	
Fluency in English						●	

	Mississippi Title 73	Missouri Title 22	Montana Title 37	Nebraska Chapter 71	Nevada Title 54	New Hampshire Title 30	New Jersey Title 45	New Mexico Section 61	New York Education Law	North Carolina Chapter 90
	b	a	a	a	b	b	a	b	b	b
		●		●	●	●	●		●	
					●	●				●
		●	●	●			●	●		
	●	●	●	●	●	●	●	●	●	●
							●			
		19					18		18	
	●	●								
		●		●	●	●	●		●	
		●			●	●				●
	●	10th grade	●	●	●	●	10th grade	●	●	
	●	●	●	●	●	●	●	●	●	●
							●			
		18		18	18		18		17	
	●									

(continued)

State Nurse Practice Acts:
Qualifications for Licensure (continued)

	North Dakota Chapter 43	Ohio Title 47	Oklahoma Title 59	Oregon Title 52	Pennsylvania Title 63	Rhode Island Chapter 5-34	South Carolina Title 40	
Frequency of license renewal (annual or biennial)	a	b	b	b	b	a	a	
RNs								
Good moral character		●	●		●	●	●	
Good physical and mental health				●			●	
High school graduation (or equivalent)		●	●		●	●	●	
Completion of basic professional nursing education program	●	●	●	●	●	●	●	
No drug/alcohol addiction								
Minimum age					18		18	
Fluency in English								
LPNs/LVNs								
Good moral character		●	●		●	●	●	
Good physical and mental health				●		●	●	
High school graduation (or equivalent)			10th grade		●	*	10th grade	
Completion of basic professional nursing education program	●	●	●	●	●	●	●	
No drug/alcohol addiction								
Minimum age		18			18		18	
Fluency in English								

* Determined by Board

	South Dakota Title 36	Tennessee Title 63	Texas Title 71 (Health)	Utah Title 58	Vermont Title 26	Virginia Title 54	Washington Chapter 18	West Virginia Chapter 30	Wisconsin Title 40A	Wyoming Title 33
	a	b	b	b	b	a	a	a	b	a
				●				●		
		●		●						
	●	●				●		●	●	
	●	●	●	●	●	●	●	●	●	●
	●			●		●	●	●	●	
		●		●			●			
	●	●	10th grade			10th grade	10th grade	●	10th grade	
	●	●	●	●	●	●	●	●	●	●
							18		18	

In most states, the board of nursing (often called the state board of nursing examiners) consists of nurses like you—experienced, currently licensed, and practicing. Many boards also include LPNs/LVNs, hospital administrators, and consumers—usually financial or legal experts. The state legislature decides on the board's mix; in almost every state, the governor appoints members from a list of nominees submitted by the state nursing association. One state, North Carolina, recently replaced this appointment process with an elective one—allowing licensed nurses to elect their own board members.

Your practice act also lists violations that can result in disciplinary action against a nurse. Depending on the nature of the violation, a nurse may face not only state board disciplinary action but also liability for her actions.

Interpreting your nurse practice act

Nurse practice acts tend to be broadly worded, and their wording varies from state to state. Your nurse practice act's general provisions help you stay within the legal limits of nursing practice in your state. But you should be aware of problems in interpreting nurse practice acts. For example, one problem stems from the simple fact that nurse practice acts are statutory laws. Any amendment to a nurse practice act, then, must be accomplished via the inevitably slow legislative process. Because of the time involved in pondering, drafting, and enacting laws, amendments to nurse practice acts usually lag well behind the progress of changes in nursing. What does this mean to you? For one thing, you may be expected to perform tasks that seem to be within the accepted scope of nursing but, in fact, violate your nurse practice act.

Maybe that seems unlikely to you. After all, who would knowingly break a law and put herself in legal jeopardy? Well, consider that most nurses now regularly make nursing diagnoses although their state nurse practice acts don't spell out whether they legally may do so.

Unfortunately, some nurse practice acts that *do* permit nursing diagnosis fail to define what they mean by the term. For instance, the Pennsylvania Nurse Practice Act defines the practice of professional nursing as "*diagnosing and treating* human responses to actual (or potential) health problems through such services as case finding, health teaching, health counseling, and provision of care supportive to or restorative of life and well-being, and executing medical regimens as prescribed by a licensed physician or dentist. The foregoing shall not be deemed to include acts of medical diagnosis or prescription of medical therapeutic or corrective measures, except as may be authorized by rules and regulations jointly promulgated by the [Medical Board] and the [State] Board [of Nurse Examiners]." This definition and others like it don't distinguish clearly between medical and nursing diagnoses.

What does this mean to you? Essentially, it means that the law can't be all things to all nurses. Your state nurse practice act isn't a word-for-word checklist on how you should do your work. You must rely on your own education, training, and knowledge of your hospital's policies and procedures. For example, you know that a nursing diagnosis is part of your nursing assessment. It's your professional evaluation of the patient's progress, his responses to treatment, and his nursing care needs. You perform this evaluation so you can develop and carry out your nursing care plan. And you know that nursing diagnosis is not a judgment about a patient's medical disorder. So, if your state nurse practice act permits you to make nursing diagnoses, your sound judgment in applying its provisions should help you avoid legal consequences. If your state practice act doesn't permit nursing diagnoses, or its wording permitting nursing diagnoses is unclear, request an official interpretation from your state board of nursing.

Obviously, making nursing diagnoses can be risky under a law that permits them without clearly defining them. Because the language of nurse practice acts is so broad, in many instances a decision on whether certain nursing conduct is a violation must be based on analysis of whether that conduct was intended to be included within conduct permitted by the act.

Here's some simple but important legal advice: Be sure you're familiar with the legally permissible scope of your nursing practice, as it's defined in your state's nurse practice act, and never exceed its limits. If you do, you're inviting legal problems.

Here's an example. Pennsylvania's Nurse Practice Act forbids a nurse to give an anesthetic unless the patient's doctor is present. The case of *McCarl v. State Board of Nurse Examiners* (1979) involved a hospital nurse who administered an anesthetic to a patient whose doctor was *not* present. The Pennsylvania Board of Nurse Examiners received a complaint about the incident and conducted a hearing. The nurse admitted to knowing about the law's requirement but argued that the requirement was satisfied by the presence of another doctor—although this doctor wasn't supervising the nurse during the procedure. The board ruled that the nurse had willfully violated a section of the Pennsylvania Nurse Practice Act and issued a reprimand. The nurse appealed the reprimand, but the court upheld it.

Most nurse practice acts also pose another problem: They state that you have a legal duty to carry out a doctor's or a dentist's orders. Yet, as a licensed professional, you also have an ethical and legal duty to use your own judgment when providing patient care.

In an effort to deal with this problem, some nurse practice acts give guidance on how to obey orders and still act independently. For example, the Delaware Nurse Practice Act says a nurse must administer "medications and treatments as prescribed by a licensed physician or dentist" while using "substantial specialized judgment and skill . . . based on knowledge and application of the principles of biological, physical and social science." This wording may be interpreted to mean that a nurse practicing in Delaware is required to follow a doctor's or dentist's orders, unless those orders are clearly wrong or he's unqualified to give them. When you feel an order is clearly wrong, tell the doctor. If you're confused about an order, ask the doctor to clarify it. If he fails to correct the error or to answer your questions, inform your head nurse or supervisor of your doubts.

A related problem arises when you deal with physician assistants (PAs). Nurse practice acts in some states say you may only follow orders given by doctors or dentists—but those states' medical practice acts may allow PAs to give orders to nurses. Washington and Florida, for example, have decided that a PA is a doctor's agent and may legally give orders to nurses (*Washington State Nurses Ass'n. v. Board of Medical Examiners,* 1980, and 1977 *Fla. Att'y. Gen. Ann. Rep.).* Find out if your hospital policy allows PAs to give you orders. If it doesn't, you should *not* follow such orders. If hospital policy *does* permit PAs to give you orders, check if such orders must be verified or countersigned by the doctor. (This same question of verification may arise over a nurse practitioner's orders written in a patient's chart.) For further clarification, check with your state board of nursing.

You may be asking, why don't nurse practice acts and hospital policies always agree? Hospital licensing laws require each hospital to establish policies and procedures for its operation. So the nursing service department develops detailed policies and procedures for staff nurses. Usually these policies and procedures specify the allowable scope of nursing practice within the hospital. The scope may be narrower than the scope described in your nurse practice act, but it can't be broader. Remember, your employer *can't* legally expand the scope of your practice to include tasks prohibited by your nurse practice act. You have a legal obligation to practice within your nurse practice act's limits. Except in a life-threatening emergency, you can't exceed these limits without risking disciplinary action. To protect yourself, compare your hospital policies and your nurse practice act.

You may have concluded, by now, that the substance of most nurse practice acts lies not in what they say, but in what they *don't* say. Most don't specify your day-to-day legal responsibilities with respect to specific procedures and functions. For instance, along with nursing diagnosis, many nurse practice acts don't specify such things as your responsibility for patient teaching or the legal limitations on nurse-patient discussions about treatment. Yet, in a recent case in Idaho (*Tuma v. Board of Nursing*, 1979), a state board of nursing took disciplinary action against a nurse who discussed, at a patient's request, the possibility of using Laetrile as alternative therapy. The board suspended her license on the grounds of unprofessional conduct. However, the Supreme Court of Idaho revoked the suspension and ordered the board to reinstate the nurse's license. Why? Because the Idaho Nurse Practice Act contained no provision stating that such a nurse-patient discussion would constitute a violation of the nurse practice act.

Keeping nurse practice acts up to date

To align nurse practice acts with current nursing practice, professional nursing organizations and state boards of nursing have lobbied for two types of legislation affecting the acts: amendments and redefinitions.

An *amendment* may be used to add to or subtract from a nurse practice act or its regulations, specifically giving nurses legal permission to perform certain procedures or functions that have become part of accepted nursing practice. These amendments have the same legal force as the original act.

Compared to redefinition, though, amendments do have a disadvantage: They represent a piecemeal approach that may remain in effect.

Redefinition, on the other hand, is a rewriting of the fundamental provision of a nurse practice act—the definition of nursing practice. This approach changes the basic premise of the entire act without the necessity to amend or repeal it. Redefinition might be used, for example, to reverse a definition of nursing practice that prohibits diagnosis. How? By clarifying the term *diagnosis* to allow nurses to make nursing diagnoses. This type of change helps nurses understand exactly what is and isn't prohibited.

To help protect yourself legally, you need to understand your nurse practice act thoroughly and keep up with any changes in it. Be sure you're up to date on your hospital's policies and procedures, too. Only when you know the legal limits of your responsibilities can you practice your profession safely.

Standards of nursing care affect you legally

Are standards of nursing care merely pie-in-the-sky ideals that have little bearing on the tasks you perform daily? Absolutely not. You're expected to meet standards of nursing care for every nursing task you perform. And any time your care falls below standard, you're risking malpractice liability.

Standards of nursing care set minimum criteria for your proficiency on the job, enabling you—and others—to judge the quality of care you and your nursing colleagues provide.

For example, if you're a medical-surgical staff nurse, minimal standards require that you develop a nursing care plan for your patient based on the nursing process—assessment, planning, intervention, and evaluation—including nursing diagnoses, nursing goals, and nursing actions for implementing the care plan. Standards also call for documentation, in the patient's record, of your completion and evaluation of the plan. When you document your patient care, you're really writing a record of how well you've met these standards.

Before 1950, nurses had only Florence Nightingale's early treatments, plus reports of court cases, to use as standards. But as nursing gradually became recognized as an independent profession, nursing organizations stressed the importance of having recognized standards for all nurses. Then, in 1950, the American Nurses' Association (ANA) published the "Code of Ethics for Nursing," a general mandate stating that nurses should offer nursing care without prejudice and in a confidential and safe manner. The code wasn't very specific, but it was the beginning of written nursing standards. In 1973, the ANA Congress for Nursing Practice established the first generic standards for the profession—standards that could be applied to all nurses in all settings. (See *The American Nurses' Association's Stan-*

dards of Nursing Practice, pages 16 to 19.) The Canadian Nurses Association (CNA) has established similar nursing standards.

By 1974, each of the ANA divisions of nursing practice (Community Health, Geriatrics, Maternal-Child, Mental Health, and Medical-Surgical) had established distinct standards for its specialty. The ANA Congress called these *specialty standards*. State nursing associations also helped develop specialty nursing standards.

ANA specialty standards are really national in nature because they can apply wherever nurses practice. But the courts may also use local standards—reflecting a community's accepted, common nursing practices—to judge the quality of nursing care. Use of local standards is becoming less common, however, as national standards receive increasing endorsement.

As you may know, local standards are established in two ways: by individual hospitals, through their policies and procedures, and by expert witnesses who testify in court cases involving nurses. Every hospital establishes standards to fit its own community's needs. An expert witness interprets local standards by testifying about how nursing is commonly practiced in her community.

You can see that a number of nursing institutions and organizations have contributed to the development of nursing standards. The ANA and the CNA established standards for nurses and recommended that state and provincial boards of nursing endorse them for incorporation into nurse practice acts. The Joint Commission on Accreditation of Hospitals also has developed nursing standards to be used in hospital audit systems. And state nursing associations and the specialty-nursing organizations actively work with hospital nursing administrators for adoption of standards.

Federal regulations for staffing Medicare and Medicaid services influence the development of standards, especially nursing home standards. By suggesting ethical approaches to nursing practice, ethics codes written by the ANA, the CNA, and the International Council of Nurses also influence how nursing care standards are developed.

Nursing standards will change as technology advances and nurses' responsibilities expand. Hospital audit committees and professional nursing associations continually monitor nursing standards to be sure they're up to date.

How courts apply nursing standards in malpractice lawsuits

The allegation that a nurse failed to meet appropriate standards of care is the basic premise of every nursing malpractice lawsuit. During the trial, the court will measure the defendant-nurse's action against the answers it obtains to the following question: *What would a reasonably prudent nurse, with like training and experience, do under similar conditions in the same community?* To answer this question, the plaintiff-patient, through his attorney, must determine that certain standards of care exist that the defendant-nurse should have applied to him, prove the appropriateness of those standards, and show how the nurse failed to meet them—and so caused him injury—in giving her nursing care.

When local standards are at issue, usually the plaintiff-patient uses expert-witness testimony to support his claims. This is known as the *locality rule*. The defendant-nurse and her attorney, of course, will also arrange for expert-witness testimony—in support of her claim that her actions did *not* fall below accepted standards of care and that she acted in a reasonable and prudent manner.

The court can also draw on sources of written standards in examining the standards of care involved in a nursing malpractice lawsuit. The court will seek information about all the national and state standards applicable to the defendant-nurse's actions. The court may also seek applicable information about the policies of the defendant-nurse's employer.

What if state and national standards contradict each other? When that happens, the court must decide which standards apply in the case, often giving state standards top priority. But sometimes courts favor the national standards. Why? Because two trends—toward uniform nursing educational requirements and

The American Nurses' Association's Standards of Nursing Practice

AMERICAN NURSES' ASSOCIATION

Standards of Nursing Practice

STANDARD I

THE COLLECTION OF DATA ABOUT THE HEALTH STATUS OF THE CLIENT/PATIENT IS SYSTEMATIC AND CONTINUOUS. THE DATA ARE ACCESSIBLE, COMMUNICATED, AND RECORDED.

Rationale

Comprehensive care requires complete and ongoing collection of data about the client/patient to determine the nursing care needs of the client/patient. All health status data about the client/patient must be available for all members of the health-care team.

Assessment Factors

- Health status data include:
  - Growth and development
  - Biophysical status
  - Emotional status
  - Cultural, religious, socioeconomic background
  - Performance of activities of daily living
  - Patterns of coping
  - Interaction patterns
  - Client's/patient's perception of and satisfaction with his health status
  - Client/patient health goals
  - Environment (physical, social, emotional, ecological)
  - Available and accessible human and material resources
- Data are collected from:
  - Client/patient, family, significant others
  - Health-care personnel
  - Individuals within the immediate environment and/or the community
- Data are obtained by:
  - Interview
  - Examination
  - Observation
  - Reading records, reports, etc.
- There is a format for the collection of data which:
  - Provides for a systematic collection of data
  - Facilitates the completeness of data collection
- Continuous collection of data is evident by:
  - Frequent updating
  - Recording of changes in health status
- The data are:
  - Accessible on the client/patient records
  - Retrievable from record-keeping systems
  - Confidential when appropriate

The American Nurses' Association developed the following standards of nursing practice in 1973 to give the courts, hospitals, nurses, and patients guidelines for determining quality nursing care. The standards are based on the steps of the nursing process: assessment, planning, implementation, and evaluation. Each standard is followed by a rationale—explaining the standard—and assessment factors for use in determining if the standard has been met.

STANDARD II
NURSING DIAGNOSES ARE DERIVED FROM HEALTH STATUS DATA.

Rationale
The health status of the client/patient is the basis for determining the nursing care needs. The data are analyzed and compared to norms when possible.

Assessment Factors
- The client's/patient's health status is compared to the norm in order to determine if there is a deviation from the norm and the degree and direction of deviation.
- The client's/patient's capabilities and limitations are identified.
- The nursing diagnoses are related to and congruent with the diagnoses of all other professionals caring for the client/patient.

STANDARD III
THE PLAN OF NURSING CARE INCLUDES GOALS DERIVED FROM THE NURSING DIAGNOSES.

Rationale
The determination of the results to be achieved is an essential part of planning care.

Assessment Factors
- Goals are mutually set with the client/patient and pertinent others:
  —They are congruent with other planned therapies.
  —They are stated in realistic and measurable terms.
  —They are assigned a time period for achievement.
- Goals are established to maximize functional capabilities and are congruent with:
  —Growth and development
  —Biophysical status
  —Behavioral patterns
  —Human and material resources

STANDARD IV
THE PLAN OF NURSING CARE INCLUDES PRIORITIES AND THE PRESCRIBED NURSING APPROACHES OR MEASURES TO ACHIEVE THE GOALS DERIVED FROM THE NURSING DIAGNOSES.

Rationale
Nursing actions are planned to promote, maintain and restore the client's/patient's well-being.

Assessment Factors
- Physiological measures are planned to manage (prevent or control) specific patient problems and are related to the nursing diagnoses and goals of care, e.g. ADL, use of self-help devices, etc.

(continued)

The American Nurses' Association's
Standards of Nursing Practice *(continued)*

- Psychosocial measures are specific to the client's/patient's nursing care problem and to the nursing care goals, e.g. techniques to control aggression, motivation.
- Teaching-learning principles are incorporated into the plan of care and objectives for learning stated in behavioral terms, e.g. specification of content for learner's level, reinforcement, readiness, etc.
- Approaches are planned to provide for a therapeutic environment:
  —Physical environmental factors are used to influence the therapeutic environment, e.g. control of noise, control of temperature, etc.
  —Psychosocial measures are used to structure the environment for therapeutic ends, e.g. paternal participation in all phases of the maternity experience.
  —Group behaviors are used to structure interaction and influence the therapeutic environment, e.g. comformity, ethos, territorial rights, locomotion, etc.
- Approaches are specified for orientation of the client/patient to:
  —New roles and relationships
  —Relevant health (human and material) resources
  —Modifications in plan of nursing care
  —Relationship of modifications in nursing care plan to the total care plan
- The plan of nursing care includes the utilization of available and appropriate resources:
  —Human resources (other health personnel)
  —Material resources
  —Community
- The plan includes an ordered sequence of nursing actions.
- Nursing approaches are planned on the basis of current scientific knowledge.

STANDARD V
NURSING ACTIONS PROVIDE FOR CLIENT/PATIENT PARTICIPATION IN HEALTH PROMOTION, MAINTENANCE AND RESTORATION.

Rationale
The client/patient and family are continually involved in nursing care.

Assessment Factors
- The client/patient and family are kept informed about:
  —Current health status
  —Changes in health status
  —Total health-care plan
  —Nursing care plan
  —Roles of health-care personnel
  —Health-care resources
- The client/patient and family are provided with the information needed to make decisions and choices about:
  —Promoting, maintaining and restoring health
  —Seeking and utilizing appropriate health-care personnel
  —Maintaining and using health-care resources

STANDARD VI
NURSING ACTIONS ASSIST THE CLIENT/PATIENT TO MAXIMIZE HIS HEALTH CAPABILITIES.

Rationale
Nursing actions are designed to promote, maintain and restore health.

Assessment Factors
- Nursing actions:
  - —Are consistent with the plan of care.
  - —Are based on scientific principles.
  - —Are individualized to the specific situation.
  - —Are used to provide a safe and therapeutic environment.
  - —Employ teaching-learning opportunities for the client/patient.
  - —Include utilization of appropriate resources.
- Nursing actions are directed by the client's/patient's physical, physiological, psychological and social behavior associated with:
  - —Ingestion of food, fluid and nutrients
  - —Elimination of body wastes and excesses in fluid
  - —Locomotion and exercise
  - —Regulatory mechanisms — body heat, metabolism
  - —Relating to others
  - —Self-actualization

STANDARD VII
THE CLIENT'S/PATIENT'S PROGRESS OR LACK OF PROGRESS TOWARD GOAL ACHIEVEMENT IS DETERMINED BY THE CLIENT/PATIENT AND THE NURSE.

Rationale
The quality of nursing care depends upon comprehensive and intelligent determination of nursing's impact upon the health status of the client/patient. The client/patient is an essential part of this determination.

Assessment Factors
- Current data about the client/patient are used to measure his progress toward goal achievement.
- Nursing actions are analyzed for their effectiveness in the goal achievement of the client/patient.
- The client/patient evaluates nursing actions and goal achievement.
- Provision is made for nursing follow-up of a particular client/patient to determine the long-term effects of nursing care.

STANDARD VIII
THE CLIENT'S/PATIENT'S PROGRESS OR LACK OF PROGRESS TOWARD GOAL ACHIEVEMENT DIRECTS REASSESSMENT, REORDERING OF PRIORITIES, NEW GOAL SETTING AND REVISION OF THE PLAN OF NURSING CARE.

Rationale
The nursing process remains the same, but the input of new information may dictate new or revised approaches.

Assessment Factors
- Reassessment is directed by goal achievement or lack of goal achievement.
- New priorities and goals are determined and additional nursing approaches are prescribed appropriately.
- New nursing actions are accurately and appropriately initiated.

standardized medical treatment regimens—are making national standards widely applicable. This court bias has made the ANA's standards more influential than local standards or the standards of other organizations.

The court may also allow nonnursing professionals, including doctors, to speak as expert witnesses about nursing practice. This has happened in several key cases. For example, in *Hiatt v. Groce* (1974), a patient sued an obstetric nurse for failing to notify a doctor when the patient was about to deliver a baby. The court permitted a doctor to testify about the adequacy of the nurse's care. In *Gugino v. Harvard Community Health Plan* (1980), the court allowed a doctor to testify about the standards for a nurse practitioner.

The case of *Pisel v. Stamford Community Hospital* (1980) provides a good example of how courts consider local, state, and national standards in nursing malpractice lawsuits. In this case, nurses at a mental health hospital left a young psychotic patient unattended in a locked seclusion room. The patient forcibly wedged her head between the bed frame and side rail, suffering permanent neurologic damage. The patient's relatives sued the nurses and the hospital for malpractice. In the absence of hospital policies that might have applied to this case, the court relied on expert-witness testimony, ANA standards, and federal regulations to judge the nurses' care. The court found the nurses and the hospital guilty of violating applicable standards of care according to the following evidence:

• failure to remove a steel bed from a seclusion room
• failure to constantly observe the patient
• failure to completely assess the patient's status
• failure to notify the attending psychiatrist of the patient's acutely psychotic condition
• failure to implement medical orders.

As further evidence against the hospital, testimony revealed that the nursing notes describing the incident had been destroyed and that new notes had been written. This falsified record was considered evidence that the hospital was conscious of its negligence. (For detailed information on the legal risks involved in falsifying medical records, see "The altered medical record," page 187.)

Nurses may also be judged by standards of care that ordinarily aren't considered nursing standards. For example, in the California case of *Fein v. Permanente Medical Group* (1981), a patient who went to a medical clinic complaining of chest pain sued the clinic and the nurse practitioner who attended him for failing to diagnose his myocardial infarction. Although diagnosis is normally considered a medical rather than a nursing function, the court found the nurse negligent. The reasoning? In directing the jury, the judge stated, "I instruct you that the standard of care required of a nurse practitioner is that of a physician and surgeon duly licensed to practice medicine in the state of California when the nurse practitioner is examining a patient or making a diagnosis." In other words, the nurse practitioner could be presumed to have the knowledge and skills to make a diagnosis.

This court decision was appealed. The higher court examining the case on appeal noted that although the roles of a nurse practitioner and a doctor differ, the plaintiff was entitled to the same standard of care a doctor would give when the plaintiff went to the clinic with his complaint of chest pain. So the higher court sustained the lower court's decision.

In another case, *Jones v. Hawkes Hospital* (1964), the court ruled against a nurse's request to have expert testimony used to judge her action. The nurse was sued for malpractice when she left a sedated patient, who was in labor, to assist a doctor with another patient in labor. She did this because the hospital had a rule that no doctor could attend a woman in labor unless a nurse was present. Left alone, the plaintiff-patient got out of her bed, fell, and suffered serious injuries. The nurse wanted the court to allow expert testimony to establish the standard of care that should have been applied. But the court ruled that any reasonably prudent person could determine this case on the basis of ordinary experience and knowledge, so the jurors could decide on their own whether the defendant-nurse's nontechnical nursing tasks met reasonable standards of care. The jury found the nurse negligent.

A similar case was *Larrimore v. Homeopathic Hospital Association* (1962) in which a nurse was found liable for failing to read a new order or for reading it negligently. The court stated that the jury could apply ordinary common sense, without an expert witness, to establish the applicable standard of care.

A nurse who administers medication when the prescribing doctor isn't present is legally responsible for clarifying the doctor's instructions. What amount of medication should she give? How should she give it—by what route? In the Louisiana case *Norton v. Argonaut Insurance Co.* (1962), a doctor left an incomplete order for administration of 3 cc of digoxin to a young patient. A nurse supervisor, helping out on the pediatric floor, picked up the order. Unsure of the amount of digoxin the doctor had prescribed, she asked two other doctors (who were on the ward) if 3 cc was an excessive dose. These two doctors, believing the nurse was describing an *oral* dose, told her 3 cc was correct. The nurse gave the patient 3 cc of digoxin *by injection,* and the young patient died.

In a subsequent malpractice lawsuit against the nurse, the court ruled that she breached her duty and violated a standard, which holds that each nurse has the duty to make absolutely certain that the dose and route of administration of every medication she administers are correct. The court made this decision based on the following evidence:
• The nurse attempted to administer a medication with which she wasn't familiar.
• The nurse failed to call the attending doctor for clarification of his orders.

(For more information on your legal risks when administering medications, see "Legal risks in drug administration," page 117.)

Conclusion

Without standards of care, nursing couldn't claim to be a profession. Why? Because standards, by establishing minimum levels of quality for performing nursing tasks, provide the criteria for placing nursing practice on a professional level. Your profession and the courts have taken a firm position regarding standards of nursing care. Both have insisted that your practice be held up to—and when necessary judged by—specific standards. Meeting these standards will protect you legally, ensure that your patients receive quality care, and strengthen the standing of your profession.

Nursing licensure

Your nursing license entitles you to practice as a professionally qualified nurse. But as with most privileges, your nursing license imposes certain responsibilities on you. As a licensed professional—registered nurse (RN) or licensed practical/vocational nurse (LPN/LVN) in the United States or Canada—you're responsible for providing quality care to your patients. To do this, *and* to protect your right to practice, you need to know the professional and legal meaning of your nursing license.

What licensing laws do

Licensing laws are contained within each nurse practice act. They establish qualifications for obtaining and maintaining a nursing license. They also broadly define the legally permissible scope of nursing practice.

Licensing laws, which vary somewhat from state to state, generally specify the following:
• the qualifications a nurse needs in order to be granted a license
• license-application procedures for new licenses and reciprocal (state-to-state) licensing arrangements
• application fees
• authorization to grant use of the title *registered nurse* or *licensed practical/vocational nurse* to applicants who receive their licenses
• grounds for license denial, revocation, or suspension
• license-renewal procedures.

Licensing laws generally do not prohibit nursing students, a patient's friends, or members of his family from caring for him (as long as no fee is involved), nor do the laws prohibit a nurse licensed in one state from caring for a patient traveling with her

through another state. The laws also usually permit a newly graduated nurse to practice for a specified period while her license application is being processed, and they allow unlicensed persons to give care in an emergency. According to state and federal constitutional requirements, state laws *must* exempt the following types of nurses from state licensure requirements:
• nurses working in federal institutions
• nurses practicing in accordance with their religious beliefs
• nurses traveling with patients from one state to another.

By defining the scope of your professional nursing practice, licensing laws help you avoid the civil and criminal liabilities that can result if you practice beyond the limits specified by your nursing license.

If you're named in a malpractice lawsuit, your state licensing laws will be used as partial evidence in determining if you acted within the legally permissible scope of nursing practice.

Consider *Vassey v. Burch* (1980), in which a patient sued an emergency department nurse for failing to recognize his signs and symptoms of appendicitis. The court reviewed the state licensing law and determined that the nurse had not violated the applicable standard of nursing care. The court ruled that the nurse had acted properly by notifying the attending doctor of the patient's signs and symptoms and that she was under no obligation to diagnose a patient's condition.

In *Barber v. Reinking* (1966), the court used the licensing laws in the Washington State nurse practice act to rule against the defendant-nurse. In this case, a boy age 2 was taken to a doctor's office for a polio booster shot. The doctor (who was also named in the suit) delegated this task to the LPN who worked in his office. While the nurse was administering the shot, the child moved suddenly and the needle broke off in his buttock. Despite attempts to remove it surgically and with a magnet, the needle remained lodged in the child's buttock for 9 months.

During the lawsuit that followed, the licensing law for practical nurses became the controlling factor in the court's decision. According to the Washington State nurse practice act, a practical nurse can't legally give an injection. The court declared that the nurse had violated the nurse practice act by performing services beyond the legal limit of her practice. The nurse's attorney attempted to introduce as evidence the "fact" that LPNs/LVNs commonly gave injections in the town where she practiced. This contention wasn't allowed as evidence, however. Instead, the judge instructed the jury to consider the violation of the nurse practice act along with other evidence in the case, including the doctor's liability under the *respondeat superior* doctrine, to determine if the nurse was negligent.

Canadian licensing laws

Nursing practice in Canada is regulated within each province. Each province has its own nurse practice act, so the laws vary somewhat from province to province. Licensing laws in all provinces except Prince Edward Island and Ontario require nurses to join provincial nursing associations in order to obtain their licenses.

In all provinces, Canadian licensing laws establish the following:
• qualifications for membership in the provincial nursing association
• examination requirements
• applicable fees
• conditions for reciprocal licensure
• penalties for practicing without a license
• grounds for denial, suspension, or revocation of a nurse's license.

Within those provinces that license practical nurses, licensing laws for LPNs/LVNs are similar to those for RNs.

Keeping your license current

When you begin a new job, your employer is responsible for checking your credentials and confirming that you're properly licensed. Make sure that your nursing license is always current, and be prepared to furnish proof that you've renewed your license in the past, when necessary, in order to keep it current.

If you fail to renew your license, you can no longer legally practice nursing. In the United States and Canada, you can be prosecuted and fined for practicing without a license. Fines vary from state to state. For example, section 223 of the Professional Nursing Law of Pennsylvania stipulates a $300 fine for nurses who violate the licensing law or practice nursing without a license; if a nurse doesn't pay the fine, she faces a 90-day prison term. In the United States and Canada, fines generally range from as little as $5 to as much as $2,000.

The courts have occasionally addressed the question of failure to renew a nursing license, usually for an appeal proceeding concerning a state board of nursing's disciplinary action. In some cases, the courts have disagreed with boards' decisions. *Kansas State Board of Nursing v. Burkman* (1975) is one such case. A registered nurse failed to renew her license and continued to practice nursing. No evidence showed that she had intentionally failed to renew her license or knowingly practiced without it. Ruling that her failure to apply for renewal was a violation of state licensing laws, the state board of nursing suspended her license for 6 months. After several appeals, a high court ruled that the board of nursing had erred in suspending the nurse's license and instructed the board to renew it.

In *Oliff v. Florida State Board of Nursing* (1979), the court again disagreed with the state board of nursing and ruled in favor of the nurse. In this case, the board of nursing refused to renew an LPN's certificate because it had not received her application by a particular date. Evidence indicated that the nurse had mailed her application before the date specified by the state board of nursing. The court ruled that the date adopted by the board was a deadline for applications to be mailed, not received.

If you discover that you've forgotten to renew your license, several simple measures will help you avoid serious legal consequences. First, notify your employer. Then, find your original license application and immediately notify the state board of nursing of your oversight. Ask them for a temporary license or for authorization to continue nursing until you receive your license. If you can't find your license application, write to the state board of nursing for a renewal application and instructions on how to proceed. Then, follow the board's instructions exactly.

License suspension and revocation

Your nursing license may be revoked or suspended for cause in most states and Canadian provinces. Grounds for suspension or revocation include inability to function competently because of alcohol intake or drug addiction, lack of mental or physical well-being, and failure to abide by the standards and requirements of the nurse practice act of the particular state or province.

Moving? Make sure your license remains valid

Before the American Nurses' Association and the National League for Nursing established a national standardized examination for nursing licensure (the National Council Licensure Examination, or NCLEX), qualifications for entry into nursing practice were not consistent from state to state. As a result, a nurse had a difficult time arranging for a license in one state on the basis of her license in another state. NCLEX established standard qualifications for entry into nursing throughout the country, so nurses now are able to move more freely to new jobs in other states.

When you move to another state to practice nursing, you must obtain a license or temporary practice permit from that state before you can legally practice nursing there.

Most state boards of nursing will license you if you're currently licensed to practice nursing in another state or territory or, in Canada, if your education fulfills the issuing state's requirements. This is called *endorsement.* Many state boards waive reexamination if you're licensed in Canada and wish to practice in the United States. The same usually applies if you hold a U.S. license and wish to move to a Canadian province.

If you must move to another state before its board of nursing has had time to approve your application, you'll probably be granted a temporary license. Be sure to check both the time limit of the temporary license and the specific nursing functions it authorizes.

Remember, if you must travel with a patient from one state to another, your license is valid for the duration of the trip in most states (and Canadian provinces). For example, you might be assigned to care for a patient who's being transferred to a medical facility in another state or province.

If the state board finds that you don't have the necessary qualifications to practice nursing in that state, it may reject your application or require that you complete a written examination—regardless of your education or the laws of the state where you presently live.

In *Richardson v. Brunelle* (1979), an LPN who'd practiced in Massachusetts for 15 years brought suit because she was refused a license to practice in New Hampshire. In her New Hampshire application, she requested a decree of educational equivalency. (Although she'd originally taken and passed a Massachusetts state licensing examination, she'd never graduated from an approved school of practical nursing.) At that time, only nursing-school graduates were permitted to practice in New Hampshire, so her request was denied. Her lawsuit was unsuccessful in reversing the New Hampshire decision, and subsequent appeals upheld the original ruling.

Snelson v. Culton (1949) is a similar case involving Maine's licensing requirements, which also specify that an applicant must be a graduate of a state-approved school of nursing.

How federal laws affect your nursing license

In some instances, federal laws can affect nursing licensure (although no federal law has jurisdiction over state boards of nursing). For example, if you're a nurse in the armed forces who is often subject to transfer, you're required by federal law to hold a current state license—but not necessarily in the state to which you are assigned.

And a recently enacted federal public health code requires all state boards that license health-care professionals to develop systems for verifying those professionals' continued competence.

Foreign licensure

If you move to a foreign country, your U.S. nursing license will be reviewed by the appropriate authority, which will either reject or endorse (accept) it (possibly with conditions). If you're a nurse in the American armed forces working in an American installation, you're exempt from this review.

In a non-English-speaking country, the licensing authority may require you to complete a language-proficiency examination.

If you're an RN or an LPN/LVN licensed in a foreign country, you can't practice nursing in any state, territory, or Canadian province until the appropriate licensing authority has approved your application and issued a nursing license to you. When you're granted licensure in the United States or Canada, you function at the same legal status, depending on your level of expertise, as a U.S.- or Canadian-educated RN or LPN/LVN. You're also equally accountable for your professional nursing actions.

Many states are beginning to require that foreign nurses take and pass the examination prepared by the Commission on Graduates of Foreign Nursing Schools (the so-called CGFN examination). If a foreign nurse successfully completes this examination—which includes an English-proficiency segment—she may then take the NCLEX examination. If she passes that, she qualifies for licensure (and for a visa that allows her to work).

Conclusion

Your nursing license guarantees that you've satisfied your state's minimum requirements for entry into nursing practice. It also provides proof of your nursing qualifications and protects the public by allowing *only* qualified persons to enter the nursing profession. Be sure to keep your license in a safe place at all times—and keep it current. (For further discussion of licensure, see *Institutional Licensure: Yes or No?*, pages 26 and 27.)

Safeguarding your nursing license

Your state board of nursing can take disciplinary action against a nurse for any violation of your state's nurse practice act. In all states and all Canadian provinces, the board of nursing has authority to discipline a nurse if she endangers a patient's health, safety, or welfare.

Depending on how severe a nurse's violation is, a state board may formally reprimand her, place her on probation, refuse to renew her license, suspend her license, or even revoke her license. The list of possible violations varies from state to state. The most common are:

• conviction of a crime involving moral turpitude, if the offense bears directly on whether the individual is fit to be licensed

• use of fraud or deceit in obtaining or attempting to obtain a nursing license

• incompetence because of negligence or because of physical or psychological impairments

• habitual use of, or addiction to, drugs or alcohol

• unprofessional conduct, including (but not limited to) falsifying, inaccurately recording, or improperly altering patient records; negligently administering medications or treatments; performing tasks beyond the limits of the state's nurse practice act; failing to take appropriate action to safeguard the patient from incompetent health care; violating the patient's confidentiality; taking on nursing duties that require skills and education beyond one's competence; violating the patient's dignity and human rights by basing nursing care on prejudice; abandoning a patient; and abusing a patient verbally or physically.

Here's how a state board of nursing typically investigates when a nurse is accused of professional misconduct: It conducts an *administrative review.*

You probably know that your state board of nursing is an administrative body that wields broad discretionary powers. But do you know that it can't issue a *final* decision? This is because it doesn't have legal authority, although court proceedings— and possibly legal penalties—may result from the board's administrative-review findings. And a state board's decision to reprimand a nurse or suspend or revoke her license isn't final. She always has the right to appeal, through the court system, for reversal of the nursing board's decision. (See *Disciplinary Proceedings for Nurse Misconduct: Typical Steps,* page 29.)

The administrative-review process

In most states and Canadian provinces, the nurse practice act specifies the steps the board of nursing must follow during an administrative review. In some states, however, a general administrative procedure act (separate from the nurse practice act) specifies the steps; in still other states, the board of nursing decides them.

In Canada, the process for administrative review of complaints against nurses is similar to the U.S. process. In some Canadian provinces, a complaints committee of the provincial nursing board hears the complaint first and either dismisses or endorses it. If the complaints committee endorses it, the complaint is sent along to a discipline committee for a full hearing. In other provinces, only a discipline committee hears the complaint.

An administrative review begins when a person, a health-care facility (the nurse's employer), or a professional organization files a signed complaint against a nurse with the state board of nursing—or when the board itself initiates such action. The board then reviews the complaint to decide if the nurse's action appears to violate the state's nurse practice act.

If it decides the nurse's action does appear to violate the act, the board prepares for a formal hearing, including subpoenaing witnesses. When these preparations begin, the accused nurse's due-process rights include the right to receive timely notice of both the charge against her and the hearing date. At the hearing, these are her rights under due process:

• to have an attorney represent her

• to present evidence and cross-examine witnesses

• to appeal the board's decision to a court.

In many Canadian provinces, an employer (except a patient) who terminates

Institutional Licensure: Yes or No?

Just the mention of institutional licensure triggers emotional responses from advocates and opponents of the process. Here's why:

As you know, the vast majority of nurses today practice under professional licensure. State law gives a nurse legal permission to engage in a profession that involves public health and safety. With this permission come practice guidelines designed to protect the public.

Institutional licensure means an institution, such as a hospital, is licensed and granted the authority to regulate its staff members' practice directly. Its professional employees don't have their own licenses. The institution's self-regulation is overseen, but not controlled, by an independent monitoring agency (such as the state agency charged with licensing institutions) or a national organization (such as the Joint Commission on Accreditation of Hospitals).

Suppose staff nurse Mary Owens and hospital administrator Ellen Gardiner find themselves discussing this issue over lunch one day. Mary is a staunch defender of professional licensure; Ellen thinks institutional licensure might work. Here's their conversation:

MARY Ellen, look at licensure in a historical perspective! The whole thrust of the nursing movement in this century has been to ensure the quality of patient care. Institutional licensure would throw us back to the days when anyone could practice as a registered nurse—just by saying she *was* one.

ELLEN Why do you say that? Institutional licensure doesn't let just anyone walk in off the street and start giving nursing care. We're talking about an elaborate system of accountabilities. Each hospital will go overboard to protect its license. I can assure you, administrators won't leave one stone unturned when they're checking out prospective employees. And do you think a hospital would be crazy enough not to monitor its staff's performances very carefully? After all, it'd be the hospital that would lose its license if any of its staff violated the terms. I can tell you, Mary, not a hospital in the country would want that to happen.

MARY The way you describe it, institutional licensure sounds safe, theoretically. But *are* all hospitals concerned enough about patients to provide more than minimal care? And remember, all those checks and reviews would cost the hospitals a bundle.

ELLEN Well, first of all, no system could cost as much as individual licensure, with its state boards of nursing and elaborate testing and licensing procedures. Besides that, every hospital already has a credential review system set up and working. Institutional licensure would just mean expanding that system.

MARY Wait a minute, Ellen. First of all, quality health care is worth whatever it costs—within reason, of course! And I've got my doubts about how useful credential reviews would be for institutional licensure—are those reviewers qualified to judge nursing practice?

ELLEN Mary, quality care isn't the question. Everyone agrees about that. The question is, how do we *get* quality care? We need more freedom to *pursue* quality care. Imagine how much more innovative we could be if we didn't have so many outside boards on our backs.

MARY I was waiting for that. "Innovation" could mean that maintaining minimum qualifications to practice nursing would go out the window. To save money, the hospital could theoretically use *anyone* to do *any* tasks, instead of paying qualified nurses. I wouldn't want to be a patient in *that* hospital!

ELLEN If we misused our staff by putting them in positions they couldn't fill, we'd be putting our own necks on the block. That just doesn't make any sense, and I don't think it'd happen.

MARY Well, we do have a precedent, you know. What do you think hospitals all over the country have done with associate degree nurses? That's a classic case of the way hospitals take people trained for one position and force them into other positions with only on-the-job training.

ELLEN Come on, Mary. That's a poor example. You know as well as I do that the distinctions between nursing degree programs are all on paper, not in practice. Associate degree programs all over the country teach students things that technically aren't part of an associate degree. What do you expect us to do? Ignore skills an employee has because she's not *supposed* to have them?

MARY That's not how it happened. Administrators plugged nurses into holes, period. They never considered their qualifications. What's the issue? It's that a nurse is licensed to perform her job in a professional way. You take away that licensure and you open the door to misuse of staff *and* abuse of patients. We're not talking about hospital convenience. We're talking about ensuring safe care and protecting the public.

ELLEN That's the hospital's goal, too! I think institutional licensure will promote safe care not only because the hospital's license is on the line but also—and more importantly—because employees will have incentives and fewer restrictions on broadening their skills. The health-care profession has been dominated too long by this "I don't do windows" mentality. Break through that thinking and people will want to learn more. Mary, I'm not saying the hospital will give an inexperi-

enced nurse a scalpel and point her toward surgery. We're talking about easing restrictions, making limits on practice more flexible, letting employees learn and use what they learn. All medicine is based on testing skills. And give people more credit! They're not going to perform tasks they know nothing about. With institutional licensure, instead of saying, "My license won't permit me to do that," a nurse can honestly say, "I'm sorry. I don't know how to do that. Could you show me?"

MARY You're saying that licensing restrictions are why there hasn't been teamwork in hospitals? Even doctors would laugh at that one. Mark my word, if you take away licensure guidelines, you're going to create a *more* defensive atmosphere. People are going to guard what they consider to be their prerogatives as if they were gold.

ELLEN You've got a point there, Mary. I suppose that could happen. But I still think the benefits would outweigh the costs. Just look at it personally. Wouldn't you prefer a system that's more responsive to you—that rewards you directly for your achievements and has room for you to grow to your potential? Basically, institutional licensure introduces a free marketplace for talent in the hospital.

MARY I'm just not sure, Ellen. I guess I'd rather take my chances with other nurses, instead of administrators, controlling my practice.

a nurse's employment for incompetence, misconduct, or incapacity must report the termination to the board of nursing in writing. If the employer fails to do this, the board may impose a fine.

At the formal hearing, an impartial attorney may act as a hearing officer (in lieu of a judge), or the board itself may hear the case. A court reporter documents the entire proceeding, or it may be taped. Members of the board are present, acting as the plaintiffs bringing the claim against the defendant-nurse. Witnesses—including co-workers—testify for the board and the nurse. If the board or hearing officer finds her guilty, she may be fined or reprimanded or have her license suspended or revoked.

The judicial review process

In every state, as you know, nurses have the right to challenge the boards' disciplinary decisions by the process of appeal through the courts. This basic right cannot be revoked by any means. In many states, the nurse practice act guarantees this right. But even when it isn't spelled out, this right is guaranteed to every nurse.

Of course, each state and court jurisdiction sets its own rules on how to file this type of appeal. In some jurisdictions, the nurse (through her attorney) must appeal to a special court that only handles cases from state agencies. In other states, she must appeal to the lowest-level court.

In an appeal, the court is reviewing the legality of the state board's original decision against the nurse—not the nurse's allegedly improper conduct. The court should only attempt to determine whether the board of nursing exceeded its legal powers or conducted the hearing improperly. It decides if the state board's decision is unlawful, arbitrary, or unreasonable according to law, or whether it constitutes "abuse of discretion" (meaning the board didn't have enough evidence to determine unprofessional conduct, and so made a decision without proper foundation). The court may also review the original evidence before deciding whether to sustain or reverse the board's decision.

The court may also allow a *trial de novo*, in which the appellate court hears the board's complete case against the nurse,

as though the administrative review had never happened. New evidence, if it exists, may be introduced by the plaintiff (the board) or the defendant-nurse, through her attorney. The court hears the case and then either sustains or reverses the board's original decision.

If the defendant-nurse loses this appeal, she may—depending on the jurisdiction—appeal to a higher court. (Of course, if the nurse wins, the board of nursing can appeal to a higher court, too.) To begin her new appeal, the nurse's attorney must file it with the lower court that ruled against her; this court will send the trial transcript and the appeal to the higher court. (Note that all states have rules and regulations governing appeals, and abiding by them is an attorney's legal responsibility.) The higher court then decides whether to hear the case, based on the merits of the grounds for appeal. Usually, these must establish that the lower court made an error of law in admitting (or not admitting) certain evidence. If the appeal doesn't establish this, the higher court may dismiss it. The higher court will *not* hear the case again, but the defendant-nurse and her attorney may continue to appeal through all higher courts up to the state's highest court. (Only exceptional cases can be heard by the United States Supreme Court.) (See *Nurse Practice Acts: Grounds for License Denial, Revocation, or Suspension*, pages 32 to 39.)

Two illustrative cases

Now, let's look at two actual cases that went through the administrative and judicial review processes.

In *Leib v. Board of Examiners for Nursing of the State of Connecticut* (1979), a nurse was accused of conduct that failed to meet accepted standards of the nursing profession. Her conduct? Charting the administration of meperidine hydrochloride to her patient, but using the drug herself. After voluntarily admitting to this action, she testified on her own behalf at the board hearing. The board issued an order revoking her nursing license. The nurse appealed the revocation order to the court of common pleas. When this court dismissed her appeal, she appealed to the Supreme Court of Con-

Disciplinary Proceedings for Nurse Misconduct: Typical Steps

SWORN COMPLAINT FILED

A sworn complaint is brought before a state board of nursing by:
- a health-care agency
- a professional organization
- an individual.

If the board finds sufficient evidence, it will conduct a formal review.

STATE BOARD OF NURSING REVIEW

The board:
- reviews the evidence
- calls witnesses
- determines if the nurse is guilty of misconduct.

DISCIPLINARY ACTION

If the board finds the nurse guilty of misconduct, it can take disciplinary action.

The board can:
- issue a reprimand
- place the nurse on probation
- refuse to renew her license
- suspend her license
- revoke her license.

If the nurse wants to challenge the board's decision or disciplinary action, she can file an appeal in court.

COURT REVIEW

The court will do one of two things, depending on the jurisdiction:
- examine the board's decision and decide if it conducted the hearing properly
- conduct a trial.

APPELLATE REVIEW

If the nurse wants to challenge the court's ruling, she can appeal to a higher court. If the board wants to appeal the court's ruling, it too can appeal to a higher court.

Nurse or board can appeal for a reversal of the lower court's ruling.

necticut. This higher court also ruled that the evidence supported the board's findings of unprofessional conduct. The nurse's license was revoked. Other cases in which courts upheld boards' decisions include *Tighe v. Commonwealth of Pennsylvania, State Board of Nurse Examiners* (1979) and *Ullo v. Commonwealth of Pennsylvania, State Board of Nurse Examiners* (1979).

In *Colorado State Board of Nurse Examiners v. Hohu* (1954), a doctor filed a complaint of incompetence against a nurse, claiming that her failure to admit a patient quickly and to contact the doctor caused the patient's injury. The board of nursing ordered the nurse's license revoked. But when the nurse appealed, the court reversed the board's revocation order. This court ruled that the board of nursing had abused its discretionary powers because the evidence did not support the doctor's charges.

License reinstatement

License revocation, if sustained despite all appeal efforts, is usually permanent. (Check to see if your state's nurse practice act provides for revoked-license reinstatement.) A nurse whose license is suspended usually may petition for reinstatement. Every nurse practice act contains a provision allowing reinstatement of a suspended license, and some license-suspension orders specify a date when the nurse may apply. In most states, after a suspension has been in effect for more than a year, the board of nursing will consider reinstating the license.

If *your* license were suspended, would you know how to get it back? Your first step would probably be to petition the board for reinstatement. Then the board would have to decide whether you're qualified to practice nursing again. (In some states, you have the right to another hearing before the board makes this decision.) After weighing the evidence, the board would issue its ruling.

The board will usually base its decision on current evidence of the nurse's fitness to practice. (For example, in a drug violation case, the board may consider whether a nurse has successfully completed a drug rehabilitation program.)

Conclusion

As you know, you can't stop someone from accusing you of unprofessional behavior or of practicing beyond the scope of your nursing license. A state board of nursing must consider every such complaint it receives. Your best defense against having this happen to you, of course, is prevention—practicing nursing according to the appropriate care standards and the provisions of your state nurse practice act. If you ever *do* have to defend yourself against a complaint about your nursing care, be sure you know your legal rights, so you can use them to defend yourself.

Comparing nursing and medical practice

Could you describe, in a simple sentence, how nursing practice and medical practice relate to each other? Don't try. You probably know that each state's (and Canadian province's) nurse practice act and medical practice act are intended to distinguish the two professions. But in fact—as you probably also know—social, professional, and judicial forces have blurred the distinction. More and more, the public expects you to perform many tasks formerly reserved for doctors. And the law allows you to perform them. Sometimes.

Because nursing practice and medical practice have blurred into each other in some areas, you need to know the legal risks involved in *not* knowing where your practice begins and where it ends. One key to this is knowing where the two practice acts differ and where they overlap— keeping in mind the lack of specific detail that characterizes most such acts. (See *Practicing Medicine without a License?*, pages 42 and 43.)

When state legislatures began writing medical and nursing practice acts, a doctor could legally perform any task a nurse performed. That remains true, although doctors today are likely to be unfamiliar with some nursing practices. Legislatures also reserved certain tasks exclusively for doctors. In theory, as a nurse, you perform such actions at your own legal peril. How-

Defining the Boundaries of Nursing Practice

You can characterize your state's nurse practice act (NPA) as traditional, transitional, or modern, depending on how it defines the boundaries of nursing practice.

States with *traditional* NPAs allow only the most conventional nursing roles. These states limit registered nursing activities to traditional patient care, disease prevention, and health maintenance. Very few states now have such limited NPAs.

States with *transitional* NPAs have broader boundaries, often including a "laundry list" of permitted nursing functions. For example, Maine's act lists six specific registered nursing activities: traditional patient care, collaboration with other health professionals in planning care, diagnosis and prescription delegated by doctors, delegation of tasks to LPNs/LVNs and aides, supervision and teaching, and carrying out doctors' orders. This list of duties—particularly the expanded duties of diagnosis and prescription—make Maine a state edging toward a modern type of nurse practice act. Other states with transitional acts, such as Massachusetts, broaden nurses' roles by including a separate definition for RNs who are nurse practitioners. These states recognize that these nurse practitioners may indeed diagnose and treat patients.

States with *modern* NPAs—New York, for example—allow registered nurses to diagnose and treat health problems as well as provide traditional nursing care. New York's definition of registered nursing is so broad it encompasses not only what nurses in the state do today but also much of what they're likely to do in the future.

---

ever, the blurring of nursing and medical responsibilities has forced corresponding changes in the law. Some of the causes for this are:
• patients' expectations of which health-care tasks nurses should perform
• hospitals' and doctors' increased inclination to delegate medical tasks to nurses.

How have patients forced nursing to broaden? By increasingly filing (and winning) lawsuits that express their expectation that you provide expanded patient care, including some forms of medical diagnosis, treatment, and referral. The law traditionally reserves diagnosis and treatment for doctors, but this is changing. (See *Defining the Boundaries of Nursing Practice.*)

In *Fein v. Permanente Medical Group* (1981), the court agreed with a patient's claim that a nurse erred when she failed to diagnose the patient's myocardial infarction—even though doctors reserve the professional duty to diagnose. (See page 20 for a discussion of this case.)

Hospitals and doctors have delegated more authority to nurses—for example, in intensive-care units (ICUs) and critical-care units (CCUs). Nursing in those units today includes diagnosis (reading EKGs) and treatment (performing cardiopulmonary resuscitation).

Reductions in health-care funding have also led to increased responsibilities for nurses, whose lower salaries make them less expensive than doctors.

In many Canadian provinces, the boards of nursing and medicine jointly determine which medical tasks may be delegated to nurses and specify the requirements for appropriate delegation.

Defining medical practice
Medical practice acts may be divided into two types: those that define medical practice and those that don't. Both types forbid non-MDs from practicing medicine. (No Canadian law related to medical practice defines it.)

Nurse Practice Acts: Grounds for License Denial, Revocation, or Suspension

	Alabama Title 34	Alaska Title 8	Arizona Title 32	
Obtaining or attempting to obtain nursing license by fraud or deceit	●	●	●	
Impersonating a licensed nurse		●		
Denial, suspension, revocation of license in another jurisdiction			●	
Conviction of felony	●	●	●	
Conviction of crime involving moral turpitude	●		●	
Habitual intoxication or drug addiction	●	●	●	
Possessing, selling, distributing controlled substances	●			
Negligence		●	●	
Violating patient privacy				
Falsifying patient records				
Mental/physical unfitness		●		
Involvement in criminal abortion			●	
Unprofessional conduct	●	●	●	
Professional incompetence		●	●	
Violating any provision of nurse practice act and regulations	●	●	●	
False, misleading, deceptive advertising				
Failing to report persons who violate nurse practice act				
Failing to report suspected child abuse or neglect				
Practicing while knowingly infected with contagious disease				
Failing to obtain U.S. citizenship during time allotted				
Practicing beyond scope of nursing				
Discriminating against patients on grounds of age, race, sex				

A recent review of each state's statutes indicates that any of the following violations may constitute grounds for license denial, revocation or suspension. Some states have others not listed here. Check with your board of nursing.

	Arkansas Title 72	California Business and Professions Code	Colorado Chapter 12	Connecticut Title 20	Delaware Title 24	District of Columbia Title 2	Florida Chapter 464	Georgia Title 43	Hawaii Title 25	Idaho Title 54
	•	•	•	•	•	•	•	•	•	•
		•								
		•	•		•		•	•		•
		•	•		•	•		•		•
	•		•		•			•	•	•
	•	•	•		•	•	•	•	•	•
							•			
	•	•	•	•	•					•
			•							
			•				•			
	•		•	•	•	•	•	•	•	•
		•								
	•	•				•	•	•	•	
		•		•	•				•	
	•	•	•		•	•	•	•	•	•
							•			
		•					•			
		•								

(continued)

Nurse Practice Acts: Grounds for License Denial, Revocation, or Suspension *(continued)*

	Illinois Chapter 111	Indiana Section 25	Iowa Title 8	
Obtaining or attempting to obtain nursing license by fraud or deceit	●	●		
Impersonating a licensed nurse				
Denial, suspension, revocation of license in another jurisdiction	●		●	
Conviction of felony	●		●	
Conviction of crime involving moral turpitude				
Habitual intoxication or drug addiction	●	●	●	
Possessing, selling, distributing controlled substances				
Negligence	●			
Violating patient privacy				
Falsifying patient records				
Mental/physical unfitness		●	●	
Involvement in criminal abortion				
Unprofessional conduct	●			
Professional incompetence	●	●		
Violating any provision of nurse practice act and regulations	●	●	●	
False, misleading, deceptive advertising				
Failing to report persons who violate nurse practice act			●	
Failing to report suspected child abuse or neglect	●			
Practicing while knowingly infected with contagious disease				
Failing to obtain U.S. citizenship during time allotted				
Practicing beyond scope of nursing		●		
Discriminating against patients on grounds of age, race, sex				

	Kansas Title 65	Kentucky Title 26	Louisiana Title 37	Maine Title 32	Maryland Health Occupations	Massachusetts Chapter 112	Michigan Chapter 333	Minnesota Chapter 148	Mississippi Title 73	Missouri Title 22
	●	●	●	●	●		●	●	●	●
										●
		●			●				●	●
	●	●	●	●	●		●	●	●	●
				●	●				●	●
	●	●	●	●	●		●	●	●	●
							●			●
	●	●	●		●			●	●	●
							●			
		●			●				●	
	●	●	●	●	●	NO STATUTE	●		●	●
	●			●	●		●		●	●
		●		●			●	●	●	●
	●	●	●	●	●		●	●	●	●
					●		●			●

(continued)

Nurse Practice Acts: Grounds for License Denial, Revocation, or Suspension (continued)

	Montana Title 37	Nebraska Title 71	Nevada Title 54	
Obtaining or attempting to obtain nursing license by fraud or deceit	●	●	●	
Impersonating a licensed nurse			●	
Denial, suspension, revocation of license in another jurisdiction		●		
Conviction of felony		●	●	
Conviction of crime involving moral turpitude	●	●	●	
Habitual intoxication or drug addiction	●	●	●	
Possessing, selling, distributing controlled substances		●		
Negligence	●	●	●	
Violating patient privacy				
Falsifying patient records			●	
Mental/physical unfitness	●	●	●	
Involvement in criminal abortion			●	
Unprofessional conduct	●	●	●	
Professional incompetence	●	●	●	
Violating any provision of nurse practice act and regulations	●	●	●	
False, misleading, deceptive advertising		●		
Failing to report persons who violate nurse practice act				
Failing to report suspected child abuse or neglect				
Practicing while knowingly infected with contagious disease				
Failing to obtain U.S. citizenship during time allotted				
Practicing beyond scope of nursing			●	
Discriminating against patients on grounds of age, race, sex				

	New Hampshire Title 30	New Jersey Title 45	New Mexico Chapter 61	New York Education Law	North Carolina Chapter 90	North Dakota Title 43	Ohio Title 47	Oklahoma Title 59	Oregon Title 52	Pennsylvania Title 63
	●	●	●	●	●	●	●	●	●	●
	●			●		●			●	●
	●		●	●	●	●	●	●	●	●
	●	●				●	●	●	●	
	●		●	●	●		●	●	●	●
							●			
	●			●	●	●		●	●	●
	●	●	●	●	●	●	●	●	●	●
	●	●	●	●	●	●		●	●	●
	●	●	●	●	●			●	●	
	●	●	●			●	●	●	●	●
										●
										●
				●						
				●						

(continued)

Nurse Practice Acts: Grounds for License Denial, Revocation, or Suspension *(continued)*

	Rhode Island Chapter 5	South Carolina Title 40	South Dakota Title 36	
Obtaining or attempting to obtain nursing license by fraud or deceit	●	●	●	
Impersonating a licensed nurse			●	
Denial, suspension, revocation of license in another jurisdiction		●	●	
Conviction of felony		●	●	
Conviction of crime involving moral turpitude	●			
Habitual intoxication or drug addiction	●	●	●	
Possessing, selling, distributing controlled substances		●		
Negligence	●		●	
Violating patient privacy				
Falsifying patient records	●			
Mental/physical unfitness	●			
Involvement in criminal abortion				
Unprofessional conduct	●	●	●	
Professional incompetence	●	●		
Violating any provision of nurse practice act and regulations	●			
False, misleading, deceptive advertising				
Failing to report persons who violate nurse practice act				
Failing to report suspected child abuse or neglect				
Practicing while knowingly infected with contagious disease				
Failing to obtain U.S. citizenship during time allotted				
Practicing beyond scope of nursing				
Discriminating against patients on grounds of age, race, sex				

	Tennessee Title 63	Texas Title 71 (Health)	Utah Title 58	Vermont Title 26	Virginia Title 54	Washington Chapter 18	West Virginia Chapter 30	Wisconsin Title 40A	Wyoming Title 33
	●	●	●	●	●	●	●	●	●
		●					●		
			●	●	●	●			●
	●	●		●	●	●	●		●
		●			●		●		
	●	●	●	●	●	●	●	●	●
	●					●			
	●		●			●	●		●
	●								
	●	●	●	●	●	●	●	●	●
	●								
	●	●	●		●	●	●	●	●
	●		●	●	●	●	●		
	●	●	●	●	●	●	●	●	●
	●								
	●					●			

When a state's medical practice act includes a definition, it typically defines medicine as any act of diagnosis, prescription, surgery, or treatment. Not every definition includes all four elements, and some states' definitions add other elements.

Whether or not a state's medical practice act defines medical practice, the courts are regularly called upon to decide if a specific action constitutes medical practice. In the past, one area of considerable overlap between nursing and medicine was midwifery; the courts usually decided that delivering babies was a medical rather than nursing function. For example, in *Commonwealth of Massachusetts v. Porn* (1907), a state court upheld the conviction of a nurse-midwife for practicing medicine without a license. The legislature could have created a midwifery practice act, the court said, but hadn't done so. Obstetrics was therefore reserved for doctors.

How state legislatures deal with nursing-medical overlap

Some states have solved the problem of overlap between the nursing and medical professions by passing laws making some functions common to both. New York's law, for example, allows both registered nurses and doctors to diagnose and treat patients—with the proviso that a nursing diagnosis should not alter a patient's medical regimen. And, as you probably know, almost all states permit you to perform any patient care a doctor requests, as long as a written or oral order exists. Some court decisions have concluded that a doctor's presence during patient care isn't necessary once he's delegated a task to a nurse. These decisions have also been interpreted as meaning that a nurse may perform some medical tasks on the basis of standing orders and nursing protocols, as well as on the basis of doctors' written and oral orders. This means that a nurse's scope of actions, when working under standing orders or nursing protocols, can be very broad in certain practice settings, no matter how restrictive her state nurse practice act may seem. Orders such as these form the basis for ICU/CCU practice, I.V. team practice, and similar practice circumstances in all states where the nurse practice acts don't grant nurses

clear-cut independent authority to treat patients.

Some state medical practice acts limit doctors' rights to delegate tasks. For example, Texas' medical practice act permits doctors to delegate tasks only to "any qualified and properly trained person or persons," and then only if doing so is "reasonable and prudent," and then only if the delegating doesn't violate any other state laws. Most state courts would probably interpret their state medical practice acts similarly, even if this restriction isn't written into the acts. Texas makes these limits explicit.

Remember, you can perform tasks that involve overlap of nursing and medical practices—such as ICU functions—even if your nurse practice act doesn't state that you can, through standing orders and through nursing protocols.

How the courts deal with nursing-medical overlap

In recent years, the two most common areas of nursing practice/medical practice overlap concern anesthesia treatment and emergency-department diagnosis. Interestingly, courts rarely give more than a passing reference to their state practice acts when dealing with these problems.

In *Mohr v. Jenkins* (1980), the patient sued a nurse anesthetist, claiming she incorrectly injected Valium into his arm and so caused phlebitis. The court dismissed the suit, saying the nurse "performed the procedure correctly and conformed to accepted medical practice." The patient appealed, but the appellate court affirmed that the standard for "specialists in similar circumstances" is "accepted medical practice," and that the defendant-nurse had met the appropriate standards.

A similar result occurred in *Whitney v. Day* (1980): In this case, a Michigan court said—without reference to the practice acts—that nurse anesthetists are professionals with expertise in an area akin to medical practice. As such, the court said, they can be held to the same practice standards—those of the "similar specialist."

In a North Carolina case that involved a question of licensure, *Maloney v. Wake Hospital Systems* (1980), the court refused to let a nurse testify as an expert witness, on a patient's behalf, about the correct practice in I.V. potassium chloride administration. The court said the nurse wasn't qualified to testify because the action in question belonged to medical practice. But an appellate court reversed the ruling because the nurse, although not a doctor, had acquired skills that qualified her to form an opinion. The appellate court decided that the nurse's "expertise is different from, but no less exalted than, that of the physician."

In *McKinney v. Tromly* (1964), a family sued their son's surgeon because the nurse anesthetist administered ether while the surgeon used an electrical surgical instrument, causing an explosion. The boy died from the burns that resulted. The Texas court said: "The administration of an anaesthetic . . . constitutes the practice of medicine. Although the nurse could not practice medicine, . . . she was trained . . . and knew how to administer an anaesthetic." The court also found that the administration of anesthesia by nurses was common practice in that locality. Based on these facts, the court ruled that the case be tried solely on the basis of whether the nurse was practicing as a hospital employee or as the surgeon's "borrowed servant." Thus, the issue of whether she was practicing medicine without a license became irrelevant.

In some situations, of course, you have no alternative to practicing medicine without a license, and the courts expect you to do so when a patient requires treatment. In *Cooper v. National Motor Bearing Co.* (1955), a California nurse was accused of failing to make a medical diagnosis of cancer in one of her patients. The nurse defended herself by arguing that state law at that time prohibited her from making diagnoses of any sort. The court ruled against her, finding that nurses were supposed to have sufficient training to tell whether a patient had signs or symptoms of a disease that would require a doctor's attention.

A federal court in Illinois reached a similar conclusion when a nurse failed to recognize that her patient's complaint resulted from a subdural hematoma rather than drunkenness. In *Stahlin v. Hilton Hotels Corp.* (1973), the court said the nurse "failed to exercise the degree of care required" even though doing so could be considered medical diagnosis—a task the Illinois nurse practice act forbids.

Can you safely assume, then, that courts will generally ignore the difference between medical practice and expanded nursing roles—for example, a nurse practitioner's role? Unfortunately, no. A case in point is *Hernicz v. State Dept. of Professional Regulation* (1980), which involved a registered nurse practitioner who examined and treated two patients without doctors' orders. The state board of nursing suspended his license, and the court decision upheld the suspension.

In general, the courts will tend to interpret the law in ways most likely to protect patients. If protecting patients means not strictly interpreting nursing and medical practice acts, the courts will usually follow that course.

Conclusion

You should have a keen interest in how your state defines nursing practice and in how your practice overlaps with medical practice. Why? Because you'll improve your chances of avoiding a malpractice lawsuit. And if you know your nurse practice act, you can help your state's nursing association to lobby for any needed changes.

Legislatures tend to resist amending nurse practice acts to reflect expanded roles. You can overcome that tendency through united professional activity—working together with hospital administrators, nursing home operators, and doctors to convince legislators to pass practice acts that incorporate present practices and future needs. Then you can concentrate on the key questions: What should we be doing for this patient? And who can do it best?

Nurse practitioners

If you're a nurse practitioner, you regularly perform functions that formerly were doctors' exclusive responsibilities. You're an RN who's specially trained to make independent judgments about a patient's condition (under a doctor's direction or

Practicing Medicine without a License?

Doctor's orders, but not nurse's job

For 5 years, I've been office nurse to a very fine doctor. Professionally, he's taught me many new things—including suturing.

He now has me cover for him when he's called out, and on these occasions I've often done minor suturing.

At a recent nursing seminar, the lecturer was an attorney. In his discussion, he described my job situation to a "T." Then he said that any nurse doing such suturing was leaving herself wide open for a lawsuit!

I reported this to the doctor I work for. He said that as long as he's taught me to suture correctly and I do it in his office, I have nothing to worry about because he'll be responsible for me. I'd appreciate another opinion, though.—RN, Mo.

Suturing is not ordinarily an accepted nursing procedure, and nurses ordinarily may not do it. However, a nurse *may* suture under certain circumstances—for example, if the nurse is a nurse clinician practicing in a state whose statutes permit her to suture; or if the nurse is a particular part of a health-care delivery team (say, an operating room nurse) who works under the immediate direction, control, and supervision of a doctor.

Since you're not working in either of these circumstances, you're in legal jeopardy and subject to disciplinary action by your licensing board—to say nothing of what the outcome could be if you were sued by a patient claiming injury because of your suturing. In such a situation, losing the case would seem bad enough—but you might also find that your professional liability insurance doesn't cover your legal fees or the damages assessed against you.

Who may read lab values?

A question about laboratory values came up at a recent nursing standards meeting. Some of our nurses think nurses should read a patient's lab values and act on them. Other nurses say that's a medical responsibility—and too much to ask of nurses. What do you say?—RN, Ariz.

Reading laboratory values *used to be* strictly the doctor's responsibility. Today, though, most nurses consider lab values an essential part of the nursing assessment, particularly when the test results are obviously going to affect treatment. For example, if a doctor orders hematocrit and hemoglobin tests for a GI bleeder, the nurse caring for that patient should make sure the tests are done and notify the doctor if the results warrant it.

In some hospitals, the charge nurse takes responsibility for laboratory tests, but more often staff nurses are responsible. Since most laboratories list normal values next to the patient's actual value, you needn't memorize all the numbers.

Standing orders for the school nurse

I'm a school nurse for a small private college. Once a month, a doctor comes on campus to teach a class and see pa-

order)—for example, forming a diagnosis and prescribing treatment.

Or maybe you're not a nurse practitioner—but you're interested in what's required to become one. You know that this expanded role offers nurses exciting new challenges. For example, besides diagnosing, prescribing, and treating, nurse practitioners evaluate patients' therapeutic procedures, assess changes in their health status, and manage their medical-care regimens. (Of course, nurse practi-

tients. He leaves standing orders for me to follow when he's not here. The orders generally involve only routine prescription medications, because our dispensary doesn't stock any controlled substances.

I enjoy my work but sometimes wonder if I'm not really diagnosing and prescribing by using these standing orders. The doctor almost never sees any of the patients. And although I can and do talk to the doctor frequently by phone, I can't send patients to his office—150 miles (240 km) away. I do, of course, refer any patients I'm in doubt about to local doctors.

Several doctors have assured me that what I'm doing is perfectly legal and standard procedure for small schools, but I'd appreciate your opinion.—RN, Calif.

Unfortunately, in medicine, a long distance call isn't "the next best thing to being there." By adapting the doctor's standing orders for patients he "almost never sees," you are diagnosing and prescribing.

True, standing orders have been routine procedure in many small schools. But lately these orders have been disappearing from college campuses. However, doesn't common sense tell us that even a small school should have a doctor on campus at least twice a week, if only for an hour?

If you were to misdiagnose a student's condition and treat it with a medication—even if it's what you call a "routine prescription medication"—the student could sue you and the college if he has an adverse reaction.

Although most institutions say they'll stand behind a nurse unless she errs grossly, you can't afford to take this for granted. When confronted with an actual lawsuit, the school could claim you're responsible for any error. You should definitely have your own professional liability insurance.

Check with college personnel to find out exactly what the doctor's contract calls for and whether he is or isn't living up to his full obligation. If he isn't, take the matter up with the proper college authority. If he is doing exactly what his contract calls for, insist that the college hire someone closer to the campus who can give more hours to the health service.

In the meantime, protect yourself: Refer students to a doctor in the area. If the students are miffed at the unexpected expense and inconvenience, that may help to light a small fire under the college authorities and move them to make better arrangements for the students' health care. And get that professional liability insurance!

These letters were taken from the files of *Nursing* magazine.

---

tioners also perform many tasks that hospital staff nurses perform.) And becoming a nurse practitioner means choosing a specialty. You could choose to become certified in such important nursing specialties as mental health, critical care, emergency care, neonatal care, family planning, rural health, and many others.

History of the nurse practitioner role

In 1965, Loretta Ford, RN, Ed.D., and Henry Silver, MD, began a program at the

University of Colorado that taught expanded nursing roles—roles that would place nurses into new practice settings and increase their traditional patient-care responsibilities. (Viewing shortages of doctors around the country, some health-care experts saw nurse practitioners as a means of providing medical care in places where doctors were scarce, such as extremely rural areas and inner-city neighborhoods.) That program provided a model for subsequent nurse practitioner programs around the country. In 1970, the American Nurses' Association (ANA) amended its definition of nursing to include nurses' right to take on expanded roles, with the proper preparation.

During the 1970s, many states amended their nurse practice acts to recognize nurse practitioners. By 1973, nurse practitioners were numerous enough to organize their first national convention. And by 1980, all 50 states had certification programs for nurse practitioners.

In 1973, Canadian nurses and doctors also endorsed nurses' expanded roles. In a joint statement, associations for both professions declared that expanding the nurse's role would improve Canadian health care.

Today, nurse practitioners work in a variety of settings, including nursing homes, hospital emergency departments, industrial medical offices, rural clinics, and remote and sparsely populated areas. Some nurse educators even work part-time as nurse practitioners.

Once the value of nurse practitioners' services was demonstrated, state legislatures took steps to legalize this expanded role. They amended their nursing and medical practice acts to allow nurses to perform nurse practitioner tasks, and they expanded the formerly limited right of doctors to delegate medical tasks to nurses. The amended nurse practice acts gave nurse practitioners the rights to diagnose, to prescribe (with a doctor's cosignature), and to treat their patients. Some states—such as Idaho, Indiana, Alaska, Pennsylvania, and Florida—set up guidelines for joint nursing-medical practices.

Becoming a nurse practitioner

What's involved in becoming a nurse practitioner? Because certification requirements vary, the ANA has begun a move to establish national qualifications. But for now, you'll need to check your state's certification program. Remember, you must meet all of a state's certification requirements before you may practice there. However, this may cause problems when you move to a different state. State boards of nursing can give you details about their nurse practitioner certification programs.

Among the most common certification requirements, you must:
• be a registered nurse
• have a college or university degree
• have at least 2 years of experience working as a nurse
• choose a nursing specialty.

Many certification programs also require that you obtain approval from a hospital's medical board if you want to work in that hospital.

Here's another requirement in many states: If you work in a nursing home or clinic, you must meet with the facility's administrator and doctors at least once a year. The reason? To review procedures, standing orders, and documentation regulations concerning your job.

Interpreting the limits of nurse practitioner practice

Because expanded roles for nurses are fairly new, few questions about a nurse practitioner's role and liability yield clear-cut answers. So complaints settled both in and out of court are important right now in defining the limits of the nurse practitioner's expanded role—and they will continue to be important in the future.

So far, complaints and lawsuits involving nurse practitioners have usually been based on alleged unauthorized medical practice. For example, the New Jersey Board of Medical Examiners reviewed the complaints of two patients who charged two nurse practitioners in a health maintenance organization with prescribing drugs and making a medical diagnosis. The ANA supported the nurses, stating that they were acting well within the nurse practice act. Although the parties settled out of court, the board cited the complaints as the basis for issuing stricter definitions of doctors' and nurse practitioners' responsibilities.

In another New Jersey complaint, the Board of Medical Examiners inquired about four school nurse practitioners said to be performing physical assessments of students. Even though the nurse practitioners were trained to do physical assessments, they agreed to stop when the school district's medical director gave them a written order, at their request, to do so.

In Missouri, doctors on the Board of Registration of Healing Arts accused two nurse practitioners, who provided family planning services, of practicing medicine. And two consulting doctors were accused of contributing to the nurses' alleged illegal practice by delegating medical tasks to them. The tasks included performing pelvic examinations and pap smears, treating vaginitis, counseling, providing contraceptives, and inserting intrauterine devices. The nurses claimed that their tasks were valid under protocols signed by their consulting doctors.

Remember: When disputes about nurse practitioner practice arise, your nurse practice act probably won't be enough help. You'll find that court decisions on medical or nursing board rulings provide more current and descriptive legal clarifications of the nurse practitioner's role.

Assessing the legal risks

Many states' nurse practice acts now legally permit nursing in an expanded role, but you should be aware that serious legal concerns exist for nurse practitioners. One legal concern is simply the fact that some states have not amended their practice acts to recognize nurse practitioners. In those states, functioning as a nurse practitioner is illegal. A nurse practitioner's responsibility to practice only under a doctor's direction or with his orders also has legal significance. Without a doctor's order, she can perform only traditional nursing tasks.

You may already know about another legal concern of nurse practitioners—the fact that their liability depends on whether they provide their services:
• as an employee of an institution, such as a hospital or public health agency

• as an employee of a doctor; sometimes as part of a joint practice
• as an independent contractor.

If you work for an institution or a doctor and you're sued for malpractice (and lose), the court will apply the traditional nurse-employer doctrine—respondeat superior—to determine liability. The doctrine doesn't necessarily relieve you of professional liability. But if you were working within the scope of your employment, application of the doctrine makes your employer responsible for all damages a court may award to the plaintiff.

If you're sued for malpractice while working as an independent contractor, however, you carry the full responsibility for your liability. That means you'll have to pay the entire cost of any cash damages the plaintiff may be awarded. (See *Should You Practice as an Independent Contractor?* page 46.)

You can see that the circumstances of your employment as a nurse practitioner are important in determining the type and amount of professional liability insurance you'll need.

Legal protection for the nurse practitioner

You now know that a number of state nurse practice acts have expanded-role provisions that give a nurse practitioner legal protection. You should also be aware of other forms of protection. For example, a *written contract* can offer some protection. In any practice setting, have an attorney draw up a contract before you begin caring for patients. Be sure it defines such important conditions as what services you're expected to perform, your fees, how and when you'll be paid, the amount of professional liability insurance (if any) your employer will carry, and how disputes will be handled. To be valid, the contract must have a legal purpose and the willing consent of both parties.

Professional liability insurance is important, but you can't beat the protection that comes with maintaining the highest competence in your practice. You may even want to take advanced courses and classes to improve your professional credentials and to strengthen your defense if you're sued.

Should You Practice as an Independent Contractor?

Thousands of nurses in the United States, including nurse practitioners and private-duty nurses, have chosen to become independent contractors. They work directly for patients (or patients' families) and bill their patients (or third-party insurers) on a fee-for-service basis. If you're considering practicing on an independent-contractor basis, you'll want to weigh the pros and cons.

PROs	CONs
• You can schedule your work hours to suit your life-style.	• You'll lose the security that continuous employment provides.
• You can put your nursing philosophy into practice by independently planning each patient's nursing care.	• You may experience strained working relationships with professionals who feel threatened by your autonomy and status.
• You'll be relatively free from institutional politics and bureaucracy.	• You'll have to compete for work with other nurses working as independent contractors.
• You can negotiate your own contract with each patient and set your own fee for nursing services.	• Your patients may sometimes be admitted to hospitals (or other health-care institutions) where you don't have privileges.
• You may improve your working relationship with other professionals because you'll assume a more prestigious role in the health-care community.	• You'll have to deal with unclear legal definitions of your practice.
• You'll keep more of the money you make, because tax laws favor self-employment.	• You'll have to educate yourself about the financial and legal aspects of running a business.
• You can tailor your benefits package to your own personal needs.	• You'll have to deal with getting patients to pay their bills.
• You can become more involved in the total care of your patient.	

Financial concerns

Nurse practitioners have to consider some possible financial problems. For example, you may know that many third-party insurance carriers won't provide reimbursement for a nurse practitioner's services, even though state and professional nurse organizations have lobbied to persuade carriers to do so. If you're a nurse practitioner, or if you become one, always have your patient check that his health insurance covers your services. If it doesn't, he may not want your services after all—or you may have difficulty collecting your fee.

Remember that if you work as an independent contractor, no employer withholds taxes (federal, state, or local), unemployment compensation, or social security payments. You're solely responsible for keeping track of these obligations and making payments on schedule.

If you have your own office, you'll also need property liability insurance. This will protect you if someone's injured on your property. Also, establish contact with an accountant who's familiar with business-finance regulations. And consider asking an attorney to help set up your business along sound legal lines.

Professional concerns

A nurse practitioner's professional concerns differ from a staff nurse's. For example, to be most effective as a nurse practitioner, you'll need a certain degree of cooperation and acceptance from the community you choose to practice in. Some communities will oppose your practice because people feel uncomfortable with your increased responsibilities.

If you work as a nurse practitioner on an independent-contractor basis, you'll have to get local hospitals and health-care institutions to grant you patient-care privileges. But what if one of your patients is admitted to a hospital that won't grant you privileges? You can appeal the hospital's decision through the hospital's nursing department committee, depending on your state laws. The hospital has a legal responsibility to tell you how its appeal process works. By appealing the hospital's decision, you can learn the reason why your request for privileges was denied—whether it was because the privilege requested isn't in the scope of your nursing practice or for some other reason. If the denial is found to be baseless, designed to limit competition with medical staff, or obliged by an exclusive contract between the hospital and another practitioner, then you have grounds for charging the hospital with unfair competition or restraint of trade.

Remember, you may face opposition from staff nurses who are concerned that your expanded role could implicate them in a malpractice lawsuit. You'll have to work at winning their trust and confidence.

Conclusion

You may wonder whether more job opportunities will exist for nurse practitioners in the future. No one can say for sure, although some believe that a surplus of doctors may have a significant impact. And although the nurse practitioner's expanded role appeals to many nurses, they must examine their willingness to deal with the special legal, financial, and professional concerns nurse practitioners face. Probably, as the nurse practitioner's ex-

panded role gains more acceptance, her legal risks will decline—although they'll always be higher than a staff nurse's—and third-party reimbursement for nurse practitioner services will become more common.

In the last analysis, economics might determine the extent of the nurse practitioner's influence on health care. If nurse practitioners can provide efficient medical and nursing services at reduced cost to consumers, chances are this expanded role for nurses will find a secure place in our health-care system.

Private-duty nurses

No doubt you've been frustrated, sometimes, when you've had to divide your attention and skills among many patients. Well, would you like a job that lets you devote all your nursing skills to the care of one patient? That's one advantage of working as a private-duty nurse (PDN).

Who's a private-duty nurse? She's any RN or LPN/LVN that a patient (or his family) hires for total nursing care. The patient pays her directly, or she bills a third-party insurer directly. She's an *independent contractor*, not an employee (except of her patient). This employment status is the major factor in distinguishing the private-duty nurse from the agency nurse. (Of course, a hospital or other health-care institution may also hire a private-duty nurse. See the discussion of *Emory University v. Shadburn*, 1933, page 48.)

Besides focusing all your skills on one patient, the other advantages of working as a private-duty nurse include choosing where you work, when you work, the type of patient you care for, and the fee you feel your skills are worth—although your community's prevailing fees will influence this decision.

Patients are referred to a private-duty nurse through nurse registries and referrals from other nurses and doctors familiar with the nurse's practice. Many hospitals maintain referral lists of private-duty nurses. If you work as a private-duty nurse long enough, you can expect that you'll build up a list of hospitals, other health-care institutions, nurses, doctors, and families who will call you when they need a private-duty nurse.

A private-duty nurse performs most of the tasks a hospital staff nurse performs, and she's expected to have the same degree of skill. She plans a patient's care, observes and evaluates his condition, reports signs and symptoms, carries out treatments under a doctor's direction, and keeps accurate records so that the patient's doctor has the data he needs to diagnose and prescribe. It is a private-duty nurse's obligation to perform her job within the scope of her state nurse practice act—the same as a staff nurse. And as you probably know, a private-duty nurse working in a hospital can expect the hospital to provide her with adequate *equipment* and *support services* for proper patient care.

But private-duty nursing poses unique *legal risks* and problems you ordinarily wouldn't face as a hospital staff nurse. For example, a private-duty nurse doesn't retain professional liability insurance through an employer. As an independent contractor, she's solely liable for any damages assessed as the result of a lawsuit—although a court may decide a hospital shares liability for her actions. So she (and you, if you work as a private-duty nurse) must obtain her own professional liability insurance.

Besides the additional legal risks, you must manage certain financial burdens if you work as an independent contractor. For example, you'll be responsible for making social security payments and for paying federal, state, and local taxes on schedule. And you won't be eligible for workmen's compensation benefits if you're injured on a job. The courts have repeatedly rejected private-duty nurses' claims for workmen's compensation. For example, in a Maryland case, *Edith Anderson Nursing Homes, Inc. v. Bettie Walker* (1963), a private-duty nurse was hurt caring for a nursing home patient who was in a wheelchair. The nurse attempted to collect workmen's compensation benefits from the nursing home because her injury occurred there, but her claim was denied. The nurse was an independent contractor who was paid by the patient's family, did no work for the home, and took her orders only from the patient's doctor. As an independent contractor, the court ruled, she wasn't entitled to the benefits available to the nursing home's employees. A subsequent appellate court decision upheld the denial of the nurse's claim.

Your legal risks working as an independent contractor

If you work as a private-duty nurse for a patient, you're legally considered an independent contractor. In this situation, your legal risks are highest when you care for a patient in his home. Why? Because you're responsible not only for giving proper patient care but also for obtaining and correctly using any equipment the patient care requires. These added responsibilities naturally increase your chances of making a mistake. And because you're self-employed, legally you're solely responsible for paying court-ordered damages if you're sued and found negligent.

Making written contracts with your patient can help reduce your legal risks as an independent contractor. A contract spells out the conditions of your employment—but remember, having a contract doesn't prevent a lawsuit, nor can it provide evidence that definitely will exonerate you if you're sued.

The case of *Emory University v. Shadburn* (1933) set the precedent for a hospital's liability for a private-duty nurse's wrongful conduct. A patient jumped out of a window after the assigned private-duty nurse—who had reason to know that his condition warranted continuous watching—left him unattended. The court ruled that the hospital was liable for this nurse's negligence because the hospital had hired and paid the nurse on a private-duty basis.

A hospital will usually insist on tight control of a private-duty nurse's practice, both to protect patients and to demonstrate "reasonable supervision" if the hospital is sued. Because of the trend to make hospitals share liability, you'll probably face liability alone only if you commit a negligent act *despite* the hospital's reasonable supervision.

Hospital controls include checking every private-duty nurse's credentials and approving her nursing qualifications. The case of *Ashley v. Nyack Hospital* (1979) established that a hospital has the right to refuse practice privileges to a nurse if the hospital doesn't approve her qualifications. Hospitals generally also establish policies to govern how private-duty nursing practice will relate to hospital nurses' practice. Hospitals are obligated to inform all health-care team members about private-duty nurses' responsibilities and rights in the hospital.

Your legal risks when working with a private-duty nurse

If you're working on a unit where a private-duty nurse is working, you're responsible for seeing that the PDN receives any help she needs. However, your responsibility doesn't end there. Even though a PDN is caring for one of her patients, remember that you're responsible for the patient as well.

Monitor the PDN's care. If you're a staff nurse and you see the PDN performing care negligently, inform your charge nurse. If you're the charge nurse, intervene immediately. If you see the PDN negligently performing emergency care when the patient's life is in danger—regardless of your staff position—you must intervene immediately. You're protecting your patient, yourself, and your hospital. If you ignore the PDN's negligence, you and the hospital could be liable for negligence if the patient (or the patient's family) files a malpractice lawsuit.

If you're a charge nurse, remember that the PDN's contract outlines her responsibilities. Read over that contract and keep its provisions in mind when you make assignments. Never assign a PDN a job that involves responsibilities not included in her contract.

Conclusion

Private-duty nursing offers you the opportunity to work in different practice settings and to give complete nursing care to individual patients. If you're a "take-charge" person who seeks new challenges, you may decide that the rewards of private-duty nursing are worth the increased legal risks.

Nurses in geriatric facilities

America is growing gray. U.S. census statistics show that the number of Americans over age 65 is growing. By 1990, they'll probably make up about 12% of the population; by 2000, about 13%.

As you know, this trend means that more and more patients will be cared for in geriatric facilities, including nursing homes and extended-care facilities. In fact, surveys already show that more patients are in geriatric facilities than in hospitals.

This growth in the number of patients in geriatric facilities began in 1965, when Congress passed the Medicare and Medicaid amendments to the Social Security Act. Because these amendments provided government reimbursement for geriatric care, the number of nursing homes (and their patients) began increasing dramatically.

The Medicare and Medicaid amendments also provided reimbursement for skilled nursing care in extended-care facilities. These were initially planned to deliver short-term nursing care to elderly patients who no longer needed intensive medical and nursing care in a hospital. Today, about 80% of the patients admitted to extended-care facilities do come directly from hospitals or other health-care facilities. But because many patients remain in extended-care facilities for long periods of time, the distinction between extended-care and geriatric facilities has blurred.

Geriatric care today

You're probably aware that all geriatric facilities should provide nursing and medical care that is preventative, protective, restorative, and supportive. Unfortunately, the care provided today in many geriatric facilities falls short of these goals. (See *Helping Your Patient Select an Extended-Care Facility,* page 51.) A 1974 U.S. Department of Health, Education, and Welfare survey showed that many geriatric facilities failed to meet standards for patients' safety, nutrition, medical care, and rehabilitation. This survey also discovered frequent violations of patients' rights. The relatively small number of licensed nurses employed by geriatric facilities may be a large part of this problem. A recent Institute of Medicine study states that sickness and disability have increased among nursing home patients, but that employers' demands for nursing services haven't kept pace. Why? Because Medicare and Medicaid payments aren't sufficient to pay for the nursing staff that would be needed. So Medicare and Medicaid payments, begun by Congress to help elderly patients, have inadvertently resulted in substandard care for many of them.

Many RNs and LPNs/LVNs working in geriatric facilities are aware of this problem, and most are concerned about their legal rights and responsibilities. The three areas these nurses are most concerned about are staffing patterns, quality of care, and ensuring patients' rights.

Staffing patterns in geriatric facilities
Health-care professionals use the term *minimal licensed-personnel staffing* to describe the current staffing situation in many geriatric facilities. The following are characteristic of nursing homes:

• Only about 1 of every 20 nursing home employees is an RN.

• Only about 1 licensed health-care professional is employed for every 100 nursing home patients.

• Doctors spend only about 2 hours a month with their nursing home patients.

• Licensed nurses usually must process the paperwork while comparatively untrained aides provide most of the patient care.

In some extended-care facilities, about 6 of 10 charge nurses on the 3 p.m. to 11 p.m. shift and about 7 of 10 charge nurses on the 11 p.m. to 7 a.m. shift are LPNs/LVNs.

Health-care experts testifying before the Select Committee on Aging of the U.S. House of Representatives have alleged that Medicare's regulations created the staffing patterns that are causing inadequate care. For instance, federal Medicare regulations only require geriatric facilities to have one LPN/LVN on all shifts and one RN on the day shift. This means that many such facilities hire only this minimum number of licensed nurses to qualify for federal funds. Few state Medicaid programs provide reimbursement to geriatric facilities for additional licensed nurses.

In most geriatric facilities, RNs hold administrative positions, shouldering broad supervisory responsibility for the quality of care. LPNs/LVNs often work as charge nurses, performing most nursing procedures and supervising nurses' aides. Obviously this arrangement creates potential legal problems concerning both supervision and the scope of nursing practice.

Legal risks of staffing problems
As you know, every nurse is legally responsible for her own actions. A supervisor is responsible for her supervisory acts and decisions. Suppose a supervisor knows—or should know—that a subordinate is inexperienced, untrained, or unable to perform a task safely. A court may find that supervisor liable in a malpractice lawsuit for delegating such a task to the subordinate. Of course, if the subordinate performs that task negligently, she'll be liable, too. And if the court finds that the supervisor and the subordinate were working within the scope of their employment, the nursing home may share liability under the doctrine of respondeat superior.

The courts judge lawsuits involving nursing malpractice by determining whether the defendant-nurse's actions met professional standards for her position. As part of this determination, the courts may review details of the staffing situation. For example, a New York court found that nurses were negligent when an unsupervised patient jumped from a balcony (*Horton v. Niagara Falls Memorial Medical Center*, 1976). The court reached this conclusion after reviewing evidence detailing the number of patients on the unit, the number of staff members, and what each staff member was doing. During this review, the court discovered that a charge nurse had permitted the only available aide to go to supper when she had the authority to prevent it, leaving the disoriented patient unsupervised.

Whether you're an RN or an LPN/LVN working in a geriatric facility, you *must* practice within the legal limits set by your

Helping Your Patient Select an Extended-Care Facility

Your elderly or disabled patient may need the care provided at an extended-care facility. As a nurse, you can help the patient and his family choose a facility by explaining the three types of extended-care facilities available and what type of care each offers.

RESIDENTIAL CARE FACILITY

Best for a patient who needs minimal medical attention, this type of facility provides meals, modest medical care, and a life-style free of most housekeeping responsibilities. Some offer recreational and social programs as well. Federal and state subsidy programs don't usually cover the cost of residential care facilities.

INTERMEDIATE-CARE FACILITY

The best choice for a patient who can't manage independently, this type of facility provides room, board, and daily nursing care. The cost may be covered by government subsidy programs. Some offer rehabilitation programs as well as recreational programs.

SKILLED NURSING FACILITY (SNF)

Best for a patient who needs constant medical attention, this type of facility provides 24-hour nursing care, medical care when needed, and such rehabilitation services as physical and occupational therapies. Depending on the patient's eligibility, both Medicare and Medicaid may pay the cost of the patient's care.

state nurse practice act, meet professional standards for your position, and be familiar with state regulations for the type of facility in which you work. If you're an RN, be sure you possess the management and supervisory skills that your job requires. Keep in mind that if you're sued for malpractice, you'll be judged according to how a reasonably prudent nursing supervisor would act in similar circumstances. You can't defend yourself by claiming that you weren't trained to supervise.

If you're an LPN/LVN working in a geriatric facility, remember that no individual or institution can force you to practice beyond the limits of nursing care outlined in your state nurse practice act. If you do exceed the legally permissible scope of nursing in your state, your state board of nursing can suspend or revoke your license. You won't be able to use your employer's expectations to excuse your actions.

Under the law, an LPN/LVN who performs a nursing function legally restricted to RNs will be held to the RN standard if she's sued for malpractice. In *Barber v.* *Reinking* (1966), involving an LPN who had performed an RN function, the court stated, "In accordance with public policy of this state, one who undertakes to perform the services of a trained or graduate nurse must have the knowledge and skill possessed by the registered nurse."

Quality of patient care

RNs and LPNs/LVNs working in geriatric facilities are concerned about the quality of patient care they're able to provide. They're particularly concerned about fragmentation of the nursing process; although an RN *remains responsible* for overall patient assessment and evaluation, an LPN/LVN decides on the daily assessments, planning, and evaluation, and a nurse's aide *implements* the assessment plan. This fragmentation of the nursing process can greatly reduce the quality of patient care. And it can also have legal consequences if nursing actions are performed improperly—or not performed at all. Here's a list of legally risky actions that occur more frequently in geriatric facilities, largely because of inadequate staffing:

- failing to make a nursing diagnosis
- observing a patient's condition carelessly
- failing to document
- writing illegibly when documenting
- failing to keep up with geriatric-nursing knowledge
- failing to use nursing consultants
- delegating improperly
- failing to insist on clear institutional policies
- failing to question a doctor's order
- taking a dangerous patient-care shortcut
- excluding family from patient care
- failing to call the doctor whenever nursing judgment indicates that a patient needs medical attention.

Protecting patients' rights in geriatric facilities

In recent years, a number of states have enacted patients' rights legislation patterned after the Patient's Bill of Rights published by the American Hospital Association. Twenty-eight of these states have passed laws that make reporting maltreatment of patients a legal responsibility. Some states have even established an ombudsman's office that has the authority to investigate complaints of abuse and the obligation to post complaint procedures in all geriatric facilities. So in most states, RNs and LPNs/LVNs working in geriatric facilities have a professional obligation (and in some states, a legal responsibility) to protect their patients' rights.

If you work in a geriatric facility, you should request that your institution adopt patient's rights policies that:

- require a patient's signature for any release of information
- clearly specify who has access to medical records and impose penalties for unauthorized disclosure of patient information
- restrict the use of chemical (drug) and physical restraints, which should be used only when the patient's physical or mental status gives evidence that they're necessary; and even then, of course, only with a doctor's order
- foster a patient's right to know about his condition and provide for informed consent for his treatment

- help combat drug abuse and misuse by requiring that nurses administering drugs know the drugs' effects and know how to assess a patient's changing needs
- ensure prompt, effective communication between doctors and nurses
- acknowledge and respect a patient's right to refuse treatment
- encourage nurses to evaluate the quality of nursing services and to work cooperatively with patient representatives and accreditation agencies in the evaluation process.

Most health-care professionals are patient-rights advocates, but the patient-rights issue can create an adversary relationship between a nurse and a doctor or between a nurse and an institution. This situation presents a paradox for nurses: You have a professional obligation to protect your patient's constitutional rights—but doing so could cost you your job. Unfortunately, your legal protection in this situation is limited. If you're an employee working without a contract, you can be dismissed for any reason your employer wants to give. You do have legal grounds to protest your dismissal if:

- your contract clearly states you can't be fired on these grounds
- your hospital guarantees you the right to notice and a hearing prior to dismissal
- your state's laws prevent your employer from retaliating if you report violations to the appropriate agency
- you're a government employee and can claim the First Amendment right to free speech.

Conclusion

In a geriatric facility, where doctors' involvement with patients is limited, RNs and LPNs/LVNs have a good opportunity to grow professionally and to affect the quality of patient care. If you're an RN, you'll need to learn not only geriatric nursing but also good management. If you're an LPN/LVN, you may have the chance to fill a charge-nurse position and to expand your nursing skills. (Depending on the limits of your nurse practice act, you may also learn how to perform nursing assessment and patient teaching.) For all nurses, along with opportunity comes responsibility—for practicing within legal limits and for continuing your education to meet professional standards for your position.

Nurses in alternative settings

Practicing nursing outside of traditional settings—such as hospitals, clinics, and nursing homes—isn't new. In fact, in the 19th century, *most* nurses worked outside hospitals: in doctors' offices, in patients' homes, and on battlefields. Today, many nurses are practicing in *alternative settings*. Their employers include factories, schools, community public health services, insurance companies, and claims review agencies. Some nurses—such as those working in schools and factories— may choose their alternative settings because they offer more independence and a challenging variety of responsibilities. Others—such as nurses in public health agencies—may want to devote themselves to public service.

These nurses find that along with benefits come additional responsibilities and legal risks. For instance, a nurse working alone doesn't have the daily support of senior nurses, doctors, and specialized equipment that a hospital setting offers. And of course, greater individual responsibility for patient care means greater legal risks. In this sense, a nurse working in an alternative setting is similar to a private-duty nurse.

As you know, two of the most important challenges for a nurse working in *any* setting are to know her legal responsibilities and to minimize her legal risks. A nurse must be particularly careful when working in an alternative setting—she may not have anything like the legal services of a hospital's administration to help her.

Professional standards for licensure

As you probably know, your state nurse practice act defines professional qualifications for RN and LPN/LVN licensure. But nurse practice acts generally don't describe professional standards for nurses working in various settings. If you work in an alternative setting, you must meet the same practice standards as a hospital nurse. If you violate those standards, your state board of nursing may suspend or revoke your license, just as it would if you were a hospital nurse, and your patient may be able to sue you for malpractice.

Few court cases involving nurses working in alternative settings have been reported. In one such case, *Stefanik v. Nursing Education Committee* (1944), a state board of nursing recommended that the state revoke the license of a district welfare department nurse. The board found that the nurse, who saw patients without their doctors' consent and contradicted their doctors' orders, was guilty of unprofessional conduct. The nurse appealed to the court, which sustained the board's decision. In reaching its decision, the board of nursing judged this nurse's conduct by the state's standards for nursing practice. Neither the court nor the board considered that this nurse could be judged by any special standards because she worked in an alternative setting.

Your liability in alternative settings

A few legal differences exist between nurses working in traditional settings and in alternative settings.

Usually, if you work for a privately owned business (such as a manufacturer, an insurance company, or a small medical practice group), you may be sued by anyone who believes you're guilty of failing to meet standards of nursing care or of practicing beyond the scope of your license. In some states, however, you can't be sued by a fellow employee you've treated for a job-related injury. That's because state workmen's compensation laws, which protect the employer from excessive business costs, also protect you. (For additional information, *see Hospice Care: Some Legal Considerations,* page 54.)

If you work for certain government agencies, you may be immune from lawsuits because of the doctrine of sovereign immunity. Depending on the state in which you're working, this immunity may be complete or partial. Check with your personnel office or agency attorney to find out if you have this legal protection.

Hospice Care:
Some Legal Considerations

As you probably know, a hospice is a health-care facility that provides terminally ill patients with therapy and psychosocial and spiritual services until life ends. If you work in a hospice, you assume the same patient-care responsibilities as nurses in other settings. Your legal responsibilities, however, differ as follows:

• *Standing orders.* A hospital staff nurse can follow standing orders for pain medication. When working in a hospice, however, you should never rely on standing orders as authorization to administer pain medication. Always obtain specific orders signed by the patient's doctor.

• *Advice on making a will.* In a hospice, never give your patient advice concerning his will. If he asks you about it, tell him you can't help him, but suggest that he discuss it with his attorney or family.

• *Living wills.* Unlike the hospital nurse, whose duty with respect to living wills varies from state to state, the nurse who works in a hospice *must* respect the patient's living will. Don't violate it in any way, unless a court order instructs you to do so.

You know that a nurse in an alternative setting must meet the same practice standards as a hospital staff nurse. A California malpractice case, *Cooper v. National Motor Bearing Co.* (1955), illustrates this point. The lawsuit concerned an occupational health nurse who failed to diagnose suspected cancer and so didn't refer the patient for further evaluation and treatment. At the trial, the court ruled that the only point of law to be considered in deciding the case was whether the nurse met the standards of nursing practice in her area. When expert testimony showed that she'd breached those standards, the court found her guilty of negligence. Her occupational setting was irrelevant to the court's decision. Similar court cases illustrating this principle include *Johnston v. Black Co.* (1939); *Barber v. Reinking* (1966; see page 22); and *Stahlin v. Hilton Hotels Corp.* (1973; see page 41).

The Canadian approach to such cases is similar to the American approach. In *Dowey v. Rothwell* (1974), a nurse who worked in a doctor's office knew that an epileptic patient was about to have a seizure, yet she failed to stay with the patient. This patient did have a seizure, fell, and fractured an arm. The court found that the nurse failed "to provide that minimum standard of care which a patient has a right to expect in an office setting." The court based its findings on testimony about the expected performance standards of experienced RNs in many settings.

Should you buy your own professional liability insurance?

Private *medical* employers generally have coverage that includes the nurses they employ, but private *industrial* employers, especially small companies, may not. Check your employer's coverage thoroughly: If you've any doubt about whether you're fully protected, consider buying your own insurance.

You may also need your own professional liability insurance if you work for a peer review organization or a state or federal government agency, unless the law grants you complete immunity from job-related lawsuits.

Your rights as an employee

Can you join a union if you work in an alternative setting? It depends on the setting—but usually you can. In fact, if you work as an occupational health nurse in a factory with a closed shop, you may be required to join a union.

If you work for a state or local government, state laws may permit you to join a union but forbid your union to strike. Remember that the National Labor Relations Act exempts state and local governments, and so doesn't protect government nurses—such as community health nurses and public school nurses—in unionization disputes.

If you work in an alternative setting, can you be fired? That depends on whether or not you have a contract. If you don't have one, your employer may fire you at his discretion. Actually, your situation is the same as that of the hospital nurse—nothing but a contract clause, a union agreement, or a civil service law can legally protect you from being fired. Even if you have such protection, you may be vulnerable to discretionary firing until after an initial probationary period. Following this period, however, any of these forms of protection guarantees you the right to appeal your employer's decision.

If you work in an alternative setting, you should know what coverage your employer as well as your state, federal, or Canadian provincial government provides for on-the-job injuries. Generally, workmen's compensation will cover you. But not always.

The majority of states and Canadian provinces require that most *privately owned businesses* participate in workmen's compensation plans. If you work for such a business, you'll probably receive workmen's compensation for job-related injuries. But you should be aware that if the money you receive from this fund is inadequate, workmen's compensation laws prevent you from suing your employer for additional compensation.

If you work for *an employer with few employees or limited income* (for instance, a doctor with a small-scale practice), you may not be covered by workmen's compensation. That's because some states don't require such employers to participate in the workmen's compensation plan. If you're in this situation, you *can* sue your employer directly for any job-related injury. Most of these employers buy their own insurance to cover workers' injuries. If your employer doesn't have such insurance, you can buy your own insurance.

If you work for *a state or federal government agency*, you may receive compensation from the state workmen's compensation plan or by making a claim under a state or federal tort claims act, depending on the applicable laws. However, if the sovereign immunity doctrine applies, you may not be eligible for any compensation.

The doctrine of sovereign immunity goes back to the days when a person couldn't sue a sovereign (or his agents) unless the sovereign consented. In the United States the courts transferred this privilege, applicable in most circumstances, to the elected government and its appointed agents—government employees. So government employees ordinarily can't be sued for their on-the-job mistakes.

In the past, this immunity has had some unfair results: A patient harmed in a private hospital could sue the hospital and its employees, but a patient harmed in a municipal or state hospital could not.

Perhaps because of this immunity, public hospitals gained a reputation for substandard practice; the public suspected that because public hospitals couldn't be sued for malpractice, their standards of care were lax.

In recent decades, most state legislatures have recognized the unfairness of this system. Many have passed laws that allow patients to sue public hospitals and other government agencies. In some states, legislatures have created special courts—often called courts of claims—in which such lawsuits must be heard. In other states, legislatures have set dollar limits on the amount a patient can recover from a government agency if he wins his suit. Some states have done both.

No matter what kind of compensation plan you have, it usually covers *any* on-the-job injury. For example, if you're a school nurse and a student kicks you, workmen's compensation will normally cover you. Typically, you also have the legal right to sue the person who caused the injury. If you win your lawsuit, the court will consider any money you've already received, either from workmen's compensation or other insurance, in deciding the amount of damages you should receive. (Because these lawsuits are costly and can take years to resolve, most nurses don't sue.)

Do you know what to do if your employer violates your legal rights? If the employer's violation is an action—such as a breach of a contract or civil service regulation, sexual harassment, or racial discrimination—you should see an attorney or your union's legal counselor. Usually, he'll explain your rights and the legal actions you can take according to applicable state, national, or Canadian provincial laws. Under most laws that protect employees' rights, however, you must file a complaint quickly (as dictated by state or provincial law) or risk losing your right to compensation.

Choosing an alternative setting

Many options exist for the nurse who wants to work outside traditional practice settings (see *Providing Nursing Care In Alternative Settings*, page 57). First, know what you want. Then, look for the alternative setting that can give it to you.

If you want more independent responsibility, for example, look into school nursing or occupational health nursing. You'll probably be the only health-care professional on duty. (Working in a doctor's office offers little opportunity for independent decision making.)

Or maybe your chief desire is plenty of patient contact. Then a doctor's office may be the place for you. Other settings where you'd see plenty of patients include schools, industry, and public-health agencies.

If your main interest is public service, check out public health agencies and social service departments. If you get a job with one of these organizations, you may be able to influence policy and thus improve the quality of health-care services for a large number of people.

Conclusion

Of course, if you accept a nursing position in an alternative setting, you'll also be accepting the special challenges of knowing your legal responsibilities and minimizing your legal risks. But if an alternative setting appears to offer you the job satisfaction you want, these challenges shouldn't discourage you.

Agency nurses

How'd you like a job that lets you continuously choose not only where you work but also the hours and the days you work? You can get that kind of work-schedule flexibility if you work for a temporary-nursing service agency. And agencies generally pay higher salaries than hospital staff nurses receive.

Keep in mind, however, that the professional relationships and responsibilities of agency work are still evolving, and no set of uniform policies and procedures has yet been formally identified or administratively defined. For example, if an RN and an LPN/LVN are assigned to care for the same patient in his home but on different shifts, what responsibility does the RN have for the LPN's/LVN's work? Does the RN have the responsibility for supervising home health aides? Also, should communication between the RN and the patient's doctor be direct or channeled through an agency supervisor?

Large agencies, especially those with nationwide placement, may have specific policies for how RNs and LPNs/LVNs should function in situations like these. But smaller, more regional agencies may not. So when you work as an agency nurse, you may have few clear-cut guidelines. Sometimes you may have to rely heavily on your professional nursing judgment when you care for patients. *But remember: The courts will generally apply the same traditional legal principles governing staff-nurse malpractice cases to agency nurses as well.* This policy means you need to be thoroughly aware of the legal risks involved in agency nursing and how you can minimize them.

Your legal status as an agency nurse

When you work for an agency, you have an employee-employer relationship. The agency charges, for your services, a fee from which it pays your salary. It may also provide such benefits as social security and other tax deductions, workmen's compensation, sick pay, and professional liability insurance. (Traditional nursing registries, of course, also refer nurses to

Providing Nursing Care in Alternative Settings

The lists below detail how nurses work in four alternative practice settings—schools, industry, community health, and business.

SCHOOL NURSE
• Provides nursing care for sick or injured students
• Gives first aid in emergencies
• Gives students medications (when authorized by the school doctor)
• Helps school doctor give routine examinations
• Gives annual screening tests—for example, vision, audiometry, and scoliosis tests—and refers students for further testing or treatment when appropriate
• Counsels parents and students
• Meets with teachers and other staff members about health problems and health education programs
• Enforces state immunization policies for school-age children
• Visits sick or injured students at home when necessary
• Helps identify and meet special needs of handicapped students.

OCCUPATIONAL HEALTH NURSE
• Provides nursing care for sick or injured employees
• Gives first aid in emergencies
• Performs medical screening tests or helps doctor perform them
• Refers sick or injured employees for appropriate treatment
• Counsels employees on health matters
• Meets with employer regarding health-related issues
• Develops and maintains employee medical records
• Maintains records for government agencies such as workmen's compensation agencies, the Occupational Safety and Health Administration, and state or federal labor and health departments

• Alerts employer to potential health and safety hazards.

COMMUNITY HEALTH NURSE
• Provides nursing care for community patients; visits sick or injured persons in their homes
• Refers patients for treatment, when appropriate
• Coordinates patient-care services with patient, family, and health-care staff
• Communicates regularly with patients, families, and other health-care staff
• Supervises home health aides and other community health workers
• Helps in agency planning by helping to define and set priorities
• Works with other professionals to identify and evaluate threats to community health, such as communicable diseases
• Works with private-sector community health workers, such as visiting nurses
• Works as a public school nurse, when needed.

NURSING CASE COORDINATOR FOR AN INSURANCE COMPANY
• Screens incoming patients by reviewing records and assessing insurance claims
• Helps assess an insurance claim by talking to the patient, his doctor, his family, and his employer
• Helps design patient-care plans, including medical, nursing, social service, and payment goals
• Monitors the patient's progress and prognosis by talking to the patient and his doctors
• Helps coordinate medical, rehabilitation, and other services to improve the insured patient's physical condition so he can return to work
• Supervises other nursing case reviewers
• Develops and maintains insurance company records.

Working with an Agency Nurse

Suppose you're a hospital staff nurse and an agency nurse is assigned to your unit. At first, she handles herself well and seems to have no problem performing her nursing duties. But later, you see her performing a procedure in a way that may harm her patient. In this situation, you have the same responsibility—to *stop the procedure*—that you'd have when working with your regular health-team colleagues. If an agency nurse performs a procedure incorrectly but without potential harm to the patient, you should report your observation to your nursing supervisor.

What legal responsibility do you have when working with her? Actually, your responsibility when working with her isn't any different than when working with others on the health-care team. If the patient may be harmed, you have a responsibility to stop the procedure.

clients. But they refer private-duty nurses, who don't have employee-employer relationships with the registries.)

A nurse is *always* liable for her own wrongful conduct. She can't escape liability if a court makes that decision. But if an agency nurse is judged to have been working within the legally permissible scope of her employment, then she's still liable. The agency is held *vicariously liable* and is required to pay any damages awarded to the plaintiff. The court can use the doctrine of *respondeat superior* to interpret the nurse's legal status. This doctrine makes an employer responsible for the negligent acts of his employees—so the agency is responsible for the actions of the nurses it employs. The situation is different, however, if the court finds that the nurse was *exceeding* the scope of her employment. This makes her solely responsible for paying any damages.

As an agency employee, you may be assigned to work in a patient's home, to care for a single patient in a hospital or other health-care institution, or to temporarily supplement an institution's staff. These different practice circumstances can influence how a court decides who's liable in a lawsuit. At present, any malpractice lawsuit involving an agency nurse will probably name as defendants the nurse, the temporary-nursing service agency, and (if applicable) the hospital or other health-care institution where the alleged malpractice happened. *When you work as an agency nurse in a patient's home,* your agency-employee status is generally clear-cut. This is also true *when you care for a single patient in a hospital or other health-care institution.*

The courts have more difficulty assigning legal liability, however, in cases involving agency nurses *working as supplemental hospital or institutional staff.* In this situation, you're still an agency employee, of course, but you're also in the "special service" of another "employer"—the hospital or institution. Courts frequently apply the *borrowed-servant* doctrine to these situations, holding that the regular employer (the agency) isn't liable for injury negligently caused by the employee ("servant") while in the special service of another "employer." When a court interprets a case this way, the legal liability shifts from the agency to the hospital or institution.

To help protect yourself against a lawsuit, be sure you fully understand what's expected of you when you accept an agency job. And be prepared to have your practice scrutinized in court.

Professional guidelines for agency nursing

As you try out the new job opportunities agencies offer, be prepared to adjust to different policies and procedures. When you work in a patient's home, for example, your *agency's* policies and procedures govern your actions. Be sure you understand them thoroughly and follow them carefully. How competently you follow them can affect such important matters as whether a claim for workmen's compensation is allowed or whether your agency will be included as a defendant with you in a malpractice suit. Don't perform any nonnursing functions when you work in a patient's home or arbitrarily change his nursing-regimen policies and procedures from what your agency has specified. If you do, and the patient or his family decides to sue, you may find yourself solely liable if you can't prove you acted the way a reasonable and prudent nurse would ordinarily have acted under similar circumstances.

The American Nurses' Association has issued guidelines outlining the responsibilities of temporary-nursing agencies and agency nurses. These guidelines say that an agency has a duty to select, orient, evaluate, and assign nurses and to provide them with professional development. Agency nurses, according to these guidelines, should:
• keep their licenses current
• select reputable employers
• maintain their nursing skills
• observe the standards of professional nursing practice
• document their nursing practice
• adhere to the policies and procedures of their agencies and clients.

The last point is particularly important if an agency assigns you to work in a hospital or other health-care institution. As always, you must be sure you understand the hospital's or institution's policies and procedures for the nursing tasks you're expected to perform. Get to know the head nurse or unit supervisor, and seek clarification from her whenever you're in doubt.

The hospital or institution, in turn, is obligated to supply equipment you need for patient care and to keep its premises and equipment in safe condition. (See *Working with an Agency Nurse,* page 58.)

Agency nursing: Pro and con
Today's nursing shortages dictate that health-care institutions will suffer frequent imbalances in the number of nurses available to work regularly scheduled shifts. In this situation, temporary-nursing service agencies provide a valuable service by supplying skilled nurses on short notice. You should be aware, however, that use of agency-provided RNs and LPNs/LVNs as supplemental staff in hospitals, nursing

homes, and extended-care facilities is a fairly new and controversial practice. Critics point out problems—for example, the morale problems that inequities in salaries between hospital and agency nurses—performing the same functions—can cause. Proponents of agency-based supplemental staffing, on the other hand, stress the cost-effectiveness of the practice and believe its flexibility helps keep nurses working and prevents nurse burnout. Proponents and critics alike urge that nursing administrations *plan* supplemental staffing programs, instead of bringing in agency nurses on a few hours' notice before a shift begins. This policy would help maintain the quality and continuity of patient care and would aid long-term planning for nursing services.

So far, no plaintiff in a lawsuit has ever charged a hospital with inadequate staffing caused by a failure to obtain available supplemental staff from an agency. But observers of the nursing profession feel that this may happen soon. Already, in the Louisiana case *McCutchon v. Mutual Insurance Co.* (1978), a court has required an insurance company to pay the agency fees of two LPNs/LVNs recruited to care for a critically ill patient whose doctor had ordered RNs (and whose insurance policy allowed payment only for RNs). The court reached its decision after reviewing evidence that neither the temporary-nursing service agency, the hospital, nor the insurance company could locate any available RNs at the time the LPNs/LVNs were assigned. Also considered was the fact that the assigned LPNs/LVNs were closely supervised by an RN at all times.

Conclusion
Temporary-nursing service agencies represent an innovative approach to the delivery of nursing services—one response to the need for practical, efficient, and cost-effective nursing care. If you, as a nurse, continue your efforts to understand the economic, professional, and legal basis of your practice, you'll be able to evaluate such new approaches accurately. And you'll be able to decide how *you* can influence the direction of nursing—and benefit from its growth and change.

Selected References

Brown, S.P. "Some Concerns on Certification," *AORN Journal* 31(1):51-52, January 1980.

Bullough, Bonnie, ed. *The Law and the Expanding Nursing Role,* 2nd ed. East Norwalk, Conn.: Appleton-Century-Crofts, 1980.

Cazalas, Mary W. *Nursing and the Law,* 3rd ed. Rockville, Md.: Aspen Systems Corp., 1979.

Chaska, Norma, ed. *The Nursing Profession: A Time to Speak.* New York: McGraw-Hill Book Co., 1983.

Cohn, Sarah D. "Revocation of Nurses' Licenses: How Does it Happen?" *Law, Medicine and Health Care* 11(1):22-24, February 1983.

Creighton, Helen. *Law Every Nurse Should Know,* 4th ed. Philadelphia: W.B. Saunders Co., 1981.

Creighton, Helen. "Law for the Nurse Supervisor: Licensure Problems," *Supervisor Nurse* 11:68-69, January 1980.

Curtin, Leah, and Flaherty, M. Josephine. *Nursing Ethics: Theories and Pragmatics.* Bowie, Md.: Robert J. Brady Co., 1981.

Cushing, M. "When Medical Standards Apply to Nurse Practitioners," *American Journal of Nursing* 82:1274, August 1982.

Cushing, Maureen. "A Judgment on Standards: Circumstances Under Which a Patient Should Be Placed in Seclusion," *American Journal of Nursing* 81:797-98, April 1981.

Fenner, Kathleen M. *Ethics and Law in Nursing.* New York: Van Nostrand Reinhold Co., 1980.

Gunn, I.B. "Certification for Specialty Practice," *AORN Journal* 31(1):48-51, January 1980.

Hemelt, M., and Mackert, M. *Dynamics of Law in Nursing and Health Care,* 2nd ed. Reston, Va.: Reston Publishing Co., 1982.

Hollowell, E.E. "Legal Liability and the LPN/LVN," *Journal of Practical Nursing* 32:30, February 1982.

Howe, Marilyn, et al. *A Plan for Implementation of the Standards of Nursing Practice.* Kansas City, Mo.: American Nurses' Association, 1977.

Kelly, Lucie Y. *Dimensions of Professional Nursing,* 4th ed. New York: Macmillan Publishing Co., 1981.

McDowell, Doris. "How Well Do You Know Your Board of Nursing?" *Nursing and Health Care* 2:557-63, December 1981.

Markowitz, Lucille A. "How Your State Board Works for You," *NursingLife* 2:25, May/June 1982.

Murchison, Irene, et al. *Legal Accountability in the Nursing Process,* 2nd ed. St. Louis: C.V. Mosby Co., 1982.

Reid, D., and Deane, A.K. "Licensure: For Whose Protection?" *Dimensions in Health Service* 59:30-32, January 1982.

Schwartz, Bernard. *Administrative Law: A Casebook,* 2nd ed. Boston: Little, Brown & Co., 1982.

Swansburg, R.C. "The Consumer's Perception of Nursing Care," *Supervisor Nurse* 12:30-32, May 1981.

2

Patients' Rights

Today's patient is different. He's more aware, assertive, and involved in his health care than the patients you used to care for. He questions his diagnosis, seeks corroboration through a second opinion, expects assurances that the treatment chosen is appropriate, and takes action when his care doesn't meet his expectations. Sometimes this action is a lawsuit, and it may involve you.

Patients' bills of rights, endorsed by major health-care providers and consumer groups across the country, have increased the awareness and reinforced the assertiveness of today's patients.

The courts have sometimes used these documents as standards for judging nursing care. Chapter 2 discusses professional obligations and potential liabilities regarding patients' rights of informed consent, privacy, and confidentiality.

A new perspective on consent

If you've been in nursing for several years, you remember when nurses were forbidden to give a patient even the most basic information about his care or his health. Answering a patient's questions about his condition was the doctor's domain.

The consumer movement of the 1960s changed these rules in a hurry. Encouraged by patients' bills of rights, which first appeared in the late 1950s, patients began demanding to know more about their care. And, because nurses were available almost constantly, patients began demanding the information from them.

You and patients' rights

Like all nurses, you face issues involving patients' rights every day. How you re-

spond depends partly on your legal responsibilities set forth by your state's nurse practice act. But it also depends on your ethical responsibility to respond when questions arise about a patient's rights.

This chapter will help you apply your legal and ethical responsibilities regarding patients' rights to your everyday nursing practice.

Elements of patient's bill of rights

A patient's bill of rights defines a person's rights while he's receiving health care. It helps protect his basic human rights at a time when he's most vulnerable.

Some consumers, civil rights activists, and attorneys feel that a patient's bill of rights is unnecessary. They claim it simply reiterates the basic rights that courts and laws recognize anyway.

In institutions that have prepared patients' bills of rights, the bills make patients aware that they have recourse to the institutions' grievance procedures.

Generally, patients' bills of rights are designed to protect such basic rights as human dignity, privacy, confidentiality, informed consent, and refusal of treatment. And they assert the patient's right to explanations about medical costs—and medical research, if he's asked to consent to experimental treatments.

Consumer-promoted bills emphasize the patient's right to decide and control his health care. These bills also include the patient's right to information about all as-

The Development of Patient's Rights

1959: National League for Nursing issues first patient's bill of rights, outlining 7 points to help patients understand nursing care.

1973: American Hospital Association (AHA) draws up patient's bill of rights, listing 12 patient rights.

1973: Pennsylvania Insurance Department issues the "Citizens Bill of Hospital Rights," the first bill developed by a government agency that told patients what they had a right to expect from hospitals.

1973: Minnesota passes a patient's bill of rights, modeled after the AHA bill, becoming the first state to establish a bill of rights as law.

pects of his care.

The trend toward guaranteed rights

The concept of patient's rights is a relatively recent development in the health-care field. (See *The Development of Patient's Rights.*) The first professional group to publish a statement on patients' rights, in 1959, was the National League for Nursing (NLN). In its position statement, "What People Can Expect of Modern Nursing Practice," the NLN called the patient a partner in health care whose ultimate goal is self-care.

Patients' rights received increasing public support during the 1960s as more people became aware of their rights as consumers. In a 1962 message to Congress, President John F. Kennedy further heightened this awareness when he outlined four basic consumer rights: the right to safety, the right to be informed, the right to choose, and the right to be heard.

The American Hospital Association (AHA) responded to the consumer movement in 1973 with its "Statement on a Patient's Bill of Rights." The statement—the result of a study the AHA had conducted with consumer groups—listed 12 patient rights. (See *AHA Patient's Bill of Rights,* page 65.)

That same year, the Pennsylvania Insurance Department (PID) issued "Citizens Bill of Hospital Rights," the first patient's bill of rights formulated by a government agency. This bill outlined the kinds of treatment a patient should expect in a hospital. And it pointed out omissions in the AHA bill. The PID also warned that it would enforce this bill by stopping Blue Cross/Blue Shield payments to hospitals and other health-care institutions that failed to protect the rights mentioned in the bill.

Also in 1973, Minnesota became the first state to make patients' rights a law. That law requires all state health-care facilities to post Minnesota's bill of rights conspicuously and to distribute it to their patients.

Since these first milestones, other states and groups have developed their own bills of rights. (See *ACLU Patient's Bill of Rights,* pages 68 and 69.)

Patients' bills of rights—legally binding or not?

As with any standard, formal or informal, written or verbal, a bill of rights has only as much authority as the group that issues it.

Bills of rights that have become laws or state regulations have the most authority because they give the patient legal recourse. If a patient believes a hospital has violated his legal rights, the patient can report the violation to the appropriate legal authority, usually the state health department. If an investigation shows that the hospital violated the patient's rights, the state will demand that the institution modify its practices to conform to state law. (In Canada, the courts usually accept a professional tribunal's decisions about patients' rights violations.)

Some bills of rights protect the rights of specific types of patients. Canada has a Charter of Rights and various provinces have Human Rights Acts. And, in the United States, the Rehabilitation Act was passed by Congress in 1973. This act guarantees the physically or mentally handicapped person the right to any service available to a nonhandicapped person. This may require a health-care institution to redesign its facilities or equipment, transfer a handicapped patient to a better-equipped facility, offer home visits, hire an interpreter of sign language for a deaf patient, or supply auxiliary aids for a patient with impaired vision or manual skills.

Bills of rights issued by health-care institutions and professional associations aren't legally binding. But hospitals could jeopardize certain federal fundings, such as Medicare and Medicaid reimbursement or research funding, if they violated federal regulations or the standards of the Joint Commission on Accreditation of Hospitals, which establishes industry-wide standards.

Patients' bills of rights are also professionally binding on you. If your hospital has a bill of rights, you're required to uphold those rights.

You're also expected to uphold the bills of rights published by professional organizations such as the NLN.

Interpreting the patient's rights

The theory is clear, but the practice is full of conflict. That's why defending a patient's rights without exceeding the bounds of nursing practice isn't easy. The case of *Tuma v. Board of Nursing* (1979) shows how the bounds of nursing practice are sometimes unclear.

In the Tuma case, a patient with myelogenous leukemia was admitted to a hospital in Idaho for chemotherapy. Although she had agreed to the chemotherapy, she was openly distressed about it. But instead of asking her doctor about alternative treatment, she asked Jolene Tuma, RN, MSN, a nursing instructor at the College of Southern Idaho who supervised nursing students at the hospital. Ms. Tuma had asked to be assigned to the patient because of her interest in the needs of dying patients.

Ms. Tuma told the patient, in detail, about alternative treatments. She discussed laetrile therapy and various natural food and herbal remedies, comparing their side effects with those of chemo-

therapy. She also gave the patient the name of a therapist who practiced alternative treatments and offered to arrange an appointment with the therapist.

At no time did Ms. Tuma encourage the patient to alter her treatment plan or indicate that alternative treatments were better than the prescribed therapy or would cure her.

At the patient's request, Ms. Tuma also discussed the alternative treatments with the patient's son and daughter-in-law. They told the patient's doctor, and, as a result, he interrupted the chemotherapy until he could discuss the situation with the patient. The next day the patient, again, agreed to undergo chemotherapy. Two weeks later, she went into a coma and died.

The patient's doctor demanded that the hospital remove Ms. Tuma from her position as clinical instructor at the College of Southern Idaho.

At the hospital's request, the board of nursing conducted an investigation and hearing. The board interpreted Ms. Tuma's behavior as unprofessional, under the Idaho Code. They agreed that she'd interfered with the doctor-patient relationship, and that this constituted unprofessional conduct. And they suspended her nursing license for 6 months.

Ms. Tuma appealed, lost, and appealed again. This time, 3 years after the incident, the Idaho State Supreme Court ruled that she couldn't be found guilty of unprofessional conduct because the Idaho Nurse Practice Act neither clearly defines unprofessional conduct nor provides guidelines for avoiding it.

This decision illustrates the nurse's evolving role in protecting patients' rights. But the decision fails to define the nurse's specific role in upholding a patient's right to information, and that leaves many troubling questions unanswered. For example, Ms. Tuma's patient asked her, not the doctor, for information about alternative therapies. The doctor testified that he wasn't knowledgeable about these therapies, so what recourse did that give his patient? If a doctor can't or won't answer such questions, does the patient have the right to get answers from a knowledgeable nurse?

Until the courts or legislatures address such questions, you won't find any easy answers. But guidelines are available.

Your responsibilities in patient's rights

The best guideline you can follow to protect your patient's interests is the NLN's position statement on nursing's role in patients' rights. (See *NLN Patient's Bill of Rights*, page 71.) According to the NLN statement, you begin by viewing your patient as a partner in the health-care process. That's the underlying premise of all patients' bills of rights.

In planning your patient's care, recognize his right to participate in the decisions. Help him set realistic goals for his health care, and teach him the various approaches he can use to achieve them.

Throughout the decision-making process, keep assessing the patient's understanding of his illness. When he needs and wants more information, first determine if you or the doctor should provide it. Then, let the patient decide on his care plan. A care plan you formulate with your patient helps you communicate and demonstrates your respect for his wishes and rights.

Such supportive nursing practice also has the long-term benefit of opening health care to new ways of doing things. For example, nurse-midwives and other maternity nurses have acted as advocates for patients who challenge traditional childbirth practices. The results? Many hospitals have introduced birthing rooms, as an alternative to traditional delivery rooms; use less intervention and medication during delivery; and allow patients to use a birthing chair, walk at will during labor, and enjoy the company and support of a "coach"—husband, other relative, or friend—during labor and delivery.

You aren't alone in your efforts to protect your patient's rights. Increasing interest in patients' rights has led many hospitals to employ full-time patient advocates, or ombudsmen. They mediate between the patient and the hospital when a patient is dissatisfied with the care he's receiving. Patient advocates are your ally, helping you uphold your responsibilities to your patient. But patient advocates don't diminish those responsibilities. Whether you're an RN, LPN, or LVN, you must respect and safeguard your patient's rights.

Consent requirements for treatment

Suppose you're caring for a patient scheduled for surgery. He's talked to his doctor and signed the consent form. But the night before surgery, he doesn't seem to understand the implications of the procedure. What should you do? This question arises from a more fundamental question: What *is* informed consent?

What is informed consent?

Informed consent has two elements: *informed* refers to information given to the patient about a proposed procedure or treatment; *consent* refers to the patient's agreement to the procedure or treatment. To be informed, a patient must receive, in terms he understands, *all* the information that would affect a reasonable person's decision to consent to or refuse a treatment or procedure. The information should include:
• a description of the treatment or procedure
• the name and qualifications of the person who'll perform the treatment or procedure
• an explanation of the potential for death or serious harm (such as brain damage, paralysis, or disfiguring scars) or for discomforting side effects during or after the treatment or procedure
• an explanation and description of alternative treatments or procedures
• an explanation of the possible effects of not having the treatment or procedure.

The patient must also be told that he has a right to refuse the treatment or procedure without having other care or support withdrawn, and that he can withdraw his consent after giving it.

The origins of informed consent

The right of *informed* consent didn't exist at the beginning of this century. At that time, a patient had no established legal right to *information* about his medical treatment. If a doctor performed surgery

AHA Patient's Bill of Rights

Most hospitals design their own patient's bills of rights. The American Hospital Association's bill of rights, shown below, is one of the bills they use as a model.

A Patient's Bill of Rights

1. The patient has the right to considerate and respectful care.

2. The patient has the right to obtain from his physician complete current information about his diagnosis, treatment, and prognosis in terms the patient can be reasonably expected to understand. When it is not medically advisable to give such information to the patient, it should be made available to an appropriate person in his behalf. He has the right to know, by name, the physician responsible for coordinating his care.

3. The patient has the right to receive from his physician information necessary to give informed consent prior to the start of any procedure and/or treatment. Except in emergencies, such information for informed consent should include but not necessarily be limited to the specific procedure and/or treatment, the medically significant risks involved, and the probable duration of incapacitation. Where medically significant alternatives for care or treatment exist, or when the patient requests information concerning medical alternatives, the patient has the right to such information. The patient has the right to know the name of the person responsible for the procedures and/or treatment.

4. The patient has the right to refuse treatment to the extent permitted by law and to be informed of the medical consequences of his action.

5. The patient has the right to every consideration of his privacy concerning his own medical care program. Case discussion, consultation, examination, and treatment are confidential and should be conducted discreetly. Those not directly involved in his care must have the permission of the patient to be present.

6. The patient has the right to expect that all communications and records pertaining to his care should be treated as confidential.

7. The patient has the right to expect that within its capacity a hospital must make reasonable response to the request of a patient for services. The hospital must provide evaluation, service, and/or referral as indicated by the urgency of the case. When medically permissible, a patient may be transferred to another facility only after he has received complete information and explanation concerning the needs for and alternatives to such a transfer. The institution to which the patient is to be transferred must first have accepted the patient for transfer.

8. The patient has the right to obtain information as to any relationship of his hospital to other health-care and educational institutions insofar as his care is concerned. The patient has the right to obtain information as to the existence of any professional relationships among individuals, by name, who are treating him.

9. The patient has the right to be advised if the hospital proposes to engage in or perform human experimentation affecting his care or treatment. The patient has the right to refuse to participate in such research projects.

10. The patient has the right to expect reasonable continuity of care. He has the right to know in advance what appointment times and physicians are available and where. The patient has the right to expect that the hospital will provide a mechanism whereby he is informed by his physician or a delegate of the physician of the patient's continuing health-care requirements following discharge.

11. The patient has the right to examine and receive an explanation of his bill, regardless of source of payment.

12. The patient has the right to know what hospital rules and regulations apply to his conduct as a patient.

without the patient's consent, the patient could sue for battery. (As you know, battery means one person touching another without consent.) However, a patient could claim battery only if he'd refused consent or hadn't been asked to give it—not because he hadn't had enough information to make an appropriate decision.

Most battery lawsuits were unsuccessful, because courts usually took the doctor's word over the patient's. Two cases that patients did win were *Mohr v. Williams* (1905)—in which the patient consented to surgery on one ear, but the doctor performed it on both—and *Schloendorff v. Society of New York Hospitals* (1914)—in which the patient consented to an abdominal examination, but the doctor performed abdominal surgery.

The right to give an informed consent wasn't introduced until 1957, when the California Supreme Court introduced the theory in the case of *Salgo v. Leland Stanford, Jr. Univ. Board of Trustees* (1957). This case involved a doctor and a patient who had acute arterial insufficiency in his legs. The doctor recommended diagnostic tests, but he did *not* describe the tests or their risks. The day after the patient underwent aortography, his legs became permanently paralyzed. The court found the doctor negligent *for failing to explain the potential risks of aortography to the patient.*

This decision established the basic rule: A doctor violates "his duty to his patient and subjects himself to liability if he withholds any facts that are necessary to form the basis of an intelligent consent by the patient to the proposed treatment."

Since this landmark ruling, a patient can sue for negligent nondisclosure if his doctor fails to give him enough information to make an informed decision.

But the ruling also raised a difficult question: How much information is enough? To help answer this question, the courts have developed two standards—the reasonable doctor standard and the reasonable patient standard.

Today, most state courts use the reasonable doctor standard (also called the malpractice model). Essentially, this standard is based on what another doctor would disclose to a similar patient under

similar circumstances. A famous example is *Natanson v. Kline* (1960). In this case, the doctor failed to inform the patient of the side effects of cobalt radiation therapy. The patient suffered the side effects and sued the doctor. The court ruled that the doctor had a duty to disclose information "which a reasonable medical practitioner would [disclose] under the same or similar circumstances."

In *Kinikin v. Heupel* (1981), a Minnesota court provided a variation on the reasonable doctor standard. It ruled that a doctor must disclose as much information as any reasonable doctor would under similar circumstances who knew the *particular patient's ability to understand.*

The other standard courts use to judge how much information a patient should be given is the reasonable patient standard. The landmark decision using this standard occurred in *Canterbury v. Spence* (1972). In this case, a patient had a laminectomy, then fell and developed paralysis. The patient sued the doctor for failing to warn him of the inherent risks. The court ruled that the doctor had a duty to disclose as much information as he knew—or should have known—a reasonable patient would need to know to make an informed decision.

Courts may eventually develop variations of this reasonable patient standard based on the information a *particular* patient needs to make his decision. If so, the courts might weigh such personal factors as a patient's intelligence, educational level, hopes, fears, and idiosyncrasies.

Laws that require informed consent

Recently, many state legislatures have passed laws that support the standards of informed consent set by the courts. Several states have substantive laws—laws that define informed consent or specify the claims and defenses that can be made in informed consent cases. (These include: Alaska, Delaware, Hawaii, Kentucky, Nebraska, New Hampshire, Oregon, Pennsylvania, Tennessee, Texas, Utah, and Vermont.)

Some states have procedural laws on informed consent—laws that describe the tort of negligent nondisclosure and possible defenses to such a lawsuit. (These include: Florida, Maine, New York, North Carolina, and Rhode Island.) In comparison, Washington State has a law that is both substantive and procedural.

Other states (including Mississippi, Arkansas, Louisiana, Georgia, and Missouri) have laws that deal with consent but not *informed* consent. And still others (including Idaho, Iowa, Nevada, and Ohio) have laws limited to the legal effect of documents, such as consent forms.

Among state laws on informed consent, Georgia's is noteworthy. It says that a signed consent form disclosing the treatment in general terms is *conclusive* proof of a valid consent. Thus, in Georgia, a patient who signs a consent form has no legal right to claim he didn't fully understand a medical treatment or that the doctor didn't explain the information in the consent form.

In many other states, a signed consent form is *evidence* of informed consent, but it's not *conclusive proof*. Even if a patient signs a form, he may still challenge his consent's validity in court—claiming, for example, that he didn't understand the information or that he wasn't given relevant information. Most state laws don't even *require* a signed consent form. Some states accept as evidence of informed consent a doctor's handwritten progress notes, stating that he discussed the proposed procedure, its risks, benefits, and alternatives with the patient, and that the patient understood and consented to the procedure.

When is informed consent required?
Informed consent is required before any treatment or procedure. As a nurse, you get this kind of consent by explaining the procedure before you perform it. At that point, any conscious, mentally competent adult has a right to refuse to let you perform the nursing treatment or procedure. The controversy over informed consent centers on medical and surgical treatments and procedures that are invasive, risky, experimental, or unlikely to succeed. For these, the doctor must obtain express consent for treatments and procedures unless delaying necessary treatment to get consent will adversely affect the patient's health.

The doctrine of informed consent assumes that an informed patient can act in his own best interests. But what if information about his condition seems likely to act against his interests—if the information itself would jeopardize his health? Sometimes, in these situations, the law may recognize a doctor's *therapeutic privilege*. This legal concept permits the doctor to withhold information he believes would jeopardize the patient's health. This concept of therapeutic privilege may be extended to allow the doctor to provide care to the patient before obtaining his informed consent. But after the risk has passed, the doctor must inform the patient.

Who's responsible for obtaining informed consent?
The responsibility for obtaining a patient's informed consent rests with the person who'll carry out the treatment or procedure. Usually this is the attending doctor.

Ideally, each doctor should disclose the information necessary for informed consent, then have the patient sign a consent form. The doctor should also sign the form to indicate that he witnessed the patient's signing. In reality, however, some hospitals have a policy requiring their nurses to witness patients' signatures. If your hospital has such a policy, you need to understand your responsibilities as a witness.

What your signature means
Your signature as a witness indicates that you saw the patient sign the consent form and that he appeared to be awake, alert, and aware of what he was signing. So, before you give a consent form to a patient to sign, check his records to be sure he hasn't recently received any preanesthetic drugs, narcotics, barbiturates, or anesthesia. If he has, put the unsigned form back in his chart, and notify your supervisor and the attending doctor.

If the patient is alert, have him read the consent form, or read it to him, before he signs it. If the patient doesn't understand the information or wants more information, you can answer any questions that are within the scope of your knowledge. However, you *aren't* obligated to answer any of the patient's questions. Your role as

ACLU Patient's Bill of Rights

The American Civil Liberties Union has developed this patient's bill of rights as a model for any health institution wishing to develop its own.

Preamble: As you enter this health care facility, it is our duty to remind you that your health care is a cooperative effort between you as a patient and the doctors and hospital staff. During your stay a patients' rights advocate will be available to you. The duty of the advocate is to assist you in all the decisions you must make and in all situations in which your health and welfare are at stake. The advocate's first responsibility is to help you understand the role of all who will be working with you, and to help you understand what your rights as a patient are. Your advocate can be reached at any time of the day by dialing _____. The following is a list of your rights as a patient. Your advocate's duty is to see to it that you are afforded these rights. You should call your advocate whenever you have any questions or concerns about any of these rights.

● The patient has a legal right to informed participation in all decisions involving his/her health care program.

● We recognize the right of all potential patients to know what research and experimental protocols are being used in our facility and what alternatives are available in the community.

● The patient has a legal right to privacy regarding the source of payment for treatment and care. This right includes access to the highest degree of care without regard to the source of payment for that treatment and care.

● We recognize the right of a potential patient to complete and accurate information concerning medical care and procedures.

● The patient has a legal right to prompt attention, especially in an emergency situation.

● The patient has a legal right to a clear, concise explanation in layperson's terms of all proposed procedures, including the possibilities of any risk of mortality or serious side effects, problems related to recuperation, and probability of success, and will not be subjected to any procedure without his/her voluntary, competent and understanding consent. The specifics of such consent shall be set out in a written consent form, signed by the patient.

● The patient has a legal right to a clear, complete, and accurate evaluation of his/her condition and prognosis without treatment before being asked to consent to any test or procedure.

● We recognize the right of the patient to know the identity and professional status of all those providing service. All personnel have been instructed to introduce themselves, state their status, and explain their role in the health care of the patient. Part of this right is the right of the patient to know the identity of the physician responsible for his/her care.

● We recognize the right of any patient who does not speak English to have access to an interpreter.

● The patient has a right to all the infor-

---

a witness doesn't include the legal responsibility for disclosing all relevant information to the patient. That's the doctor's legal responsibility, and he *cannot* delegate it to you.

That doesn't mean that you have no legal responsibility to the patient regarding informed consent. If you *see* that a patient is confused about explanations he's received, and *you* don't provide the information he needs, you're responsible for documenting your observation in the patient's chart and making sure the patient gets the information from his doctor or another appropriate source. (See *Patient Consent: Acting Legally and Responsibly,* pages 72 and 73.)

mation contained in his/her medical record while in the health care facility, and to examine the record on request.

• We recognize the right of a patient to discuss his/her condition with a consultant specialist, at the patient's request and expense.

• The patient has a legal right not to have any test or procedure, designed for educational purposes rather than his/her direct personal benefit, performed on him/her.

• The patient has a legal right to refuse any particular drug, test, procedure, or treatment.

• The patient has a legal right to privacy of both person and information with respect to: the hospital staff, other doctors, residents, interns and medical students, researchers, nurses, other hospital personnel, and other patients.

• We recognize the patient's right of access to people outside the health care facility by means of visitors and the telephone. Parents may stay with their children and relatives with terminally ill patients 24 hours a day.

• The patient has a legal right to leave the health care facility regardless of his/her physical condition or financial status, although the patient may be requested to sign a release stating that he/she is leaving against the medical judgment of his/her doctor or the hospital.

• The patient has a right not to be transferred to another facility unless he/she has received a complete explanation of the desirability of and need for the transfer. If the patient does not agree to transfer, the patient has the right to a consultant's opinion on the desirability of transfer.

• A patient has a right to be notified of his/her impending discharge at least one day before it is accomplished, to insist on a consultation by an expert on the desirability of discharge, and to have a person of the patient's choice notified in advance.

• The patient has a right, regardless of the source of payment, to examine and receive an itemized and detailed explanation of the total bill for services rendered in the facility.

• The patient has a right to competent counseling from the hospital staff to help in obtaining financial assistance from public or private sources to meet the expense of services received in the institution.

• The patient has a right to timely prior notice of the termination of his/her eligibility for reimbursement by any third-party payor for the expense of hospital care.

• At the termination of his/her stay at the health care facility we recognize the right of a patient to a complete copy of the information contained in his/her medical record.

• We recognize the right of all patients to have 24-hour-a-day access to a patient's rights advocate, who may act on behalf of the patient to assert or protect the rights set out in this document.

Reprinted with the permission of the American Civil Liberties Union.

The legal risk involved in doing nothing

If you know a patient hasn't been informed and you do nothing, you and your hospital can be held legally responsible.

Usually, the courts won't hold the hospital responsible if the patient sues the doctor for battery for performing a procedure without the patient's consent. But the courts might hold you responsible if you took part in the battery by assisting with the treatment or if you knew it was taking place and didn't try to stop it.

Similarly, the courts won't usually hold the hospital responsible if the patient sues the doctor for negligent nondisclosure for failing to provide adequate information for consent. But, again, the court might hold you responsible if—knowing the doctor hasn't provided adequate information to a patient—you don't perform your professional and legal duty to try to stop the procedure by informing your supervisor.

Usually though, you can meet your legal obligation for informed consent by ensuring that the consent form has been signed and witnessed and that it's attached to the patient's chart.

Informed consent to treat the sedated or comatose patient

If you know a doctor is going to seek consent from a patient receiving a sedative, narcotic, or tranquilizer, make sure the doctor is aware of the patient's medication schedule. Then the doctor can select an appropriate time to explain the procedure or treatment and thus ensure that a valid consent has been obtained.

If the patient receives such medication before the doctor explains the procedure or treatment, the doctor should evaluate the patient's mental status. If his mental status is impaired, his consent will be invalid, and someone else will have to give consent for him.

If the patient is comatose from a long-term disease process, the doctor should ask the court to appoint a guardian for the patient. But if immediate treatment is needed, the doctor may, as a practical matter, seek consent from the nearest relative. However, such a consent by a relative who is not a court-appointed guardian will not protect the doctor from liability if the patient wakes up and later decides to sue.

Informed consent to treat incompetent adults

A patient who's been declared incompetent by a court (such a patient is called an *adjudicated incompetent*) cannot give a valid consent. In such instances, a court-appointed guardian must give consent: consent from a relative or friend is *not* legally binding.

When a patient is incompetent but hasn't been adjudicated as such, the doctor has two alternatives. He may seek consent from the patient's next of kin—usually his spouse. (Note that determining who's the next of kin is a legal question and varies from state to state.) Or the doctor or hos-

pital may petition the court to appoint a legal guardian for the patient. When to appoint a legal guardian remains a controversial issue. Generally, doctors go to court when they don't feel comfortable with the next of kin's decision.

The decision that a patient is incompetent can be very difficult, particularly with a mentally ill patient: don't make the mistake of assuming that mental illness is the same as incompetence. An increasing number of courts have upheld the constitutional right of the alert, involuntarily confined mental patient to refuse medication and treatment even if the treatment might ameliorate the mental illness. Even a committed mental patient can be forcibly medicated *only* in an emergency when he may cause harm to himself or others.

Obtaining informed consent to treat minors

In most situations, a minor's consent to treatment is legally invalid, so the doctor must obtain *substitute consent* from the parents or legal guardians. In these instances, the doctor is legally obligated to disclose all relevant information to the parents or legal guardians to ensure that their consent is informed.

In some situations, minors *can* give valid consent. For instance, some states let a minor give consent to treatment of a sexually transmitted disease. And most states let an emancipated minor—one who's married, a parent, pregnant, or financially independent—give legal consent to treatment.

To avoid difficult judgments on whether a minor is legally emancipated, a doctor usually tries to get informed consent from both a minor and his parents.

Two exceptions to the need for informed consent

There are two situations in which the legal requirement for obtaining informed consent is waived. In one situation, the patient himself waives the requirement. In the other, the urgent nature of a medical or surgical emergency supercedes the requirement.

A patient's rights include the right *not* to be informed. If a patient exercises that right by telling his doctor that he doesn't

NLN Patient's Bill of Rights

The National League for Nursing believes nurses are responsible for upholding these rights of patients:

• People have the right to health care that is accessible and that meets professional standards, regardless of the setting.

• Patients have the right to courteous and individualized health care that is equitable, humane, and given without discrimination as to race, color, creed, sex, national origin, source of payment, or ethical or political beliefs.

• Patients have the right to information about their diagnosis, prognosis, and treatment—including alternatives to care and risks involved—in terms they and their families can readily understand, so that they can give their informed consent.

• Patients have the legal right to informed participation in all decisions concerning their health care.

• Patients have the right to information about the qualifications, names, and titles of personnel responsible for providing their health care.

• Patients have the right to refuse observation by those not directly involved in their care.

• Patients have the right to privacy during interview, examination, and treatment.

• Patients have the right to privacy in communicating and visiting with persons of their choice.

• Patients have the right to refuse treatments, medications, or participation in research and experimentation, without punitive action being taken against them.

• Patients have the right to coordination and continuity of health care.

• Patients have the right to appropriate instruction or education from health care personnel so that they can achieve an optimal level of wellness and an understanding of their basic health needs.

• Patients have the right to confidentiality of all records (except as otherwise provided for by law or third-party payer contracts) and all communications, written or oral, between patients and health care providers.

• Patients have the right of access to all health records pertaining to them, the right to challenge and to have their records corrected for accuracy, and the right to transfer of all such records in the case of continuing care.

• Patients have the right to information on the charges for services, including the right to challenge these.

• Above all, patients have the right to be fully informed as to all their rights in all health care settings.

The National League for Nursing urges its membership, through action and example, to demonstrate that the profession of nursing is committed to the concepts of patient's rights.

Reprinted with permission of the National League for Nursing.

---

want to know the details regarding a treatment or procedure, the doctor has two responsibilities. He must make sure that the patient understands that risks and alternatives do exist. And he should clearly document the patient's waiver of his right to receive information.

A doctor can legally treat a patient without getting his consent if the patient needs immediate treatment to save his life or to prevent loss of an organ, limb, or function, and the doctor can't get consent because the patient is unconscious or, in the case of a minor, the family can't be reached. In such situations, the law assumes that if a patient could decide, he would choose to receive treatment.

This exception is very limited, however. It doesn't apply if the doctor knows the patient has previously said he'd refuse such treatment if and when offered. And it also doesn't apply if he can wait for a proper consent from the patient or his family without increasing the patient's risk. For example, a doctor may admit a minor patient with acute appendicitis, but he

Patient Consent: Acting Legally and Responsibly

Consent before or after sedation?
We have an ongoing conflict with the anesthesiologist on our short-stay surgical unit. The problem is, some patients arrive for surgery without signed consent forms. (Their surgeons bring the forms to the hospital just before surgery.)

The anesthesiologist wants us to sedate the patient before the surgeon arrives with the consent form. We contend that we can't legally sedate the patient before we see the signed consent. The anesthesiologist argues that we shouldn't clinically withhold sedation because the patient needs it to be properly prepared for general anesthesia.

Should we give the sedative after we inform him there's no consent, or should we continue to refuse to sedate the patient until the consent arrives?—RN, Ariz.

Check your hospital's preoperative checklist. If it requires a signed operative consent before a patient is sedated, then the surgeon, the anesthesiologist, and *you* must abide by this policy. You must continue to refuse to sedate the patient until *you* see the signed consent.

If you don't have a preoperative checklist (or the checklist doesn't require a consent form before sedation), document the problem, and ask the administration's help. In the meantime, have the patients bring their own consents. Or the surgeons can have their secretaries deliver the consents well ahead of surgery.

Nonconsensual procedures
For the past year, I've been working in the emergency department (ED) of a large metropolitan hospital, where we frequently treat victims of assault. We're sometimes asked to cooperate with investigating police officers by obtaining blood specimens for legal evidence.

Just last month I was asked to take a blood smear from a patient, allegedly involved in a murder, whose arm was streaked with blood. I did it, but I was unsure whether my action was legal.

Since the man was fully conscious, should I have obtained his consent before I took the blood sample? Since the procedure was noninvasive, was his verbal or written consent necessary at all? Should he first have been informed of his rights?—RN, Vt.

An informed consent signed by the patient is always your best protection against liability. Ideally, the consent form should describe *what* the procedure is, *why* it's being done, and *how* the results will be used. Then, there is no question of the patient having been misled.

A 1966 U.S. Supreme Court decision *(Schmerber v. California)* held that you could obtain a blood sample against the patient's wishes *only if the patient was under arrest and the test was likely to produce evidence.* If these criteria are met, we suspect that a noninvasive procedure like taking a blood smear sample

---

can't do emergency surgery without consent if he has time to obtain the parents' informed consent.

If you assist in emergency treatment without consent, make sure the doctor documents his reasons for proceeding, including the specific risks the patient would face without treatment.

What should you do if the doctor wants to provide emergency care without consent, but you feel the patient could wait? First, tell the doctor why you feel that way. If the doctor insists on treating the patient anyway, evaluate the likely consequences of two courses of action:
• If your refusal to help would harm the patient or create an unsafe situation (a

would be legally permissible. You should tell the arresting officer you'll get the sample after he reads the patient his legal rights.

Overstepping my bounds?

As an operating room nurse, I explain preoperative procedures to patients scheduled for next-day surgery.

Recently, I stopped in to see a middle-aged man scheduled for a bilateral orchiectomy. I explained the preoperative procedures to him and then, almost routinely, asked if he had any questions. I couldn't believe my ears when he asked, "Exactly what is a bilateral orchiectomy?"

When I explained that it was removal of both testicles, the patient was clearly shaken. He said he hadn't fully realized what the surgery involved because the doctor had described it in vague terms.

I tried to reassure the patient, and I advised him not to sign the surgical consent form until he'd talked to his doctor again.

I reported the conversation to my charge nurse and my supervisor. They advised me to call the patient's doctor at once and explain the problem to him.

The doctor accused me of "practicing medicine" and said he had told the patient "all he needed to know." Then he warned me: "If you ever overstep your bounds again, I'll file a complaint against you."

*If the patient had signed the consent form and went into surgery without realiz-*ing what it entailed, couldn't he have sued the doctor and the hospital? (By the way, the patient did sign the consent form, but I understand that the doctor had a lot of talking to do first.) What's your viewpoint?—RN, Ill.*

The doctor shouldn't have accused you—he should've *thanked* you. Were you overstepping your bounds? The answer—a very definite *no*. The patient could've looked up "orchiectomy" in a medical dictionary and found the answer to his question. But he didn't. He asked you, and you answered him truthfully.

The doctor is responsible for getting the patient's informed consent. So he took a big risk when he failed to explain the procedure adequately. If the patient had signed the form without an explanation, the consent would not have been "informed." The patient might have sued—and won.

If you encounter this problem again, do just what you did before. Reassure your patient, tell him *not* to sign the consent form until he talks to the doctor again, and tell your supervisor and the doctor about your action. Next time, *document* everything in your nurses' notes.

Chances are the doctor won't thank you *next* time, either. But good documentation will ensure your administration's support if the doctor complains.

These letters were taken from the files of *Nursing* magazine.

doctor caring for a patient without assistance), you should assist, even if you know you're right.

• In all other situations, you should refuse to participate and then notify your nursing supervisor. She, in turn, should report to hospital administration.

When does a patient's informed consent become invalid?

You should know that informed consent can become invalid if a change in a patient's medical status alters the risks and benefits of the treatment he consented to. In such situations, the doctor must explain the new risks and benefits to the consenting patient to be sure he still consents to the treatment. And the doctor must explain any new risks or benefits to a non-consenting patient to be sure he still wants to refuse the treatment.

In summary, remember that the patient has a legal right to determine the treatment he receives, and you have a professional responsibility to protect that right. (See *The Right to Consent: From Birth to Adulthood.*)

The patient who refuses treatment

You're in the business of saving lives, so you probably have a hard time accepting a patient's decision to refuse treatment. You may be very disturbed, for example, when a patient refuses treatment he can't live without—just to avoid unpleasant side effects. But as a professional, you know you must respect that decision. Laws and court rulings give almost all patients the right to refuse treatment.

When your patient refuses treatment, you must understand his right and your responsibilities. (See *When a Patient Says No*, page 77.) If you don't, you increase your legal risks on the job.

Your patient's legal right to refuse treatment

Most right-to-refuse-treatment court cases have involved patients or their families who want to discontinue life-support treatment for a terminal illness. In one of the best-known cases, Karen Ann Quinlan's parents argued that unwanted treatment violated their comatose daughter's constitutional right to privacy. In 1976, the parents successfully petitioned the court to discontinue her life-support treatment.

Many other court cases have involved the right of freedom of religion, and often the patients are Jehovah's Witnesses. Members of this sect oppose blood transfusions because a section of the Bible forbids "drinking" blood. Some sect members believe that even a life-saving transfusion given against their will deprives them of everlasting life. The courts

usually respect their refusals because of the constitutionally protected right to religious freedom. In the case of *Osborne* (1972), for example, the court respected a Jehovah's Witness' right to refuse consent.

Most other religious freedom court cases involve Christian Scientists, who oppose many medical interventions, including medicines. For example, in *Winters v. Miller* (1971), a psychiatric patient claimed she involuntarily received treatment and medications at a New York state hospital. After her discharge, she sued for damages based on a violation of her religious freedom as a Christian Scientist. The trial court dismissed her complaint, but an appeals court ordered a new trial on the grounds that the unwanted treatment might have violated her rights.

Besides court rulings, most patients' bills of rights also support the right to refuse treatment—starting with the bill of rights adopted by the American Hospital Association in 1973.

State laws provide another legal authority for the right to refuse treatment. Twenty-three states have informed-consent laws that require you to explain the risks of nontreatment to a patient who refuses nursing treatment. Twenty-two states and the District of Columbia have right-to-die laws (also called *natural death laws* or *living-will laws*). These laws recognize the patient's right to choose death by refusing extraordinary treatment when he has no hope of recovery. For example, they would support a terminally ill patient's (or his family's) insistence that a hospital discontinue life support.

Each state has established its own guidelines, so ask your employer for a summary of your state's right-to-refuse-treatment laws. In general, the same right-to-refuse-treatment laws apply in Canada and the United States.

Reasons to challenge the right to refuse

Any mentally competent adult can legally refuse treatment if he's fully informed about his medical condition and about the likely consequences of his refusal. This leaves you two grounds for challenging a patient's right to refuse. You can claim that

The Right to Consent: From Birth to Adulthood

As you know, a minor's rights in making independent decisions about medical treatment are more restricted than an adult's rights. However, in certain instances, a doctor or judge may decide a minor is mature—has a sufficiently developed awareness and mental capacity. In these instances, the minor, not his parents, has the right to make decisions about his medical treatment. This chart details how medical rights change from birth to adulthood.

From birth, everyone has the right to:
• confidentiality concerning medical records
• privacy during treatment
• legal protection from malpractice.

A minor—anyone under the age of 18 or 21, depending on the state where he lives—has the right to:
• consent to treatment for sexually transmitted diseases, serious communicable diseases, and drug or alcohol abuse (although the minor's parents may have to be notified).

A mature minor—a minor that a doctor or judge considers *mature*—has the right to:
• consent to, or refuse, medical experimentation and emergency care, as well as routine care
• obtain contraceptives and advice about contraception (although the minor's parents may have to be notified)
• obtain an abortion (although the minor's parents may have to be notified)
• request a second opinion if his parents have him committed to a mental health facility.

An adult—anyone who's reached majority or who's legally emancipated—has the right to:
• consent to, or refuse, medical treatment
• consent to, or refuse, medical treatment for children in most circumstances.

---

the patient is incompetent, or you can claim that compelling reasons exist to overrule his wishes.

The courts consider a patient incompetent when he lacks the mental ability to make a reasoned decision, such as when he's delirious. (For further discussion, see *When the Court May Overrule the Patient*, page 79.)

The courts also recognize several compelling reasons to overrule a patient's refusal of treatment. Here are some of the reasons:
• Refusing treatment endangers the life of another. For example, a court may overrule a pregnant woman's objection to treatment in order to save her unborn child's life.
• A relative wants to withhold treatment of an incompetent patient and has not been appointed legal guardian.

• A parent wants to withhold lifesaving treatment from his child. For example, a court may overrule parents' religious objections to their child's treatment when the child's life is endangered. When the child's life isn't in danger, however, the courts are more likely to respect the parents' religious convictions. For example, in the *Green* case (1972), the court upheld the parents' wish to withhold treatment from their 16-year-old child. The treatment was not lifesaving, but rather was for correction of scoliosis.
• The patient links his refusal of treatment with a strong indication that he wants to live, by making statements to you such as that he fears death. For example, some Jehovah's Witnesses who oppose blood transfusions say or imply that they won't prevent the transfusions if a court takes responsibility for the decision. In *Powell*

v. Columbian-Presbyterian Medical Center (1965), the court authorized transfusions when a Jehovah's Witness indicated she wouldn't object to receiving blood, although she'd refused to give written consent.

• Public interest outweighs the patient's right. For example, the law requires school-age children to receive polio vaccine before they can attend classes.

What to do when a patient refuses treatment

A patient planning to refuse treatment may tell you first. When he tells you he's going to refuse treatment or he simply refuses to give consent, stop preparations for any treatment at once. Then immediately report your patient's decision to your supervisor. She'll notify the doctor and hospital administrator. Never delay informing your supervisor, especially if a delay could be life-threatening. Any delay you're responsible for will greatly increase your legal risks. The doctor and hospital have the responsibility to take action, such as trying to convince the patient to accept treatment or asking him to sign a release form. This form relieves the hospital and its health team of liability for any consequences the patient might suffer by refusing treatment. (However, the release form doesn't release the health team from its obligation to continue providing other forms of care.)

If the patient has refused life-sustaining treatment and you're asked to participate in terminating treatment, be sure you fully understand your state's right-to-die law first. Otherwise—even with a signed release form—you could face criminal or civil charges for honoring *or* violating the request. For example, some states could prosecute you on criminal charges if you allowed a patient to die by withholding the life-support treatment he refused. In other states, a patient or his family could sue you for battery for continuing life-support measures they refused.

A patient can sue you for battery—intentionally touching another person without authorization to do so—for simply doing what a doctor has ordered. Here's a fictional example:

Albert Proxy, age 69, is hospitalized with a gastrointestinal disorder. He's also depressed and uncooperative. His day-shift nurse, Bernice Bransted, reads on his chart that the doctor ordered an enema.

Disgruntled and surly, Mr. Proxy has other ideas. He bluntly tells the nurse: "Leave me alone. I'm not getting an enema now!"

Despite his protests, Ms. Bransted insists. She gently turns him in his bed and administers the enema.

Later, Mr. Proxy's son becomes angry when his father tells him what happened. The son confronts the nursing supervisor and warns her that he intends to pursue the matter.

Does Mr. Proxy have a case for battery against the nurse? Yes. As a conscious, coherent adult, even though depressed, Mr. Proxy has the right to refuse treatment. After he—or any other adult patient—refuses any nursing treatment, giving it will make the nurse liable for battery.

How to challenge the patient's refusal

To overrule the patient's decision, the doctor or your hospital must obtain a court order. Only then are you legally authorized to administer a treatment a competent patient doesn't want.

If the doctor or hospital tries to convince the court to overrule the patient on the grounds that he's incompetent, they'll need proof that he lacks the mental ability to make a reasoned decision. Some of that proof can come from your documented observations about your patient's mental status.

The refusal itself, no matter how serious the patient's condition, isn't evidence of incompetence. In *Lane v. Candura* (1978), for example, a diabetic patient first agreed to have her leg amputated, then changed her mind and refused the surgery. The doctors applied for a court order, arguing that by changing her mind the patient had shown incompetence. The court disagreed. It upheld the patient's right to withdraw her consent as long as she understood.

When a Patient Says No

As you know, a patient must give his consent before you can perform any treatment. Do you know what to do if he refuses?

If the patient refuses, start by telling him the risks involved in not having the treatment done. If the patient understands the risks but still refuses, notify your supervisor and the doctor. Record the patient's refusal in your nurses' notes.

Next, ask the patient to fill out a refusal-of-treatment release form, like the one shown below. The signed form indicates that the appropriate treatment would have been given had the patient consented. This form protects you, the patient's doctors, and your institution from liability for not providing treatment.

If the patient refuses to sign the release form, document this in your nurses' notes. For additional protection, your institution's policy may require you to get the patient's spouse or closest relative to sign another refusal-of-treatment release form. Document whether or not the spouse or relative does this.

REFUSAL OF TREATMENT
RELEASE FORM

I, _____,

(patient's name)

refuse to allow anyone to

_____

(insert treatment)

The risks attendant to my refusal have been fully explained to me, and I fully understand the results for this treatment and that if the same is not done, my chances for regaining normal health are seriously reduced and that, in all probability, my refusal for such treatment or procedure will seriously endanger my life.

I hereby release the

_____

(name of hospital)

its nurses and employees, together with all doctors in any way connected with me as a patient, from liability for respecting and following my express wishes and direction.

_____   _____
Witness   Patient or
                                     Legal Guardian

_____   _____
Date   Age of
                                     Patient

How emergencies affect the right to refuse

A competent adult has the right to refuse even emergency treatment. His family can't overrule his decision, and his doctor may not give the expressly refused treatment even if the patient becomes unconscious.

Sometimes, however, *not* giving emergency treatment that the patient has refused can incur liability. For example, a patient who refuses treatment in an irrational way—with disjointed statements and gestures—actually could be legally incompetent. In that situation, the doctor could be held liable for not treating him.

Obviously, for your protection as well as your patient's, you need to exercise great care when dealing with a difficult patient in an emergency. Make sure the doctor waits till he has consent, if that's possible. And make sure he has a court order before you assist in giving emergency care to a competent patient who refuses treatment.

If there are no grounds for seeking a court order to overrule your patient's refusal, you have an ethical duty to defend his right to refuse treatment in the face of all opposition, even his family's. If they disagree with his decision, try to explain why he made it. But emphasize that the decision is his as long as he's competent.

You also have a responsibility to continue to inform your patient about treatment, because he may change his mind.

Patient privacy

Have you ever had to obtain highly personal, even embarrassing, information from a patient to care for him properly? If so, you probably remember how uncomfortable you both felt. You may have tried to put him at ease by reassuring him that you'd keep his information confidential. But did you stop to think about the complexities of that responsibility?

How do you exercise that responsibility when your patient's spouse, other healthcare professionals, the media, or public health agencies ask you to disclose confidential information? Find out by reading this entry on your responsibility to maintain your patient's privacy.

In the eyes of the law

Privacy and confidentiality were first proposed as basic legal rights in 1890 in a *Harvard Law Review* article entitled "The Right to Privacy."

The U.S. Constitution doesn't explicitly sanction a right to privacy. But in *Griswold v. Connecticut* (1965), *Katz v. United States* (1967), *Stanley v. Georgia* (1969), and *Roe v. Wade* (1973), the U.S. Supreme Court cited several constitutional amendments that imply the right to privacy.

Essentially, the right to privacy is the right to be left alone—and to make personal choices without outside interference. In the landmark case of *Griswold v. Connecticut* (1965), for example, the U.S. Supreme Court recognized a married couple's right to privacy in contraceptive use. In *Eisenstadt v. Baird* (1972), the Supreme Court extended the privacy right to include unmarried persons. In *Carey v. Population Services International* (1977), the Supreme Court said a state law that prohibited the sale of contraceptives to anyone under age 16 was unconstitutional. The court held that the decision to bear a child is a fundamental right and that the state law could only be justified if it protected a compelling state interest.

Recently, the Department of Health and Human Services tried to modify the Court's ruling in the *Carey* case. The department published a regulation, "Parental Notification Requirements Applicable to Projects for Family Planning Services." Also known as the "squeal rule," it proposes that any federally funded clinic or health agency that gives contraceptives to a minor must inform the minor's parents or guardian. A New York federal district court has already declared that divulging such confidential information invades the minor's privacy and is unconstitutional.

The Supreme Court ruling in *Roe v. Wade* (1973) protects a woman's right to privacy in having an abortion during the first trimester. The ruling permits a woman and her doctor to decide to terminate the pregnancy free from state intrusion until the end of the first trimester. After the first

When the Court May Overrule the Patient

Can your patient refuse life-support treatment under any circumstances? Can a relative of an unconscious adult patient force you to withhold treatment? Can parents stop you from treating their child?

Usually, the court respects a patient's right to refuse treatment if the patient is capable of making a reasoned decision. And it usually lets the parent or legal guardian of a child decide about the child's care, provided that the parent doesn't refuse lifesaving treatment. But the court will intervene in certain circumstances, even when the patient's or parent's decision rests on constitutionally protected grounds, such as religious beliefs. If you ever get caught between a patient or his family and a court, you'll be better prepared to deal with the situation if you know about previous court rulings in this area. Here are some delicate legal situations the court has ruled on:

● If an adult patient becomes physically or mentally incapacitated, a relative can't always refuse treatment for him. The court reserves the right to overrule even a spouse in the patient's behalf. For example, in *Collins v. Davis* (1964), the court overruled the wife's refusal of surgery for her unconscious husband.

● If a patient who's responsible for the care of a child refuses lifesaving treatment, the court may reverse the patient's decision. In *Application of the President and Directors of Georgetown College, Inc.* (1964), the court ordered a blood transfusion for a Jehovah's Witness who was the mother of an infant and who refused to give consent for the transfusion. In the *Melideo* case (1976), the court said that it might have ordered a lifesaving transfusion for the patient if she had had a child.

● If a patient who's pregnant refuses treatment, thereby threatening not only her health but also that of her unborn child, the court has reversed the patient's decision. In *Jefferson v. Griffin Spalding County Hospital Authority* (1981), the court awarded temporary custody of the unborn child to a state agency. The mother had a complete placenta previa but had refused to consent to a cesarean section. The court's custody award included full authority to give consent for a surgical delivery.

● If a patient is a minor, the court will allow his parents or legal guardian to consent to medical treatment, but not allow them to deny him lifesaving treatment. *In re Sampson* (1972) was such a case.

---

trimester, a state may regulate abortion to protect the mother's health. And the state may prohibit an abortion if the fetus is judged able to live outside the womb.

The *Roe v. Wade* decision played an important role in getting abortion rights extended to minors.

In *Planned Parenthood of Central Missouri v. Danforth* (1976), the Supreme Court overruled a law that prevented first trimester abortions for minors without parental consent. Its decision hinged on the *Roe v. Wade* decision that a state could not interfere with a woman's personal choice to abort her pregnancy during the first trimester.

In a similar case, *Bellotti v. Baird II* (1979), the Court acknowledged that the privacy rights of a minor are not equal to the constitutional rights of adults. But it held that a state law requiring a minor to obtain parental consent for an abortion infringed on the minor's rights.

In some cases of abortion involving minors, parental notification may be necessary. In *H. L. v. Matheson* (1981), the Supreme Court ruled that a state may require parental notification before an abortion if the minor is immature or unemancipated. The law has been judged to be constitutional because it doesn't prohibit a minor from getting an abortion.

How the states support the patient's right to privacy

The right to privacy has received even more attention at the state level. Ten states—Alaska, Arizona, California, Florida, Hawaii, Illinois, Louisiana, Montana, South Carolina, and Washington—have written some type of privacy provision into their constitutions. And nearly all states have recognized the right to privacy through statutory or common law.

The state courts have been strong in protecting the patient's right to not have confidential information revealed about him. Even in court, your patient is protected by the privilege doctrine. According to this doctrine, people who have a protected relationship—such as a doctor and patient—can't be forced, even during legal proceedings, to reveal communication between them unless the person who'd benefit from the protection—usually the patient—agrees to it.

State law determines which relationships are protected by the privilege doctrine. Most states include husband-wife, lawyer-client, and doctor-patient relationships.

At present, only a few states (including New York, Arkansas, Oregon, and Vermont) recognize the nurse-patient relationship as protected. But some courts have said the privilege exists when a nurse is following doctor's orders. Whether the privilege applies to LPNs/LVNs as well is uncertain.

Some courts have allowed a hospital or doctor to withhold confidential information on the patient's behalf. But the hospital's motive cannot be self-protection, as it was in *People v. Doe* (1978). In this case, a nursing home was being investigated for allegedly mistreating its patients. The court ruled that the nursing home's attempt to invoke patient privilege was unjust, since the issue at hand was the patient's welfare.

How far does the privilege extend?

State laws also determine the extent of the privilege in protected relationships. In some states, a patient automatically waives his right to doctor-patient privilege when he files a personal injury or workmen's compensation lawsuit.

The purpose of the privilege doctrine in patient relationships—doctor-patient, nurse-patient—is to encourage the patient to reveal confidential information that may be essential to his treatment. The doctrine guarantees that no one will reveal his confidential information without his permission. In *Hammonds v. Aetna Casualty and Surety Co.* (1965), the court reinforced that guarantee by declaring that protecting a patient's privacy is a doctor's legal duty. It further ruled that a patient could sue for damages any unauthorized person who disclosed confidential medical information about him. Similarly, a patient can sue for invasion of privacy any unauthorized personnel, such as student nurses, who observe him without his permission. The only hospital personnel who have a right to observe a patient are those involved in his diagnosis, treatment, and related care.

Canada's view of patient privacy

Canadian common law recognizes the privilege doctrine in doctor-patient relationships, but not in nurse-patient relationships. (Cases that suggest the doctor-patient privilege include *Dembie, 1963; Re SAS, 1977;* and *Geransky, 1977.*) However, the Canadian Nurses Association and the provincial licensing authorities have adopted the International Council of Nurses Code of Ethics. (See *International Council of Nurses Code of Ethics*, page 267.) The code requires you to keep confidential any personal information you receive from a patient during the course of your nursing care. Consequently, although violation of a patient's right to privacy isn't subject to criminal prosecution in Canada, it is deemed professional misconduct. So in Canada, a nurse who violates a patient's right to privacy can lose her nursing license.

Nurses' responsibilities in protecting patient privacy

Despite the *legal* uncertainties regarding nurses' responsibilities under the privilege doctrine, you have a professional and ethical responsibility to protect your patient's

How to Handle a Reporter's Questions

Imagine this: A reporter approaches you in the hospital and asks if a local government official is being treated for cancer. Would you know how to answer?

Usually, you'd answer a reporter's question directly and honestly. As a general rule, you can release the patient's name, age, address, and condition—as good, fair, serious, or critical—with one exception: Don't release a patient's name until you know that his family has been notified.

But what do you say when a direct, honest answer would violate your patient's right to confidentiality?

The best answer is, "Call my nursing supervisor or the hospital's public relations officer." If neither is available, answer as honestly as you can *without releasing confidential information*. Here are some sample answers to some tough questions:

Q. Is the sheriff being treated at your hospital for cancer?

A. The sheriff *is* being treated at our hospital. He's listed in fair condition. I can't release the nature of his problem because that's confidential information.

Q. The sheriff is a community leader. The public has a right to know if he's seriously ill. Can't you just tell me if he has cancer?

A. I'd like to help you, but you know that our hospital can't release confidential patient information. I'll be happy to tell the sheriff you'd like more information about him. If he gives the okay, someone will contact you.

Q. Mary Jones was brought to your hospital by ambulance tonight. The police say she was raped. Can you confirm that?

A. We never confirm whether a patient has been raped. I'm sure you can understand the harm this could cause a patient.

Q. Did you treat Mary Jones?

A. Yes. Mary Jones was treated and released.

Q. Did you treat a child-abuse victim today?

A. We can't confirm that a patient is a victim of child abuse. That's for courts to decide.

Q. But this child was brought by ambulance. That makes the case a public record. Can you confirm that you treated a child who was the victim of child abuse?

A. If you can provide the child's name, I can only confirm whether he was treated here, and I can tell you whether he's listed in good, fair, serious, or critical condition.

Adapted from Ann Doll, "What to Say (and Not to Say) When Reporters Ask Questions," *NursingLife*, May/June 1982.

privacy, whether you're an RN or an LPN or an LVN, a Canadian or an American.

This responsibility requires more of you than sealed lips. You may have to educate your patients about their right to privacy. Some of them may be unaware of what their right to privacy means, or that they even have such a right. In such situations, you must inform the patient of his rights and make sure his wishes are carried out. Explain that he can refuse to allow pictures to be taken of his disorder and its treatment, for example. And tell him he can choose to have information about his condition withheld from others, including family members.

Disclosing confidential information

If your patient is exercising his right to privacy in such a way that others' well-being is threatened, you may have to violate his privacy and reveal confidential information.

Under certain circumstances, you can lawfully disclose confidential information about your patient. For example, the courts allow disclosure when the welfare of a person or a group of people is at stake.

Consider the patient who's diagnosed as an epileptic and asks you not to tell his family. Depending on the circumstances, you may decide this isn't in the patient's and his family's best interest, particularly in terms of safety. In that situation, inform the patient's doctor; he may then decide to inform the family of the patient's condition to protect the patient's well-being.

You're also protected by law if you disclose confidential information about a patient that's necessary for his continued care, or if your patient consents to the disclosure. But be sure you don't exceed the specified limit of a patient's consent. Taking pictures is the largest single cause of invasion of privacy lawsuits. In *Feeney v. Young* (1920), a woman consented to the filming of her cesarean delivery for viewings by medical societies. But the doctor incorporated the film into a generally released movie entitled *Birth*. The court awarded damages to the woman under the state's privacy law.

The courts have also granted immunity to health-care professionals who, in good faith, have disclosed confidential information to prevent public harm. In *Simonsen v. Swenson* (1920), a doctor who believed his patient had syphilis told the owner of the hotel where the patient was staying about the patient's contagious disease. The court ruled that doctors are privileged to make disclosures that will prevent the spread of disease.

A controversial California case established a doctor's right to disclose information that would protect any person whom a patient threatened to harm. In *Tarasoff v. Regents of the University of California* (1976), a woman was murdered by a mentally ill patient who had told his psychotherapist that he intended to kill her. The victim's parents sued the doctor for failing to warn their daughter. The Supreme Court found the doctor liable because he didn't try to avert the danger posed by the patient's condition. The Court ruled similarly in *McIntosh v. Milano* (1979).

In some situations, the law requires you to disclose confidential information. For example, all 50 states and the District of Columbia have disclosure laws for child abuse cases. Except for Maine and Montana, all states also grant immunity from legal action for a good-faith report on suspected child abuse.

Courts may also order you to disclose confidential information in cases of child custody and neglect. One case involving such an order was *D. v. D.* (1969). Despite the doctor-patient privilege, the court ordered the doctor to turn the mother's medical records over to the court for a private inspection. The mother had a history of illness, and the court said the inspection would help it decide which parent should be granted custody. The courts made a similar ruling in the custody case of *In re Doe Children* (1978). The court stated that the children's welfare outweighed the parent's right to keep their medical records private.

Some laws create an exemption to the privilege doctrine in criminal cases so that the courts can have access to all essential information. In states where neither a law nor an exemption to the law exists, some courts will *find* an exemption to the doctrine in criminal cases.

Certain government agencies can also order you to reveal confidential information. Federal agencies that can do so include the Internal Revenue Service, the Environmental Protection Agency, the Department of Labor, and the Department of Health and Human Services. State agencies that can do this include revenue, or tax, bureaus and public health departments. For example, most state public health departments require reports of all communicable diseases, births and deaths, and gunshot wounds.

The newsworthiness of an event or person can also make disclosure acceptable. In such circumstances, the public's right to know must outweigh an individual's right to privacy, as in the assassination attempt on President Ronald Reagan in 1981. Another example was the precedent-setting implantation of an artificial heart in 1982 into Seattle dentist Barney Clark. (See *How to Handle a Reporter's Questions,* page 81.)

Even when the public has a right to know about a confidential matter, the courts will not allow the public disclosure to undermine a person's dignity. In *Barber v. Time, Inc.* (1942), *Time* magazine was sued by a woman whose picture and name they published in an article which said the patient suffered from an illness that caused her to eat as much food as 10 people could eat. The court ruled that publishing the patient's name and picture was an unnecessary invasion of her privacy and that ethics required keeping such information confidential.

Doe v. Roe (1977) is a similar case: a patient sued a psychiatrist for publishing the patient's biography and thoughts verbatim. Even though the doctor didn't use the patient's name, the court said the patient was readily identifiable by the article. It found the doctor liable for violating the doctor-patient privilege.

Conclusion

Other court cases that involve violations of patients' confidences include *Griffin v. Medical Society* (1939) and *Bazemore v. Savannah Hospital* (1930). As these cases and the others discussed show, you're responsible for protecting patients' privacy even when the circumstances allow some disclosure. Clearly, your patient's right to privacy is one that you must carefully uphold. (See *Confidentiality: Does It Ever End?*.)

The patient who demands his chart

Suppose your patient says to you, "I'm paying for the tests; I have a right to know the results." Does he have the legal right to know what's in his medical records?

Yes. And because patients increasingly want explanations about what's being done to them and why, you should know what to do when your patient asks to see his medical records.

The disclosure debate: Pro and con

For years, health-care experts have debated the merits of letting a patient see his medical records. Proponents argue that knowing the information helps the patient better understand his condition and care and makes him a more cooperative patient.

Confidentiality: Does It Ever End?

A former nursing home patient was recently charged with murder, and our local paper published several interviews with nurses who had known him in the home. These nurses gave very personal information about their patient, and I was upset at their breach of professional confidentiality. I asked the newspaper editor about the ethics of publishing the interviews. He said the nurses interviewed no longer worked at the home, so they were free to say whatever they wished. Is this true? Does confidentiality end with the job? What's being taught in nursing schools today?—RN, Calif.

A nursing school dean reassured us that nursing schools are still teaching that no nurse is free to reveal confidential patient information without the patient's permission. The nurses and the editor were wrong in thinking that this responsibility ended when the patient was discharged or the nurses changed their jobs.

Unfortunately, some professionals, including nurses, do reveal confidential information. But they never do so ethically, and they may face legal action.

This letter was taken from the files of *Nursing* magazine.

Opponents—usually doctors and hospitals—argue that the technical jargon and medical abbreviations found in medical records will confuse and perhaps frighten a patient. In addition, opponents claim that opening medical records to a patient will increase the risks of malpractice lawsuits. However, evidence to support this contention doesn't exist.

Legally, the right-to-access debate has centered on other issues. The first issue the courts had to answer involved ownership.

Who owns a patient's medical records?

The hospital owns the hospital medical records, and the doctor owns his office records, according to court decisions. Generally, the courts have decided that a patient sees a doctor for diagnosis and treatment, not to obtain records for his personal use.

The second issue the courts had to resolve involved access. While granting ownership of medical records to doctors and hospitals, the courts have expressed their own right to get the records anytime they need them for a case review.

For this reason, any patient in any state can file a lawsuit to subpoena his medical records. But some court decisions and some states' laws have given patients the right to direct access. Nine states' laws guarantee a patient's right to his medical information. And in states without such laws, the courts have recognized a patient's right to see the information.

In *Cannell v. Medical and Surgical Clinic S.C.* (1974), the court ruled that a doctor had the duty to disclose medical information to his patient. However, the court said doctors and hospitals needn't turn over the actual files to the patient. Instead, they need only show the complete medical record—or a copy—to the patient.

The court based the patient's limited right to access on two important conclusions:

• A patient has a right to know the details about his medical treatment under common law.

• A patient has a right to the information in his records because he pays for the treatment.

Despite the laws and court decisions, hospitals don't always make access to records easy. Some hospitals discourage a patient from seeing his medical records by putting up bureaucratic barriers. For example, requiring the patient to have an attorney make the request can stifle a patient's attempt to gain access to his records.

Other hospitals charge high copying fees in an effort to discourage patient record requests. Some states, such as Pennsylvania, have passed laws requiring reasonable copying fees.

In rare circumstances, hospitals can legally deny a patient access to his medical record information. For example, in *Gotkin v. Miller* (1975), a patient wanted access to all her medical records for the 8 years she spent in various New York mental hospitals. She wanted the information for a book she was writing about treatments for mental illness. The court said Mrs. Gotkin's records possibly contained many references to and statements by other patients. Since releasing the Gotkin records would violate the privacy of the other mental patients, the courts said the hospitals didn't have to give Mrs. Gotkin access to her records.

What to do when your patient asks to see his records

A patient's request should, first, make you question whether you and your colleagues have done enough to communicate with him. When you get such a request, try to assess why. Your patient could simply be curious; but his request may reflect hidden fears. For example, maybe he feels that he isn't being told enough about his treatment.

Next, notify your nursing supervisor that the patient has asked to see his medical records. Also, notify the risk manager, if your facility has one. Why? To alert administrative staff—and legal counsel, if necessary—so they can protect the hospital's interests.

After your patient gets approval to see his records, stay with him while he reads them. Explain to him that state laws prohibit him from changing or erasing information on his records, even information he considers incorrect. Tell him to show you any information he considers incorrect. Offer to answer any of his questions you can; assure him that his doctor will answer questions, too. In fact, encourage the patient to write down specific questions for his doctor, and offer to contact his doctor for him.

Documenting AMA Incidents

An AMA (against medical advice) form differs from the paperwork you deal with every day in one very important way. It's not a medical record; it's purely a legal document that's designed to protect you, your co-workers, and your institution should any problems result from the patient's unapproved discharge or escape.

To document an AMA incident, begin by getting your institution's AMA form. The form may look like the one shown below. You'll notice the form clearly states that the patient:
- knows he's leaving against medical advice
- has been advised of and understands the risks of leaving
- knows he can come back.

Discuss this form with the patient and ask him to sign it. You should sign it, too, as a witness. The patient, of course, doesn't *have* to sign the form, so don't try to force him.

Add the AMA form to the patient's medical chart, and write a detailed description of how you first learned of the patient's plan to leave AMA, what you and the patient said to each other, and what alternatives to the patient's action were discussed.

Also, check your institution's policy concerning incident reports. If the patient leaves without anyone's knowledge, or if he refuses to sign the AMA form, you'll probably be required to file an incident report. Be sure to include the names of any other employees involved in the discovery of the patient's absence. Hospital administration or your head nurse may also want to solicit corroborating reports from other employees, such as other RNs, LPNs/LVNs, doctors, aides, orderlies, and clerical staff.

RESPONSIBILITY RELEASE

This is to certify that I, _____,
a patient in _____,
am being discharged against the advice of my doctor and the hospital administration. I acknowledge that I have been informed of the risk involved and hereby release my doctor and the hospital from all responsibility for any ill effects that may result from such a discharge. I also understand that I may return to the hospital at any time and have treatment resumed.

_____
(Patient's signature)

_____
(Witness' signature)

_____
(Date)

RE: _____ Patient # _____
(Name of patient)

While your patient reads, help him interpret the abbreviations and jargon used in medical charting. One patient hospitalized for hypertension was greatly relieved when her nurse explained that the "malignant hypertension" notation on her chart had nothing to do with cancer.

Observe how the patient responds while he reads. If he becomes apprehensive, puzzled, or angry, try to provide him with calm, professional explanations about what he's read in his records. He may simply seem relieved: some patients want to read their records just to be sure you and the doctors aren't hiding any information. For example, one patient who demanded to see her medical records merely flipped through the pages. The hospital's willingness to share information about her treatment apparently satisfied her.

Can a patient's relative see the records?

A relative can see a patient's medical records under any of these conditions:
• The relative is the patient's legal guardian, and the patient is incompetent.
• The relative has the patient's approval.
• Circumstances indicate that the patient routinely involves the relative in treatment discussions and decisions.

Patient discharge AMA

The patient's bill of rights and the laws and regulations based on it give a competent adult the right to refuse treatment for any reason without being punished or having his liberty restricted.

Some states have turned these rights into law. And the courts have cited the bills of rights in their decisions.

The right to refuse treatment includes the right to leave the hospital against medical advice (AMA) any time, for any reason. Since the law prohibits you from detaining most patients and upholds their right to leave, all you can do is try to talk them out of it.

But if you think your responsibilities to your patient end if he leaves AMA, you're

mistaken. You still have a legal and professional responsibility to your patient and to the hospital to manage the situation properly.

Managing an AMA situation

Because you have more contact with your patient than any other health-care professional, you're likely to be the first person to suspect that a patient is contemplating leaving AMA.

His complaints or hostile behavior may indicate his extreme dissatisfaction with hospital routine or with the care he's receiving—valid reasons, in his mind, for getting out. By carefully observing, listening, and talking with him, you may be able to resolve the problems by giving him a new perspective on his situation that will change his mind about leaving.

If you discover that a specific problem has caused his dissatisfaction, try to resolve it. If the problem lies outside the scope of your practice, call the patient's doctor or the house doctor.

Recognize, too, that a patient may tell you he's changed his mind about leaving just to divert your attention. If you suspect this, check on him more often and ask other nurses to do the same. And stay with him when you escort him to another part of the hospital.

Suppose, however, your patient insists on leaving AMA. If your hospital has a policy on managing the patient who wants to leave, follow it exactly. It's designed to protect the hospital, your co-workers, and you from the risk of a lawsuit for malpractice (unlawful restraint, false imprisonment). If you don't have a policy, follow these steps:
• Contact the patient's family (if you or the patient hasn't already called them) to explain that the patient is getting ready to leave. If you can't reach the family, contact the person listed in the patient's records as being responsible for him (or for his body and valuables if he should die).
• Explain the hospital's AMA procedures to the patient if hospital policy delegates this responsibility to you. If it doesn't, have the house officer or other appropriate person do it.
• Give the patient the AMA form to sign (see *Documenting AMA Incidents,* page

85). His decision to leave is the same as a refusal of treatment, so make sure he's aware of the implications of his decision. Tell him the medical risks if he leaves the hospital and explain the *alternatives available at the hospital* and at other locations, such as regular visits to the hospital's outpatient clinic or admission to another facility. His signature on the AMA form is evidence of his refusal of treatment. You should witness the signature.

• Provide routine discharge care. Even though your patient is leaving AMA, his rights to discharge planning and care are the same as those for a patient who's signed out with medical advice. So if the patient agrees, escort him to the door (in a wheelchair, if necessary), arrange for medical or nursing follow-up care, and offer other routine health-care measures. These procedures will protect the hospital as well as the patient.

When your patient refuses to sign out or escapes

What if your patient refuses to sign the AMA form? In this situation, you're responsible for documenting his refusal in his medical chart. Be sure to include what you told him about signing the form, his response, and your efforts to involve his family in his decision.

What if you discover that the patient is missing from the hospital? Your first priority is to notify the hospital and nursing administrations immediately. If the patient was in police custody or if he poses a threat to anyone outside the hospital, the administration should contact the police. Subsequently, the hospital administration may ask you to notify the patient's family or friends, collect the patient's belongings, and document the escape in the patient's medical chart and incident report. (See *Documenting AMA Incidents,* page 85.)

False imprisonment

At no time should you attempt to detain a competent adult who has a right to leave. Any attempt to detain or restrain him may be interpreted as unlawful restraint or false imprisonment, for which you can be sued or prosecuted.

Your hospital's policy should reflect your state's laws and should specifically answer such questions as: How long and for what reasons may a patient be detained? When can you use forcible restraints? Who may order the use of restraints? Who may apply the restraints? Know the policies and the court rulings they're based on.

In general, the courts disapprove of detaining a patient arbitrarily or for an unreasonably long time, which may be ruled false imprisonment. Some court cases involving false-imprisonment charges resulted when institutions threatened to hold patients or their personal belongings until bills were paid. In most cases of this type, the courts ruled against the institutions.

A hospital or nursing home can, however, delay a patient's discharge until routine paperwork is complete—if the delay is reasonable. *Bailie v. Miami Valley Hospital* (1966) was a case in which the court ruled in favor of a hospital.

A typical case in which the courts found an institution guilty of false imprisonment was *Big Town Nursing Home v. Newman* (1970).

Mr. Newman, 67, had Parkinson's disease, arthritis, heart trouble, hiatus hernia, a speech impediment, and a history of alcoholism. Four days after his nephew signed him into the nursing home, Mr. Newman decided to leave. But employees at the nursing home stopped him, locked away his suitcase and clothes, restricted his use of the phone, and restricted his right to visitors. When Mr. Newman tried to walk off the grounds, employees locked him in a wing with severely emotionally disturbed patients and patients addicted to drugs and alcohol. He made other unsuccessful escape attempts, so staff tied Mr. Newman to a chair for long periods of time. Twenty-two days after his admission, Mr. Newman escaped. Eventually, he sued.

The court ruled in favor of Mr. Newman. Despite his physical infirmities, Mr. Newman had not legally been declared incompetent and was, therefore, legally entitled to exercise his rights.

In a few cases, because of extenuating circumstances, the courts have ruled against a patient who sued on grounds of false imprisonment. The case of *Pounders v. Trinity Court Nursing Home* (1979) is one such example.

Mrs. Pounders, 75, was a disabled widow. When her niece and nephew no longer wanted her to live with them, the niece arranged for her to move to Trinity Court Nursing Home. Mrs. Pounders did not object.

During her 2 months at Trinity Court, Mrs. Pounders complained only once to a nurse's aide that she wanted to leave. Unfortunately, the aide failed to report the complaint to anyone in authority at the home.

Mrs. Pounders was finally released, through the aid of an attorney, into another niece's care. Eventually, she sued the nursing home.

But because Mrs. Pounders couldn't prove she'd been involuntarily detained, the court absolved the nursing home of the false imprisonment charges.

Lawful detention

The right to leave the hospital AMA isn't absolute. Certain patients who pose a threat to themselves or others cannot legally leave the hospital. In these situations, restraint, when necessary, is lawful:
• *The psychiatric patient or prisoner.* If a patient transferred to your hospital for medical care from a prison or psychiatric hospital threatens to escape, notify the custodial institution immediately. They're responsible for sending personnel to guard the patient or for making new arrangements for his care. Restrain the patient only if his medical condition warrants it or if the police or psychiatric hospital authorities instruct you to do so.

If the prisoner or psychiatric patient escapes, you or your hospital or nursing administration should call the authorities at the custodial institution or the police and ask them to intervene.
• *The violent patient.* If you suspect that a patient with a history of violence or violent threats is planning to leave AMA, notify hospital and nursing administrators immediately. If state law allows it, your hospital administrators may decide to get police assistance to restrain the patient.

If the violent patient has escaped, notify your nursing or hospital administration immediately. They will contact the police and mental health authorities. If the patient ever expressed an intention to harm

a known person, the administration should also contact that person.
• *The patient with a communicable disease.* If your patient with a communicable disease warns you that he's going to leave AMA, notify your nursing or hospital administration. They'll alert appropriate public health authorities and, when warranted, the police. Your hospital may decide to restrain the patient until the authorities arrive or until a court issues a restraining order. The hospital will determine how to restrain the patient and how long to detain him, depending on the seriousness of his disease and the risk it presents to the general population. For example, leprosy, smallpox, bubonic plague, and an untreated sexually transmitted disease present different risks of contagion to the community.

When a patient dies

When a patient dies, his rights don't end— they transfer to his estate. But in recent years, legally determining when death has occurred has become very difficult. That, in turn, makes your role difficult.

How can you be sure a patient is legally dead? Who has the right to pronounce death? What are your responsibilities after the patient dies? This entry will answer those questions.

The changing definition of death

Determining death used to be fairly simple. When a person's circulation and respiration stopped, he was dead. But in the last 30 years or so, advances in medical technology have made death pronouncements more difficult. Because medical equipment (such as respirators, pacemakers, and intraaortic balloon pumps) can maintain respiration and circulation, some patients continue to "live" even after their brains have died.

To help doctors determine death in such cases, an ad hoc committee at Harvard Medical School published a report, in 1968, defining brain death. This report set the following criteria for death:
• a failure to respond to the most painful stimuli

Can a Nurse Pronounce Death?

When a patient in our nursing home dies, my nursing supervisor pronounces death if a doctor isn't available. She says the RN on duty or the supervisor can legally pronounce death if no doctor is available.

Can a nurse pronounce a death, or is this illegal?—RN, Ohio.

In almost all states, including your own, a nurse *can't* legally pronounce a patient dead—only the doctor can do this. But if the doctor can't be there in person, he can pronounce death over the telephone.

You're considered qualified to determine whether a patient exhibits *evidence* of death. Based on your findings, the doctor can pronounce a patient officially dead.

As a precaution, be sure to chart the fact that the *doctor* pronounced the patient dead after you'd relayed the necessary information to him. And be sure to check whether your institution has a written policy on the matter.

By the way, telling the family about the patient's death is usually the job of the doctor or an administrator. Check your institution's policy on this matter.

One last detail: If the doctor pronounces a death on the basis of your report, but the patient is not really dead, the doctor could be liable for malpractice. You, however, would *not* be liable, because you merely reported your physical findings.

This letter was taken from the files of *Nursing* magazine.

• an absence of spontaneous respirations or muscle movements
• an absence of reflexes
• a flat EEG.

The committee recommended that all the above tests be repeated after 24 hours and that hypothermia and the presence of central nervous system depressants, such as barbiturates, be ruled out.

Other groups also issued definitions of brain death, and several court decisions have been based on such definitions.

In the case of *State v. Brown* (1971), an Oregon court was among the first to recognize brain death. In this case of second-degree murder, the defendant argued that he hadn't caused the victim's death by inflicting a gunshot wound to the brain. Instead, he claimed, a doctor killed the victim by removing artificial life support. But the court ruled that the defendant caused the victim's death because the gunshot wound resulted in brain death.

In 1975, several New York hospitals initiated a lawsuit to get a legal ruling on the definition of death when the patient was a potential organ donor (*N.Y.C. Health and Hospitals Corporation v. Sulsona*).

Expert testimony in the case showed that the common-law definition of death apparently raised the failure rate of organ transplants. When death was defined as the cessation of circulation and respiration, the incidence of renal failure in kidney recipients was about 88%. But when death was defined by the brain death standard, the incidence of renal failure in recipients was only about 15%. (Bear in mind, however, that medical advances have improved the success rate of almost all types of transplant surgery since 1975.)

The court ruled it would recognize brain death in transplantation cases to encourage anatomic gifts, even though the state had no law defining brain death. This ruling applied to transplantation cases *only*.

In 1979, a Colorado court also accepted the criteria for brain death, in *Lovato v. Colorado*. In this case, a mother was charged with abusing her child. The child was comatose, with a flat EEG, with pupils fixed and dilated, and without spontaneous respirations or reflexes, or responses to painful stimuli. The mother petitioned the court to maintain the child on a respirator. But the court ruled that the child was dead because he met the criteria for brain death.

In 1980, representatives of the American Bar Association, the American Medical Association, and the Uniform Law Commission drafted the Uniform Determination of Death Act. This act states that "an individual who has sustained either irreversible cessation of circulatory and respiratory functions or irreversible cessation of all functions of the entire brain, including the brain stem, is dead. A determination of death must be made in accordance with accepted medical standards."

No state has yet adopted this act verbatim. However, many state legislatures have passed laws that describe how to determine brain death. In states without such laws—or judicial precedents—the common-law definition of death (cessation of circulation and respiration) is still used. In these states, doctors are understandably reluctant to discontinue artificial life support for brain-dead patients. If you are likely to be involved with patients on life-support equipment, protect yourself by finding out how your state defines death.

In Canada, defining the moment of death has traditionally been left to medical professionals. Human-tissue gift legislation says death is determined according to accepted medical practice.

Who's responsible for pronouncing death?

Legally, only a doctor or a coroner can pronounce a person dead. However, in some health-care facilities, such as nursing homes, nurses pronounce death when a doctor isn't available. If you work in such a facility, you should understand, however, that pronouncing death isn't a nursing responsibility (see *Can a Nurse Pronounce Death?*, page 89).

The attending doctor is usually responsible for signing the death certificate, unless the death comes under the jurisdiction of a medical examiner or coroner. State laws specify when this occurs. Usually, the coroner or medical examiner has jurisdiction over deaths with violent or suspicious circumstances: suspected homicides and suicides, and deaths following accidents, abortions, surgery, or hospital stays of less than 24 hours.

The Canadian provincial laws on autopsies are similar. Any death occurring in violent or suspicious circumstances comes under the jurisdiction of a medical examiner or coroner. Depending on the province, other types of death—including a prisoner's death, a sudden death, or a death not caused by a disease—may also come under the jurisdiction of a medical examiner or coroner.

When a patient dies, you're responsible for *accurately* and *objectively* charting all his signs and any actions you take. For example, an appropriate entry in the nurses' notes would be: "Midnight. No respirations or pulses, pupils fixed and dilated. Notified Dr. York." Don't write a conclusion that borders on a medical diagnosis, such as "Patient seems dead."

You're also responsible for notifying the doctor who can be reached most quickly. If this is the doctor on call, he should notify the patient's doctor, who should notify the family. Find out who will be notifying the family, and document it.

At the appropriate time, you should prepare the body for removal to the morgue, according to hospital procedure. When doing this, be sure you carefully identify the body. In *Lott v. State* (1962), a nurse mistagged two bodies, causing a Roman Catholic to be prepared for an Orthodox Jewish burial, and an Orthodox Jew to be prepared for a Roman Catholic burial. The court found her liable.

Obtaining consent for an autopsy

As you know, an autopsy is a postmortem examination to determine the cause of death. If the death came under the jurisdiction of a medical examiner or coroner, the decision to perform an autopsy rests solely with him, despite the family's wishes.

In all other cases, however, the patient's family has a right to give or withhold consent. (In some states, the patient can give written consent to an autopsy before he dies.) When a doctor or other hospital representative has sought consent from a patient's family, you can help by explaining why the autopsy is needed and how autopsy arrangements are made.

Who can give consent?
Most states have laws that specify who has the right to give consent to autopsies. Some laws simply list which relative can give consent. Others list relatives in descending order, according to their relationship to the deceased. The usual order is spouse, adult children, parents, brothers or sisters, grandparents, uncles or aunts, and cousins. The person with the right to consent may withhold consent or impose limits on the autopsy. If it exceeds these limits, the consenting relative may sue.

Of course, the relative with the right to consent may also sue if an autopsy is performed without any consent. Usually, the grounds for such lawsuits are mental or emotional suffering.

The family also has a right to give or withhold specific consent to practice medical procedures on a corpse. In teaching hospitals, residents and medical students practice procedures, such as intubation, on corpses. But if a hospital does not obtain proper consent, the family member responsible for consent may sue. In many states, the hospital may even face criminal charges for mistreating a corpse.

Responsibility for burial
In the United States and Canada, the family member who has the right to consent to autopsy usually has the responsibility to bury the body as well. However, in one Canadian case (*Hunter v. Hunter,* 1930), the court ruled that the deceased's son, who was the executor of the will, had this responsibility—not the wife, who was the next of kin.

If no one claims the body, despite the hospital's effort to contact the person responsible, a state or county official must dispose of it. Laws in many states direct this official to deliver unclaimed bodies to an appropriate educational or scientific institution, unless the person is a veteran or has died from a contagious disease. In these situations, the state pays for burial or cremation.

In Canada, the hospital must notify an appropriate official of an unclaimed body, and the body will be delivered to a medical school.

Conclusion
As state legislatures and courts continue to grapple with the definition of death, your responsibilities may seem unclear. Until a single, national definition of death exists, you must know your current state or provincial laws and hospital policies defining death.

In addition, you must know what to do when a patient dies. To protect yourself legally, be sure you understand which tasks are the doctor's responsibility, and which tasks are yours.

Selected References

Creighton, Helen. *Law Every Nurse Should Know,* 4th ed. Philadelphia: W.B. Saunders Co., 1981.

Doudera, A. Edward, and Peters, J. Douglas, eds. *Legal and Ethical Aspects of Treating Critically and Terminally Ill Patients.* Ann Arbor, Mich.: Health Administration Press, 1982.

Friloux, C. Anthony, Jr. "Death: When Does It Occur?" *Baylor Law Review* 27:10, 1975.

Harvard Medical School, Ad Hoc Committee to Examine the Definition of Brain Death. "A Definition of Irreversible Coma," *Journal of the American Medical Association* 205:337-40, August 1968.

"Informed Consent," Chapter 3 in *Hospital Liability and Risk Management.* New York: Practicing Law Institute, 1981.

Pozgar, George D. *Legal Aspects of Health Care Adminis-* *tration,* 2nd ed. Rockville, Md.: Aspen Systems Corp., 1983.

President's Commission for the Study of Ethical Problems in Medicine and Biomedical and Behavioral Research. *Defining Death: Medical, Legal and Ethical Issues in the Determination of Death.* Washington, D.C.: U.S. Government Printing Office, 1981.

Rocereto, LaVerne, and Maleski, Cynthia. *The Legal Dimensions of Nursing Practice: A Practical Guide.* New York: Springer Publishing Co., 1982.

Rosoff, Arnold J. *Informed Consent: A Guide for Health Care Providers.* Rockville, Md.: Aspen Systems Corp., 1981.

Rozovsky, Lorne E. *Canadian Patient's Book of Rights.* Garden City, N.Y.: Doubleday and Company, Inc., 1980.

Warren, Samuel D., and Brandeis, Louis D. "The Right to Privacy," *Harvard Law Review* 4:193, 1890.

3

Your Legal Risks in Nursing Practice

No doubt about it—as a nurse, your chances of being named a defendant or codefendant in a malpractice lawsuit are growing.

In 1976, for example, 834 registered nurses were named in lawsuits. Just 2 years later, in 1978, that number had jumped more than 440%—to 3,775. And the number of nurses involved in work-related lawsuits continues to grow.

Why this rapid and continuing increase? Certainly one reason is today's "I'm gonna sue!" climate, which suggests that lawsuits should be used to resolve grievances against anybody and everybody, including nurses. The dynamic growth within the nursing profession, however, offers another—more substantial—reason. As nursing grows professionally, nurses are taking on expanded responsibilities that inevitably lead to increased legal accountability. What does this mean for you? It means you need to thoroughly understand your basic legal rights, responsibilities, and risks in everyday nursing practice. If you don't, you may be setting yourself up for a lawsuit. (See *Preventing the Defendant-Nurse Syndrome,* page 94, and *Avoiding Legal Risks when Working with Others,* page 96.)

Understanding the issues
As you know, whether you're an RN or an LPN/LVN, you're always legally accountable for your nursing actions. In any practice setting, your care must meet these baseline legal standards:
• Does your care fall within the scope of your nurse practice act?

• Does your care measure up to established practice standards?
• Are you protecting your patient's rights?

Remember these points as you read the entries in this chapter. Each entry is designed not to restrict your patient-care options, because of legal issues, but to free you to give your patients the best care possible—because you understand those issues.

Hospital policies: The legalities

Every hospital and other health-care institution has *policies*—a set of general principles by which it manages its affairs. If you work for a hospital, you're obligated to know those policies and to follow the established *procedures* that flow from them.

But never do this blindly. As a nurse, you're also obligated to maintain your professional standards, and these standards may sometimes conflict with your employer's policies and procedures. At times, you may be forced to make decisions and take actions that risk violating those policies and procedures. At times like these, you need help balancing your duty to your patient with your responsibility to your employer. Your best help is a well-prepared nursing department policy manual, coupled with high standards of performance. This combination is the mark of a successful nursing department—one whose first concern is to deliver high-quality patient care.

What makes a good nursing department manual?

Although manuals will differ, most good ones will do the following:
• show how general hospital policies and procedures apply to the nursing department
• outline the nursing department's roles and responsibilities, both internally and in relation to other hospital departments
• identify the expected limits of nursing action and practice
• offer guidelines for handling emergency situations
• provide standing orders for nurses who work in special areas, such as the intensive care unit (ICU) or the coronary care unit (CCU)
• show the steps to be taken before—and after—arriving at nursing-care decisions. These steps can then become a well-thought-out statement of the care standards applied in the institution, and the manual itself can be used as evidence in malpractice cases. (See the discussion of *Utter v. United Health Center, 1977,* on this page.)

Any good nursing department manual should always be in the process of revision—especially today, when hospitals are rapidly revising and expanding their basic policies and procedures. Some of these procedure and policy changes result from efforts to streamline and standardize patient care. Others result from efforts to comply with new state, provincial (Canada), and federal regulations or to implement recommendations of the Joint Commission on Accreditation of Hospitals.

How hospital policies can affect court decisions

Hospital policies are meant to be followed. Policies aren't laws, but courts have generally ruled against nurses who violated their employers' policies. Courts have also held hospitals liable for poorly formulated—or poorly implemented—policies.

Take, for example, the matter of reporting doctors who fail to give their patients adequate medical care. In *Darling v. Charleston Community Memorial Hospital* (1965), the court found the attending nurses negligent because they failed to monitor the condition of a patient's broken leg that, because of improper casting, became necrotic and had to be amputated.

Specifically, the court found that because the attending nurses did not bring the patient's worsening condition to the medical staff's attention, the nurses had failed to exercise proper judgment concerning the adequacy of the patient's medical care. The nurses should have informed the attending doctor of complications; then, if he'd failed to act, they should have advised the hospital authorities of the patient's unsatisfactory medical care. These measures would have helped to ensure that appropriate action was taken.

Since the *Darling* case, the generally accepted rule of law is that staff actions that deviate from established hospital policies and procedures constitute a breach of duty. But this case also showed that a hospital can be held liable for failure to have a system for monitoring the quality of care and taking action to correct any deficiencies. Because Charleston Community Hospital didn't provide enough trained nurses and adequate hospital policy guidelines, the judge allowed the jury to evaluate standards of accreditation, state licensing regulations, and hospital bylaws in determining the applicable standard of care for deciding the case.

Although the *Darling* case and others have established a nurse's duty to report certain matters to proper authorities, how this should be done hasn't been clearly spelled out. In many instances, this reporting consists of verbally notifying the attending doctor about the problem. If he doesn't act, then the nurse can report the situation to the chief of the service. Of course, all this should be documented in the nurses' notes on the patient's chart.

In *Utter v. United Health Center* (1977), the court relied on a provision in the hospital's nursing manual, which said that if the doctor in charge—after being notified—did nothing about adverse changes in a patient's condition or acted ineffectively, the nurse was to "call this to the attention of the Department Chairman." The nurses cited in this case failed to report to the chairman and so caused a crit-

Preventing the Defendant-Nurse Syndrome

Nurses with signs and symptoms of the *defendant-nurse syndrome* may easily end up in court. What's the defendant-nurse syndrome? Basically, it's a pattern of substandard nursing care—care that consistently fails to meet current legal standards. Nurses who exhibit this syndrome are ready targets for malpractice lawsuits.

Fortunately, you can prevent the defendant-nurse syndrome by doing the following:

• *Recognize that your first duty is to defend your patient, not his doctor.* If your judgment says your patient's condition warrants a call to his doctor, don't hesitate—in the middle of the day or in the middle of the night. If your judgment says to question a doctor's order because you can't read it, don't understand it, think it's incomplete, or think it may harm your patient, don't hesitate.

If your hospital doesn't already have a policy covering nurse-doctor communications, ask for one and keep asking till you get one. Meanwhile, for your own protection, carefully record all contacts with doctors.

• *Keep your nursing know-how up to date.* Here are some effective ways: reading nursing journals, attending clinical programs, attending inservice programs, and seeking advice from nurse specialists. If your hospital doesn't offer needed inservice programs, ask for them.

Remember, ignorance of new techniques is no excuse for substandard care. If you're ever sued for malpractice, your patient care will be judged by current nursing standards.

• *Include all parts of the nursing process in your patient care.* Taking shortcuts risks your patient's well-being and your own. If you're charged with malpractice, and the court finds out you took a dangerous patient-care shortcut, the court may hold you liable for causing harm to your patient.

• *Document every step of the nursing process for every patient.* Chart your observations immediately, while facts are fresh in your mind; express yourself clearly; and always write legibly. If you're ever involved in a lawsuit, a complete patient-care record could be your best defense.

• *Audit your nursing records consistently and comprehensively, using specific criteria to evaluate the effectiveness of patient care.* Ask for a charting class—or start one yourself—to encourage staff nurses to chart patient care correctly and legibly. Use problem-oriented charting (to be sure you're documenting all parts of the nursing process) and flow sheets (to record large volumes of data). Encourage other nurses to use these documenting aids.

• *Use your nursing knowledge to make nursing diagnoses and give clinical opinions.* You have a legal duty to your patient not only to make a nursing diagnosis but also to take appropriate action to meet his nursing needs. Doing so helps protect your patient from harm and you from malpractice charges.

• *Delegate patient care wisely.* Know the legal practice limits of the people you supervise, and caution them to act only within those limits. If your delegation of skilled tasks to an unskilled person harms a patient, you can be held liable for breaching your nurse practice act.

• *Know your nursing service policies.* Review the policies at least yearly. If you think new policies are needed, ask for them. If you're ever involved in a malpractice lawsuit, good nursing service policies and your knowledge of them could be important in your defense.

• *Treat patients' families, as well as patients, with kindness and respect.* When you help relatives cope with the stress of your patient's illness and teach them the basics of home care, they'll more likely remember you with a thank-you card than with a legal summons.

ical 24-hour delay in the patient's treatment. Because of this, the judge told the jury that it could label the nurses' failure as the proximate cause of the patient's injury. So the nurses shared the blame for the inaction of the patient's doctor because they did not go a step further and make sure the patient got the needed medical attention. (For more examples, see *Following Policy and Avoiding Legal Problems,* pages 98 and 99.)

Another policy question that could arise involves exactly when to take a patient's history after he's admitted to your unit. Suppose, for example, you admit a patient who has pneumonia and, unknown to you, a history of GI bleeding. On admission, his doctor writes a stat order for aspirin for fever. Following his order, you give the aspirin right away. A half hour later, before you can take his history, the patient begins to have GI bleeding.

Who's liable in a situation like this? The doctor might be, assuming he knew the patient's history. But you might be, too, for not taking the patient's history that would have revealed the prior GI bleeding.

You know, of course, that legally you're personally and primarily responsible for everything you do while on hospital duty. But if you're sued for malpractice, the hospital will have to assume secondary responsibility in the lawsuit, provided you were practicing within the scope of your job description. Whether you've acted properly is ordinarily determined, in court, by the patient's condition on admission and the hospital's nursing service policy.

The case of *O'Neill v. Montefiore Hospital* (1960) illustrates the dilemma a nurse faces when she must choose between hospital policy and her professional standards. This case involved a nurse who, following hospital policy, refused to admit a patient because he belonged to an insurance plan her hospital didn't accept. The man returned home and died. Although the trial court ruled in favor of the nurse, the New York Supreme Court (Appellate Division) reversed the decision and ruled the hospital nurse negligent for refusing to admit the patient. (For other examples, see *What Are the Limits of Your Liability?,* pages 102 and 103.)

How laws affect hospital policies

As you probably know, many hospital policies and procedures are mandated by state or (in Canada) provincial licensing laws or by such federal regulations as the conditions for participation in Medicare. Once made law, these requirements must be embodied in hospital policy.

Many such mandatory requirements exist. In the United States, for instance, the Civil Rights Act of 1964 compels any hospital receiving federal funds to adopt policies against discrimination based on race, creed, color, national origin, handicap, or sex. (These requirements mainly refer to admitting patients, not to giving bedside care.) The Freedom of Information Act requires hospitals to give consumers and patients access to certain data previously considered privileged. And the Department of Health and Human Services' regulations require that hospitals observe strict guidelines when using patients in research studies.

In Canada, each province has its own laws governing hospitals, both public and private. According to the Ontario Public Hospitals Act, certain classes of hospitals receiving provincial aid must, with few exceptions, admit patients needing treatment.

The provincial legislatures also pass laws governing hospitalization in psychiatric facilities. Matters of criminal law, however, are in the hands of the federal parliament, so hospital policymakers look to the federal parliament for guidance on issues such as narcotics and abortions.

U.S. and Canadian policy similarities and differences

Hospital policies in the United States and Canada generally show more similarities than differences.

One difference involves control at the federal level. Federal agencies in the United States exert more power than their Canadian counterparts do.

Under English common law, people are usually not obligated to help each other—not even in emergencies. However, where hospitals are concerned, Canadian provincial legislatures have departed from this tradition. For example, the Public Hospitals Act of Nova Scotia states that when

Avoiding Legal Risks when Working with Others

To help you steer clear of legal dangers when working with the health-care team, here are some questions and answers that deal with the legal responsibilities you face:

Q. Can I be held liable for mistakes made by a student nurse under my supervision?

A. Yes, if you have primary responsibility for instructing the student and correcting her mistakes.

Q. If a student nurse performs tasks that only a licensed nurse should perform, and does so with my knowledge but without my supervision, am I guilty of breach of duty?

A. Yes, because as a staff nurse, you should know that a student nurse can perform nursing tasks *only* under the direct supervision of a nurse licensed to perform those tasks.

Q. What should I do if I see another health-team member perform a clinical procedure incorrectly?

A. If the incorrect procedure can harm the patient, you have a legal duty to stop the procedure—tactfully, when possible—and immediately report your action to your nursing supervisor. If the incorrect procedure doesn't threaten to harm the patient, don't stop the procedure—but report your observation to your supervisor.

Q. Can I face legal action if I ask a hospital volunteer to help me give patient care and she does something wrong?

A. Yes. Don't ask a volunteer to participate in any task she isn't trained and professionally qualified to perform.

---

a qualified medical practitioner makes application for a patient and the (publicly funded) hospital has room, it must admit the patient—even if he can't pay for his care. (Private hospitals, however, needn't do this.)

In the United States, if an uninsured patient tries to get emergency treatment in a hospital but is turned away, the hospital subsequently can be found negligent if the patient's condition becomes significantly worse. This is so even if he seeks treatment elsewhere. One such case was *Hunt v. Palm Springs General Hospital* (1977). It involved a patient who died from brain damage due to prolonged seizures after one hospital refused to admit him because he hadn't paid past-due bills. He wasn't treated until another hospital admitted him, 4 hours later.

Hospital policies affect your job as a staff nurse

Remember that top management originates policies specifically to guide workers in the hospital's daily operations. Policies stem from the hospital's philosophy and objectives and are part of the hospital's planning process. So they affect your job very directly.

If you're considering employment at a hospital, study its policies carefully. If they're well defined, they may give you an indication of how satisfied and secure you can expect to be in your job.

If you're working in a specialized nursing area, such as the ICU or CCU, give special attention to any policies that directly or indirectly apply to you. Make sure your specialty is clearly defined in keeping with your state or provincial nurse practice act—and with the standards recommended by accrediting agencies and professional medical and nursing associations.

Besides reading policies—the general principles by which a hospital is guided in its management—read the hospital's rules, too. These describe the actions that employees should or should not take in specific situations. "No smoking in the patient's room," for example, is a rule and must be enforced without exception.

If you feel reasonably comfortable with the hospital's philosophy, objectives, policies, rules, and quality of care, you'll probably feel comfortable on the job. But if the hospital's policy calls for nursing procedures that conflict with your personal nursing standards or ethics, then you'll probably do better if you look elsewhere for employment.

When hospital policy and your nurse practice act conflict

You must refuse to follow hospital policy when it conflicts with your nurse practice act. Why? Because your state legislature has given the board of nursing power to define and monitor nursing practice in the interest of public health and safety. Any willful violation of board rulings, even with your hospital's knowledge and encouragement, could result in suspension or revocation of your license.

So if your hospital policy calls for nurses to remove sutures from postoperative patients, but your state board of nursing says you may not, don't do it. (In Pennsylvania, the state board of nursing sent a notice to all RN licensees stating that suture removal was not a nursing function. The notice also stated that a nurse who removed a patient's sutures would be violating the Pennsylvania Nurse Practice Act.) But *do* tell your hospital administration about the discrepancy.

Hospital policies that apply to LPNs and LVNs

LPNs and LVNs aren't RNs. They shouldn't be asked to exceed limits that law and education place on their practice. You'll find exceptions to this, of course. Both state law and national health commissions have recognized LPNs/LVNs' right to perform in an expanded role—for example, to administer drugs, if the LPN or LVN is properly trained for the task and it's one that other nurses perform in the hospital where she works.

But you should protect yourself. Make sure the conditions for your doing this work are included in your hospital's *written* policies. And make sure the policies have been established by a committee representing the medical staff, the nursing department, and the administration, and that the written version is available to all medical and nursing staff members. If these LPN/LVN policies *aren't* stated in writing, you'd better not administer drugs. If you're sued on this basis and can't back up your actions with written hospital policy, you could be found liable.

How to get hospital policies changed

You have two ways to bring nursing policy problems to your hospital administration's attention. You can involve your health-team colleagues by discussing policy problems at committee meetings, conferences, and interdepartmental meetings. Or you can communicate directly with your hospital administration via the grievance procedure, counseling, attitude questionnaires, and formal and informal unit management committees. Both ways give you a voice in determining the policies that affect your job.

The liability of understaffing

Understaffing—failure to provide enough professionally trained personnel to meet a patient population's needs. If you're like most nurses, you're very familiar with understaffing and the problems it can cause.

Statistics about understaffing are sketchy, but the fact that a number of court cases have addressed this issue suggests not only that understaffing is widespread but also that understaffing results in substandard bedside care, increased mistakes and omissions, and hasty documentation—all of which increase nurses' (and their employers') liability.

For example, if during hospitalization a patient is harmed and can demonstrate that the harm resulted from the hospital's

Following Policy and Avoiding Legal Problems

When in doubt, stick with policy

I'm a new nursing graduate, working the night shift on an oncology floor. Maybe because this is my first nursing job, I've read the hospital's policy manual carefully and I try to follow instructions. But not everybody does the same. Let me explain.

According to our hospital's written policy, only certified chemotherapy nurses may administer any chemotherapeutic drug. This regulation also stipulates that if a chemotherapy nurse isn't available, the attending doctor must administer the drug himself.

The policy couldn't be clearer. But on our floor, uncertified nurses do hang 5-fluorouracil (5-FU) when a chemotherapy nurse isn't available.

I checked with my supervisor about this practice. She took out and read her policy manual and then said "Look— everyone else hangs 5-FU. It's not a potent chemotherapeutic drug and won't cause damage if it should infiltrate. If we don't have a chemotherapy nurse available, the attending doctor isn't about to come in to hang a bottle of 5-FU at midnight."

She was telling me, without using the words, to hang the drug if I had to—despite what the manual said.

What should I do now? If I follow my supervisor's advice and I run into trouble, will my malpractice insurance protect me?—RN, Mass.

You're in a precarious position. If a written hospital policy says one thing and a nurse does another, she's probably liable for any trouble that may arise. Nurses *have* been sued for administering drugs improperly. What's more, if a nurse is acting contrary to hospital policy, she's *not* acting as an agent of the hospital. Therefore, the hospital's insurance doesn't have to cover her.

If you're going to correct this situation, you'll have to document all the facts. Then take your documentation through channels to the patient's doctor, to the hospital and nursing administrators, and to the hospital's policy committee.

---

failure to provide enough qualified personnel to care for him, the hospital may be found liable in a malpractice lawsuit.

What constitutes adequate staffing?

You won't find many legal guidelines to help you answer this question. So if you want to determine whether your floor has too few nurses, you may have a problem. The few guidelines that do exist vary from state to state and are limited mainly to specialty care units (such as intensive care, coronary care, and recovery room care). Even the Joint Commission on Accreditation of Hospitals (JCAH) offers little help. The JCAH staffing standard sets no specific nurse-patient ratios. It just states generally that "nursing personnel staffing shall... be sufficient to assure prompt recognition of an untoward change in a patient's condition and to facilitate appropriate intervention by the nursing, medical, or hospital staffs."

In the absence of well-defined staffing guidelines, the courts have had no reliable standard to use in deciding cases where understaffing is alleged. So each such case has been decided on an individual basis.

The first case decided partly on the basis of this issue was *Darling v. Charleston Community Memorial Hospital* (1965). A young man broke his leg while playing football and was taken to Charleston's emergency department, where the on-call doctor set and cast his leg. The patient began to complain of pain almost im-

Put it in writing

I'm writing for myself and for three other RNs in a hospital outpatient clinic. We're all concerned about our role in giving immunizations at the clinic. Usually, a local doctor gives the injections. But some days, he can't get to the clinic. On those days, his receptionist sends a typewritten note, saying the doctor won't be in and giving us the hospital phone number where we can reach him in an emergency. She always signs his name and initials the signature.

When the doctor isn't there, he expects us to give the immunizations ourselves. So far, we've done as he wishes, and we haven't had any problems. But we're worried about our liability. Our state doesn't allow nurses to prescribe drugs, and we don't have standing orders for administering immunizations. We've talked with the doctor, and he says we don't need to worry. But we'd like another opinion. Is the receptionist's note adequate authorization? Will it protect us legally if something goes wrong?—RN, Mich.

No. You definitely need a written protocol to handle this situation. In the current situation, you're administering prescription drugs without a doctor's order, and the receptionist's note wouldn't protect you legally if someone accused you of practicing medicine without a license.

Here's what you can do to protect yourselves and your patients: Ask your state health department to send you current immunization recommendations from the Centers for Disease Control in Atlanta. (Or contact the centers yourself: Centers for Disease Control, 1600 Clifton Rd., NE, Atlanta, Ga. 30333.)

Put the information in a manual, and ask the clinic doctor to review and sign it. Revise the manual every year, and get the doctor's signature after each revision. The result: You'll have *a procedure manual,* as well as a standing order for immunizations. Clinic nurses who've prepared such manuals say they can offer excellent protection in touchy situations.

These letters were taken from the files of *Nursing* magazine.

---

mediately. Later, his toes grew swollen and dark, then cold and insensitive, and a stench pervaded his room. Nurses checked the leg only a few times a day, and they failed to report its worsening condition. When the cast was removed 3 days later, the necrotic condition of the leg was apparent. After several surgical attempts to save the leg, it had to be amputated below the knee.

After an out-of-court settlement with the doctor who'd applied the cast, the court found the hospital liable for failing to have enough trained nurses available at all times to recognize the patient's serious condition and to bring it to the attention of the medical staff.

Since the *Darling* case, several similar cases have been tried (for example, *Cline v. Lund,* 1973, and *Sanchez v. Bay General Hospital,* 1981). Almost every case involved a nurse who failed to continuously monitor her patient's condition—especially his vital signs—and to report significant changes to the attending doctor. In each case, the courts have emphasized:

• the need for sufficient numbers of nurses to continuously monitor a patient's condition

• the need for nurses who are specially trained to recognize signs and symptoms that require a doctor's immediate intervention.

The hospital's liability for understaffing

Courts hold hospitals primarily liable in lawsuits where nursing understaffing is the key issue. A hospital can be found liable for patient injuries if it accepts more patients than its facilities can accommodate or its nursing staff can care for. The hospital controls the purse strings and, in the courts' view, is the only party that can resolve the problem.

Hospitals accused of failing to maintain adequate nursing staffs have offered various defenses. Some have argued they acted reasonably because their nurse:patient ratio was equal to that found in other area hospitals. This argument fails if any applicable rules and regulations contradict it.

Other hospitals have defended understaffing by arguing that no extra nurses were available. The courts have hesitated to accept this defense, however, especially when hospitals have knowingly permitted an unsafe condition to continue despite their inability to correct it. And the day may come when a hospital is charged with failing to use the nursing personnel available from temporary-nursing service agencies or nursing registries during understaffed periods.

Still other hospitals have excused understaffing by pleading lack of funds. The courts have repeatedly rejected this defense.

Of course, hospital liability for understaffing isn't automatic. Suppose a hospital finds itself understaffed on the night shift and assigns one nurse to cover two adjacent units. If a patient is injured because of the nurse's unmanageable work load, the hospital may be held liable if it could have reasonably provided adequate staff. But if it couldn't—because, for example, a nurse suddenly called in sick and no substitute could quickly be found—the hospital may escape liability. This is known as a *sudden emergency exception* when used as a defense during a trial. The emergency could not have been anticipated—in contrast to chronic understaffing.

Except for the sudden emergency exception defense, a hospital has only two alternatives for avoiding liability for understaffing: either hire sufficient personnel to staff an area adequately or else close the area (or restrict the number of beds) until adequate staff can be found.

The charge nurse's liability

Any nurse who's put in charge of a unit, even temporarily, may find herself liable in understaffing situations, including the following:

• She knows understaffing exists but fails to notify the hospital administration about it.

• She fails to assign her staff properly and then also fails to supervise their actions continuously.

• She tries to perform a nursing task for which she lacks the necessary training and skills.

In *Horton v. Niagara Falls Memorial Center* (1976), the charge nurse, one LPN, and one nurse's aide were responsible for 19 patients on a unit. During their shift, one patient became delirious and tried to climb down from a balcony off his room. The attending doctor, when notified, ordered that someone stay with the patient at all times to keep him from going out on the balcony again.

The charge nurse, instead of calling for additional help from within the hospital or notifying the hospital administration, called the patient's wife and summoned her to the hospital to sit with him. The wife agreed to send her mother but said her mother would need a while to get there. During this period, the charge nurse provided no supervision of the patient, who did go out on the balcony again. He jumped and sustained injuries. In the lawsuit that followed, the court held the charge nurse liable.

In *Norton v. Argonaut Insurance Company* (1962), a temporary staff shortage led the assistant director of nurses to volunteer her nursing services on a pediatric floor. Because she had been an administrator for several years and was unfamiliar with pediatric care, she proceeded to give a newborn 3 ml of Lanoxin (digoxin) in injectable rather than elixir form. The infant died of cardiac arrest, and the court held the assistant director liable.

Assignment of liability to the charge nurse isn't automatic, however, in lawsuits where understaffing is a factor. The charge nurse isn't necessarily liable unless she

knew, or should have known, that the nurse who made the mistake:
- had previously made similar mistakes
- wasn't competent to perform the task
- had acted on the charge nurse's erroneous orders.

And remember, the plaintiff-patient has to prove two things: that the charge nurse failed to follow customary practices, thereby contributing to the mistake; and that the mistake actually caused the patient's injuries.

Coping with a sudden overload

You know it happens. You begin your shift and suddenly you find yourself assigned more patients than you feel you can reasonably care for. What can you do to protect yourself?

First of all, make every effort to protest the overload and get it reduced. Begin by asking your supervisor or director of nursing service to supply relief. (See *Floating: When Can You Refuse?*) If they can't or won't, notify the hospital administration. If no one there will help either, write a memorandum detailing exactly what you did and said and the answers you got. Don't walk off the job (if you do, you may be liable for abandonment), but do the best you can. After your shift is over, prepare a written report of the facts and file it with the director of nursing.

Filing a written report isn't guaranteed to absolve you from liability if a patient is injured during your shift and sues you for malpractice. You may still be found liable, especially if you could have foreseen and prevented the patient's injury. But a written report will impress a jury as a sincere attempt to protect your patients. And the report could provide you with a defense if the alleged malpractice involves something you should have done, but didn't do, because of understaffing.

If you're faced with a sudden patient overload, you may have only two choices: tolerate the situation or refuse to work under such conditions and suffer suspension from duty without pay. Consider the Canadian case of *Re Mount Sinai Hospital v. Ontario Nurses Association* (1978).

This case involved three nurses in the hospital's intensive care unit. Because they were already caring for many critically ill

Floating: When Can You Refuse?

An order to float to an unfamiliar unit can cause worry and frustration in the best of nurses—and understandably so. It may cause you worry about using skills that have grown rusty since nursing school, or frustration at being pulled away from work you enjoy.

Unfortunately, floating is necessary. Hospitals must use it to help solve their understaffing problems. And you'll have to go along with it unless:
- you have a union contract that guarantees you'll always work in your specialty
- you can prove you haven't been taught to do the assigned task.

Legally, you can't refuse to float simply because you fear that the skills you need for the assignment have diminished or because you're generally concerned about legal risks in the assigned unit. However, if your supervisor gives you a task you definitely haven't been taught to do, *tell* her that. Usually, she'll accommodate you by changing your assignment. But if she insists that you perform the task you don't know how to do, refuse the assignment. If the hospital reprimands or fires you, you may be able to appeal the action taken against you in a court of law.

patients, they refused to accept still another from the emergency department. The nurses argued that admitting the new patient would endanger the patients already under their care. The hospital disagreed and suspended them for three shifts without pay.

The case was settled in favor of the hospital, on the premise that a hospital is legally obligated to provide care for patients it admits and can insist that certain instructions be carried out. If the hospital

What Are the Limits of Your Liability?

As a nurse, do you know the limits of your professional responsibility—and liability? Most nurses think they do. But a large number of your colleagues who took part in a recent staff-nurse survey, which tested this knowledge, were in for a surprise.

In this survey, each question was based on an actual court case that measured nursing performance against current standards. For each case, the nurses surveyed were asked to judge whether or not the court found the defendant-nurse (or nurses) liable. The survey respondents averaged only about 11 correct answers out of 20.

Below are five questions selected from the survey. To test yourself, jot down *Yes* if you think the court considered the nurse or nurses liable. Jot down *No* if you think the court did not consider the nurse or nurses liable. Then read the court decisions and the corresponding survey results.

1. A boy, age 19, was hospitalized after his leg was broken in a football game. Nurses reported signs of infection to the doctor and charted them. The doctor took no action and the leg eventually had to be amputated. Were the nurses liable?

2. A staff nurse took a patient, on a stretcher, to the radiology department and left him with several other patients in the crowded hall. The patient was injured when his stretcher was knocked against the wall. Was the nurse liable?

3. A staff nurse called a medical resident when a patient complained of soreness in her jaw and difficulty opening her mouth, 3 days after she'd had a cesarean section. The resident examined the patient and ordered treatment. The staff nurse documented these events, treated the patient as ordered, and stayed in constant communication with the resident when the patient's condition worsened. She did not call the patient's doctor. The patient developed a serious postoperative complication and sued. Was the nurse liable?

4. An operating room (OR) nurse prepared a 17-year-old boy's left leg instead of the right one, and the surgeon operated on a normal knee. Was the OR nurse liable?

5. A nurse wasn't familiar with one of the medications ordered. So she talked to two available doctors about it. After they told her the dosage "wasn't out of line," she gave the medication. The patient died as a result of the medication. Was the nurse liable?

---

had to defer to its employees' opinions, the decision stated, it would be placed in an intolerable legal position.

Chronic understaffing

Chronic understaffing, if it occurs on your unit, presents you with a dilemma. On the one hand, your conscience tells you to try your best to help every patient. On the other hand, you feel compelled to protect yourself from liability in case a patient is harmed.

The best protection, as you might expect, is prevention—action taken to remedy the understaffing situation (see *Staffing Suggestions*, page 107). If you and your colleagues act responsibly and col-

lectively to try to bring about institutional change, the law protects you in several important ways.

A case in point is *Misericordia Hospital Medical Center v. N.L.R.B.* (1980), which involved a charge nurse who was discharged from her job because her employer found her activities "disloyal."

She belonged to a group of hospital employees called the Ad Hoc Patient Care Committee. The committee was formed after the JCAH, which intended to survey the hospital, had invited interested parties—including hospital staff—to submit at a public meeting information on whether accreditation standards were being met. One complaint lodged by the

The courts found that, in all five cases, the nurses were liable. Here's a summary of each court decision, along with the corresponding survey results:

1. The court ruled that the nurses' failure to report the *doctor* for doing nothing about the patient's deteriorating condition was one of the reasons the patient lost his leg. They were found negligent even though they documented their observations and had communicated them to the doctor several times.

Only about 11% of the respondents recognized a nurse's responsibility to follow up when the primary doctor doesn't provide proper medical attention.

2. The court ruled that although the hospital administration and the housekeeping and maintenance departments were also liable for unsafe conditions, the nurse's education and experience should have made her familiar with acceptable standards. Failure to meet these standards constituted malpractice.

Many of the survey respondents—about 75%—knew that nurses can be held liable for an unsafe environment.

3. The court found the nurse and the resident liable—the nurse, for failure to notify the primary doctor of his patient's condition.

Only about 27% of the respondents knew they could be held liable for failing to call a patient's primary doctor in such circumstances.

4. The court held the nurse liable for the injuries the patient suffered after she prepared the wrong leg. (Of course, the surgeon was liable, too.)

Most of the respondents—about 81%—recognized the nurse's liability.

5. In this case, the court found the nurse negligent because she failed to question the *prescribing* doctor and because she administered a drug with which she was unfamiliar.

A majority of the respondents—about 69%—answered this question correctly.

---

nurse and her committee was insufficient coverage on many shifts—a situation the hospital had failed to remedy.

Even though the JCAH examiners approved the hospital, the nurse was fired shortly afterward. When the National Labor Relations Board (NLRB) ordered the hospital to reinstate the nurse, the hospital appealed. The appeals court upheld the NLRB order, citing a U.S. Supreme Court ruling that employees don't lose protection "when they seek to improve terms and conditions of employment or otherwise improve their lot as employees through channels outside the immediate employee-employer relationship."

This decision offers nurses considerable protection in conflicts with employers, especially those in which working conditions directly affect the care given patients.

Of course, you must be sure you follow the appropriate channels of communication. If you can't get help to remedy a dangerous understaffing situation, first go through all hospital channels, up to and including the board of trustees. Simply report what the problem is, the number of hours you've been forced to work without relief, the number of consecutive days you've been forced to work, and any other relevant facts. Then, if you still can't get help, and if your complaint involves an alleged unfair labor practice, you can contact the NLRB.

Conclusion

Given the present uncertainty about future numbers of nursing graduates, and in view of hospitals' financial woes, understaffing probably will continue in many health-care institutions. Some hospitals are experimenting with ways to ensure adequate staffs, however, and others will surely follow. Ideas include letting nurses choose their own work schedules and hiring part-time nurses through agencies or on a private-duty basis. But don't look for this issue to disappear any time soon.

Witnessing and signing documents

You can't escape it. As a nurse, you'll sometimes be asked to witness the signing of documents, such as deeds, bills of sale, powers of attorney, contracts, and wills. You'll also find yourself—intentionally or otherwise—witnessing patients' (or others') oral statements that may have legal significance. Your actions at times like these are important. They can influence whether what you witnessed has the force of law, and they can also expose you to certain legal consequences. You may even have to testify, later, in court about the signing and the circumstances surrounding it.

What signing as a witness means

When you sign as a witness, you're usually certifying only that you saw the person, known to you by a certain name, place his signature on the document. You're not certifying the primary signer's mental competence (although you should *not* sign if you believe he's incompetent), nor are you certifying the presence or absence of duress, undue influence, fraud, or error.

If you're ever called to testify about the signing, don't underestimate the importance of your testimony. A court looking into charges of fraud or undue influence used in executing a document often gives great weight to a nurse's perception. You may be asked about the patient's physical and mental condition at the time of the signing, and the court may ask you to describe his interactions with his family, his attorney, and others.

Which laws apply to signing documents?

In the United States and Canada, as you know, nurse practice acts are the laws that establish nurses' scope of professional and legal accountability. When you witness a document, other laws also apply. For example, all states have laws setting out the legal requirements for written and oral wills, dying declarations, and gifts *causa mortis* (in expectation of death). These laws establish the format of wills, the number of witnesses needed, who can be a witness, what makes a will valid or invalid, how to make a will inoperative, and how to contest a will. (See *Requirements for a Valid Will*, pages 108 and 109.)

In many states, your signature on a will certifies not only that you witnessed the will signing but also that you heard the maker of the will declare it to be his will, and that all witnesses and the maker of the will were actually present during the signing.

By attesting to these last two facts, you help ensure the authenticity of the will and the signatures. Your signature doesn't certify, however, that the maker of the will is competent.

If a patient asks you to serve as a witness when he draws up his will, follow these precautions:
• Don't forget to notify the patient's doctor and your supervisor before you act as a witness.
• Don't give the patient any legal advice.
• Don't offer to assist him in phrasing the document's wording.
• Don't comment on the nature of his choices.
• Don't forget to document your actions in your nurses' notes.

The laws also cover dying declarations and gifts *causa mortis,* specifying when they're valid and when they aren't.

In the case of a living will, your state law may prohibit you from acting as a witness. (See "Your responsibility for a patient's living will," page 147.)

What's your liability?

You can be liable and in violation of the prevailing standards of care if the signature you witness is false or if you sign knowing the patient is incompetent or has given uninformed consent. You can also be held liable if you knowingly allow a minor, nonguardian, or other ineligible person to sign a document.

If you're the only person who informs a patient about a planned medical procedure and you then witness his signature, you can be liable for practicing outside your nurse practice act, for practicing medicine without a license, or both. And your hospital may be liable for negligence under the doctrine of respondeat superior. If you've given the patient false information in an attempt to deceive him, you may be guilty of fraud or misrepresentation.

Before you sign—read!

Before you sign any document, read at least enough of it to make sure it *is* the type of document the primary signer represents it to be. Usually you won't have to read all the text, and legally this isn't necessary for your signature to be valid. But always examine the document's title and first page, and give careful attention to what's written immediately above the place for your signature. (The place for your signature, by the way, should be clearly labeled as such.)

How to sign

When signing a document, write legibly and use your full legal name. When signing on hospital forms, add your title. On other documents the title is optional, but adding it will establish why you're in the hospital.

When—and when not—to sign

When you're asked to sign as a witness, do so only if you believe the patient to be both mentally and physically competent. Legally, as you know, you don't need to have knowledge of exactly what's contained in the documents you witness. But professionally, as when you witness the signing of an informed consent form, you should know. You also should make sure the patient knows what procedure or treatment he's consenting to when he affixes his signature.

When should you not sign? Here are some instances:

• when the patient is not legally able to give consent—for example, when he's a minor or a nonguardian

• when the patient is not who he says he is, or you can't be sure

• when the patient has no power of free choice; for example, when he's being blackmailed or otherwise pressured into signing by his family

• when the patient is uninformed about what he's consenting to because he's been given misleading information, doesn't understand the information given, or hasn't been told of the risks involved

• when a patient is obviously incompetent—for example, when he's suffering from advanced senility and is being pressured to sign a deed transferring a real estate title to someone else.

In such situations, simply explain that you choose not to act as a witness. Then record the incident in your nurses' notes, using a chronologic format. Chart the setting, the patient's mental and physical condition, the reason for the refusal, what you saw and heard, and what happened after your refusal (for instance, that someone else witnessed or someone else gave consent).

Finally, report the incident to other staff members affected by your refusal to sign—for example, your supervisor and the patient's doctor.

Writing your nurses' notes

When you record in your notes that you've witnessed a patient's signature on any type of document, always include something about his apparent perceptions of his health and general circumstances.

When you witness a *written will,* document that it was signed and witnessed, who signed it, who else was present, what was done with it after signing, and what the patient's condition was at the time.

When you witness *oral statements* such as dying declarations or oral wills, document what the patient says as close to word-for-word as you can. Also document the names of other witnesses, the patient's physical and mental condition at the time, and the patient's reaction to the statement afterwards. Make your notes carefully: remember, they could be used in court for probating the will, for resolving creditors' claims, or for prosecuting alleged criminals. The notes will also refresh your memory if you're called to testify in court.

Besides recording the event in your own notes, write up or type a copy of the patient's oral statement and, if possible, get him and other witnesses to sign it. Report the matter to the patient's doctor and to your supervisor, too. This will keep them informed and alert them that an item in the patient's medical record may have legal importance.

Canadian procedures

The formalities of signing and witnessing documents differ between the United States and Canada. But because both countries' legal systems are based primarily on English common law, the U.S. and Canadian laws governing how a witness should sign legal documents are essentially the same.

Special risks in special-care units

As you know, recent decades have witnessed dramatic changes in the nurse's role. In many patient-care circumstances, nurses now perform tasks that only doctors used to perform. This is particularly true in special-care units, such as the emergency department (ED), operating room (OR), recovery room (RR), intensive care unit (ICU), and coronary care unit (CCU). Here, patient care offers exciting nursing challenges, increased nursing responsibilities—and extra risks of liability.

For example, if you're an ED nurse, you'll sometimes have to employ triage in patient selection; that is, you may have to classify patients according to the seriousness of their medical problem. If you make a mistake, a seriously injured patient's treatment may be needlessly delayed. And you may be liable.

In the OR, you must confirm that the patient has given his informed consent and that his consent is documented. As you

work with the operating team (work that today involves much more than worrying about missing instruments and sponges), you can't help but be aware of the legal risks involved.

If the RR is your assignment, you know you must watch your patients for signs and symptoms of adverse anesthetic effects, of postoperative cardiac and pulmonary complications, and of shock caused by hypoxia, hemorrhage, or infection. The same concerns apply if you work in an ICU or CCU. In these units, you may also have to administer sophisticated drugs or perform sophisticated procedures, such as passing a stylet through a patient's subclavian line to determine patency. In any of these special-care units, you must be able to take appropriate and effective action when a patient's survival depends on your judgment.

Where you stand legally

If you work in a special-care unit, you must take the possibility of increased liability seriously. Remember, even though hospital policy requires that you perform certain tasks, or you perform them under doctor's orders as a doctor's *borrowed servant,* your individual liability continues. If a patient sues for malpractice, all the persons involved can be held separately and jointly liable. This suggests that you carefully evaluate the jobs you're asked to do. If any task is beyond your training and expertise, don't attempt it. And even if you can do it, make sure you're permitted to do it according to hospital policy and your state or Canadian provincial nurse practice act. (See *Exercising Caution in Special-Care Units,* pages 112 and 113.)

Role expansion and the law

Many nurse practice acts recognize nurses' expanded roles.

One such role involves diagnoses. In general, a nurse can't legally make a medical diagnosis or prescribe medical, therapeutic, or corrective measures, *except as authorized* by the hospital and the state where she's working. This means that if you perform a tracheotomy while working on a postoperative orthopedic floor (especially if you could have called a doctor), you may be found liable, if the patient

Staffing Suggestions

Our 85-bed hospital has no recovery room nurse. Every day, one of the RNs from the day shift is "floated" to the recovery room. We feel this is dangerous, for a couple of reasons:

Only one RN is assigned, no matter how many patients are there. Shouldn't the hospital maintain a certain nurse:patient ratio in the recovery room?

Also, the nurse assigned to the recovery room must work 8 to 10 hours without a break. Surely this isn't right.

Our director of nursing knows the whole situation but has made no improvements.—RN, Tex.

The acceptable nurse:patient ratio varies with the types of surgical procedures and the patients' expected conditions. For example, in a large hospital one or two RNs may be needed for each open-heart surgery patient, but one RN could safely care for three or four patients after less complicated procedures.

To determine daily averages in your re-

covery room, record the number and types of operations performed daily and the number of patients in the recovery room each hour. With these figures, you can document any times when the patient load is too great for one nurse.

Regarding the RN's working 8 to 10 hours without a break, if this happens frequently, check your state wage-and-hour division to find out whether your hospital can legally require such a schedule.

Why not ask for a meeting with the director of nursing after compiling the information suggested? Even if your figures don't indicate the need for a full-time recovery room nurse, you might be able to make other staffing arrangements, such as floating a second nurse into the recovery room during peak periods or for breaks or limiting nurses who can be floated to two or three nurses who've received appropriate inservice training.

This letter was taken from the files of *Nursing* magazine.

---

sues, for performing a medical function. But you probably wouldn't be liable if you performed the tracheotomy in the ED during a disaster.

In Canada, several provinces, including Ontario and Quebec, have passed medical acts that permit the delegation of specific medical functions to nurses. Some provinces require that a nurse obtain special training or certification to perform these functions. In the United States, however, current laws provide little guidance for nurses who daily face situations like these.

Suppose, for example, you're working in an ICU, where you must often act on standing orders and without a doctor's supervision. How can you be sure that when you perform quasi-medical functions, even with standing orders, that you're not violating your nurse practice act?

You can't be sure, of course, because nurse practice acts don't provide specific guidelines. Treating patients on the basis of standing orders is a matter of judgment. In such situations, be sure you're qualified to recognize the problem; then follow established medical protocol. (See *Protecting Yourself When Working in Special-Care Units,* page 115.)

How nursing standards apply

In general, a nurse working in a special-care unit is subject to the same general rule of law as her staff-nurse colleagues: she must meet the standard of care that a reasonably well-qualified and prudent nurse would meet in the same or similar circumstances.

However, in deciding whether a specialty nurse has acted reasonably, if she's

Requirements for a Valid Will

	Age when a person can make a will disposing of real property	Age when a person can make a will disposing of personal property	Number of persons required to witness a will	Holographic wills recognized
Alabama	18	18	2	Yes
Alaska	19	19	2	Yes
Arizona	18	18	2	Yes
Arkansas	18	18	2	Yes
California	18	18	2	Yes
Colorado	18	18	2	Yes
Connecticut	18	18	2	No
Delaware	18	18	2	No
D.C.	18	18	2	Yes
Florida	18	18	2	Yes
Georgia	14	14	2	Yes
Hawaii	18	18	2	No
Idaho	18	18	2	Yes
Illinois	18	18	2	No
Indiana	18	18	2	Yes
Iowa	19	19	2	No
Kansas	18	18	2	Yes
Kentucky	18	18	2	Yes
Louisiana	16	16	2	Yes
Maine	18	18	2	Yes
Maryland	18	18	2	Yes
Massachusetts	18	18	2	No
Michigan	18	18	2	Yes
Minnesota	18	18	2	No
Mississippi	18	18	2	Yes
Missouri	18	18	2	No

Here are the 50 states' requirements for preparing legally acceptable wills. As a nurse, you won't often deal with patients who are preparing their wills. And when this does happen, your function's likely to be limited to signing as a witness.

	Age when a person can make a will disposing of real property	Age when a person can make a will disposing of personal property	Number of persons required to witness a will	Holographic wills recognized
Montana	18	18	2	Yes
Nebraska	18	18	2	Yes
Nevada	18	18	2	Yes
New Hampshire	18	18	3	No
New Jersey	18	18	2	Yes
New Mexico	18	18	2	No
New York	18	18	2	No
North Carolina	18	18	2	Yes
North Dakota	18	18	2	Yes
Ohio	18	18	2	Yes
Oklahoma	18	18	2	Yes
Oregon	18	18	2	No
Pennsylvania	18	18	2	Yes
Rhode Island	18	18	2	No
South Carolina	18	18	3	Yes
South Dakota	18	18	2	Yes
Tennessee	18	18	2	Yes
Texas	18	18	2	Yes
Utah	18	18	2	Yes
Vermont	18	18	3	No
Virginia	18	18	2	Yes
Washington	18	18	2	No
West Virginia	18	18	2	Yes
Wisconsin	18	18	2	Yes
Wyoming	21	21	2	Yes

Adapted with permission from the Reader's Digest Association, Inc., *You and the Law* (Reader's Digest Association, Inc., 1984).

the defendant in a malpractice lawsuit, the court won't consider what the average LPN/LVN or RN would have done. Instead, the court will seek to determine the standard of care that an LPN/LVN or RN *specifically trained to work in the special-care unit* would have met. Thus, the law imposes a higher standard of conduct on persons with knowledge, skill, or training superior to that of other persons in the profession.

Hunt v. Palm Springs General Hospital (1977) illustrates how the courts evaluate the reasonable-person standard in light of prevailing practices.

The patient, Mr. Hunt, was rushed to the ED with convulsions. Once he was examined, his doctor concluded that Mr. Hunt, a known drug addict, was experiencing convulsions because he'd gone without drugs for several days. Although the doctor advised the hospital administration that the patient's condition wasn't critical, he nevertheless requested hospitalization.

The hospital refused to admit Mr. Hunt because of a history of unpaid bills. During the next 4 hours, while Mr. Hunt sat in the ED waiting area, the doctor tried to find hospitalization for him elsewhere in the city. Eventually, Mr. Hunt was admitted to a neighboring hospital. He lived for 26 hours before dying from brain damage caused by prolonged seizures.

During the lawsuit that followed, the court examined the practice of ED nurses elsewhere and found that the Palm Springs Hospital nurses had acted unreasonably. Their duty was to monitor Mr. Hunt's condition periodically while he awaited transfer to another hospital. If this duty had been carried out, the court concluded, the nurses would have noted his elevated temperature—a clear indication that he needed immediate hospitalization.

Similarly, in *Cline v. Lund* (1973), the patient, Ms. Cline, was sent to a CC stepdown unit after problems developed following a hysterectomy on July 10. Except for one bout with nausea, she appeared to be making satisfactory progress. At about 2:30 p.m. on July 11, a nurse dangled Ms. Cline's legs from the side of her bed. The nurse charted that the patient tolerated the dangling well. By 3:30 p.m.,

Ms. Cline was unresponsive, her blood pressure was rising, and she was vomiting.

At 9:00 p.m., when Ms. Cline's blood pressure reached 142/90, the attending nurse notified her supervisor, who at 9:40 p.m. notified the attending doctor. He came to the hospital, examined the patient, and—suspecting an internal hemorrhage—ordered blood work and vital signs taken every 30 minutes. At 11:45 p.m., the patient's blood pressure was 160/90. Her arms and legs were stiff, her fists clenched.

Instead of summoning the doctor again, the attending nurse once more notified her supervisor. At 12:15 a.m. on July 12, when Ms. Cline's blood pressure had reached 230/130, the doctor was called. The patient stopped breathing at 12:40 a.m., suffered a cardiac arrest at 12:45 a.m., and died at 4:45 a.m.

In the ensuing lawsuit, the court found the nurse liable, stating that her care had fallen below that of a reasonably prudent nurse in the same or similar circumstances. "Nurses," the court decision said, "should notify the doctor of any significant change or unresponsiveness."

How Canadian nursing standards apply

As you're probably aware, a Canadian nurse's performance is also measured against the appropriate standard of care.

For example, in *Laidlaw v. Lions Gate Hospital* (1969), the court held that both the RR nurse who left for a coffee break and the supervisor who permitted her to leave should have anticipated an influx of patients from the OR.

When the nurse left on her break, only two patients and the supervisor nurse were in the RR. In a short time, however, three more patients arrived—including the plaintiff, Mrs. Laidlaw. Because only one nurse was on duty to care for five patients, Mrs. Laidlaw did not receive appropriate care and suffered extensive, permanent brain damage as a result of anesthesia-related hypoxia.

When the resulting lawsuit came to trial, another nursing supervisor testified that usually two nurses were present in the RR and that nurses were not permitted to take breaks after new patients arrived. Other testimony revealed that RR nurses should know the OR schedule and so should anticipate when new patients will arrive.

The court found the nurse who left, and her supervisor, negligent in leaving only one nurse on duty in the RR.

Staying within nursing practice limits

You know that when you work in special-care units, you mustn't presume that your increased training and broadened authority permit you to exceed nursing's legal limits. This is especially important in an area such as diagnosis, where you can easily cross the legal boundary separating nursing from medicine.

One place this sometimes happens is in the ED, where an on-call doctor may refuse to see a patient himself, instead ordering care based on a nurse's observations of the patient. Similar situations may occur in the RR, ICU, and CCU, where split-second patient-care decisions are sometimes made on the basis of nurses' phone calls to attending doctors.

If you find yourself in this situation, remember that all state and Canadian provincial nurse practice acts prohibit you from medically diagnosing a patient's condition. You can tell the doctor about signs and symptoms you've observed—but you may not make the decision about what care should be given. If you do, you'll be practicing medicine without a license. And you'll be held at least partly liable for any harm to the patient that results.

Consider the case of *Methodist Hospital v. Ball* (1961). Young Mr. Ball was brought to the ED with injuries sustained in an automobile accident. Because of a sudden influx of critically ill patients, the ED staff was unable to care for him immediately. While lying on a stretcher in the hospital hallway, Mr. Ball became boisterous and demanded care. Apparently the attending nurse decided he was drunk. Instead of being treated, Mr. Ball was put into restraints and transported by ambulance to another local hospital. There, 15 minutes after arriving, he died from internal bleeding.

An autopsy revealed no evidence of alcohol in Mr. Ball's system. The court that heard the resulting lawsuit found the attending nurse and medical resident negligent because they failed to diagnose Mr.

Ball's condition properly, to give supportive treatment, and to alert personnel at the second hospital about Mr. Ball's critical condition.

Conclusion

If and when you practice in a special-care unit, be sure you know—and follow—hospital policies and procedures. Know your own limitations, too—never perform a procedure you feel unsure about. Remember, admitting to inexperience is never improper. But performing a procedure that may exceed your capabilities could be, especially if it results in a patient's serious injury or death.

If you're an LPN or LVN working in a special-care unit, the same precautionary watchword applies. As you help RNs care for acutely ill patients and carry out doctors' orders, remember that you assume a significant legal risk when you perform a task that an RN ordinarily performs. If you injure the patient in the process and he sues you for malpractice, your care will be measured against what a reasonably competent RN would do in the same or similar circumstances.

Legal responsibility for patients' safety

As a hospital nurse, one of your most important responsibilities is patients' physical safety. To prevent falls, for example, you have to make sure bed side rails are up for debilitated, elderly, confused, or medicated patients. You also have to help weak patients walk, use proper transfer methods when moving patients, and sometimes use restraining devices to immobilize patients.

In the interest of patient safety, you also have to keep an eye on your hospital's facilities and equipment. If you spot loose or improperly functioning side rails, water or some other substance on the unit floor, or an improperly functioning respirator, you have a duty to report the problem and call for repairs or housekeeping assistance. Failure to do so may not only endanger patients but also make you—and

Exercising Caution in Special-Care Units

Risky practice in the emergency department

I enjoy working in the emergency department (ED) of a small community hospital near my home, but I don't enjoy one of the practices there. Our nurses routinely take doctors' telephone orders for narcotic injections.

What am I making a fuss about? Well, what usually happens is that, when a patient comes in complaining of a headache, a staff doctor is consulted by phone, and he orders a narcotic. The patient receives his injection, then leaves without ever seeing a doctor. Supposedly, the doctor will come by the next day to sign the verbal order he gave. But many doctors here "forget" this step.

Several months ago, one of the ED doctors reported this practice to the hospital administration and said he felt it was ill-advised and illegal. The administration responded with a letter to all staff doctors indicating that the ED would continue to honor telephone orders as a service to staff doctors. (We were also told doctors would sign their telephone orders the next day.)

Maybe I'm bucking the system, but I'm not satisfied. I've discussed our policy and practice with ED nurses at other hospitals and with several staff doctors here who also work in other EDs. Everyone tells me the same thing: other hospitals consider our practice illegal.

I'd like to refuse to give narcotic injections under these circumstances, but I need some backup.—RN, Tenn.

This practice is illegal. It violates the federal government's conditions for nurses' participation in medical care. And it runs counter to numerous court decisions supporting the requirement that a doctor examine every patient who comes to the ED before the patient receives treatment.

Document the telephone orders as they occur (with facts only; leave your opinions aside), and then send a memo with the facts, and the reasons for your concern, through proper channels. If you're attempting to change your hospital's policy, why not join forces with the ED doctor who's already protested the unsafe practice?

Guarding the postoperative patient

I've just started to work in the recovery room (RR) of our local hospital, but I'm already up in arms about an unsafe practice I see going on.

When a postoperative patient is ready to return to the medical/surgical unit, one of our nurses places the stretcher near the RR door to wait for an orderly. No nurse accompanies the patient back to the unit—just an orderly who isn't even trained in cardiopulmonary resuscitation.

---

the hospital—liable if patients are injured.

Patient-safety standards of care

In any malpractice lawsuit against a nurse, she's judged on how well she performed her duty as measured against the appropriate standards of care. This means that if you're ever sued for malpractice, the court, in reaching its judgment, will analyze whether you gave the plaintiff-patient care equal to that of a reasonably well-qualified and prudent nurse in the same or similar circumstances. (To learn how courts establish standards, see page 15.)

Where patient safety is involved, your duty includes anticipating foreseeable risks. For example, if you're aware that the floor in a patient's room is dangerously slippery, you must report the condition to the appropriate hospital department. If you

But that's not all that's bothering me. If all the orderlies are busy, the patient may wait as much as half an hour at the RR door. During this time, no one's checking his vital signs. If one of these patients should run into trouble before he reached the medical/surgical unit, who'd be responsible?

Our charge nurse claims the hospital would be responsible. I checked the hospital's policy book, and it's vague about transport and about the RR nurse's role in discharging a patient.

Of course I'm worried about these patients. But I'm also worried about my responsibility as an RR nurse. I'd like to know: is transporting a patient without a nurse being present standard policy in most hospitals?—RN, Vt.

At no time should an RR patient be left unattended. The responsibility for that patient remains with the RR staff until that patient has been turned over to the staff of the medical/surgical unit and an appropriate report has been given.

The hospital *is* liable; but so is the RR staff, because they *know* about the dangerous practice of leaving the patient unattended but have neither documented nor remedied it.

Ideally, an RN should accompany all patients leaving the RR. In hospitals where this is routine practice, the RR nurses love it. They feel secure about the patients and about their own responsibilities.

If a nurse can't go with *every* patient, *at least* a nurse should accompany a high-risk patient—say, one with chest tubes. An orderly could accompany a patient less likely to develop difficulties.

For every departing RR patient, an RR nurse should call the medical/surgical unit, tell the staff the patient is on his way, and inform them of his progress and condition.

To remedy the situation in your hospital, try to get a detailed policy in writing. Begin by finding out how the transfer of postoperative patients is handled in other hospitals in your area. Then document the risks of your hospital's current practice. Bring all this information to the attention of your immediate supervisor. If she doesn't take action, keep going up the chain of command.

In calling attention to this risky nursing practice, you may get some flak. Just tell yourself you're not *making* trouble—you're *preventing* it. If you need professional support, consult the Association of Operating Room Nurses (AORN), 10170 E. Mississippi Ave., Denver, Colorado 80231.

These letters were taken from the files of *Nursing* magazine.

don't, and a patient falls and is injured, you could be held liable for failing to protect that patient.

In fact, you might be held liable even if you *didn't* know the floor was slippery. Using accepted standards of care, a court might reason that part of your duty as a reasonable and prudent nurse was to check the floor of your unit regularly and report any patient hazard immediately.

The standards of care that you meet will vary with your job or the training you've had. A staff nurse's actions, for example, will be measured against staff-nurse standards, and a gerontologic nurse's actions will be measured against standards that gerontologic nurses must meet.

Special safety concerns

You're always on guard, of course, to prevent *patient falls.* You know that almost anything can cause a patient to fall, particularly if he's elderly or receiving medication. Elderly patients are in many instances confused, disoriented, and weak. Medications can cause (or increase) confusion and lessen a patient's ability to react in situations when he might fall. Here are some important ways you can protect your patient from falls:

• Make sure his bed's side rails are kept up, when indicated.

• Orient him to where he is and what time it is, especially if he's elderly.

• Monitor him regularly—continually, if his condition makes this necessary.

• Provide adequate lighting and a clean, clutter-free environment.

• Make sure that someone helps and supports him whenever he gets out of bed and that he wears proper shoes when walking.

• Make sure adequate staff are available to transfer him, if necessary.

Elderly patients and patients taking medications need special nursing care when doctors' orders require them to be "up in chair for 15 minutes x 3 daily" or "up in chair for meals." If you can't supervise such a patient while he's sitting up, at least make sure another member of the health-care team does so.

Restraining devices, often prescribed to ensure a patient's safety, unfortunately can also endanger it. So when a doctor prescribes a Posey belt or other restraining device for a patient, keep in mind that such devices don't remove your responsibility for the patient's safety. In fact, they increase it. For example, when a patient wears a Posey belt, you have to make sure he doesn't undo it or inadvertently readjust it; if he does, it could choke or otherwise injure him. You also have to make sure the belt is fitted properly; if it's too tight, it could restrict the patient's breathing or irritate his skin.

You may have to decide when the belt is no longer necessary. Failure to do this could result in an accusation of false imprisonment against you.

Be sure to document carefully any use of a restraining device. Note why the patient needed it, when you first applied it, how you supervised its use, and when and why you stopped using it. As long as you can demonstrate that the restraint is lawful—that is, clinically necessary—you're protected from false-imprisonment accusations. (See *When Can You Legally Restrain a Patient?,* page 116.)

Preventing suicides is another very important aspect of patient safety for every nurse. Not all self-destructive, suicidal patients are cared for by psychiatric nurses.

If a suicidal patient is in your care, your first obligation is to provide close supervision. He may require one-on-one, 24-hour-a-day supervision until the immediate threat of self-harm is over. Take from him all potentially dangerous objects, such as belts, bed linens, glassware, and eating utensils. And make sure he swallows pills when you give them; otherwise, he may retain them in his mouth and save them for use—and abuse—later.

Check his hospital environment carefully for possible dangers. If he can easily open or break his room windows, or if escape from your unit would be easy, you may have to transfer him to a safer, more secure place—if necessary, to a seclusion room.

Remember, whether you work on a psychiatric unit or a medical unit, you'll be held responsible for the decisions you make about a suicidal patient's care. If you're sued because he's been harmed while in your care, and the case is brought to court, you'll be judged on the basis of:

• whether you knew (or should have known) that the patient was likely to harm himself

• whether, knowing he was likely to harm himself, you exercised reasonable care in helping him avoid injury or death.

Ensuring the safety of equipment, making sure that the equipment used for patient care is free from defects, is an important duty. You also need to exercise reasonable care in selecting equipment for a specific procedure and patient and then help maintain the equipment. Here again, your patient care must reflect what the reasonably well-qualified and prudent nurse would do in the same or similar circumstances. This means that if you know a specific piece of equipment isn't func-

Protecting Yourself when Working in Special-Care Units

If you're working in a special-care unit of a hospital—the emergency department, intensive care unit, operating room, or recovery room—your expanded responsibilities make you extra vulnerable to malpractice lawsuits. To protect yourself, take the following precautions:

● Request a clear, written definition of your role in the hospital. Your hospital should have an overall policy and an individual, written job description for you that specifies the limits of your nursing role. You'll be better protected if guidelines for advanced nursing competencies are formally established.

● Document everything you do, so there's no question later about your actions. Your notes, of course, should reflect the nursing process: document your assessment of the patient, your care plan, your actual care, and your evaluation of the plan's effectiveness.

● Make sure of your own competence. If your role expands, your skills have to grow, too. If this requires advanced courses and supervised clinical experience, make sure you get both.

● Insure yourself. Damages awarded to patients can be very high, and high legal fees may mean you can't afford even to *win* a lawsuit. If you don't have your own professional liability insurance, and your hospital doesn't help defend you against a lawsuit, you could face a starting bill even after all claims against you are proven groundless and dropped. (You might never even get to court—but you could still find yourself with a large bill for legal consultation.)

tioning properly, you must take steps to correct the defects and document the steps you took. If you don't, and a patient is injured because of the defective equipment, you may be sued for malpractice.

Selecting proper equipment and maintaining it also means making sure it's not contaminated. When cleaning equipment, always follow hospital procedures strictly, and document your actions carefully. This will decrease the possibility that you could be held liable for using contaminated equipment.

Similarly, be sure *you* don't cause contamination or cross-infection of patients. In *Helman v. Sacred Heart Hospital* (1963), staff nurses were held responsible for causing the plaintiff-patient's *Staphylococcus* infection. According to the court decision, the nurses were negligent because after caring for the plaintiff's roommate (who originally had the infection), they did not wash their hands before caring for the plaintiff.

You can also be held liable for improper use of equipment that's functioning properly. This liability occurs in many instances with equipment that can cause burns—for example, diathermy machines, electrosurgical equipment, and hot water bottles. When you use such equipment, carry out the procedure or therapy carefully, observe the patient continually until the procedure or therapy is completed, and ask the patient frequently (if he's awake during the procedure or therapy) whether he's comfortable or having any pain.

The hospital's responsibility for patient safety

Patient safety, of course, isn't only your responsibility. Your hospital is responsible, too. This institutional responsibility for patient safety rests on the two most frequently used doctrines of malpractice liability.

The first doctrine, *corporate liability*, holds the hospital liable for its own wrongful conduct—for any breach of its duties as mandated by statutory law, common law, and applicable rules and regulations. The hospital's duty to keep patients safe

When Can You Legally Restrain a Patient?

Recently, we had a confused elderly patient who kept wandering off the unit. We kept a "sitter" with him for several days, but that taxed our staff. Finally, our nurse said we couldn't spare anyone to sit with him anymore and told me to put restraints on him.

I told her I was afraid I'd get in trouble if I restrained a patient without his doctor's orders. She told me I was insubordinate and did it herself.

I still think I was right. Is a nurse ever justified in restraining a patient without his doctor's orders?—RN, Calif.

Yes. In fact most hospitals expect nurses to restrain a patient if that's necessary to protect him from injury. In one court case, a patient's family accused nurses of negligence because they *didn't* restrain a patient. The family won.

Read your hospital's policy on restraints immediately, so you'll know what's expected of you next time. You were right to *question* an order you weren't sure was proper. But you weren't right to refuse it without checking further.

Despite your hospital's policy, you may still have questions about a restraint order—and rightly so. With or without a doctor's order, restraints are legal only if they're necessary to protect the patient or others from harm. You can be charged with false imprisonment or battery if you use restraints on a competent patient simply because he refuses to follow orders.

Were restraints called for in the situation you mentioned? The patient's safety clearly required some method of restraining his wandering, so no one's likely to challenge the need for restraint. If you had adequate staff to provide a sitter, that would have been the best form of restraint—because it was the least restraining. If you couldn't spare a staff member, applying a soft restraint would probably have been the safest course to take. With proper documentation explaining the need to protect the patient, the use of restraints in this situation probably wouldn't have exposed you to liability. (Presumably you contacted the doctor as soon as possible and obtained an order to continue the restraint.)

This letter was taken from the files of *NursingLife* magazine.

---

includes the duty to provide, inspect, repair, and maintain reasonably adequate equipment for diagnosis and treatment. The hospital also has a duty to keep the physical plant reasonably safe. Thus, if a patient is injured because the hospital alone breached one of its duties, the hospital is responsible for the injury.

In recent years, the courts have expanded the concept of an institution's liability for breaching its duties. In a landmark case, *Darling v. Charleston Community Memorial Hospital* (1965), the Illinois Supreme Court expanded the concept of hospital corporate liability to include the hospital's responsibility to supervise the quality of patient care given to its patients. (For a discussion of this case, see "The liability of understaffing," pages 97 to 104.)

The second doctrine of institutional malpractice liability is *respondeat superior*. Under this doctrine, the liability for an employee's wrongful conduct is transferred to the institution. This means that both the employee and the institution can be found liable for a breach of duty to the patient—including the duty of ensuring his safety.

Establishing liability for patients' safety
You may be wondering which breaches of the duty to protect patients will result in liability for a hospital alone and which will result in a nurse's sharing the liability. The answers depend on the facts involved. If, for example, a court can determine that the duty to monitor patient-care equipment and to repair any discovered defects rests with the hospital and the nurse, then both could be held liable for a breach of that duty. In *May v. Broun* (1972), the plaintiff-patient sued the hospital, the circulating nurse, and the doctor for burns she sustained when an electric cautery machine's electrode burned her during a hemorrhoidectomy.

Although the machine had been used successfully earlier in the day, when the doctor began to use it on the plaintiff, he noticed that its heat was not sufficient to cauterize blood vessels. So, he asked the circulating nurse to check the machine. She did, and after that it apparently worked properly. Nevertheless, the plaintiff was burned where the electrode had touched her body. She later sued the hospital, the circulating nurse, and the doctor.

Because the hospital and the nurse settled with the plaintiff out of court, the doctor was the only one to stand trial. The court held the doctor not liable for the patient's injuries because the hospital had the duty to monitor the equipment and to provide trained personnel to operate it. This meant that the hospital had to bear responsibility for the defective equipment and any wrongful conduct by the nurse. In this case, the hospital and the nurse were liable for the plaintiff's injury.

In *Story v. McCurtain Memorial Management, Inc.* (1981), the outcome was different. This case involved the delivery of one twin by the mother herself when she was left unattended in a shower room. The patient continuously called for help, but her calls went unanswered and the baby the mother delivered herself died.

The mother sued both the hospital and the nurse on duty at the time. The court found the nurse not liable, but it held the hospital liable (under the doctrine of corporate liability) for failing to provide safeguards in the shower room and adequate supervision on the unit. Here, then, the hospital alone was liable for breaching its duty to protect patients from harm.

Conclusion
As a nurse, you have an important duty to ensure your patients' safety. Remember, all your actions directed toward patient safety must be in line with your hospital's policies and procedures, so be sure you know what these are. If no policies exist, or if they're outdated or poorly drafted, bring this to your supervisor's or head nurse's attention. Consider volunteering to help write or rewrite the policies. By getting involved in efforts to improve patients' safety, you may decrease your potential liability and, at the same time, improve the quality of patient care.

Legal risks in administering drugs

Administering drugs to patients continues to be one of the most important—and, legally, one of the most risky—tasks you perform as a nurse.

For many years, U.S. and Canadian nurses were only permitted to give drugs orally or rectally. If a patient needed to receive a drug by injection, the prescribing doctor injected it himself.

Gradually, however, the nurse's role expanded. Today you give subcutaneous and intramuscular injections, induce anesthesia, and use I.V.s. In some states you may even prescribe drugs, with certain limitations.

In general, the law has kept pace with nurses' expanding role in administering drugs. You must meet high practice standards and adhere to the long-standing *five rights formula*:
• the right drug
• to the right patient
• at the right time
• in the right dosage
• by the right route.

And you'd be wise to add a sixth right to this checklist:
• by the right technique.

Drug-control laws

Legally, as you probably know, a *drug* is any substance listed in an official state, Canadian provincial, or national formulary. It may also be any substance (other than food) "intended to affect the structure or any function of the body . . . (or) for use in the diagnosis, cure, mitigation, treatment, or prevention of disease" (N.Y. Educ. Law).

A *prescription drug* is any drug restricted from regular commercial purchase and sale. Why? Because a state, provincial, or national government has determined that it is, or might be, unsafe unless used under a qualified medical practitioner's supervision.

Two federal laws mainly govern the use of drugs in the United States: the Comprehensive Drug Abuse Prevention and Control Act (incorporating the Controlled Substances Act), which regulates those drugs thought to be most subject to abuse; and the Food, Drug, and Cosmetic Act, which restricts interstate shipment of drugs not approved for human use and outlines the process by which drugs are tested and approved.

On the state and (in Canada) provincial level, the main laws affecting the distribution of drugs are the pharmacy practice acts. These laws give pharmacists (and sometimes doctors, in Canada) the *sole legal authority* to prepare, compound, preserve, and dispense drugs. *Dispense* refers to taking a drug from the pharmacy supply and giving or selling it to another person. This contrasts with *administering* drugs—actually getting the drug into the patient. As you know, your nurse practice act is the law that most directly affects how you administer drugs.

In general, most nursing, medical, and pharmacy practice acts first define the tasks that belong uniquely to the profession being regulated and then state that anyone who performs such tasks without being a licensed or registered member of the defined profession is breaking the law. In some states and Canadian provinces, certain tasks overlap. For example, both nurses and doctors can provide bedside care for the sick and, in Canada, both doctors and pharmacists can prepare medicines.

In many states, if a nurse prescribes a drug, she's practicing medicine without a license; if she goes into the pharmacy or drug supply cabinet, measures out doses of a drug, and puts the powder into capsules, she's practicing pharmacy without a license. For either action, she can be prosecuted or lose her license (or both), even if no one is harmed by what she does. In most states and Canadian provinces, to practice a licensed profession without a license is, at the very least, a misdemeanor.

In *Stefanik v. Nursing Education Committee* (1944), a Rhode Island nurse lost her nursing license in part because she'd been practicing medicine illegally: she'd changed a doctor's drug order for a patient because she didn't agree with what had been prescribed. No one claimed she had harmed the patient. But to change a prescription is the same as writing a new prescription, and Rhode Island's nurse practice act didn't—and still doesn't—consider that to be part of nursing practice.

The federal Food, Drug, and Cosmetic Act and the federal and state drug-abuse laws are less important to nursing practice than the state nursing, medical, and pharmacy practice acts. Why? Because most nurses don't test drugs, prescribe them, compound them, or dispense them. But you should know what the federal and state drug-abuse laws do. They seek to categorize drugs by how dangerous they are (forbidding the use of some, limiting the use of others), and they provide for rehabilitating drug-abuse victims.

Randal v. California State Board of Pharmacy (1966) involved a state's nursing, medical, and pharmacy practice acts as well as its drug-control laws. In that case, a pharmacist lost his license to practice partly because he'd taken telephone orders for controlled substances (amphetamines) from a nurse. The law in his state clearly treats telephone orders as prescriptions and, as such, requires that they be taken only from a doctor.

Nurses' involvement in drug-related lawsuits

Unfortunately, lawsuits involving nurses' drug errors are common.

Taking Drug Orders and Carrying Them Out: How to Protect Yourself

When a doctor writes a drug order for his patient and signs it—or when another health-care professional writes an order and the doctor countersigns it—the courts usually will not question the legality of the order. But if a doctor gives you an oral drug order—either in person or by telephone—protect yourself legally, as follows:

● Write down the order *exactly* as he gives it.

● Repeat the order back to him so that you're sure you heard the doctor correctly.

Once you've given the drug to the patient, make sure you document all necessary information:

● Record *in ink* the type of drug, the dosage, the time you administered it, and any other information your institution's policy requires.

● Sign or initial your notes.

If your institution keeps drug orders in a special file, make sure that you transfer the doctor's drug order, which you wrote on the patient's chart, to that file.

If a doctor orally gives a drug order during an emergency, your first duty is to carry it out at once. When the emergency is over, document what you did.

Here's what can happen if you don't document drug orders:

● You could face disciplinary measures for failing to document.

● You could damage your defense or your hospital's in any malpractice lawsuit.

● Other nurses, not knowing what drugs have been given, may administer other drugs that could have harmful interactions.

In *Derrick v. Portland Eye, Ear, Nose & Throat Hospital* (1922), an Oregon nurse gave a young boy a pupil-contracting drug when the doctor had ordered a pupil-dilating drug. As a result, the boy lost his sight in one eye, and the nurse and the hospital were found negligent.

As you're probably aware, a diagnostic drug can also prompt a lawsuit. In a 1967 case in Tennessee, *Gault v. Poor Sisters of St. Francis Seraph of Perpetual Adoration*, a nurse was supposed to give a patient a saltwater gastric lavage in preparation for a gastric cytology test. Instead, she gave the patient dilute sodium hydroxide, causing severe internal injuries. The hospital lost the verdict and also an appeal.

Getting the dose right is also important. In a Louisiana case, *Norton v. Argonaut Insurance Co.* (1962), a nurse inadvertently gave a 3-month-old infant a digitalis overdose that resulted in the infant's death. At the malpractice trial that followed, the nurse was found liable, along with the hospital and the attending doctor.

Similarly, in *Dessauer v. Memorial General Hospital,* a 1981 New Mexico case, an emergency department doctor ordered 50 mg of lidocaine for a patient. But the nurse, who normally worked in the hospital's obstetrics ward, gave the patient 800 mg. The patient died, the family sued, and the hospital was found liable.

In *Moore v. Guthrie Hospital,* a 1968 West Virginia case, a nurse made a mistake in the administration route, giving the patient two drugs intravenously rather than intramuscularly. The patient suffered a seizure, sued, and won.

All the court decisions in these cases were based on, and in turn help to define, the standard of care you must apply when administering drugs to patients. In some of these court cases, if the nurse had known more about the proper dose, administration route, or procedure connected with giving the drug, she might not have made the mistake that resulted in the lawsuit. But even when a nurse can demonstrate her competence, one point still stands: The courts will not permit carelessness that harms the patient.

Your liability for dispensing drugs

In rare instances, adequate patient care may require that you give a certain drug that isn't available on the floor. Normally, of course, you'd call the hospital pharmacist and ask that the drug be sent. But what can you do if you're working on the night or weekend shift and no pharmacist is available?

In this situation, a nurse can't escape liability if she dispenses the drug herself and a lawsuit results. Some hospitals and nursing homes have written policies that permit the charge nurse under special circumstances to go into the pharmacy and dispense an emergency dose of a drug. But whether the institution has a written policy or not, a nurse who dispenses drugs is doing so unlawfully—unless her state's pharmacy practice act specifically authorizes her to do so. If she makes an error in dispensing the drug and the patient later sues, the fact that she was practicing as an unlicensed pharmacist can be used as evidence against her.

You can, of course, choose to disregard the laws that govern your practice if you think your patient's well-being requires it. But clearly you do so at your own risk. And even if you don't harm your patient, you can still be prosecuted and you can still lose your license. In extraordinary circumstances —when ethics and the law conflict, and you have to weigh concern for your patient's life or health against concern for your license—you must make up your own mind about what action you're going to take.

Your role in drug experimentation

At times, you may participate in administering experimental drugs to patients or administering established drugs in new ways or at experimental dosage levels. Your legal duties in these situations are the same as when you normally administer drugs. But if you have any questions, you'll get your answers from the experimental protocol, not your usual sources (books, product labels, or package inserts). You'll also need to make sure no drug is given to a patient who hasn't consented (in writing, if it's a federally funded experiment) to taking part in the experiment.

Your responsibility for knowing about drugs

Once you have your nursing license, you're expected—by law—to know about any drug you administer. This means you're expected to know a drug's safe dosage limits, toxicity, side effects, potential adverse reactions, and indications and contraindications for use. If you're an LPN or LVN, you assume the same legal responsibility as an RN once you've taken a pharmaceutical course or have some other authorization to administer drugs.

Increasingly, judges and juries expect nurses to know what the appropriate observation intervals are for a patient receiving any type of medication. And they expect you to know this even if the doctor doesn't know or if he doesn't write an order stating how often to check on the newly medicated patient. A case that was decided on this basis is *Brown v. State*, a 1977 New York case. After a patient was given 200 mg of Thorazine, the nurses on duty left him largely unobserved for several hours. When someone finally checked on the patient, he was dead. The hospital and the nurses lost the resulting lawsuit.

In *LaMade v. Wilson* (1975), a nurse applied Ophthaine to the eye of an ophthalmology-unit patient. The anesthetic stopped his eye from hurting, but it also stopped it from healing. And the hospital and attending nurses were sued.

When the case was appealed, the appellate court presumed that a reasonably experienced nurse specialist would know a great deal about the drugs she was ordered to give—including contraindications. The burden was on the nurse and on the hospital to prove that the appropriate standard of care was lower. The appellate court decided that the lower court should have heard evidence to determine whether the nurse knew, or should have known, that Ophthaine might be contraindicated in posttrauma and postoperative situations. If she did know or should have known and she hadn't at least questioned the order, the court implied, she and the hospital would be liable.

Giving Injections: A Sticky Legal Question

I'm a nurse in a small-town general practitioner's office. When the doctor is out of town, he expects me to give injections—for instance, penicillin—to his regular patients who are complaining of sore throats or colds. He also expects me to give vitamin and allergy shots to those patients who receive them regularly.

The last time the doctor left town, he even asked me to give flu and pneumococcus injections to patients after I'd examined them—but then have each patient sign a statement saying he wouldn't hold me responsible for any side effects.

I've never felt comfortable giving these injections, and I've told the doctor this. But he just shrugs off my remarks.

What can and can't I do while the doctor is gone? Will a statement signed by the patient really protect me? The doctor says "Yes," but I disagree."—RN, Del.

You're right—release statements can't absolve you of professional responsibility for your actions.

Aside from the issue of responsibility, what would you do if a patient *did* have an unexpected reaction to an injection? Is there another doctor on call to handle these emergencies?

And what if a patient does sign a statement releasing you from responsibility? Who'll accept responsibility? Your boss?

You may administer certain injections during the doctor's absence—but only under specific conditions. Give injections only if the doctor left standing orders for those patients who need vitamin or allergy shots for preexisting conditions; and even then, only if another doctor is available to handle any emergencies.

Don't ever administer injections for *new* conditions. For example, don't give penicillin shots to patients complaining of sore throats or colds. If you do, you're diagnosing patients and prescribing medicine without the required licenses.

Discuss this problem with your boss immediately—and don't let him shrug off your concern. Protect yourself now. If an emergency ever does occur, you'll need all the protection you can get.
This letter was taken from the files of *Nursing* magazine.

When you're not sure—ask!
If you question a drug order, follow your hospital's policies. Usually they'll tell you to try each of the following actions until you receive a satisfactory answer:
• Look up the answer in a standard drug reference.
• Ask your charge nurse.
• Ask the hospital pharmacist.
• Ask your nursing supervisor or the prescribing doctor.
• Ask the chief nursing administrator, if she hasn't already become involved.
• Ask the prescribing doctor's supervisor (service chief).

• Get in touch with the hospital administration and explain your problem.

When you must refuse to administer a drug
All nurses have the legal right not to administer drugs they think will harm patients.

You may choose to exercise this right in a variety of situations:
• when you think the dosage prescribed is too high
• when you think the drug is contraindicated because of possible dangerous interactions with other drugs, or with substances such as alcohol

• because you think the patient's physical condition contraindicates using the drug.

In limited circumstances, you may also legally refuse to administer a drug on grounds of conscience. Some states and Canadian provinces have enacted *right-of-conscience laws*. These laws excuse medical personnel from the requirement to participate in any abortion or sterilization procedure. Under such laws, you may, for example, refuse to give any drug you believe is intended to induce abortion.

When you refuse to carry out a drug order, be sure you do the following:

• Notify your immediate supervisor so she can make alternative arrangements (assigning a new nurse, clarifying the order).
• Notify the prescribing doctor if your supervisor hasn't done this already.
• If your employer requires it, document that the drug wasn't given, and explain why.

Protecting yourself from liability

If you make an error in giving a drug, or if your patient reacts negatively to a properly administered drug, protect yourself by documenting the incident thoroughly. (See *Taking Drug Orders and Carrying Them Out: How to Protect Yourself,* page 119, and *Giving Injections: A Sticky Legal Question,* page 121.)

Some of the documentation belongs in the patient's chart. In addition to normal drug-charting information, include information on the patient's reaction and any medical or nursing interventions taken to minimize harm to the patient.

Other documentation should be confined to the incident report. Here, identify what happened, the names and functions of all personnel involved, and what actions were taken to protect the patient after the error was discovered.

The LPN's/LVN's role in administering drugs

A few states' and Canadian provinces' nurse practice acts don't permit LPNs/LVNs to administer drugs to patients at all, even under supervision. If you're an LPN or LVN working under such a law, don't administer any drugs—ever.

Most nurse practice acts, however, now permit LPNs and LVNs to give drugs un-

der the supervision of an RN, a doctor, or a dentist, assuming that the LPN or LVN has the appropriate educational background or on-the-job training. What constitutes appropriate training or educational background? No clear-cut definitions exist, but most courts probably would be satisfied if an LPN or LVN could prove that her supervising RN or doctor had watched her administer drugs and had judged her competent.

Conclusion

Both U.S. and Canadian laws restrict the nurse's role in regard to drugs. And within that narrow role, the laws impose exceptionally high standards. The standards probably won't be lowered—but the role may expand.

No matter what the future holds, the legal watchword for nurses where drugs are concerned is still "Take care." (See *When Your Patient Is Abusing Drugs.*)

Legal responsibilities in patient teaching

Anytime you give a patient information about his care or treatment, you're involved in patient teaching—a professional nursing responsibility *and* a potential source of liability. This entry explains your legal risks in patient teaching and how you can minimize them.

You teach patients both formally and informally. You teach *formally* when, for example, you prepare instructions on stoma care for a colostomy patient. Before giving the patient this detailed information, you follow a typical patient-teaching process that includes these steps:

• assessing what the patient wants or needs to know
• identifying goals that you and the patient want to reach
• choosing teaching strategies that will help reach the goals
• evaluating how well you've reached the goals.

You teach *informally* when, for example, you answer your postoperative patient's question about the fact that he has

When Your Patient Is Abusing Drugs

If you suspect your patient is abusing drugs, you have a duty to do something about it. If such a patient harms himself or anyone else, and a lawsuit results, the court may hold you liable for his actions. However, your legal responsibilities vary, depending on how much you know about the patient's drug or alcohol abuse.

For instance, suppose you know for certain that a patient is abusing drugs—if you're an emergency department nurse, you may find drugs in a patient's clothes or handbag while looking for identification. Your hospital's policy may obligate you to confiscate the drugs and take steps to see that the patient doesn't acquire more.

What if a patient's erratic or threatening behavior makes you *suspect* he's abusing drugs, but you have no evidence? Your hospital's policy may require that you conduct a drug search. The legal question here is whether your search is justified. As a rule of thumb, if you strongly believe the patient poses a threat to himself or others, and you can document your reasons for searching his possessions, you're probably safe legally.

Before you conduct a search, review your hospital's guidelines on the matter.

Then follow those guidelines carefully. Most hospital guidelines will first direct you to contact your supervisor and explain why you have legitimate cause for a search. If she gives you her approval, next ask a security guard to help you. Besides protecting you, he'll serve as a witness if you do find drugs. When you're ready, confront the patient, tell him you intend to conduct a search, and tell him why.

Depending on your hospital's guidelines, you can search a patient's belongings as well as his room. If you find illegal drugs during your search, confiscate them. Remember, possession of illegal drugs is a felony. Depending on your hospital's guidelines, you may be obligated to report the patient to the police.

If you find alcoholic beverages, take them from the patient and explain that you'll return them when he leaves the hospital.

After you've completed your search, tell the patient's doctor about it and record your findings in your nursing notes and in an incident report. Your written records will be an important part of your defense (and your hospital's) if the patient decides to sue.

---

a 100° temperature. When you explain to him that a low-grade temperature is common for a day or two after surgery, you're reassuring him and teaching him that this sign isn't unusual.

For best results, patient teaching should include the family and others involved in the patient's care. The family that understands the reason for a patient's treatment will support him as he acquires new information and skills.

Nurses' role in giving health-care information

You know, of course, that people have traditionally turned to nurses as important sources of health-care information in and out of the hospital. Informally, friends often ask nurses about such concerns as caring for a child with a fever, why grandmother has been prescribed certain drugs, and what immunizations are needed for traveling overseas. Community health nurses, in particular, teach families how to maintain good health. And, of course, hospital nurses give patients information about their care, such as when a nurse tells a patient what to expect when he undergoes a diagnostic test.

The trend toward nurses doing patient teaching has accelerated in recent years, largely because patients are spending less time in hospitals. Now that patients are being discharged earlier, they need more understanding of their illness and how to manage it at home. And so do their families.

How the law defines nurses' patient-teaching responsibilities

Most nurse practice acts in the United States and Canada contain wording about promoting patient health and preventing disease or injury. But they don't specify a nurse's responsibility for patient teaching. Nurses can find this information in the practice standards developed by professional organizations, in nursing job descriptions, and in statements about nursing practice from national commissions.

The nursing practice standards published in 1973 by the American Nurses' Association (ANA) provide a good example. Standard IV states, "The plan of nursing care includes priorities and the prescribed nursing approaches or measures to achieve the goals derived from the nursing diagnoses." To help nurses understand this standard, the ANA suggests making sure that "teaching-learning principles are incorporated into the plan of care and objectives for learning stated in behavioral terms."

The standard clearly recognizes the dynamic nature of the teaching-learning process: that it is a means to an end, and that its effectiveness is measured by an objective goal. The standard merges the patient-teaching process into the expected outcome.

The patient's right to health-care information

Both statutory law and common law support the patient's right to have information about his condition and treatment. In fact, when a patient is admitted to a hospital, he may be handed a patient bill of rights that clearly indicates his right to such information. The doctrine of informed consent further supports the patient's right to know.

Despite RNs' deep involvement in patient teaching (RNs, not LPNs/LVNs, are primarily responsible for patient teaching), the courts have rarely addressed nurses' liability in this area of patient care.

Why? Perhaps because, in the past, patients have usually sued doctors rather than nurses. But some legal experts believe that nurses will increasingly become the target of such lawsuits, in part because of their increasing patient-teaching responsibilities.

One case that did address the question of a nurse's liability for patient teaching was *Kyslinger v. United States* (1975). In that case, a veterans' hospital sent a hemodialysis patient home with an artificial kidney. He eventually died (apparently while on the machine), and his wife sued the federal government—because a veterans' hospital was involved—alleging that the hospital and its staff had failed to teach either her or her late husband how to properly use and maintain a home hemodialysis unit.

After examining the evidence, the court ruled against the patient's wife, as follows:

"During those 10 months that plaintiff's decedent underwent biweekly hemodialysis treatment on the unit (at the VA hospital), both plaintiff and decedent were instructed as to the operation, maintenance, and supervision of said treatment. The Court can find no basis to conclude that there was any course of conduct on the part of the defendant or any of its personnel which would support the finding of any liability or any evidence which would lead the Court to conclude that the plaintiff or plaintiff's decedent were not properly informed on the use of the hemodialysis unit."

According to present law, a court faced with a question involving a nurse's responsibility for patient teaching will probably examine the question under the general category of a patient's right to know (*Gerety v. Demers*, 1978, and *Canterbury v. Spence*, 1972). Health care requires the patient's participation and cooperation, so this right to know becomes an inherent part of successful treatment. When the right to know becomes critical to the patient's health (as in the home-hemodialysis situation described above), a court is likely to view patient teaching as a health-care provider's legal duty.

Suppose you begin teaching a patient about the medications he's taking, only to hear him say, "Oh, just tell my wife; she gives me all my pills." When something like this happens, be sure to document the incident. Include the patient's exact words; then describe what you taught his wife, and how.

Suppose you're sued for malpractice, and your alleged wrongful act involves patient teaching. The court will consider whether patient teaching was your legal duty to the patient—the standard of care you should have met—and whether you met or breached it. If the evidence indicates you did breach your duty to the patient and so caused him harm, you could be found liable.

What's the LPN's/LVN's role in patient teaching?

Unlike RNs, LPNs and LVNs aren't taught the fundamentals of patient teaching as part of their school curriculum—nor is patient teaching included in their scope of practice. RNs are primarily responsible for patient teaching and may delegate to LPNs/LVNs only the responsibility to reinforce what has already been taught. For example, if an RN is preparing a patient for a barium enema, she could ask an LPN or LVN to tell the patient about the X-ray room and what to expect there. (The LPN/LVN should know what to tell the patient, because LPNs/LVNs are trained in the technical aspects of patient care.) The RN could add to the information as necessary.

The benefits of patient teaching

What you teach a patient while he's in the hospital can help him adjust to the medical regimen or altered life-style he may have to follow after returning home—and benefit more from it, too. Be prepared to arrange for a community health nurse to continue the teaching program you've begun.

Patient teaching also helps patients being admitted to other health-care agencies. For example, when an elderly patient is transferred into a nursing home, he needs information about the home's rules and regulations, its recreational opportunities, and the paramedical support systems available. If a social service worker doesn't provide such information, an RN can.

RNs can also teach children who are being moved to foster or adoptive homes. And if you're a nurse involved in community education programs, you can help families adjust to healthier life-styles by teaching them about good nutrition, regular exercise, and the use of health resources.

Patients taught about their health care are more cooperative because they recognize the reasons for their treatments, medications, and restrictions. They also adapt more readily to changes resulting from medical regimens or new health routines. All this helps reduce patients' stress and the tensions that stem from dependence on health-care personnel.

Patient teaching also helps reduce the likelihood of medical emergencies. For example, diabetic patients who've been taught to assess their urine for ketones generally require fewer admissions to emergency departments for treatment of ketoacidosis. And when community health nurses teach the mothers of young children ways to prevent accidents at home, those children also require fewer emergency department visits.

Last, but not least, patient teaching saves patients money. For example, the mother who's taught to manage her child's colostomy or orthopedic prosthesis will need fewer costly doctor's visits. And the patient who's taught to manage his permanent central venous catheter (for nutrition or chemotherapy) will spend less time in the hospital.

Avoiding conflicts about patient teaching

Doctors, nurses, and other health-team members sometimes disagree about how patient teaching should be done and who should do it. To avoid conflict, always consult doctors and other health-team members (if appropriate) when you're preparing routine patient-teaching protocols. A team approach to patient teaching not only decreases conflicts but also ensures continuity in teaching—and a better educated patient.

You can also avoid conflicts by listening to the instructions that doctors, respiratory therapists, dietitians, and others give the patient. Then, you'll know exactly what's already been said to him, and you can structure your teaching accordingly.

Candor and diplomacy, of course, also help reduce conflict. Everyone profits when health-team members share their patient-teaching approaches and work together to achieve patient-teaching goals.

Conclusion
As a nurse, you provide the most constant care to patients and can best evaluate how well they understand what they're taught. Your responsibility for patient teaching is steadily increasing. And it will continue to increase as people become more aware of their rights and grow more knowledgeable about health and illness.

Handling patient incidents

Many times, despite the best training and intentions, "incidents" occur in the hospital. As you know, these incidents are events that are inconsistent with the hospital's ordinary routine. In most hospitals (and other health-care institutions), *any* injury to a patient requires an incident report. Besides patient injuries, patient complaints, medication errors, and injuries to employees and visitors require incident reports.

An incident report serves two main purposes:
• to inform hospital administration of the incident so it can consider changes that will help prevent future similar incidents (risk management)
• to alert the administration and the hospital's insurance company to the possibility of liability claims and the need for further investigation (claims management). Even when the incident isn't investigated, the report helps identify witnesses if a lawsuit is started months or even years later.

Of course, an incident report is useful only if it's filed promptly, thoroughly, and appropriately.

Your legal duty to report patient incidents
Whether you're an RN, an LPN, or an LVN, a staff nurse or a nurse manager, your legal duty is to report any incident of which you have first-hand knowledge. Failure to report an incident not only can lead to your being fired, it can also expose you to personal liability for malpractice—especially if the breach of your duty to report the incident causes injury to a patient.

Only a person with first-hand knowledge of an incident should report it. And only the person making the report should sign it. *Each person with first-hand knowledge should fill out and sign a separate report.* Never sign a report describing circumstances or events you haven't personally witnessed.

What—and what not—to include in an incident report
An incident report should include only the following:
• the identities of the patient and any witnesses
• information about what happened and what were the consequences to the patient (supply enough information so the hospital administration can decide whether the matter needs further investigation)
• any other relevant facts.

Statements like these should never be included in an incident report:
• mention of events not seen by the reporter (such as something another employee said happened)
• opinions (such as the reporter's opinion of the patient's prognosis)
• conclusions or assumptions (such as what caused the incident)
• suggestions of who was responsible for causing the incident
• suggestions to prevent the incident from happening again.

Including this type of information in an incident report could seriously hinder the defense in any lawsuit arising from the incident.

Remember, the incident report serves only to notify the administration that an incident has occurred. In effect, it says, "Administration: please note that this incident happened, and please decide whether you want to investigate it further." Such items as detailed statements from witnesses and descriptions of remedial action are normally part of an investigative follow-up, so don't include them in the incident report itself.

Be especially careful that the hospital's reporting system does not lead to improper incident reporting. For example, some hospitals require nursing supervisors to correlate reports from witnesses and then to file a single report. And some incident report forms invite inappropriate conclusions and assumptions by asking, "How can this incident be prevented in the future?"

Avoid these potential pitfalls by following the guidelines given above. If your hospital's reporting system or forms contain such potential pitfalls, alert the administration to them.

Processing incident reports

As you're probably aware, an incident report doesn't become part of the patient's medical record. In fact, the record shouldn't even mention that an incident report has been filed. The record should include *only* clinical observations relating to the incident. (Again, avoid value judgments.)

By the way, entering your observations in the nurses' notes section of the patient's record doesn't take the place of completing an incident report. Nor does completing an incident report take the place of proper documentation in the patient's chart.

An incident report, once it's filed, may be reviewed by the nursing supervisor, the doctor called to examine the patient, appropriate department heads and administrators, the hospital attorney, and the hospital's insurance company. (See *What Happens to an Incident Report?*, pages 128 and 129.) The report may be filed under the involved patient's name or by the type of injury, depending on the hospital's policy and the insurance company's regulations. Reports are rarely placed in the reporting nurse's employment file.

A currently controversial question concerns whether a patient's attorney may "discover" (request and receive a copy of) an incident report and introduce it into evidence in a malpractice lawsuit. The law on this issue varies from state to state. To avoid discovery, the hospital may send copies of the incident report to its attorney, or the hospital attorney may write a letter stating that the report is being made for his use and benefit only.

Actually, concern about incident-report discovery should be minimal if an incident report contains only properly reportable material. After all, the information in a properly completed incident report is readily available to the patient's attorney through many other sources. Only when an incident report contains second-hand information, opinions, conclusions, accusations, or suggestions for preventing such incidents in the future does discovery of the incident report become an important issue for attorneys and the courts.

What to do when your error causes a reportable incident

If an incident results from an error you made, you have the duty to file an incident report immediately. Making a mistake is serious and may invite corrective action by your hospital, but attempting to cover it up is worse—and so are the potential consequences.

For one thing, the likelihood that an incident report will be used against you is slight. A hospital wants its nurses to report incidents and to keep proper records. They may not do this consistently if they're always reprimanded for even small errors. Most hospitals, in fact, will reprimand a nurse severely for *not* filing an incident report if irreversible injury is done to the patient.

Of course, if an incident results from your act of gross negligence or irresponsibility or is one of a series of incidents in which you've been involved, then the hospital may take action against you. And that possibility increases if the patient sustains irreversible injury because of your error.

If a fellow employee's error causes a reportable incident, your safest course is to factually and objectively report what you observed. Remember, the truth isn't libel. By properly fulfilling your duty to your patient and your hospital, you'll also minimize any potential liability if the em-

What Happens to an Incident Report?

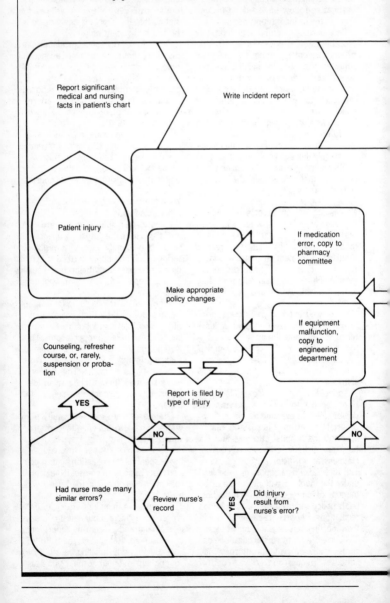

Do you know what happens to an incident report after it's filed? This chart gives you a comprehensive overview of incident-report routing.

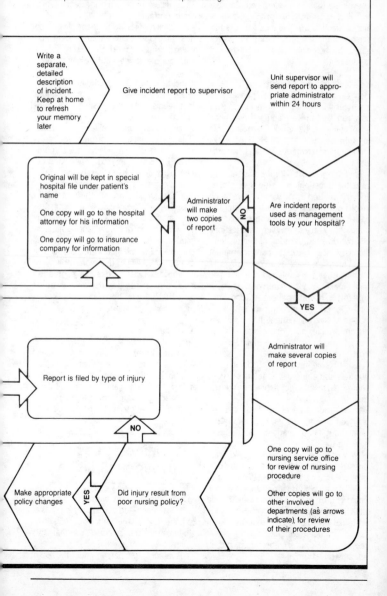

Write a separate, detailed description of incident. Keep at home to refresh your memory later

Give incident report to supervisor

Unit supervisor will send report to appropriate administrator within 24 hours

Original will be kept in special hospital file under patient's name

One copy will go to the hospital attorney for his information

One copy will go to insurance company for information

Administrator will make two copies of report

Are incident reports used as management tools by your hospital?

NO

YES

Administrator will make several copies of report

Report is filed by type of injury

NO

Make appropriate policy changes

YES

Did injury result from poor nursing policy?

One copy will go to nursing service office for review of nursing procedure

Other copies will go to other involved departments (as arrows indicate) for review of their procedures

ployee files a lawsuit against you.

Here's another point to remember: Most states have laws granting "qualified privilege" to those who have a duty to discuss or evaluate their co-workers, employees, or fellow citizens. This privilege means that no liability for libel exists unless the person giving the information knows it's false or has acted with a reckless disregard for the truth.

Risk-management strategy

How can you minimize the chances that a patient will sue after an incident? And how can you protect yourself and your hospital in case he does? The best way is to follow the "three Rs" of risk-management strategy: rapport, record, and report.

Maintain rapport with the patient. Answer his questions honestly. Don't offer any explanation if you weren't personally involved in the incident; instead, refer the patient to someone who can supply answers. If you try to answer his questions without direct knowledge of the incident, inconsistencies could arise and the patient could interpret these as a cover-up.

Don't offer any explanation if doing so might make you visibly nervous. Ask your supervisor, hospital patient-relations specialist, or an administrator for advice on how to answer the patient. If you still feel uncomfortable, have one of them talk to the patient, but still try to maintain rapport.

Don't blame anyone for the incident. If you feel someone was at fault, tell your charge nurse or supervisor—not the patient.

If an incident necessarily changes the way you care for the patient, tell the patient about it and clearly explain the reasons for the change.

Record the incident in the medical records. Remember, truthfulness is the best protection against lawsuits. If you try to cover up or play down an incident, you could end up in far more serious trouble than if you'd reported it objectively. Never write in the medical record that an incident report has been completed. An incident report is *not* clinical information, but an administrative tool.

Report every incident. Some nurses think incident reports are more trouble than they're worth and, furthermore, that they're a dangerous admission of guilt. That's false. Here's why incident reports are important:

• Incident reports jog our memories. Much time may pass between an incident and when it comes to court. So we simply can't trust our memories—but we can trust an incident report.

• Incident reports help administrators act quickly to change the policy or procedure that seems to be responsible for the incident. An administrator can also act quickly to talk with families and offer assistance, explanation, or other appropriate support. Sometimes helpful communication with an injured patient and his family can be the balm that soothes a family's anger and prevents a lawsuit.

• Incident reports provide the information hospitals need to decide whether restitution should be made. When a patient is injured instead of helped during his hospital stay, the hospital sometimes decides it has a moral obligation to compensate the patient. In fact, this moral obligation is another reason (besides protection against having to pay damages awarded in a lawsuit) why hospitals carry professional liability insurance.

Conclusion

Incident reporting will become increasingly important as health-care consumers become more aware of their rights. Remember, a long period may elapse between an incident and subsequent court proceedings. Documentation may be the only objective proof of what happened.

Minors: Legal responsibilities

That patient you're caring for, the one who's a minor—do you know his rights as a patient? And what your legal obligations to him are? For answers to these and other questions, keep reading.

A *minor* is any person under the age of majority, which is usually 18 or 21, depending on state or Canadian provincial law. When you care for a minor, you should keep in mind the way minors' legal rights are structured. What legal rights a minor has depend largely on his age. He may also have special legal status.

Minor's rights

A minor's rights fall into three categories:

• *Personal rights that belong to everyone from birth.* Examples include the right to privacy and the right to protection against crimes.

• *Rights that can be exercised as a minor matures.* These fall into two groups. The first includes the right to drive a car, to work at a paying job, and to have sexual relations—as long as *both* partners are of legal age. These rights are granted at certain ages, according to state laws, whether or not the minor is mature enough to exercise the right intelligently.

The second group includes rights granted by the courts rather than by statutory law, which are given to any minor who shows the mental and emotional ability to handle them. (See the discussion of the nonemancipated but mature minor, below.)

• *Rights that belong to adults and can be exercised only by adults and so-called emancipated minors.* Examples include many financial and contractual rights, such as the right to consent to medical treatment. (See the discussion on obtaining consent from a minor, below, and *The Right to Consent: From Birth to Adulthood,* page 75.)

The law provides special rights for minors that they may exercise only *after* reaching the age of majority. For example, because a minor cannot sue in court, most states give minors a grace period after they reach the age of majority to bring any lawsuit relating to the time when they were of minor age. This includes suing persons their parents could have sued earlier on the minors' behalf but chose not to. Because this can include a lawsuit for medical malpractice, most hospitals keep the records of pediatric patients longer than the legally required period, which can be fairly short.

Emancipation basics

Under the laws of most states and Canadian provinces, a person can become emancipated from the legal restrictions of being a minor in the following ways:

• marrying (in which case emancipation continues after separation, widowhood, or divorce)

• becoming a parent (even if not married)

• becoming pregnant (or believing she's pregnant)

• joining the armed forces

• living away from home and earning an independent living, managing his own finances, and in general assuming an adult role.

Under most circumstances, you should treat an emancipated minor the same as if he were an adult.

Mature minor

A mature minor is a nonemancipated minor in his middle to late teens who shows clear signs of intellectual and emotional maturity. A mature minor may be able to exercise certain adult rights, depending on laws in his state.

Note that even an emancipated minor may not exercise some rights. If he's 18 and the drinking age in his state is 21, he still can't legally buy a drink. Some states set a minimum age for making a will (usually the age of majority). In those states, even if the minor is married or has a child, any will he draws up won't be valid.

The laws of most states provide that some contracts made by minors are valid but voidable. In theory, this protects the minor from recklessness. Many hospitals won't allow a minor to sign a contract to pay his hospital bills unless a parent or guardian at least guarantees his contract. This legal arrangement, of course, should not influence anything you do as a nurse.

Guardians ad litem

The court may appoint a guardian ad litem when these two conditions coexist:

• a court decision is needed for the minor

• a "diversion of interest" exists; that is, the court assumes that the interest of the minor's parents or legal guardians probably doesn't coincide with the minor's welfare.

The court may do this if one or both parents are still living and interested in the minor's welfare or even if the minor already has a guardian.

Obtaining consent

By far the most common problem with minors is obtaining proper consent for their medical care. Although the doctor bears the legal responsibility for this, you'll often be involved in the process. Here are 11 different situations you may face in helping to obtain a minor's consent:

Under normal circumstances. If the minor isn't emancipated, his mother, father, or legal guardian has the right to refuse or consent to treatment for him. Whenever possible, consent should be obtained from both parents or both guardians when joint guardians have custody of the minor.

If the parents are divorced or separated, the usual policy is to obtain consent from the parent who has custody. If the custodial parent is unavailable, the other parent may be asked to make the decision.

If the minor's parents are incompetent or dead and he has no legal guardian, the court will usually appoint a legal guardian for him. The guardian can consent or refuse, just as if he were a parent.

When parents or joint guardians disagree. Problems can arise when parents (whether married, divorced, or separated) or joint guardians disagree about consenting to treatment for a minor. The hospital's only recourse may be to go to court, where a judge either makes the decision himself or assigns responsibility to one parent or guardian. You may find yourself caught in a situation where a minor's parents or guardians can't agree on consenting to his treatment. When this happens, tell the hospital administrators immediately so they can talk to the parents or guardians and, if necessary, alert the hospital's attorney.

When the minor is emancipated. An emancipated minor can refuse or consent to treatment himself. But if he's unable to do so (for example, because he's unconscious following an accident), you have to try to find someone who can give consent for him. Possibilities, in descending order of preference, include his spouse, parents or guardians, and nearest living relative.

You may waive this requirement for consent only in an emergency situation, when your failure to treat a minor immediately could result in further injury or in death.

When your patient is a nonemancipated but mature minor. In Canada, nonemancipated mature minors can consent to medical treatment themselves. For example, in *Booth v. Toronto General Hospital* (1910), the court ruled that a minor who was working for his living but residing at his parents' home could give his own consent to surgery.

In the United States, nonemancipated but mature minors' rights are not so broad. In some cases, however, even young minors' wishes have been taken into account—for example, in *Hart v. Brown* (1972), an organ-transplant case involving minor twins. And in a series of rulings on abortion and contraception, discussed below, the U.S. Supreme Court has ruled that mature minors have certain rights of consent and privacy.

When a minor needs emergency care. The legal rule here is the same as for adults: If necessary, treat first and get consent later. Some courts have held that any mature minor, emancipated or not, may give a valid and binding consent to emergency treatment. For example, in *Younts v. St. Francis Hospital and School of Nursing* (1970), a nonemancipated but mature 17-year-old was held able to consent to surgical repair of a severed fingertip.

When a minor asks for an abortion. Under common law, all pregnant minors have the right to consent to abortion. In most states, however, this common-law right has been modified or eliminated by statutory law or court decision. But recent U.S. Supreme Court rulings, including *Planned Parenthood of Central Missouri v. Danforth* (1976), *Bellotti v. Baird I* (1976), and *Bellotti v. Baird II*(1979), make clear that state laws can't stop a mature or otherwise emancipated minor from seeking and getting a legal abortion—although a judge may have to certify that the minor is mature enough to make the decision. Also, the law in some states may require notification of the parents of a minor who's seeking an abortion (*H.L. v. Matheson,* 1981).

For the rules your state requires you to follow, check with your hospital's attorney.

When a minor asks for contraceptives. In *Carey v. Population Services International* (1977), the U.S. Supreme Court ruled unconstitutional various state laws that are more stringent about providing contraceptives (to minors or adults) than the laws about abortions. This means that laws about giving minors contraceptives (or advice about contraceptives) will be equally restrictive as or less restrictive than the laws about obtaining abortions. Again, check with your hospital's attorney if you have questions.

When a minor needs treatment for sexually transmitted or other communicable diseases. Most states and Canadian provinces have laws that permit minors to consent to treatment for serious communicable diseases (including sexually transmitted diseases) without parental approval.

If you must deal with a minor who's refusing diagnosis or treatment for a communicable disease, check your state's laws. Most states permit public health authorities to deal with a nonconsenting minor as an adult, including when he must be quarantined.

When a minor needs treatment for drug abuse. State and federal laws generally permit minors to consent to take part in drug-abuse treatment and rehabilitation programs just as though they were adults. Like adults, minor patients in drug treatment programs are entitled to have their records kept confidential.

When religious beliefs conflict with a minor's treatment. If your patient or his parents or guardians are Jehovah's Witnesses or Christian Scientists, you may have special problems getting consent to treatment.

Although competent adults or emancipated minors may refuse treatment for religious reasons, unemancipated minors may not. In most states where the question has come before the courts, judges have ruled that parents and guardians can't stop a hospital from treating their child solely on religious grounds, if a reasonable chance exists that the treatment will help the patient.

Note, however, that in this situation a court will have to appoint a guardian ad litem for the sick minor. This may take some time, so to avoid delaying the minor's treatment unnecessarily, notify your hospital administration as quickly as possible.

When a minor seeks or receives mental health care. Minors, like adults, may be treated at private and state-run mental health facilities. When the minor and his parents agree to seek such treatment for the minor, the facility will follow its normal medical guidelines and procedures in deciding whether to admit him.

The U.S. Supreme Court, in *Parham v. J.R.* (1979) and in *Secretary of Public Welfare v. Institutionalized Juveniles* (1979), held that nonconsenting minors can be admitted to state-run mental health facilities at the request of either or both parents. Such minors, however, always have the right to have a psychiatrist or other trained fact finder review the request at or before admission and at least once thereafter. The fact finder may be the facility's regular admissions officer.

In many states, however, the rules controlling admission of minors to state inpatient mental facilities are more rigorous. The rules may call for a full-scale hearing, with attorneys present, within a set time after admission (if not concurrent with admission). For example, in *Melville v. Sabbatino* (1973), a minor challenged the validity of his admission to a state mental-health facility. The court ruled that the minor was entitled to a hearing. (The outcome of the hearing wasn't reported.)

As yet, no restrictions of legal rights exist for outpatient or clinic treatment of minors. And, of course, a minor's admission to any private mental-health facility concerns only the facility and a competent adult relative (or the minor's spouse, if he's married).

Conclusion

As you can see, caring for minors generally presents no special legal problems for the staff nurse. In most respects, problems in obtaining consent for nonemancipated minors' treatment are exactly the same as those in getting consent for incompetent adults.

The laws and regulations governing care of minors probably won't change much in the near future. This includes laws regarding contraception—specifically, whether parents must be told when their nonemancipated minor daughter is seeking contraceptives.

Whether or not the laws concerning minors' medical treatment change, remember that you're responsible for knowing them.

The abused child or adult—legal aspects

As you're surely aware, nurses have long had to care for abused patients. Often these are children—victims of parents, relatives, or so-called friends. But just as often they are adults.

You know that abuse takes many forms. Sometimes abuse is physical battering, such as when a son regularly beats his aging father. At other times, abuse involves verbal, sexual, or emotional attack, or neglect.

Why abuse occurs is uncertain. It may be a product of stressful situations or sudden crises. But nonabusers also face stress and crisis—so this explanation leaves much to be desired.

People who become abusers

People who abuse others come from all socioeconomic levels and all ethnic groups. No specific psychiatric diagnosis encompasses the abuser's personality and behavior. However, many abusers have a history of being abused themselves when young or of having witnessed abuse of parents or siblings. (These childhood experiences are often profound and can influence a person's behavior throughout his adult life.) Abusive persons often lack self-esteem and the security of being loved—qualities that help support nonabusive persons through stressful periods of their lives.

In times of crisis, abusers resort to the behavior they learned as children. They abuse just as they were abused—all in an attempt to restore their own feelings of self-control and to foster self-esteem. After all, if abuse was an acceptable behavior for their parents, why can't it be the same for them now?

Abusers are often unable to tolerate personal failure or disapproval from spouses, children, or friends. When an abuser's self-esteem is low, he expects rejection and often will act in ways that cause others to reject him. In turn, this allows the abuser to verbally or emotionally abuse those same people. Abusers commonly have unrealistic expectations of the people they abuse. These expectations show themselves in different ways, but the result is the same: When a person can't or won't live up to an abuser's expectations, he feels compelled to control, mortify, reject, and, if necessary, physically injure that person.

Sometimes low self-esteem will prompt an abuser to choose a partner much like himself. Each will then feed into the other's forms of abuse. If the couple has children, they often become targets of their parents' abusive behavior. And what the children witness, and suffer, begins another cycle of abused child to child abuser.

Victims of abuse

How much do you know about the types of people most likely to be abused? As a nurse, you need to familiarize yourself with the attributes that frequently characterize abuse victims.

Children, of course, are commonly abused, especially children between the ages of 4 months and 3 years. (See *Caring for the Abused Child.*) Some children are particularly vulnerable to abuse. Among them are children with behavior problems as well as those who are malformed, developmentally disabled, born prematurely, or born to unmarried parents. From the abusive parent's perspective, such a child represents an unplanned disruption or a stress-producing crisis. If the child has mental or physical defects, the parent may see this as reaffirming his own inadequacy and weakness. And if the child's defects are severe, the parent may be unable to admit that the child is his: he may pour on abuse to destroy this "alien being."

Parents may also view children as extensions of persons they hate. Sometimes this results from similarities in physical ap-

Caring for the Abused Child

You're on duty in the emergency department when Mrs. Collins comes in with her son Jeff, age 5. She tells you, "My son was in an accident while riding in a friend's car. I didn't think Jeff was injured, but later on his knee swelled up. I decided I'd better have a doctor look at it."

You look closely at Jeff for head and neck injuries. You don't see any, but you do notice some bruises on his left arm and on his legs that look several weeks old. You question Mrs. Collins about the accident, but she offers few details. Then, when you question Mrs. Collins about Jeff's injuries, she gets very defensive. Although his injuries look painful, Jeff sits quietly while you examine him.

Considering the evidence, you suspect Jeff has been abused.

If you were faced with such a situation, would you know what to do? Here are some guidelines:

• Tell the doctor that you suspect child abuse and ask him to order a total-body X-ray. If he resists your request, talk directly with the radiologist; he can do it on his own authority. Don't hesitate to take this action into your own hands. Also, inform your supervisor of the situation.
• If you suspect the child has been forced to ingest drugs or alcohol, get an order for toxicology studies of the child's blood and urine.
• If the child is severely bruised, get an order for a blood coagulation profile.
• If X-rays or other studies suggest the child has been abused, talk with the doctor about confronting the parents. Ask how you might help him do this.
• If a parent admits to abusing the child and appears to want help, supply the address and telephone number of a local group, such as the Child Abuse Prevention Effort, and encourage the parent to call.
• Whether or not the parent admits to abusing the child, report all suspected abuse to the state-designated agency empowered to investigate the situation.

pearance or similarities in behavior. If a child resembles a spouse who deserted the family, he may be blamed for the spouse's failures and abused accordingly.

Of course, adults abuse other adults as well as children. Spouses and elderly parents or relatives are the most common victims.

One important characteristic of an abused spouse is lack of self-esteem. Often an abused spouse's parents abused each other, or one parent abused the other. Having witnessed these attacks as a child, the present-day abused spouse accepts that she, or sometimes he, will be abused. By behaving passively toward their partners, such spouses make it easy for the partners to abuse them repeatedly without fear of retaliation.

Like children, adults can become abuse victims if they're viewed as too dependent, too sickly, or too much like a hated person.

Ill or elderly persons who make financial, emotional, or personal demands will often end up injured when the stress they create becomes intolerable for their abusers.

Among abusers of adults, men who abuse women seem to predominate. But sometimes the reverse is true. Abused men, married or not, often show the same low self-esteem and passivity as abused women. Sometimes an abused man is the less aggressive and more subservient member of the relationship and accepts a certain level of abuse in the hope that it won't get worse. At other times, he may be so ashamed by his inability to provide adequately that he invites abuse to give himself a feeling of atonement.

How the law relates to abusers and their victims

Until 1875, no U.S. laws specifically protected abuse victims—unless they were animals! In 1874, grossly battered "Mary Ellen," age 9, was found chained to her bed in a New York City tenement. Etta Wheeler, a church worker, tried to find help for Mary Ellen, but she quickly discovered that New York had no laws to protect children. Her only recourse was the American Society for the Prevention of Cruelty to Animals, which agreed to intervene on Mary Ellen's behalf.

A year after Mary Ellen's case reached the courts, New York State adopted the country's first child-protection legislation. This gave child-protection agencies a legal base, and it proved a breakthrough for other disadvantaged groups as well.

Since then, child abuse has gained increasing attention from the public, from legislators—and from concerned health-care professionals. In 1946, for example, radiologists reported that subdural hematomas and abnormal X-ray findings in the long bones were commonly associated with early childhood traumatic injuries. In 1961, an American Academy of Pediatrics symposium on child abuse introduced the term *battered child*.

The first statutory laws calling for mandatory reporting of child abuse resulted from a 1963 report by the Children's Bureau of the (then) U.S. Department of Health, Education, and Welfare. Most states, using the model in the report, developed protective legislation by the early 1970s. Unfortunately, the diversity of these laws makes uniform interpretation impossible.

To help remedy this, the Early Childhood Project Education Commission published a nationwide model law in 1973. During the same year, Congress passed the Child Abuse Prevention and Treatment Act. This act required states to meet certain uniform standards in order to be eligible for federal assistance in setting up programs to identify, prevent, and treat the problems caused by child abuse. The act also established a national center on child abuse and neglect.

Currently, two common features characterize most state child abuse legislation:
• empowering of a social welfare or law enforcement bureau to receive and investigate reports of actual or suspected abuse

• granting of legal immunity from liability, for defamation or invasion of privacy, to any person reporting an incident of actual or suspected abuse.

Laws protecting abused spouses are still being written. Although many domestic-relations laws exist, more are needed for the specific protection of victims of domestic violence. (See *Child Abuse Statutes* in Appendix.)

Your legal duty to report abuse

As a nurse, you play a crucial role in recognizing and reporting incidents of suspected abuse. While caring for patients, you can readily note evidence of apparent abuse. When you do, you must pass the information along to the appropriate authorities.

If you've ever hesitated to file an abuse report because you fear repercussions, remember that the Child Abuse Prevention and Treatment Act protects you against liability. If your report is bona fide (that is, if you file it in good faith), the law will protect you from any suit filed by an alleged abuser. (Caution: This protection may not be available in Maine and Montana.)

To have a bona fide belief that abuse has occurred, you must carefully assess not only the abused child's or adult's injuries but also the relationship between him and the possible abuser. Make your report as complete and accurate as possible. At the same time, be careful not to let your personal feelings affect either the way you make out a report or whether you should file the report at all. (See *Consent to Photograph the Abused Child*.)

Abuse cases often raise many difficult emotional issues. Remember, however, that not filing a report may have more serious consequences than filing one that contains an error. It is better to risk error than to risk breaching the child abuse reporting laws—and, in effect, perpetuating the abuse.

Besides your duty to report abuse, you also have a duty to teach the public about abuse. The Child Abuse Prevention and Treatment Act encourages health-care institutions to develop programs to identify, report, and ultimately prevent abuse. You can help reduce the incidence of abuse by

Consent to Photograph the Abused Child

Imagine you work in the emergency department (ED) of a hospital. One day a social worker brings in a girl, age 11, a suspected victim of child abuse. The social worker asks you to photograph the girl's injuries to document them.

Can you legally take photographs of the patient?

If your state law permits it and your hospital policy does not prohibit it, you can legally take photograhs of the patient.

In most states, either an agency caseworker or the local police can photograph child-abuse injuries without parental consent. In states that don't specifically grant the right to photograph, the examining doctor has the responsibility to authorize photographs, because the duty to report implies a responsibility to preserve any evidence. If the parents are present and object to photographs, the doctor should contact law-enforcement

officials to secure a court order.

All 50 states now have laws requiring that doctors and social workers (among other professionals) report suspected child abuse in children under age 16 or 18, depending on the state. These laws also offer professional care givers some immunity from liability, as long as they act in good faith.

Some states have designated reporting agencies. These agencies have 24-hour-a-day coverage and will send a caseworker to investigate, night or day. Find out the appropriate agency you should contact when you suspect child abuse, and post the number near the ED telephone.

Child abuse reporting laws are far from standardized, so ED personnel should request a specific procedure from the hospital administration. Obviously, the administration should design a procedure that meets all state reporting laws.

teaching people about its signs and symptoms, diagnosis, and treatment.

How to recognize signs and symptoms of abuse

You can learn to become adept at recognizing both the events that trigger abuse and the signs and symptoms that mark the abused and the abuser. Early in your relationship with an abused patient, you'll need to be adept in order to spot the behavioral and interactional clues that can signal an abusive situation. Why? Because many of the clues are subtle, or not easily distinguished from nonabusers' behavior.

For example, abused people tend to be passive and fearful. An abused child often fails to protest if his parent is asked to leave the examining area. An abused adult, on the other hand, often wants his abuser to stay with him.

Here's another clue: Abused persons often react to hospital procedures by crying helplessly and incessantly. And they tend

to be wary of physical contacts, including physical examinations.

The abuser may also give important clues. Sometimes he'll appear overly agitated when dealing with hospital personnel; for example, he'll get impatient if they don't carry out procedures instantly. At other times, he may exhibit just the opposite behavior: a total lack of interest in the patient's problems.

When you take an abused victim's history, he may be vague about how he was injured and tell different stories to different people. When you ask directly about specific injuries, he may answer evasively or not at all. Sometimes he'll minimize or try to hide his injuries.

When examining an abused victim, look for characteristic signs of abuse. Often you'll find old bruises, scars, or deformities the patient can't (or won't) explain. X-ray examinations may show the presence of many old fractures.

Always document your findings objectively; try to keep your emotions out of your charting. One way to do this is to use the SOAP technique, which calls for these steps:

• In the subjective (S) part of the note, record information in the patient's own words.

• In the objective (O) part, record your personal observations.

• Under assessment (A), record your evaluations and conclusions.

• Under plan (P), list sources of hospital and community support available to the patient following discharge.

Offering support services

Many support services have become available for both abusers and their victims. For example, if a female victim is afraid to return to the scene of her abuse, she may find temporary housing in an established shelter. If no shelter is available, she may be able to stay with a friend or family member.

Social workers or community liaison workers may also be able to offer suggestions for shelter. Another possibility is a church, synagogue, or mosque, which may have members willing to take the patient in. If no shelter can be found, the patient may have to stay at the hospital to guarantee safety.

Alert the patient to state, county, or city agencies that can help protect him. The most obvious is the police department, which should be called to collect evidence if the patient wants to press charges against the abuser. If the patient is a child, the law may require filing a report with a government family-service agency.

As a nurse concerned about abuse, you need to evaluate the abuser's ability to handle stress. He'll probably pose a continued threat to others until he gets help in understanding his behavior and how to change it. When you question him (or his family), try to get answers to questions like these:

• Has he recently lost his job or other means of support?

• Does he have problems with alcohol or drugs?

• Is his wife pregnant with a child he doesn't want? (This is often a triggering factor in wife abuse.)

• Does he have unusual problems?

For abusive fathers or mothers, a local chapter of Parents Anonymous (PA) may be helpful. (see *Organizations that Help the Abused and the Abuser,* page 141). PA, a self-help group made up of former abusers, attempts to help abusing parents by teaching them how to redirect their anger and deal with it.

Besides helping short-circuit abusive behavior, a self-help group like PA takes abusing parents out of their isolation and gives them someone to talk to. It also provides help in a crisis, when members may be able to prevent an abusive incident.

Telephone hot lines to crisis intervention services also give abusers someone to talk with in times of stress and crisis and may help prevent abuse. Commonly staffed by volunteers, telephone hot lines provide a link between those who seek help and those willing and trained to provide counseling and reassurance.

These and other kinds of help are also available through family service agencies and hospitals. Be sure you know what resources are available, nationally and in your area. Then when an abuser or his victim needs your help, you can respond quickly and authoritatively.

Conclusion

As you know, protecting patients' rights is a primary nursing responsibility. Abuse violates those rights. To protect your patients, be alert to recognize signs and symptoms of abuse. Accept your responsibility for reporting possible incidents of abuse. Learn about community resources that can help abusers and their victims. And remember, *both* need your help.

Special risks in caring for "special" patients

When your hospitalized patient is mentally ill or developmentally disabled, take care. Despite his often dependent condition, he has most of the same rights as your other patients. And if you violate these rights, even unwittingly, you could face serious legal complications.

Part of today's concern for the rights of the mentally ill and developmentally disabled stems from attempts to correct past abuses. Under the United States Constitution, a person's rights can't be limited or denied merely because of his status. Many health-care professionals still don't realize that the courts have generally interpreted the Constitution to mean that mentally ill and developmentally disabled persons have a right to fair and humane treatment, including during hospitalization. Under most circumstances, such a patient can't be kept in a hospital against his will, for example. Nor can he be denied the right to refuse treatment or to receive information so he can give informed consent to proposed surgery.

State governments have tried to assure the rights of this special population by enacting legislation specifically addressing the problems of the mentally ill and developmentally disabled. This legislation describes and authorizes specific services and provides the necessary funding. The federal government also provides for the mentally ill and developmentally disabled. The Rehabilitation Act of 1973, for example, earmarked funds specifically for rehabilitative programs. For instance, it provides cash assistance for persons who, because of their disabilities, aren't able to provide adequately for themselves or their families. The act also outlines 14 patient's rights to ensure high standards of health care. Facilities that participate in Medicare must comply with these 14 rights and make sure that the patient, his guardian, next of kin, or sponsoring agency knows about them, too.

Canada makes similar provisions for mentally ill and developmentally disabled persons. As in the United States, Canadian legislation seeks to prevent maltreatment and to fund programs that help these persons to function successfully in society.

Issues of legal responsibility

When a mentally ill or developmentally disabled child is admitted to a hospital, legal responsibility for him must be established immediately.

If the patient is accompanied by a parent, usually the parent will be legally responsible.

If the child has been institutionalized prior to entering the hospital, the institution may have responsibility. However, this is true only if the parents have waived responsibility and the institution has written evidence to prove it.

If the courts have found the parents unfit or unable to care for the child, a legal guardian will have been appointed. This person has the legal right to assume responsibility for the child.

When no guardian has been appointed for the child, the state may act as a guardian under the doctrine of *parens patriae*. This is true of mentally ill or developmentally disabled adults, as well, who must have guardians.

Whenever your mentally ill or developmentally disabled patient is an adult, check his chart to see if he requires a legal guardian and to establish who it is. It may be a parent. Or if the patient is married, it may be the patient's spouse.

Sometimes an adult patient and his guardian will seriously disagree about the patient's care. When this happens, get clarification by going through proper hospital channels.

As a nurse, you have no right to control the life of a mentally ill or developmentally disabled patient. Restricting his liberty for any reason is almost never legally permissible, except when he may otherwise harm himself or others. You must analyze each situation carefully to determine at what point the patient needs help in managing his affairs.

Obtaining informed consent

When consent is required from a patient who's mentally ill or developmentally disabled, three questions should immediately come to mind:

• Is consent for treatment or a special procedure obtained the same way it is from any other patient?

• Does the patient fully understand the procedure that he's to undergo, including risks?

• Does the patient have the authority to give his own consent, or must someone else give it?

The answers to these questions, of course, will vary with each patient. Clearly, if the patient is of unsound mind and can't understand the nature, purpose, and risks of the proposed treatment, he can't legally consent. In such a case, consent must be obtained from the patient's legal guardian.

If the legal guardian is unavailable, a court authorized to handle such matters may allow treatment.

As you know, a doctor must always explain the nature, purpose, and risks of the treatment to the person giving consent, whether it's the patient or someone else. This explanation allows the person to make an informed decision that will be in the patient's best interest. Failure to obtain a truly informed consent can result in legal action against the doctor, the nurse (if she knew the patient's consent wasn't informed), and the hospital or other health-care institution.

Sometimes a doctor or nurse may doubt a patient's capacity to consent, even though he hasn't been judged incompetent. This often happens during an illness that causes temporary incompetence. In such a situation, the nearest relative's consent must be obtained or, if none can be found, the court must authorize treatment.

In the New York case of *Collins v. Davis* (1964), a hospital administrator sought a court order to permit surgery on an irrational adult whose life was considered to be in danger. The patient's wife had previously refused to give consent, allegedly for reasons she felt served the patient's best interest. The court, after considering the entire situation—especially the patient's prognosis if surgery wasn't performed—agreed that the hospital and the doctor had only two choices: either let the patient die, or perform the operation against his wife's wishes. The court overruled the wife's refusal, holding that the patient had sought medical attention and that treatment normally given to a patient with a similar condition should be provided.

You can best protect the mentally ill or developmentally disabled patient's legal rights to informed consent by making sure a doctor has provided him or his guardian with complete, accurate information.

Of course, you know you should never help with procedures on a patient whose informed consent hasn't been obtained. If you do, you can be held liable along with the doctor and hospital. In fact, if your patient is a minor, you could face double liability: his parents could sue you now, and he could sue you when he comes of age.

Adolescents who protest their hospitalization may obtain a court review and be represented by appointed legal counsel.

Forced hospitalization and use of restraints

Mentally ill or developmentally disabled persons may be involuntarily kept in hospitals if they're at risk of taking their own lives or if they pose a threat to other persons' property or lives. However, mental illness alone is not a sufficient legal basis for detaining a patient. The U.S. Supreme Court, in *O'Connor v. Donaldson* (1975), held that a state cannot constitutionally confine a patient, without treatment or without the rehabilitation necessary to reintegrate him into society, "who is capable of surviving safely in freedom by himself or with the help of willing and responsible family members or friends."

Similar restrictions apply to physical restraint of patients. Most states require a doctor to write the restraint order and place it in the patient's medical record before restraints can be applied.

Restraint (or seclusion) may be used only to prevent a patient from seriously injuring himself or others—and only when all other physical and psychological therapies would likely fail to prevent such injuries. Whenever possible, use minimal restraint—only that amount necessary to protect the patient and safeguard the staff and others. Restraint should never be used for punishment, for the convenience of staff, or as a substitute for treatment programs. Use of restraints is usually limited to a specific period of time (see *Caring for a Patient in Restraints or Seclusion,* page 143). Except in emergencies, you may normally apply restraints only after a doctor has examined the patient and written an order to restrain him. In an emergency situation—such as a violent outburst with actual or potential harm to persons or

Organizations That Help the Abused and the Abuser

Here's one simple but important way you can help the abuse victim and his abuser. Encourage them to call the organizations listed below for support and counseling.

Child Abuse Prevention Effort	**(215) 831-8877**
National Clearinghouse on Marital Rape	**(415) 548-1770**
National Coalition Against Sexual Assault	**(612) 296-7084**
National Committee for Prevention of Child Abuse	**(312) 663-3520**
Parents Anonymous	**(800) 421-0353 in California: (800) 352-0386**
Parents United	**(408) 279-1957**

property—any person may apply restraints to the patient. But obtain an order for the restraint as soon as possible, and document the incident carefully.

As a nurse, you may be held liable in a lawsuit if you can't verify that—in your judgment—a patient needed to be restrained, and that he was restrained only as long as necessary. If you restrain or seclude a patient simply for shouting obscenities, for example, you risk a lawsuit for false imprisonment.

When applying restraints, take care to avoid undue force; otherwise, you may invite a lawsuit for battery. Even threatening to use force may be sufficient cause for legal action.

When a doctor isn't available in an emergency, you're responsible to see that restraints and seclusion are used only to the extent necessary to prevent injury. Until the doctor authorizes the use of restraints, you must provide one-to-one patient supervision. Make sure, too, that the staff uses only legally permissible forms of restraint.

Restraint is a form of imprisonment, so it should only be used as a last resort. Before restraining a patient, consider alternatives, such as constant observation or walking with the patient.

Tranquilizing drugs may be another possibility. However, use them sparingly, with caution, and of course only with a doctor's order. The patient's right to the least restrictive treatment or to an open-door policy that allows patients to move about "freely" means little if accompanied by indiscriminate drug use as a substitute for restraints.

The right to privacy

The law has tried to protect all citizens from unwarranted intrusion into their private lives. Unfortunately, mentally ill and developmentally disabled patients' right to privacy is easily violated. A good definition of privacy, first presented at the International Commission of Justice in 1970, reads: "Privacy is the ability to lead one's life without anyone: A) interfering with family or home life; B) interfering with physical or mental integrity or moral and intellectual freedom; C) attacking honor and reputation; D) placing one in a false light; E) censoring or restricting communication and correspondence, written or oral; F) disclosing irrelevant or embarrassing information; and G) disclosing information given or received in circumstances of professional confidence."

Keep this definition in mind as you work with these patients, and do all you can to protect their rights. Despite their handicaps, these patients should never be treated as second-class citizens.

The right to writ of habeas corpus

Institutionalization may, at times, breach a patient's rights, giving him cause to petition for a writ of habeas corpus. This writ seeks to ensure the timely release of any person who claims that he's being detained illegally and deprived of his liberty.

Right-to-treatment issues

In *Wyatt v. Stickney* (1972), the court upheld the legal right of a mentally ill person hospitalized in a public institution to receive adequate psychiatric treatment. This decision suggests that when a patient is involuntarily committed because he needs treatment, his rights are violated if such treatment isn't given. Furthermore, if the underlying reason for a patient's commitment is danger to himself or others, treatment must be provided to make him less dangerous.

To qualify as adequate, treatment must be given as follows:
- by adequate staff
- in the least restrictive setting
- in privacy
- in a facility that ensures the patient a comfortable bed, adequate diet, and recreational facilities
- with the patient's informed consent, prior to unusual treatment
- with payment for work done in the institution, outside of program activities
- according to an individual treatment plan.

You must ensure that any mentally ill or developmentally disabled patient knows what treatment he needs and how he will get it. To help him, you must know what his major problems are and what he can do for himself—or what others must do for him—to help him get ready for discharge. You should also involve him in formulating his treatment plan, unless you have a documented reason why he can't or won't be involved.

Sexual-rights issues

Many questions regarding the care of mentally ill and developmentally disabled patients have so far eluded definitive answers. Some have to do with sexual matters. For example, should developmentally disabled persons be given sex education? Should they be allowed to reproduce, practice contraception, undergo voluntary sterilization? Although the general inclination is to let guardians make these decisions, the issue of the individual's right to make his own decisions will not go away. If good care can be given to both the developmentally disabled and their offspring, who's to say that they should be denied the opportunity to enjoy the same satisfactions others do?

Many U.S. Supreme Court decisions have upheld the following rights of mentally ill or developmentally disabled patients:
- to marry
- to have children
- to employ contraception, abortion, or sterilization, if desired
- to follow a life-style of their own choosing.

These rights were upheld in such cases as *Sengstack v. Sengstack* (1958), *Wyatt v. Stickney* (1972), *O'Connor v. Donaldson* (1975), and *N.Y. State Association for Retarded Children, Inc. v. Carey* (1977).

Involuntary sterilization of mentally disabled patients isn't employed as often today as in previous years, although its constitutionality was upheld in *Buck v. Bell* (1927). In its ruling, the court held that the state has the right to sterilize a developmentally disabled or insane person provided that:
- the sterilization is not prescribed as punishment
- the policy is applied equally to all
- the unborn child's interest is sufficient to warrant the sterilization.

The courts apply this ruling only when absolutely necessary. When it is applied, the patient's legal guardian must consent to the procedure, and usually a separate, independent presterilization review of the case is ordered. (In New York State, an independent medical review board must review and approve every planned involuntary sterilization before it can be performed.) If the patient refuses to submit to surgery, the matter may go to court, which may call for use of a less permanent birth-control method.

Caring for a Patient in Restraints or Seclusion

Before you can keep a patient in restraints or in seclusion, you must get an order from the patient's doctor authorizing it. New York State law, typical of most states, says this order must include:

• the results of the doctor's physical examination of the patient

• a description of the patient's behavior that makes restraints or seclusion necessary

• a description of the type of restraint or seclusion you should use

• the period during which the restraint should be used

• an order indicating how frequently you should take the patient's vital signs and check on his overall safety and comfort.

In an emergency situation, if a patient becomes violent, you may need to restrain him immediately without a doctor's order to prevent him from harming himself or others. In this situation, apply the restraints, then notify the doctor to examine the patient and write the restraint order.

When you're caring for a patient in restraints or seclusion, the law says you must:

• monitor the patient's vital signs according to the doctor's order. If you can't do this because the patient is violent, explain why in your nurses' notes. Observe his level of consciousness, verbal content, activity, color, appearance, hydration, perspiration, and skin temperature, and record your findings.

• check on the patient as the doctor has ordered, paying close attention to his comfort, safety, and personal needs, including proper placement of restraints and circulation in hands and feet, if appropriate.

• release the patient in restraints every 2 hours, if he's awake. Be sure to take proper precautions. If his actions no longer threaten others or himself, tell this to the doctor immediately. He may discontinue his order.

• feed the patient in restraints in an upright position to minimize his risk of choking and aspirating food particles.

Patient participation in research

Another troublesome area involves using mentally ill and developmentally disabled persons as subjects for medical or other research—especially if risks are involved. Guidelines for consent to experimentation and drastic, questionable, or extreme forms of treatment are complicated and raise many unresolved questions. The so-called Willowbrook decision (*N.Y. State Association for Retarded Children, Inc. v. Carey*, 1977), however, decreed that both voluntary and involuntary residents of an institution have the constitutional right to be protected from harm. The proper authority (often a research-proposal review board) should allow the patient to participate in the research only if it's relevant to his needs and the needs of others like him. For example, a depressed patient shouldn't

be asked to participate in research involving anxiety and schizophrenia.

The issue of special consideration

Because of their limitations, mentally ill or developmentally disabled patients often make "ordinary" requests that require special consideration.

For example, a patient may demand to smoke a cigarette *now*. Probably his doctor hasn't written an order for the request. If the patient should smoke only under supervision because of the danger of fire, you may decide to stay with him while he does so. But if you have a duty to be elsewhere, you should refuse his request, explaining why and telling him when he'll be able to smoke. Or, if you know a refusal will agitate and anger him, you can ask another nurse to supervise the patient while he smokes.

But maybe you feel the patient's demand is really a challenge to your authority. If so, you may decide to refuse the request, explaining the need to follow the hospital's social and safety policies.

If the patient's behavior is part of a pattern that includes, for example, refusing to shower, refusing to go to bed by a certain time, and demanding to make an immediate phone call, then you need to refer the situation to the treatment team for a well-thought-out decision—one that serves the best interests of both patient and hospital. Once it's made, reinforce the decision with the patient, and ask all the health-team members to enforce it consistently.

Conclusion

When you care for patients who are mentally incapacitated or developmentally disabled, you must remember this: *They do not have any less legal protection than the rest of society has.* In fact, often the law covers these patients' rights in extra detail to ensure that they receive the proper care and treatment that they're due. As a nurse, your responsibility is to provide that care and treatment skillfully, safely, and humanely.

The patient who is a suspected criminal

Suppose you're asked to care for an injured suspect who's accompanied by police. Because the police need evidence, they ask you to give them not only the patient's belongings but also a sample of his blood. Should you comply?

If he's under arrest, you can legally handle his belongings and take the blood sample for evidence (with a doctor's order, of course). If he *isn't* under arrest, be careful. Make sure a valid search warrant is in effect before you proceed. If you don't, the patient may be able to sue you for invasion of privacy as well as assault and battery. Here's another consideration: If you assemble the requested evidence without a search warrant, the evidence

may be inadmissible in court.

Also involved here is the suspect's right to be considered innocent until proven guilty. Despite his police guard, you have no business judging him. His guilt or innocence will be for the courts to decide.

Some constitutional rights

The Fourth Amendment to the U.S. Constitution provides that "the right of the people to be secure in their persons, houses, papers and effects, against unreasonable searches and seizures shall not be violated, and no warrants shall issue, but upon probable cause." Ironically, this means that every individual, even a suspected criminal, has a right to privacy, including a right to be free from intrusions that are made without search warrants. So the Fourth Amendment doesn't absolutely prohibit all searches and seizures, only unreasonable ones.

Even after conviction, an individual doesn't forfeit all constitutional rights. Among those retained is the Eighth Amendment's proscription against cruel and unusual punishment. This implies that prison officials and health-care workers must not deliberately ignore a prisoner's medical needs.

Probably the *exclusionary rule* is the most common rule affecting nurses in relation to suspected criminals and their victims. This rule stems from the Fourth Amendment's prohibition of unreasonable searches and seizures. In the landmark case of *Mapp v. Ohio* (1961), the U.S. Supreme Court held that evidence obtained through an unreasonable or unlawful search cannot be used against the person whose rights the search violated.

A search without a warrant isn't reasonable unless an arrest is involved. A law enforcement official may conduct a search without a warrant if it's incidental to an arrest and if it doesn't extend beyond the accused person's body or an immediate area where he could reach for a weapon. Generally, *a search may not precede an arrest* unless probable cause has been established. So if evidence obtained during a prearrest search is used to *provide* probable cause for the arrest, the courts will consider that an unreasonable search. Of course, if an accused person consents to a search, any evidence found would be considered admissible in court.

Evidence in plain view can be confiscated. As a nurse, if you find a gun, knife, drug, or other item that the suspect could use to harm himself or others, you have a right to remove it. You should, however, notify the hospital administration immediately and maintain control over the evidence until you can give it to an administrator or a law enforcement official.

In *Burdreau v. McDowell* (1921), the court said that Fourth Amendment protections applied only to governmental (such as police) action and not to searches conducted by private persons. Although several courts have criticized this rule, it has been repeatedly upheld.

In *State v. Perea* (1981), a nurse took a suspect's shirt for safekeeping, then turned it over to the police even though they hadn't requested it. The court allowed the shirt to be admitted as evidence. The reason: Since no governmental intrusion was involved, the suspect's Fourth Amendment right wasn't violated.

The case of *United States v. Winbush* (1970) produced a similar result. Here the court ruled that evidence found during a routine search of an unconscious patient's pockets was admissible because the purpose of the search was to obtain necessary identification and medical information.

Commonwealth v. Storella (1978) involved a bullet that a doctor removed during a medically necessary operation. After the operation, the doctor turned the bullet over to the police. The court allowed the bullet to be admitted as evidence because the doctor was acting according to good medical practice, and not as a state agent, in removing the bullet.

This doesn't mean, of course, that doctors (and nurses) have a right to become private police forces. Generally, searches that occur as part of medical care don't violate a suspect's rights. But searches made for the sole purpose of gathering evidence—especially if done at police request—very well may. Several courts have said that a suspect subjected to an illegal private search has a right to seek remedy against the unlawful searcher in a civil lawsuit. One such case was *Stone v. Commonwealth* (1967).

The major difference between U.S. and Canadian law regarding searches is that, in Canada, evidence obtained during an illegal search is still admissible in court. However, a police officer properly should have a search warrant before searching a suspected criminal to protect his rights.

Refusal to consent

Opinions differ as to whether a blood test, such as a blood alcohol test, is admissible in court if the person refused consent for the test. In *Schmerber v. California* (1966), the U.S. Supreme Court said that a blood extraction obtained without a warrant, incident to a lawful arrest, is not an unconstitutional search and seizure and is admissible evidence. Many courts have held this to mean that a blood sample must be drawn *after* the arrest to be admissible and must be drawn in a medically reasonable manner.

So when a suspect is pinned to the floor by two police officers while a doctor draws a blood sample (as in *People v. Kraft,* 1970), or when a suspect's broken arm is twisted while a policeman sits on him to force consent to a blood test (as in *State v. Riggins,* 1977), the courts have ruled the test results inadmissible. The courts have also ruled as inadmissible—and as violative of due process rights—evidence gained by untrained, nonhospital personnel who forcibly insert a nasogastric tube into a suspect to remove stomach contents (*Rochin v. California,* 1952).

Courts have admitted blood tests as evidence when the tests weren't drawn at police request but for medically necessary purposes, such as blood typing (*Commonwealth v. Gordon,* 1968). Some courts have also allowed blood work to be admitted as evidence when it was drawn for nontherapeutic reasons and voluntarily turned over to police (*Turner v. State,* 1975). Be careful, though. As with unlawful private searches, a doctor or nurse who does blood work without the patient's consent may be liable for committing battery, even if the patient is a suspected criminal and the blood work is *medically necessary.*

Many states have enacted so-called implied-consent laws as part of their motor vehicle laws. This means that by applying for a driver's license, a person implies his consent to submit to a blood alcohol test if he's arrested for drunken driving. Many of these laws state specifically that if an individual refuses to submit to the chemical test, it may not be given, *but* the driver then forfeits his license. Check to see whether such laws exist in your state, because a blood alcohol sample is inadmissible in court if it's been drawn without a suspect's consent.

Documenting your procedures

Needless to say, be careful and precise in documenting all your procedures when you care for a suspected criminal. Note any blood work done, and list all treatments and the patient's response to them.

If you turn anything over to the police or administration, record what it was and the name of the person you gave it to. Record a suspect's statements, too, but distinguish between those that are privileged and those that aren't. If a suspect says, "I wasted four cops tonight," that's not a privileged communication. But if he says, "I think I was shot in the leg by a cop," that relates directly to his medical care and is privileged.

Safeguarding evidence

Before any evidence can be admissible in court, the court must have some guarantee of where, and how, it was gathered. Someone must account for evidence from the moment you collect it until it appears in court. You can't leave it unattended, where it might be tampered with.

If you discover evidence, mark it in some way. Before doing so, however, check with a police officer or a forensic expert, so you don't destroy valuable information.

When a suspect dies, most states provide that the coroner can claim the body. Police are free to gather any evidence that will not mutilate the body. A dead body has no constitutional rights, so no rights are violated by a search.

Working in a prison setting

If you work in a prison hospital or infirmary, remember the Eighth Amendment's prohibition against cruel and unusual punishments.

The U.S. Supreme Court, in *Estelle v. Gamble* (1976), stated that the Eighth Amendment prohibits more than physically barbarous punishment. The amendment embodies "broad and idealistic concepts of dignity, civilized standards, humanity, and decency against which we must evaluate penal measures."

The state has an obligation to provide medical care for those it imprisons. The Court concluded that: "deliberate indifference to serious medical needs of prisoners constitutes the unnecessary and wanton infliction of pain proscribed by the Eighth Amendment. This is true whether the indifference is manifested by prison doctors in response to a prisoner's needs or by prison personnel in intentionally denying or delaying access to medical care or intentionally interfering with the treatment once prescribed."

In *Ramos v. Lamm* (1980), the court outlined several ways in which prison officials show deliberate indifference to prisoners' medical needs:

• preventing an inmate from receiving recommended treatment

• denying access to medical personnel capable of evaluating the need for treatment

• allowing repeated acts of negligence that disclose a pattern of conduct by prison health staff

• allowing such severe deficiencies in staffing, facilities, equipment, or procedures to exist so that inmates are effectively denied access to adequate medical care.

Working daily with prisoners is difficult and demanding, both professionally and emotionally. Along with exhibiting a host of other unpleasant behaviors, prisoners can be abusive, manipulative, and angry. In spite of this, health-care professionals can't forget their ethical and legal duty to provide quality care.

Nurses working in a prison setting should be aware that the doctrine of "respondeat superior" does not apply to prison cases. The nurse supervisor or manager cannot be held responsible for accusations of "cruel and unusual punishment" unless she has personally acted to deprive the prisoner of medical care (*Vinnedge v. Gibbs*, 1977).

Several courts have stated that individuals have a constitutional right to privacy based on a high regard for human dignity and self-determination. This means a competent adult may refuse medical care, even lifesaving treatments. For instance, in *Lane v. Candura* (1978), an appellate court upheld the right of a competent adult to refuse a leg amputation that would have saved her life.

A suspected criminal may refuse unwarranted bodily invasions. However, an arrested suspect or convicted criminal does not have the same right to refuse lifesaving measures. In *Commissioner of Correction v. Myers* (1979), a prisoner with renal failure refused hemodialysis unless he was moved to a minimum security prison. The court disagreed, saying that although the defendant's imprisonment did not divest him of his right to privacy or his interest in maintaining his bodily integrity, it did impose limitations on those constitutional rights.

As a practical matter, inform your hospital administration anytime a patient refuses lifesaving treatments. In the case of a suspect or prisoner, notify law enforcement authorities as well.

Conclusion
Caring for a suspected criminal presents some special problems that deserve close attention. Whenever you're in this situation, be sure to check your hospital's policy on caring for suspected criminals (if one exists) and follow its guidelines carefully.

Your responsibility for a patient's living will

When a legally competent person draws up a living will, he declares the steps he wants or doesn't want taken when he's terminally ill. The will doesn't apply to initial treatment decisions; it applies only to decisions that will be made after a terminally ill patient is comatose and has no reasonable possibility of recovery. Generally, a living will authorizes the attending doctor to withhold or discontinue lifesaving procedures.

The will is called *living* because its provisions take effect before death. By clearly

stating his wishes regarding terminal-illness procedures, the patient also helps relieve any guilt his family and the health-care team might otherwise feel for having done too little (or too much) to keep him alive.

Living wills stem from action by the public, not by the medical community. Persons active in promoting living wills are often part of a "right-to-die" or "quality-of-life" movement.

State legislatures have recognized the movement's importance. In every state, a living will is considered a legal—but not necessarily legally binding—statement of the patient's wishes. California, in 1976, was the first state to adopt a living-will law (also called a natural death law). Currently, only 22 states and the District of Columbia have laws specifically governing living wills. These laws help guarantee that the patient's wishes will be carried out.

The health team's responsibility
In four of the states with living-will laws, and in the District of Columbia, the laws make living wills binding on doctors and impose penalties for noncompliance. Many of the states impose no penalties for noncompliance, and several make the wills advisory only. (See *Living-Will Laws*, pages 148 to 155.)

What living-will laws do
Generally, living-will laws address questions such as these:
• Who may execute a living will?
• When does a living will apply?
• Who's immune from liability for following a living will's directives?
• What documentation is required?
• How long is a living will valid?
• When and how should a living will be executed? (In California, for example, a living will is binding only if executed after a terminal-illness diagnosis has been made.)
• How can a living will be rescinded?

In the remaining states without living-will laws, a doctor may choose to follow or not to follow the will's provisions.

Even if the doctor must obey the living will, or would like to, he faces real difficulties in determining when it should apply. The typical wording in living wills isn't

Living-Will Laws

STATE	TESTATOR REQUIREMENTS	WITNESS REQUIREMENTS	LENGTH OF EFFECTIVENESS
Alabama	Adult of sound mind	Two witnesses, excluding relatives, heirs, persons who are financially responsible for patient	Effective until revoked
Arkansas	Adult of sound mind; proxy permitted for minor or incompetent person	Two witnesses; will must be notarized	Effective until revoked
California	Adult of sound mind	Two witnesses, excluding relatives, heirs, patient's doctor, and employees where patient is hospitalized	5 years
Delaware	Adult of sound mind	Two witnesses, excluding relatives, heirs, employees where patient is hospitalized, and persons who are financially responsible for patient	Effective until revoked
District of Columbia	Age 18 or older and of sound mind	Two witnesses, excluding spouse, heirs, relatives, patient's doctor, employees where patient is hospitalized, and persons who are financially responsible for patient	Effective until revoked
Florida	Competent adult	Two witnesses, one of whom is not a spouse or blood relative	Effective until revoked

Currently, 22 states and the District of Columbia have living-will laws. This chart shows you the details of each state's law.

LEGAL STATUS	IMMUNITY FROM LEGAL ACTION FOR OBEYING WILL	PENALTY FOR NOT OBEYING WILL	PENALTY FOR DESTRUCTION, FORGERY, CONCEALMENT, OR FALSE REPORTING
Not binding	Doctor, licensed health-care professional, medical care facility or employee	No penalty; doctor "shall permit" transfer to another doctor	Destroying will or forging revocation is a misdemeanor; forging will or concealing revocation is a felony
Not specified	Any person and health facility	No penalty	No penalty
Not binding unless executed 14 days after diagnosis of terminal illness	Doctor, licensed health professional acting under doctor's direction, and health facility	Charged with unprofessional conduct unless doctor transfers patient	Destroying will is a misdemeanor; forging or concealing revocation, causing death, is homicide
Not clear	Doctors, nurses	No penalty	Forcing patient to sign is a misdemeanor; any action that falsely implies patient wanted to prolong his life is a felony
Binding	Doctor, licensed health-care professional, health facility, or employee	Unprofessional conduct if he fails to transfer patient to doctor who will comply	Destroying will or forging revocation brings a fine and a jail term; forging will or concealing revocation, causing death, is homicide
Binding	Doctor, or person acting under doctor's direction, and health facility	No penalty	All above are felonies

(continued)

Living-Will Laws *(continued)*

STATE	TESTATOR REQUIREMENTS	WITNESS REQUIREMENTS	LENGTH OF EFFECTIVENESS
Georgia	Adult 18 years or older and of sound mind	Two witnesses, excluding relatives, heirs, patient's doctor, employees of doctor or of facility where patient is hospitalized, persons who are financially responsible for patient's medical care. If signed in a health-care facility, chief of staff or medical director must also witness	7 years
Idaho	Terminally ill adult	Two witnesses, excluding relatives, heirs, patient's doctor, and employees where patient is hospitalized	5 years
Illinois	Individual of sound mind, at age of majority or emancipated minor	Two witnesses, not relatives, heirs, or financially responsible for patient's medical care	Effective until revoked
Kansas	Adult of sound mind	Two witnesses, excluding relatives, heirs, patient's doctor, and employees where patient is hospitalized	Effective until revoked
Louisiana	Adult of sound mind	Two witnesses, excluding relatives, heirs, patient's doctor and his employees, and employees where patient is hospitalized	Effective until revoked

LEGAL STATUS	IMMUNITY FROM LEGAL ACTION FOR OBEYING WILL	PENALTY FOR NOT OBEYING WILL	PENALTY FOR DESTRUCTION, FORGERY, CONCEALMENT, OR FALSE REPORTING
Binding	Doctor, health facility, employee, or agent	No penalty; doctor must notify kin, make good faith effort to transfer, and permit kin to transfer	Concealment, obliteration, forcing person to sign, or false witnessing is a misdemeanor; forging will or concealing revocation, causing or hastening death, is homicide
Not specified	Doctor and health facility	No penalty	No penalty
Binding	Doctor, licensed health-care professional, medical care facility, or employee	No penalty, but doctor must make prompt arrangements to transfer patient	Concealment, obliteration, forgery of revocation makes one civilly liable; forging null or concealing revocation, causing or hastening death, is voluntary manslaughter
Binding	Doctor, licensed health professional, health facility, or employee	Charged with unprofessional conduct unless doctor transfers patient	Destroying will or forging revocation is a misdemeanor; forging will or concealing revocation is a felony
Binding	Doctor, person acting under doctor's direction, and health facility	No penalty, but doctor must make reasonable effort to transfer	Concealment or obliteration makes one civilly liable; forging null or concealing revocation, and hastening death may subject one to prosecution *(continued)*

Living-Will Laws *(continued)*

STATE	TESTATOR REQUIREMENTS	WITNESS REQUIREMENTS	LENGTH OF EFFECTIVENESS
Mississippi	Adult 18 years or older and mentally competent	Two witnesses, excluding relatives, heirs, doctor and his employees	Effective until revoked
Nevada	Adult of sound mind	Two witnesses, excluding relatives, heirs, patient's doctor, and employees where patient is hospitalized	Effective until revoked
New Mexico	Adult of sound mind; proxy permitted for minor or incompetent person	Same number of witnesses as for regular will; court must certify a minor's living will	Effective until revoked
North Carolina	Competent person; no age provision specified	Two witnesses, excluding relatives, heirs, patient's doctor, and employees where patient is hospitalized; will must be notarized	Effective until revoked
Oregon	Adult of sound mind	Two witnesses, excluding relatives, heirs, patient's doctor, and employees where patient is hospitalized	Effective until revoked
Texas	Adult of sound mind	Two witnesses, excluding relatives, heirs, patient's doctor, and employees where patient is hospitalized	Effective until revoked

LEGAL STATUS	IMMUNITY FROM LEGAL ACTION FOR OBEYING WILL	PENALTY FOR NOT OBEYING WILL	PENALTY FOR DESTRUCTION, FORGERY, CONCEALMENT, OR FALSE REPORTING
Not binding	Doctor	No penalty, but doctor must cooperate with transfer	Forgery of declaration or concealment of revocation, and hastening death is a felony
Not binding	Doctor, person acting under doctor's direction, and health facility	No penalty	Destroying will is a misdemeanor; forging will or concealing revocation, causing death, is murder
Binding	Doctors, employees of health facility, and health facility	No penalty, but physician must take "appropriate steps" to transfer	Destroying will, concealing revocation, or forgery is a felony
Not binding	Licensed health professional and health facility	No penalty	No penalty
Binding	Doctor, licensed health professional acting under doctor's direction, and health facility	No penalty, but doctor who disagrees with will must make a reasonable effort to transfer patient to another medical facility	Prohibited, but no penalties
Binding when executed after diagnosis	Doctor, licensed health professional acting under doctor's direction, and health facility	Charged with unprofessional conduct unless doctor transfers patient	Destroying will is a misdemeanor; forging will or concealing revocation, causing death, is criminal homicide

(continued)

Living-Will Laws *(continued)*

STATE	TESTATOR REQUIREMENTS	WITNESS REQUIREMENTS	LENGTH OF EFFECTIVENESS
Vermont	Adult age 18 or older	Two witnesses, excluding spouse, heirs, creditors, patient's doctor and other medical personnel under his supervision	Effective until revoked
Virginia	Competent adult	Two witnesses; oral declaration requires doctor and two witnesses	Effective until revoked
Washington	Adult of sound mind	Two witnesses, excluding relatives, heirs, patient's doctor, and employees where patient is hospitalized	Effective until revoked
West Virginia	Adult 18 years or older of sound mind	Two witnesses 18 years or older, excluding relatives, heirs, doctor, health facility where patient is hospitalized, or person financially responsible for patient's medical care; notarized	Effective until revoked
Wisconsin	Adult 18 years and of sound mind	Two witnesses excluding relative, heir, doctor, health-care facility where patient is hospitalized or its employees	5 years
Wyoming	Adult of sound mind	Two adult witnesses, excluding relatives, heirs, or person financially responsible for patient's medical care	Effective until revoked

LEGAL STATUS	IMMUNITY FROM LEGAL ACTION FOR OBEYING WILL	PENALTY FOR NOT OBEYING WILL	PENALTY FOR DESTRUCTION, FORGERY, CONCEALMENT, OR FALSE REPORTING
Binding	Doctor, nurse, health professional, and health facility	No penalty; doctor must inform patient and/or assist in selecting another doctor	No penalty
Binding	Doctor, person acting under doctor's direction, and health facility	No penalty	Destroying, concealing, or falsely reporting revocation is a felony
Binding	Doctor, licensed health professional acting under doctor's direction, and health facility	No penalty, but doctor who disagrees with will must make a reasonable effort to transfer patient	Destroying will is a misdemeanor; concealing revocation or forging will, causing death, is first-degree murder
Binding	Doctor, licensed health-care professional, health facility or employee	No penalty; shall transfer patient	All above are felonies
Not binding	Doctor, in-patient health-care facility, or health-care professional under doctor's direction	No penalty, but unprofessional conduct if doctor does not make good faith attempt to transfer	Obliteration means fine or jail; forgery of declaration or concealment of revocation is homicide
Binding	Doctor, licensed health-care professional, health facility or employee	No penalty; shall attempt to transfer patient	Obliteration of declaration or forgery of revocation is a misdemeanor; forgery of declaration or concealing revocation, and hastening death is a felony

much help. What, for example, is a "reasonable expectation of recovery?" And what is a "heroic" or "extraordinary" measure? These ambiguities and the difficulty in clarifying them (particularly before the situation actually arises) are among the reasons why legislatures have been reluctant to make living wills binding.

If doctors, nurses, and other health-care providers follow the wishes expressed in a living will authorized by law, they're generally immune from civil and criminal liability. In states without living-will laws, immunity is not assured. Because of the complexities involved, no matter which state you work in, you'll do well to check your hospital's policy-and-procedures manual and get advice from your hospital's legal department when a living will appears in a patient's record.

In Canada, not one province has enacted legislation covering living wills. Nor are any likely to do so, because the Canadian Law Reform Commission has rejected the living-will approach. So the status of living wills in Canada is uncertain. However, the commission has proposed changes in Canadian laws that would help recognize statements in a living will as accurately representing the patient's wishes, if he is unable to speak for himself.

May children make living wills?

Although minors can't make valid testamentary wills, and adults can't make such wills for them, living wills are another matter. In Arkansas, Louisiana, and New Mexico, adults are authorized to make living wills for their minor children.

Of course, parents don't normally plan for their child to die, so most are unlikely to make a living will before a child's terminal illness is diagnosed. Even then, a living will is usually legally unnecessary. If the parents and the child agree that no extraordinary means should be used to prolong life, or if the child is too young to understand, the parents have the legal right to act for the child. They can require that the health-care team not use extraordinary means to prolong his life. The same principle also applies in reverse: if the child wants to die but the parents want him treated, the parents' wishes prevail.

If a terminally ill adolescent doesn't want extraordinary treatment but his parents do, and the adolescent has written a living will, a doctor or hospital may use the will to petition a court in his behalf. Even though the will itself is legally invalid because it was written by a minor, its very existence may prompt the court to consult the adolescent and, in its ruling, grant the patient his wishes.

When a mentally incompetent person wants to make a living will

Of the 22 states (and the District of Columbia) that have living-will laws, only Arkansas authorizes a competent adult to make a living will on behalf of an adult who's not mentally competent. The remaining states allow only competent adults to prepare such wills for themselves. But even in these states, a living will may influence a court to grant the wishes of an adult whose mental capacity is in question.

The living will from another state or country

U.S. law applies to foreign citizens treated in the United States. This means a foreign citizen may execute a living will while in the United States, and it must be honored if executed in a state with a legally binding living-will law. A state without a living-will law may honor it, but it isn't required to.

What if a patient produces a living will executed in a foreign country? This situation is the equivalent of executing a living will in a state that doesn't have a living-will law. The patient's doctor may honor it, but the law doesn't require that he do so.

You may be wondering, what about a patient who executes a living will in one state and later finds himself terminally ill in another? If both states have living-will laws, the second state will honor the patient's living will if it has been properly prepared. A state without a living-will law may, but need not, honor a living will that was executed in another state.

The same general legal principle applies to U.S. citizens in Canada or in another foreign country. A foreign country's law applies to all persons, whether citizens of that country or not, and determines the extent to which a living will will be honored.

What invalidates a living will?
A living will needn't be honored if it's been revoked, if it's out of date, if the patient asks that it be disregarded, or if the patient asks for treatment that disagrees with statements in his living will.

In the states with living-will laws, all but Arkansas provide procedures for revocation. The procedures include deliberate destruction of the document, written revocation, and the patient's statement that he intends to revoke it.

In the states that have living-will laws, the period of time before it becomes invalidated varies. If the patient's family and attending medical personnel find that the patient made the living will many years ago and his life circumstances have changed substantially since then, they may have legal justification for disregarding the will. For this reason, publishers of living-will forms suggest reviewing the will yearly, revising it if necessary, and re-dating and re-signing it.

Remember, if a patient tells his doctor to proceed with treatment that contradicts the living will, the patient's action effectively revokes the will.

Can the family's wishes prevail?
In a state with a living-will law, the patient's family can't contradict it unless they can prove the will is invalid. Some of these states provide penalties for concealing a patient's living will or for falsely reporting that it's been revoked.

In a state that doesn't have a living-will law, the health team or a court will consider both a patient's living will and his family's wishes before deciding on treatment or nontreatment.

Drafting a living will
Like all legal documents, a living will must be written, signed, and witnessed. States with living-will laws specify the execution requirements; in states without laws, the patient may use a standardized form or have his attorney design one. (Anyone can obtain forms from Concern for Dying or The Society for the Right to Die, two groups that currently share offices at 250

W. 57th St., New York, N.Y., 10107.) Although it's not required, a patient may want to file copies of his living will in his medical record, with his doctor, and with family members who would be with him in the event of a terminal illness.

As a nurse, you may be asked to help a patient write a living will or to witness one. You may help him write it or refer him to someone else for help. If he asks you to witness the will, check to see if your state has laws that restrict you from doing this by referring to *Living-Will Laws,* pages 148 to 155. If it doesn't, ask your nursing supervisor for the procedure you should follow. Document the patient's actions in your nurses' notes, describing factually the circumstances under which the will was drawn up and signed.

Oral living wills
Patients most often make oral statements expressing their wishes about further medical treatment as follows:

Before terminal illness. When a patient has made his treatment wishes known to his family and doctor in advance, they will usually respect his wishes even if he later becomes comatose or otherwise incompetent. But if the doctor and the family disagree about what is best for the terminally ill, incompetent patient, they may have to settle the dispute in court.

Another possible alternative may be that your state's living-will law has a provision that implicitly permits another person to make medical decisions for an incapacitated (incompetent) patient. Delaware's living-will law is one such example.

Nevertheless, authority to appoint a proxy to act after a person becomes incompetent does exist in several states that have laws authorizing "durable powers of attorney." (*Durable* means that the proxy's authority to act continues after the patient is incapacitated.)

You can alert patients that durable-power-of-attorney laws exist (in certain states). And you can urge them to discuss their desires about treatment with a proxy decision maker.

During terminal illness. Every competent adult has the right to refuse medical treatment for himself, including the use of extraordinary means. If a terminally ill patient tells a doctor or nurse to discontinue extraordinary efforts, his wishes are binding.

If a patient tells you his wishes about dying, first write what he says in your nurses' notes, using his exact words as much as possible. Next, describe the context of the discussion—for example, was the patient in pain, or had he just been informed of a terminal illness? Be sure you also tell the patient's doctor about the discussion. Remember, *specifically stated oral wills are not legally enforceable,* although a patient's stated refusal of treatment is binding. Oral wills *should* be respected, however, as guidelines to how the patient feels about his treatment.

When you find a living will in a patient's chart

What do you do when a patient is admitted to your care and you discover a properly executed living will attached to his chart?

First, notify your supervisor and the patient's doctor. To protect yourself, document the existence of the living will and the fact that you notified the patient's doctor about it. Include in your documentation the date the will was signed and the names of the people who signed it.

Check your nursing policy manual, too, to see what it says about living wills. If you can't find anything there, try your hospital's policy-and-procedures manual. The hospital's legal department should be able to advise you as well, particularly about applicable state laws.

(Note: If you don't find a stated policy about living wills in either your nursing manual or your hospital's manual, consider organizing a committee to write a policy. Be sure to include representatives from the departments of nursing, medicine, risk management, legal affairs, and from hospital administration on the committee. If your hospital has an ethics committee or an intensive-care committee, you may also invite their participation.)

Next, inform the patient's doctor about the will. Ask your nursing supervisor to inform the hospital administration and the legal affairs department. Make sure (with the patient's permission) that the family knows about the will; if they don't, show them a copy.

If the patient is able to talk, discuss the will with him, especially if it contains terms that need further definition. As always, objectively document your actions and findings in the patient's record.

Beyond these actions, your responsibilities for a patient's living will will be determined by the circumstances involved—including the family's and doctor's responses to the will. If you feel strongly about the patient's right to have his wishes followed, try to talk further with those involved to come up with a unified plan of care.

Conclusion

If implementing a living will conflicts with your personal ethics or beliefs, you may wish to discuss the matter with a clinical nurse specialist, your nursing supervisor, a nursing administrator, the hospital chaplain, or a hospital administrator. Then, after talking over your feelings with one of them, if you're still unable to accept the idea, you can ask for reassignment to another patient. Chances are your request will be honored and no disciplinary action will be taken against you.

Selected References

"Abused and Neglected Children in America: A Study of Alternative Policies," *Harvard Educational Review* 143:559, November 1973.

Annas, George J. *The Rights of Doctors, Nurses and Allied Health Professionals.* Cambridge, Mass.: Ballinger Publishing Co., 1983.

Annas, George J. "When Patients are Prisoners They Lose Their Right to Refuse Life-Maintaining Treatments," *Nursing Law Ethics* 1:3, February 1980.

Beauchamp, Tom L., and Childress, James F. *Principles of Biomedical Ethics, 2nd ed.* New York: Oxford University Press, 1983.

Brown, G.C. "Medication Errors: A Case Study," *Hospitals* 53:61, October 1979.

Cazalas, Mary W. *Nursing and the Law,* 3rd ed. Rockville, Md.: Aspen Systems Corp., 1979.

Creighton, Helen. *Law Every Nurse Should Know,* 4th ed. Philadelphia: W.B. Saunders Co., 1981.

Driscoll, Dorothy L., et al. *The Nursing Process in Later Maturity.* Englewood Cliffs, N.J.: Prentice-Hall, 1980.

Grane, Nancy B. "How to Reduce Your Risk of a Lawsuit," *NursingLife* 3(1):17-20, January/February 1983.

Grosser, L.R. "All Nurses Can Be Involved in Teaching Patient and Family," *AORN Journal* 33:217-18, February 1981.

Hemelt, M., and Mackert, M. *Dynamics of Law in Nursing and Health Care,* 2nd ed. Reston, Va.: Reston Publishing Co., 1982.

Leiba, P.A. "Management of Violent Patients," *Nursing Times* 2(76):101-4, October 1980.

Lofstedt, Carol R. *Mereness Essentials of Psychiatric Nursing: Learning and Activity Guide.* St. Louis: C.V. Mosby Co., 1982.

Mikolaj, P.J. "Hospital Association Determines Nature of Closed Claims in State." *Hospitals* 52:53, February 1978.

"A Patient's Bill of Rights... American Hospital Association," *Journal of Nursing Care* 14:17, March 1981.

Porter, Sharon. "Working with a Killer," *Nursing81* 11(1):136, January 1981.

"Principles of Hospital Liability," in *Hospital Law Manual: Administrator's and Attorney's Set.* Rockville, Md.: Aspen Systems Corp., 1981.

Robertson, John A., and American Civil Liberties Union. *Rights of the Critically Ill.* Cambridge, Mass.: Ballinger Publishing Co., 1983.

Robinson, Lisa. *Psychiatric Nursing as a Human Experience, 3rd ed.* Philadelphia: W.B. Saunders Co., 1983.

Wiemerslage, D. "Professional Negligence," *Critical Care* Update 9(11):21-22, November 1982.

4

Your Legal Risks While Off Duty

When you're on duty, you have ways to check on the legal limits of your practice and the legal risks you may face. That's because you have plenty of guidelines, including professional policies and rules, statutory law, and common law.

But what about when you're off duty? Very few professional or legal guidelines exist. So the legal limits of your off-duty actions aren't clear-cut. Fortunately, though, your risk of liability is low; relatively few lawsuits are brought against nurses for off-duty actions.

Understanding legal issues
Of course, you do run some legal risks. So you should understand the legal issues surrounding nursing actions off duty. This chapter covers those issues in four key areas:
• "Good Samaritan acts"
• "When you're asked for health-care advice"
• "Donating nursing services," when you volunteer your nursing skills without compensation
• "Disasters."

Each entry also distinguishes between what the law requires and what it allows. You'll learn when your nurse practice act applies and when it doesn't apply to your off-duty actions. You'll also find a common theme running through the four entries: the general silence of the law, except for Good Samaritan acts, on the subject of off-duty nursing.

As you read these entries, you'll notice that relatively few legal cases are discussed. That's simply because relatively few exist.

If only a few legal cases exist and the chances of being named in a lawsuit are fairly slim, why have a chapter on your legal risks? Well, for one thing, the few court cases that do exist make important legal distinctions. And most states do have *some* laws that cover some of the care you provide while off duty. So whether you provide care regularly when off duty or just give advice to your next-door neighbor occasionally, this chapter will tell you what you need to know to stay on sound legal footing.

Good Samaritan acts

If you come upon an automobile accident in which a motorist is injured, what should you do? As a nurse, your conscience and compassion prompt you to offer your assistance in any health-care emergency. But you know how vulnerable nurses are to malpractice lawsuits. So while you're naturally inclined to help, you can't help thinking, "Could I get in legal trouble in this situation?"

Because you may experience this ambivalence, you need to know about Good Samaritan acts. Why? These acts address your responsibility and risk whenever you're in a position to use your nursing skills at an accident scene. This entry will explain the extent and limits of protection that Good Samaritan acts offer you.

Questions Nurses Ask about the Good Samaritan Acts

Q. Am I covered by the Good Samaritan act if I respond to an emergency outside the hospital while I'm on duty?
A. That depends on two things: the wording of the act in your state, and court decisions, if any, that interpret that act.

Q. If I'm from out of state but I decide to help in an emergency, would that state's Good Samaritan act apply to me?
A. If that state's act says it applies to "any person," you're covered. If the act specifically states that it applies only to "nurses," you're not; "nurse" in a law or act usually means an RN, LPN, or LVN licensed in that state.

Q. Does the Good Samaritan act apply if I accept money from the person I've helped?
A. The act usually doesn't apply in such a situation because, by accepting money, you've established a professional relationship with the person you've helped.

Q. When does my responsibility end toward the person I've helped?
A. Statutory law doesn't address this subject, but the courts have. Generally, common, or court-made, law says your responsibility ends:
● when the emergency ends—that is, when you're absolutely certain that the victim is no longer in danger.
● when an authorized rescue or other medical service takes over for you.
● when the victim is pronounced dead.

Q. If a doctor and I respond to the same emergency, does the Good Samaritan act provide us with the same coverage?
A. Not necessarily. In some states, the Good Samaritan act for nurses is completely different from the Good Samaritan act for doctors. Contact your state's board of nursing to find out what's true for your state.

Do you have a legal duty to rescue?

Let's return to that fictional automobile accident scene. You quickly realize that you have three options:
● You can help the accident victim at the scene.
● You can pass the scene, stop at the nearest phone, and call for an ambulance, emergency medical service (EMS), or other authorized rescue service.
● You can pass the scene and *make no attempt to call for help*.

In almost every state, you have the legal right to choose any of these options. Why does the law give you so much leeway? In the countries that inherited British common law, including the United States and Canada, nurses have no duty to rescue

anyone. The only people with a legal duty to rescue are those who perform rescues as part of their jobs, such as firemen, EMS workers, and a few other groups, such as people who operate public transportation.

As a nurse, therefore, your decision whether or not to help is strictly voluntary and personal. But if you do decide to help the accident victim, do any laws protect you? The answer is yes. In fact, two kinds of law give you protection: common (or court-made) law and statutory (or legislature-made) law—in this situation, the Good Samaritan acts. (*See Questions Nurses Ask about the Good Samaritan Acts.*)

Good Samaritan Acts by State and by Province

	Alabama	Alaska	Arizona	Arkansas	California	Colorado	Connecticut	Delaware	
Date of act or last amendment	1981	1976	1978	1979	1984	1983	1983	1974	
Covers "any person"		●	●	●		●		●	
Covers in-state nurses only	●				●		●		
Includes out-of-state nurses in coverage			●			●		●	
Requires acts in good faith	●		●	●	●	●		●	
Covers only gratuitous services	●		●	●		●	●	●	
Covers aid at scene of emergency, accident, disaster	●	●	●	●	●	●	●	●	
Covers only roadside accidents									
Covers emergencies outside place of employment, course of employment					●		●		
Covers emergencies outside of hospital, doctor's office, or other places having medical equipment									
Protects against failure to provide or arrange for further medical treatment	●	●	●					●	
Covers transportation from the scene of the emergency to a destination for further medical treatment									
Specifically mentions that acts of gross negligence or willful or wanton misconduct are not covered		●	●	●	●		●	●	
Includes "duty to rescue" statute									

Here's a handy chart you can use to familiarize yourself with your state's or province's Good Samaritan act. You should, however, check with your board of nursing to make sure your state or province hasn't passed any amendments since 1984 that would affect how this law pertains to your practice.

	Dist. Columbia	Florida	Georgia	Hawaii	Idaho	Illinois	Indiana	Iowa	Kansas	Kentucky	Louisiana	Maine	Maryland
	1977	1978	1962	1980	1980	1980	1973	1982	1977	1980	1964	1977	1983
	•	•	•	•	•		•	•				•	•
									•	•	•		
	•					•			•				
	•	•	•	•	•	•	•	•			•		
	•	•	•	•		•	•	•	•	•		•	•
	•	•	•	•	•	•	•	•	•	•	•	•	•
	•	•							•	•			
		•	•				•				•		
					•								•
	•			•	•	•	•	•	•	•	•	•	•

(continued)

Good Samaritan Acts by State and by Province *(continued)*

	Massachusetts	Michigan	Minnesota	Mississippi	Missouri	Montana	Nebraska	Nevada
Date of act or last amendment	1980	1978	1983	1979	1979	1974	1971	1975
Covers "any person"			●		●	●	●	●
Covers in-state nurses only								
Includes out-of-state nurses in coverage	●	●		●	●			●
Requires acts in good faith	●			●	●	●		●
Covers only gratuitous services	●		●		●	●	●	●
Covers aid at scene of emergency, accident, disaster	●	●	●	●	●	●	●	●
Covers only roadside accidents								
Covers emergencies outside place of employment, course of employment								
Covers emergencies outside of hospital, doctor's office, or other places having medical equipment			●					
Protects against failure to provide or arrange for further medical treatment	●						●	●
Covers transportation from the scene of the emergency to a destination for further medical treatment			●	●				
Specifically mentions that acts of gross negligence or willful or wanton misconduct are not covered		●	●	●	●	●	●	●
Includes "duty to rescue" statute			●					

	New Hampshire	New Jersey	New Mexico	New York	North Carolina	North Dakota	Ohio	Oklahoma	Oregon	Pennsylvania	Rhode Island	South Carolina	South Dakota
	1977	1968	1972	1975	1975	1981	1981	1979	1981	1978	1982	1964	1976
	●	●	●		●	●	●	●				●	
			●	●		●							
	●	●						●	●	●	●		●
	●	●	●			●		●		●		●	●
	●		●	●			●	●	●		●	●	
	●	●	●	●	●	●	●	●	●	●	●	●	●
					●								
					●						●		
				●			●			●	●		
												●	
	●												
	●		●	●	●	●	●	●	●	●	●	●	

(continued)

Good Samaritan Acts by State and by Province *(continued)*

	Tennessee	Texas	Utah	Vermont	Virginia	Washington	West Virginia	Wisconsin	
Date of act or last amendment	1976	1977	1979	1968	1984	1975	1967	1977	
Covers "any person"	●	●		●	●	●	●	●	
Covers in-state nurses only			●						
Includes out-of-state nurses in coverage									
Requires acts in good faith	●	●	●		●	●	●	●	
Covers only gratuitous services	●	●		●	●	●	●	●	
Covers aid at scene of emergency, accident, disaster	●	●	●	●	●	●	●	●	
Covers only roadside accidents									
Covers emergencies outside place of employment, course of employment		●						●	
Covers emergencies outside of hospital, doctor's office, or other places having medical equipment								●	
Protects against failure to provide or arrange for further medical treatment	●								
Covers transportation from the scene of the emergency to a destination for further medical treatment						●	●		
Specifically mentions that acts of gross negligence or willful or wanton misconduct are not covered	●	●			●		●		
Includes "duty to rescue" statute				●				●	

	Wyoming	Alberta	Brit. Columbia	Manitoba	New Brunswick	Newfoundland	Nova Scotia	Ontario	Prince Edward Is.	Quebec	NW Territories	Saskatchewan	Yukon Terr.
	1977	1970	1979			1971	1969					1978	1976
		●	●			●	*					●	●
			●										
	●												
	●		●			●	●						
	●	●	●	NO GOOD SAMARITAN ACT	NO GOOD SAMARITAN ACT	●	●	NO GOOD SAMARITAN ACT	NO GOOD SAMARITAN ACT	NO GOOD SAMARITAN ACT	NO GOOD SAMARITAN ACT	●	●
			●										
		●				●	●					●	
	●	●	●				●					●	●
	●												

* Doctors only

Being a Good Samaritan: Some Do's and Don'ts

When you stop at an accident scene to offer your assistance, you must still observe professional standards of nursing care, even in such an unsuitable setting. To reduce your malpractice risk, follow these guidelines:

DO's

- Care for the victim in the vehicle if you can do so safely.
- Move him if he's in danger and if conditions at the scene permit.
- Keep the victim's airway patent.
- Stop his bleeding.
- Keep him warm.
- Determine his level of consciousness.
- Determine the possibility of fractures.
- Ask him where he feels pain.

DON'Ts

- Don't move the victim needlessly.
- Don't try to straighten his arms and legs.
- Don't carry him or force him to walk.
- Don't speculate about who's the guilty party in the accident.
- Don't allow unskilled personnel to attend or treat the victim.
- Don't leave the scene until *skilled* personnel arrive to assume care of the victim.
- Don't give the injured person's personal property to anyone except the police or family members.

How common law protects you

Common law is the cumulative result of many court decisions over the years. According to common law, to win a malpractice lawsuit against you a patient must prove that you owed him a duty, that you breached that duty in some way, that he was harmed, and that your breach of duty caused the harm.

Let's apply these legal rules to the auto accident situation:

Duty: As long as you pass the scene—whether or not you stop down the road to call for help—you don't owe the victim any legal duty. He's not your patient, and he can't make any legal claim on your professional services. (Remember, ethical claims aren't at issue here.) But just by stopping your car at the scene, you *do* incur a legal duty. Once you do that, you can't leave the victim until he's being cared for by another health-care professional with at least as much training as you have or until the police order you from the scene. Why? Because when you stop your car, you give the appearance to other potential rescuers that you'll take care of the victim. At that point, you establish a nurse-

patient relationship. That means you owe him the normal duty you owe any patient—treatment that meets the standard of care of a reasonably prudent nurse in a similar situation.

Breach of duty: Let's assume that you've established the nurse-patient relationship because you've stopped to help. If you use the same good judgment you show on the job, you're not likely to breach your duty just because you're dealing with an off-the-job problem in a less-than-ideal situation. But what if you do breach your duty?

Harm: If you perform an act below standard, the court will ask this key question: How has your act worsened the victim's condition? If what you did hasn't made the victim measurably worse, the court is likely to find that the harm committed doesn't warrant damages. In other words, your act must cause measurable harm for the court to consider you negligent.

Cause: The victim must prove the probability is better than 50% that your error caused his injuries. The courts historically have set the 50% figure as the standard. Since the typical victim has already suffered injuries from the accident, he may

Minimizing Your Legal Risks When Giving Advice: Some Do's and Don'ts

Do you know you're assuming legal risks when you give health-care advice to your friends? In the courts' view, even a casual conversation can sometimes establish a nurse-patient relationship, making you liable for the consequences of your advice. To help minimize these risks, keep these do's and don'ts in mind:

DO's	DON'Ts
• Find out if your professional liability insurance (or your employer's) provides you with off-the-job coverage. • Know whether your state's nurse practice act discusses giving advice to friends. • Only give advice within the confines of your nurse practice act, education, and experience. • Make sure the advice you give is up-to-date. Remember, you'll be judged on current nursing standards if your advice results in a lawsuit.	• Don't speculate about your friends' illnesses or ailments. • Don't suggest that friends change or ignore their doctors' orders. • Don't give any advice about medical care. • Don't offer any advice that, if wrong, could result in serious or permanent injury.

have a hard time proving that your error caused or worsened his injuries.

Why have the courts made it so difficult for the victim to prove you negligent at an accident scene? Because, through the years, the courts have tried to balance victims' rights to justice against society's need to encourage trained professionals to use their talents in emergencies.

But many health-care professionals feel that common law doesn't sufficiently reduce the likelihood that they'll be sued. For example, common law doesn't prevent a victim from pursuing a lengthy court battle against you—a battle that could cost you considerably in time, effort, and legal fees, even if you ultimately win. As a result, these health-care professionals have lobbied for a second, stronger protection, and almost all states have obliged by enacting Good Samaritan acts.

How Good Samaritan acts work

Good Samaritan acts encourage you to volunteer your services at an accident or an emergency scene. How? By limiting your liability for any service you render.

In effect, Good Samaritan acts offer you immunity from lawsuits when you help an accident victim as long as you don't intentionally or recklessly cause the patient injury. But keep in mind that no law can protect you if you commit an act that *seriously* violates the applicable standard of care.

Most Good Samaritan acts apply only to uncompensated rescue acts. If you charge or accept money for the service you render, the law usually says that you forfeit the special protections.

Also, Good Samaritan acts vary greatly from state to state. For example, some states limit the protection to nurses trained in cardiopulmonary resuscitation. Some acts specifically include nurses, and others—such as those in Florida and British Columbia—protect any person who offers help to a victim. In some states the Good Samaritan act includes only "practitioners of the healing arts," a phrase the court has usually limited to doctors and dentists. (To learn about the Good Samaritan act that applies to you, see *Good Samaritan Acts by State and by Province,* pages 162 to 167.)

How Good Samaritan acts are used

Regardless of the kind of Good Samaritan act your state has—if it has one at all—you should know that victims rarely sue Good Samaritans. And nurses have never had to invoke a Good Samaritan act as a defense. In effect, the common law so far has served as a deterrent.

Who, then, uses Good Samaritan acts? Ironically, auto accident victims sometimes try to claim that the acts create a duty for a nurse or doctor to respond to an accident scene. The courts have rejected this argument.

In some states, doctors being sued for malpractice have tried to use the Good Samaritan act as a defense. These doctors claim that the act protects them from liability in emergency situations, even for services they provided in a hospital. Doctors have tried this argument in California, with mixed results. But the argument won't work for nurses in California, because the Good Samaritan act that applies to nurses gives them liability protection only during emergencies "outside both the place and course" of their employment.

Further limitations of Good Samaritan acts

Most Good Samaritan acts protect you only if your error is "ordinary" negligence. The acts won't protect you if you're grossly negligent. What's the distinction? That's decided by the jury, who'll determine the degree of negligence. The court will always measure your error against the standard of care, which can vary from locality to locality. For example, what might be considered ordinary negligence in a rural Georgia nursing case might be considered gross negligence in Boston.

Besides your locality, the court will also take into consideration your training and experience to measure whether you've breached the standard of care. This means that RNs—even as Good Samaritans—are held to a higher standard than LPNs/LVNs.

Beyond the Good Samaritan principle

Three states have taken the Good Samaritan principle a step further—as have most European countries—by *requiring* potential rescuers to help a victim. Vermont's law, the first of its type in the United States, defines *rescuer* as any person who knows that another is exposed to grave physical harm. The law requires anyone—whether or not he's a Vermont resident—who can help a victim to do so, provided he won't then be putting himself in danger or interfering with important duties he owes to others. Minnesota now has a law similar to Vermont's, as does Wisconsin, which has a "duty to rescue crime victims" law.

Failure to comply with the law carries a fine of up to $100. The law hasn't been tested for nurses or doctors yet. How it would be applied in a roadside accident situation is uncertain. For example, if you pass an accident on the way to your dentist, the law requires you to stop and try to help. But what if you're on your way to work? Would your nursing job be considered an important duty owed to others? Answers to these questions will eventually come from the courts. Until then, you'd be wise to help the victim—acting, of course, as prudently as possible. (See *Being a Good Samaritan: Some Do's and Don'ts,* page 168.)

Conclusion

A discussion of the legal aspects of being a Good Samaritan may ignore the likelihood that you feel an ethical and moral obligation to help someone in need. Because you have the skills to help save lives, you may naturally feel a duty to use those skills in any emergency—inside or outside the hospital. That attitude is certainly commendable. But when you provide rescue service, you should also be able to feel secure that you aren't legally jeopardizing your career. Good Samaritan acts, as well as common law, provide you with that security.

With the law on your side, when confronted with an emergency, let your conscience guide you. For example, suppose you're out having dinner and a patron at another table begins to choke. You don't just sit and watch him choke to death. You know how to perform the abdominal thrust maneuver, so without hesitation you take action. Other emergencies won't be so

Questions Nurses Ask about Giving Advice

Q. A friend and I have babies the same age. My friend isn't a nurse, and I know she relies on my judgment a lot. How can I answer her when she asks things like, "Would you take your baby with a rash like that to the doctor?"

A. If you wish to advise your friend to see a doctor, you can do so without risk because no harm can result from your advice. If your advice is "Don't see a doctor," and harm does result, you may be liable. It's your decision whether to take that responsibility. Conservative advice, in this situation, is legally safer, especially when you have any doubts.

Q. I seem to be the neighborhood ear-piercer. Of course, with children I require a parent's permission, and I warn everyone about the risks of infection and how to reduce them. Still, I'm worried: If someone got an infection and sued me, would I be considered negligent?

A. Some states have legislation or regulations governing ear piercing, so check with your state licensing board. If your state doesn't have regulations on ear piercing, your warnings about possible infection protect you only if infection results from piercing you've done according to accepted standards. The warning doesn't protect you if the infection results from your negligence.

Q. One of my neighbors comes to see me whenever one of her family members is in the hospital. She's a good friend and I'm glad to help, but I'm nervous about her habit of asking me to explain everything the doctor tells her. For example, she might say, "The doctor says my husband might have adhesions from a previous operation. What does that mean? Is that common?" And so on. Can I protect myself by saying, "I can only tell you what I know from my own experience..."?

A. You'd be better off saying, "I can only tell you what those terms usually mean but not what they mean in your husband's case." However, the best service you can render is to encourage your neighbor to ask the doctor to explain anything she doesn't understand.

clear-cut, so the decision to intervene or not to intervene won't be as easy. But, remember, the decision rests with you. You have the final say as to whether or not you should become a Good Samaritan.

Giving health-care advice

As a health-care professional, you're likely to find your family and friends depending on you, perhaps more than you'd prefer, for free advice. Because giving such help is an activity for which you can be sued

(even though such a lawsuit is extremely unlikely), you should protect yourself. Here are several ways:

• Make sure that your advice reflects accepted professional and community nursing standards.

• Don't charge or accept money for it.

• Make sure that your professional liability insurance covers such off-the-job nursing activities.

Of course, you can also decide not to give free advice at all—the law does not require you to—but this is a difficult attitude to maintain if you want continued cordial relationships with family and friends! (See *Minimizing Your Legal Risks when Giving Advice: Some Do's and*

Don'ts, page 169.)

Free advice and your NPA
Giving free advice is unusual in one way: although doing it improperly can be malpractice, doing it at all is not usually considered "practice." This is because the nurse practice acts (NPAs) in many states and Canadian provinces exempt services performed without pay. (Of course, once you accept pay for any nursing service, even if the service is as simple as giving advice, you come under the control of the state board of nursing and your NPA.) Remember, giving health-care advice—whether you're paid for it or not—can be a problem if the advice you give is inappropriately medical. You could be liable for practicing medicine without a license.

Free advice and the courts
In free-advice situations, the same legal rules apply as in other situations where malpractice may be alleged: the person who would sue you for harm caused by your giving the wrong advice has to prove that you owed him a specific duty, that you breached that duty, that he was harmed, and that the harm was a result of that breach. For a duty to exist, you must have established a nurse-patient relationship with the person asking for your advice. This rarely occurs in everyday short-lived conversations with other people. Suppose, for example, that someone at a cocktail party finds out that you're a nurse and bombards you with questions about his health. If you decide to answer, you have a duty to answer as correctly as any reasonably prudent nurse would, but you have no duty to follow up after the party is over, no duty to monitor the outcome of your advice. The person who's asking your advice hasn't established, or indicated that he intends to establish, an ongoing nurse-patient relationship with you.

The situation may be different if you decide to give advice to a neighbor. For example: The young mother next door asks you about her child's fretfulness, and you answer honestly that it doesn't appear serious enough, to you, for the mother to call the doctor. Suppose that a day later, you see the mother and child together outdoors, and the child looks particularly listless. If you go over and discover that the child is feverish or shows other signs and symptoms of illness, then legally and professionally your responsibility is to tell the mother to take him to a doctor as soon as possible. This is true no matter what your original advice was. You must respond to the mother's probable reliance on you for further advice, even though you may not originally have intended to form a nurse-patient relationship with her and her child. If you realize that she *is* relying on you for further advice, you have an obligation—a legal and professional duty—to keep your advice current as the situation changes. Or you may opt to take formal steps to break off the relationship, such as telling the mother to look elsewhere for help.

The same principles, of course, apply in your regular work: the help and advice you give your patient Monday morning may have to be changed by Tuesday afternoon, and if a patient's questions reveal that his problem may be beyond the scope of nursing practice, you have a clear duty to call in the doctor. (See *Questions Nurses Ask about Giving Advice,* page 171.)

Your professional obligations
Whenever you establish a professional relationship with a questioner—and become responsible for giving him accurate nursing advice—you must give an answer as good as any reasonably prudent nurse would give under similar circumstances. To do this, apply the same standards that you're expected to apply in your regular work. If you know the answer, you're legally free to give it. But do this only if you're certain your answer is correct and giving it is appropriately within your scope of nursing practice. To protect yourself, you might say something like, "I think your problem sounds like arthritis, but it could be something more serious, and I'm not sure. You should ask a doctor."

Obviously, you're always legally protected if you refer the questioner to his doctor. However, the law doesn't require that you make that suggestion if you're honestly convinced it isn't necessary, and a reasonably prudent nurse wouldn't make

Working with Volunteers

Suppose a volunteer is assigned to your unit in the hospital or nursing home where you work. Do you know what you can and can't ask her to do?

In general, you'll find the answer in the policies and rules of your institution, not in the laws of your state. In most hospitals, nonnurse volunteers perform many useful tasks, and the hospitals have guidelines that say what volunteers can and can't do. If you need help with one of your patients, and if the work involved is within your institution's guidelines, ask the volunteer if she's been trained in the task. If she hasn't, you should wait for a regular staff member to help you. In one case, *Marcus v. Frankford Hospital* (1971), in which the regular nurses on the floor forgot to obey this common-sense rule, the volunteer—untrained in the task she was given and emotionally unable to cope with it—fainted, fell, and injured herself. The hospital was held liable.

In general, the more training the volunteer has, the more the law allows you to rely on her. Still, regardless of her degree of training, you must respect a few common-sense limitations on asking for her help. If the volunteer is working as a private-duty nurse for a patient who needs round-the-clock care, you cannot call her away to help you with other duties. And if the volunteer is elderly or frail, you cannot have her help you with tasks that involve heavy lifting, such as moving an obese patient.

If you demand help from a volunteer that she cannot give, for whatever reason, she has a right to refuse. Even if she doesn't refuse, and your request leads to harm—either to her or to a patient—you may be liable. Remember that the volunteer will probably not be covered by your institution's insurance policy, and she may not have her own coverage. So the injured patient may turn against *you* as the most likely source for recovering damages.

it either.

Be on your guard against the temptation to say, "Don't worry," to be reassuring when family members or friends ask for advice. Reassurance is appropriate only if you're sure that nothing serious is wrong. The standard the law requires you to apply is this: If I were at work, and one of my patients asked the same question, what would I tell him? Try to imagine that an inquiring family member or friend is a complete stranger. Then give your best professionally considered answer.

Conclusion

You alone can decide if you have a professional or ethical responsibility to give health-care advice in situations outside of your paid employment. On the one hand, you have expertise that the person requesting your advice doesn't have, and your professional advice may be helpful. On the other hand, the person requesting the advice probably hasn't stopped to consider your legal position. Decisions about whether to give nursing advice will be easier for you if you plan how you'll handle such requests *before* a neighbor knocks at your door.

Donating nursing services

Many health-care professionals, including nurses, occasionally or regularly donate their health-care services to community organizations or activities. This is unpaid work, donated in the interest of supporting the community.

Of course, as a nurse, you may find yourself "volunteering" your services for pay, such as when you provide nursing services in addition to—and outside of—your regular paid job. Here, you're volunteering your personal time while being paid for your nursing services. But most often, when you volunteer your nursing services, you'll be donating nursing care, and no pay will be involved.

You might donate your nursing services to family members, friends, or such community organizations and activities as these:

• a community-run ambulance service
• a bloodmobile or hypertension outreach program
• a PTA that asks you to give a slide-lecture on children's health and development.

As a licensed nurse, whether RN or LPN/LVN, your responsibilities toward patients don't change when you donate your services, but your legal status is less well defined than when you're paid. Why? Because most states' nurse practice acts (NPAs) specify only the legal limits of *paid* nursing practice. (This also means that a nonlicensed or nonregistered person may provide nursing care for no pay without being subject to NPA regulations or discipline.)

How the courts view donated nursing services

Being exempt from your state's NPA, if you donate nursing services, *doesn't* mean you'll be exempt from being sued. In such a situation, the court can use the provisions of your state NPA—together with expert-witness testimony and applicable standards of nursing care—to determine if you acted as a prudent nurse would have under similar patient-care circumstances. If the court finds that your care didn't conform to the requirements of your state's NPA, you may be found liable for malpractice.

Even if no lawsuit results from your donated nursing services, you may be subject to discipline by your state board of nursing if the board finds your donated services to be below the accepted standard of care. In such a situation, the board may suspend or even revoke your license.

If you travel to a state in which you're not licensed to practice, you're not prohibited from donating your nursing services as long as that state's NPA covers only paid nursing care. But if you're sued, the court will probably evaluate your actions—and their consequences—against whatever standard of nursing care would apply in that situation.

Remember, too, that the Good Samaritan act won't cover you in day-to-day situations in which you donate your nursing services. These acts are applicable only to emergency situations. And not all states extend coverage to all nurses in their Good Samaritan acts.

The best protection

The best way to protect yourself legally when you donate your nursing services, as you've probably realized by now, is simply to function in this situation according to the same standards of care and scope of nursing practice you'd follow in your regular paid job. For example, be sure that you obtain a doctor's order (or a standing order), as you would in your regular practice, before giving any treatment or medication that requires it. And you'd be wise to document your care as carefully as you always do. Retain your nurses' notes so you have a permanent record of your actions should a question ever arise.

Before agreeing to donate your services to any organization, check your professional liability insurance coverage, and its limitations, from every angle. Does your personal policy cover you? Does the organization have coverage that includes you? Is the coverage adequate to cover reasonable damages and legal fees that you could be required to pay? Be sure to check whether your coverage specifically includes the type of volunteer nursing you're considering.

Conclusion

Should you donate your nursing services? It's your decision. Nothing in the law compels you to work without compensation. Base your decision on your sense of duty to your community, your enjoyment of the work (if that applies), the adequacy of patient-care conditions, and the extent of your professional liability insurance coverage. (For information about services donated by lay persons, *see* Working with Volunteers, page 173.)

Know the Law Before You Volunteer

Most of my 10 years of experience have been in psychiatric nursing. This summer, however, I've volunteered for weekend duty as nurse in charge of a first-aid tent at our summer-long outdoor religious assembly. Although we have no doctor and the assembly is too poor to provide us with professional liability insurance, the LPN and I are not too concerned because we administer only over-the-counter medications—such as aspirin and Maalox—that people can buy themselves.

Other aspects of the work do worry me, though. Suppose someone falls and I think it's just a simple sprain. Should I also recommend an X-ray just to be on the safe side?

As I said, I'm only a volunteer and not getting paid for my work.—RN, Ill.

You're right when you say the medications you're administering could be purchased by any of the patients themselves. But there's a grave difference here. You are not a clerk in a pharmacy where the *customer* assumes the risk of taking medications from the hands of a lay person.

The law has designated you a *nurse*. As such, you'll be held to the standards of care established for a nurse. This means you're expected to know the indications, contraindications, dosages, adverse reactions, and possible drug interactions of *anything* you administer.

Furthermore, even if you were completely confident in your knowledge of these medications, you might still be subject to disciplinary action for breaching the nurse practice act because you administered these medications without any orders from a doctor.

Do two things immediately: Get standing orders from a doctor, and get professional liability insurance to cover your volunteer work. Once you do that, we recommend that you set up some system of recording everything you do in the first-aid tent. Such records, even if not legally necessary, are good practice and good sense. And, of course, before handing out any medication, make appropriate medical inquiries of the patient (concerning possible contraindications, drug interactions, and so on) according to the accepted standard of nursing care.

Too many nurses think volunteer work is always covered by the Good Samaritan act. But not all states cover nurses or lay volunteers in their acts. Further, even if your state's act does cover you, such volunteer work as you describe would not ordinarily qualify as a true emergency.

Before you ever donate your nursing skills, make sure that you're performing within the guidelines of your state nurse practice act and that you're properly covered by insurance.

This letter was taken from the files of *Nursing* magazine.

Disasters

A tornado hits your community. A hurricane strikes. Heavy spring rains cause destructive flooding. A train derails, sending clouds of toxic vapor into the air in a heavily populated area. A fully loaded plane, landing in a fog, goes off the end of the runway. Any of these disastrous events can stretch local medical and nursing resources to the breaking point. As a nurse, do you know your special responsibilities, and your legal rights, in situations like these?

Minimizing Your Legal Risks During a Disaster

As you know, volunteering your services during a disaster is not without legal risks. But you can minimize those risks if you follow these suggestions:

BE PREPARED
Don't wait for an emergency to happen before you ask your charge nurse what you'll likely be required to do. Also, keep any equipment you're likely to need available and in good condition. (If you're being asked to go to your hospital for the duration of the emergency, carry a change of clothing and toiletries, if you wish, with you.)

FOLLOW INSTRUCTIONS
In any serious emergency, people in positions of public authority—such as medical personnel, public health agency staff, or governor's office staff—will probably be giving orders. Even if these people are not normally your superiors, to be truly helpful you should obey their orders as much as possible—and offer advice only when you think necessary.

TAKE EVERY PRECAUTION TO AVOID COMMITTING MALPRACTICE
If you're helping during a disaster, you're not likely to be sued, and even if you are sued, you're not likely to lose; but being careful in the first place is always the best policy.

DO NOT WORK YOURSELF BEYOND YOUR POINT OF EFFECTIVENESS
If you're so tired that you're unable to make the correct decisions, no one will profit from your care. Explain your fatigue to the person in charge and ask for a rest break.

Contract duties

When you give nursing care during a disaster, professional, ethical, and legal concerns figure heavily in every decision you make. In general, with the exception of declared emergencies, a nurse's responsibilities in a disaster don't differ legally from her everyday responsibilities. As a nurse, you may have specific duties to perform in specific kinds of disasters, and you may be legally bound to perform those duties, but this is likely to be based on your employment contract and not on laws or precedent-setting legal cases. If you work in a city hospital, for example, your employment contract may contain a provision that your administration can call you in to work whenever a government official declares a state of emergency. If you refuse to come in, you can be disciplined, suspended, or fired. And this rule applies even if the work you're being asked to do isn't normally part of your job description.

If you're already on the job when a disaster occurs, the same contractual provisions may be invoked to keep you from going home at the end of your shift. And the same penalties apply if you refuse to cooperate.

Similarly, if you're an unpaid volunteer for a community emergency service, such as the Red Cross or an emergency medical service, you may be expected to report for duty in any local disaster as long as your reporting doesn't conflict with your regular employment. If you refuse, the emergency service is entitled to drop you from its roster; if you're a paid part-time worker for such an emergency service, the service is entitled to fire you. These duties exist even if your work arrangements aren't written, but are merely part of an oral agreement.

By refusing to appear when people are expecting you to help in a disaster, you could make a bad situation even worse. Why? Because your agreement to be available may have led the emergency service or hospital to stop looking for, or not to hire, someone who would have been able and willing to do the job.

Contract defenses

Because reporting for work in an emergency, including a disaster, is usually a contract matter, specific "contract defenses" apply if you're disciplined for failing to fulfill your duties. The defense of impossibility is one such contract defense. If reporting-in is impossible for you, and you can prove it—even if you're contractually required to do so and would be paid for the work—you can't be disciplined or prosecuted. For example, if a blizzard absolutely prohibits travel from your home to the hospital, or disastrous flooding causes the governor to place a ban on all travel in your area, what your contract says doesn't matter much. If you can't come, you can't. And if you're disciplined, you have a legal defense. But watch for exceptions to travel bans—for example, a ban may be announced for all but "required" personnel (you) or "persons with medical or nursing training." In these situations, obviously you'd have to report for duty.

What the law says

No law prevents you from voluntarily donating your services, and specific statutory or common laws may protect you if you do. If you want to volunteer your help in a disaster, do it, whether or not anyone in authority has asked you (See *Know the Law Before You Volunteer*, page 175.).

Suppose you're working in a hospital that doesn't have a policy mandating that health-care personnel report to work when a disaster occurs. You can still volunteer to stay for extra shifts or to perform services outside your normal scope of employment. The hospital will almost certainly accept your offer—or it may ask you before you have a chance to volunteer. This is especially likely if emergency conditions prevent other staff nurses from reporting to work. But you can't necessarily

expect your pay to reflect the extra work; most institutions will try to pay for the overtime, but some may not. If you're curious, find out what your institution's policy is *before* such an emergency occurs. The policy may depend on union rules or, if you work in a city or state hospital, on city ordinances or state regulations.

Your location doesn't legally restrict your ability to volunteer when a disaster happens. Your nurse practice act (NPA) doesn't even stop you. For instance, suppose you're licensed in California and while you're on vacation in Oregon, a disaster occurs. You can give your nursing services during the disaster without concern that you're breaching California's or Oregon's NPA. This is because most states' NPAs have a special exemption for care given in emergencies that usually includes disasters. In an unlikely instance, suppose you volunteer your nursing services in a state that doesn't have a special exemption *and* you're charged with malpractice. You could theoretically be sued for practicing nursing without a license. This, however, has never happened to a nurse.

Taking on special duties

In a disaster, you may find yourself performing duties that you don't normally perform. If you're an LPN or LVN, you may be asked to perform duties that ordinarily would be restricted to RNs, and aides may be asked to do work you usually do. If you're an RN, you may find yourself doing tasks normally reserved for medical residents. And either you or a resident may be asked to do work an aide would normally do. Provided you have the knowledge and skill to meet minimum safety requirements, you're permitted to give such substitute care in disasters based on the same exemption in NPAs that lets an out-of-state nurse volunteer her services in a disaster. This exemption may be construed as letting you expand the scope of your practice in a disaster. Even if it can't be construed this way, usually other statutory or common laws exist that permit the regulatory authorities to decide that the public welfare comes first—ahead of strict enforcement of the letter of the law.

What if you don't want to volunteer? If your hospital policy or contract doesn't require it, or in the rare instance when you don't have a contract, you generally have the right to refuse. Although most NPAs provide special exemptions to allow emergency care in disasters, they don't *require* you to perform such care, any more than they require you to perform *any* care. They only *permit* such care. Similarly, Good Samaritan acts give you some legal immunity for giving emergency care, but they don't require you to provide that care—except in states with duty-to-rescue laws.

Civil defense laws, also known as disaster relief laws, do not apply in most states to nurses who aren't already involved in civil defense work—although in a declared national emergency, nurses (like anyone else) can be drafted. Or martial law may be imposed, which makes all citizens subject to public authority. Many civil defense laws authorize state or federal governing bodies to enforce special regulations dealing with the duties of medical and nursing personnel in a declared emergency. Some states already have such plans in final form, ready for use in a sufficiently serious disaster.

Practical considerations
Your professional responsibility in particular disaster circumstances must be determined in part by assessing your actual ability to help. For example, do you have the particular skills needed to help? Caring for the disaster victims may require knowledge of a specialty such as toxicology (as in the example of the train wreck that releases toxic gases). Or the skill required may be as simple and nonprofessional as rowing a boat in a flood.

Can you get to the disaster site or to the place where care is going to be provided? If a plane has crashed, for example, and a hundred or more badly injured passengers are being ferried by ambulance to emergency departments throughout the city, your ability to get to your hospital or *another hospital* quickly may figure in your decision whether or not to volunteer. What if the disaster is a riot taking place during a total blackout in your city, and the mayor has said, "Don't come to work unless you're within walking distance"? If you try to drive into the city from your suburban home, you'll only complicate driving conditions—and you probably won't get to your hospital in time to be of much help.

You should also consider whether volunteering in the disaster will keep you from earning your regular salary. Find out, too, whether your professional liability insurance covers off-the-job activities. (See *Minimizing Your Legal Risks During a Disaster,* page 176.)

Conclusion
Two basic questions govern your response, as a nurse, when a disaster occurs. The questions are the ethical (and sometimes contractual) "*Should* I help?" and the practical "*Can* I help?" When disaster strikes, you should be ready with your answers.

Selected References

Bullough, Bonnie, ed. *The Law and the Expanding Nursing Role.* 2nd ed. East Norwalk, Conn.: Appleton-Century-Crofts, 1980.

Cazalas, Mary W. *Nursing and the Law,* 3rd ed. Rockville, Md.: Aspen Systems Corp., 1979.

Fenner, Kathleen M. *Ethics and Law in Nursing.* New York: Van Nostrand Reinhold Co., 1980.

Fromer, Margot J. *Ethical Issues in Health Care.* St. Louis: C.V. Mosby Co., 1981.

Murchison, Irene, et al. *Legal Accountability in the Nursing Process,* 2nd ed. St. Louis: C.V. Mosby Co., 1982.

Pozgar, George D. *Legal Aspects of Health Care Administration,* 2nd ed. Rockville, Md.: Aspen Systems Corp., 1983.

Veninga, Robert L. *The Human Side of Health Administration: A Guide for Hospital, Public Health and Nursing Administrators.* Englewood Cliffs, N.J.: Prentice-Hall, 1982.

5

Documentation

You may consider medical records a 20th century phenomenon. But documentation of patient information dates back to 25,000 B.C.—when Stone Age man recorded, in cave painting, his attempts to care for the sick.

Hippocrates, the famous Greek doctor of the 5th century B.C., was probably the first person to record individual patient problems.

And, in the centuries since then, medical records—like medical and nursing practice—have become increasingly more scientific and complex. They've also become more necessary—as a link between specialists.

The key role good documentation can play

With increasing specialization in nursing and other health-care professions, now many practitioners care for every patient. A typical patient on your unit, for example, probably has several nurses besides you—and also several doctors, pharmacists, nutritionists, and therapists. With all of you observing, evaluating, and caring for the patient, careful documentation and communication are vital. And that's the key role the patient's medical record plays.

The medical record is the chief means by which you and other health-care practitioners plan, coordinate, and guarantee the continuity of each patient's care.

If you all document carefully, the medical record can help you:

• plan continuous, quality care for your patient

• coordinate the care each of you contributes

• communicate constantly to keep each other up-to-date on your patient's condition and treatment

• furnish data for continuing education and research.

The legal significance of the medical record

Each patient's medical record is also legal proof of the quality of care you provided. And the weight it carries in the courtroom can't be exaggerated.

In fact, documentation of care has become synonymous with care itself: fail to document, and the courts are likely to assume that you also failed to provide care. That's what happened to the nurse in *Collins v. Westlake Community Hospital* (1974).

The Collins boy was hospitalized with a fractured leg, which was put in a cast and placed in traction. The evening nurse recorded the condition of the boy's toes several times during her shift. The night nurse, however, didn't record the condition of his toes until 6 a.m., when she noted that they were dusky and cold and that his doctor had been contacted.

Part of the boy's leg had to be amputated, and his family sued the hospital. They claimed the amputation was necessary because the night nurse had negligently failed to observe the condition of his toes during the night.

She testified that she *had* observed them and they'd been normal. Other nurses testified that only abnormal findings needed to be documented. But the blank chart spoke louder than the experts' words: the jury inferred that no documentation meant no observation, and they found the nurse

Tips on Documentation:
How to Protect Yourself Legally

If you've ever read a malpractice case transcript, you realize how much the jury relies on documentation.

If you're ever involved in a case, how you documented, what you documented, and what you didn't document will heavily influence the outcome. Here are some tips on how to document so that your records don't tip the scales of justice against you:

• Use the appropriate form, and document in ink.

• Record the patient's name and identification number on every page of his chart.

• Record the complete date and time of each entry.

• Be specific. Avoid general terms and vague expressions.

• Use standard abbreviations only.

• Use a medical term only if you're sure of its meaning.

• Document symptoms by using the patient's own words.

• Document any nursing action you take in response to a patient's problem. For example: "8 p.m.—medicated for incision pain." Be sure to include the medication route and site.

• Document the patient's response to medications and other treatment.

• Document safeguards you use to protect the patient. For example: "raised side rails" or "applied safety belts."

• Document any incident in two places: in your progress report and in an incident report.

• Document each observation. Failure to document observations will produce gaps in the patient's records. And these gaps will suggest that you neglected the patient.

• Document procedures after you perform them, never in advance.

• Write on every line. Don't insert notes between lines or leave empty spaces for someone else to insert a note.

• Sign every entry.

• Chart an omission as a new entry. Never backdate or add to previously written entries.

• Draw a thin line through an error. Never erase one.

• Document your own care, only. Never document for someone else.

liable for malpractice.

The Importance of proper documentation

The standards of care for documenting require that you record your observations accurately, completely, and in a timely manner, and that you include normal as well as abnormal findings. The *Collins* case clearly shows how failure to meet the legal standards for documenting could lead to serious legal consequences for you. This chapter helps you avoid such consequences by giving you an overview of your legal and professional responsibilities regarding documentation.

As patient care becomes more complex, accurate documentation is likely to become an even greater legal and professional responsibility. Make sure you know how to document properly, so that your patients' medical records provide proof of your provision of quality care.

The legal importance of documentation

Good patient care is your best defense against being sued for malpractice. But if you *are* sued, clear and accurate documentation of the nursing care you provided will be your best defense in the courtroom. That's why you need to know the legal functions and implications of documentation.

What is documentation? It's the preparing or assembling of records to authenticate the care you gave your patient, as well as your reasons for giving that care. In general, you should document these kinds of information for each patient:

• therapeutic measures you and other health-care providers carry out

• doctor-prescribed measures you carry out

• the patient's health-related behavior, including body action, verbal communication (always use direct quotes and describe the emotional tone), and physiologic reactions

• the patient's specific responses to therapy and care.

How documenting became your responsibility

Doctors have been documenting their care since Hippocrates started recording his clinical observations in the 5th century B.C. For the next 2,000 years or so, doctors were thought to be the only health-care providers qualified to provide—and document—patient care. As you know, those days are gone forever.

Today, the responsibility for a major share of each patient's care rests squarely in your hands. And with that responsibility goes the responsibility for documenting accurately. (See *Tips on Documentation: How to Protect Yourself Legally,* page 180.)

What is the medical record?

Each patient's medical record is really a collection of records, including:

• patient's admission sheet and history

• doctor's order sheet and progress notes

• patient's medication record

• nursing care plan (cardex)

• nurses' notes

• laboratory test results

• X-ray reports

• flow sheets, checklists, and graphic sheets

• discharge summary

• home-care instruction sheet.

This collection of separate records grew out of a system of record keeping called *source-oriented records.* As the name implies, in this system, each *source* of information keeps a separate record. This type of record keeping was almost universal until the 1960s, with doctors charting the progress notes and nurses charting the nurses' notes. The obvious drawback of this system is that you have to consult several sources to get an accurate picture of your patient's condition. Failing to consult all the separate records could have disastrous clinical consequences for the patient and serious legal consequences for the patient's doctors and nurses. The case of *Villetto v. Weilbaecher* (1979) is an example. In this case, the nurses noticed that the patient had developed several blisters after surgery for a fractured kneecap. They recorded their observation in the nurses' notes and reported it to the doctor.

The patient later sued the doctor for failing to treat the blisters. The doctor couldn't defend himself successfully because *his* record, the progress notes, didn't mention the blisters until 6 days after the nurses charted them.

To avoid this kind of communication gap, many hospitals have switched to *problem-oriented records.* In this system of record keeping, all members of the health-care team, and even the patient, combine their information in a special format that goes by the acronym SOAP. Each note combines Subjective data (how the patient feels), Objective data (what you find), Assessment data, and Plans. For example, you might note: Problem: *Pain on ambulation.*

S "My side hurts when I walk"

O Favoring left side, appendectomy done on 8/15/83

A Stitches and local inflammation causing pain

P Assist when walking.

This type of record keeping provides a comprehensive picture of how well the patient is coping with his problem and responding to therapy.

Block charting and time charting

With both systems, you can use either block charting or time charting. When using *block charting,* you note—in paragraph form—the procedures you carried out during a block of time; for example, between 11 p.m. and 7 a.m. or between

How to Avoid Subjective Charting

Do you know the most common error nurses make when they chart? It's writing value judgments and opinions—subjective, rather than factual (objective) information. This type of information is inappropriate because it tells you how the nurse feels about the patient's condition, not about the patient's condition itself. Here are some subjective entries, with their *objective* alternatives:

SUBJECTIVE CHARTING	OBJECTIVE CHARTING
She is drinking *well.*	Drank 1,500 ml liquids between 7 a.m. and noon.
She reported *good* relief from Demerol.	Pain in R hip decreasing, now described as "like a dull toothache."
Dorsalis pedis pulse *present. Good* pedal pulses.	Peripheral pulses in legs 2 + /4 + bilaterally.
Moves legs and feet *well.*	Leg strength 5 + /5 + bilaterally all major muscle groups. Sensation intact to light touch, pin; denies numbness or tingling. Skin warm and dry. No edema.
Voiding *qs.*	Voided 350 ml clear yellow urine in bedpan.
Patient is *nervous.*	Patient repeatedly asking about length of hospitalization, expected discomfort, and time off from work.
Breath sounds *normal.*	Breath sounds clear to auscultation all lobes. Chest expansion symmetrical—no cough. Nail beds pink.
Bowel sounds *normal.*	Bowel sounds present all quadrants—abdomen flat. NPO since 12:01 a.m.
Ate *well.*	Ate all of soft diet.

3 p.m. and 11 p.m. Block charting encourages you to note the important patient care information as briefly as possible. But it may *discourage* you from including all the significant information. In *Engle v. Clarke* (1961), for example, a nurse recorded that she'd administered medication to a patient, but she failed to record the time at which the medication took effect.

Because of the danger of omitting important information, block charting isn't as popular as time charting. In *time charting,* you record the hour-by-hour care you give the patient: your observations, what you did, and when you did it.

Using Flow Sheets in Documenting

As you know, flow sheets are record-keeping forms that come in a variety of styles—blank-ruled paper, multicolumned paper, graph paper—to suit particular documenting purposes. They're perfect for recording information about routine tasks you perform throughout the day, such as giving medication or monitoring your patient's vital signs or fluid balance. Why? For four reasons. A flow sheet:

• displays a specific aspect of your patient's condition, such as his temperature, at a glance. You don't have to search through pages of notes to determine his temperature pattern over the last 48 hours.

• saves you time. You can write down the vital signs or medication given without having to write a full descriptive entry every time. You can use your nursing notes to describe how the patient is responding to treatment.

• documents that you're giving the patient the continuous care he needs. In this way, a flow sheet legally protects you and the hospital from charges of negligent care.

• provides a legal form for nonlicensed personnel to chart their care and observations. Because nonlicensed personnel can't chart in the nurses' notes, information about patient care they give may be lost. Have them enter their care and initial each entry on a flow sheet. Then, if you have a question about the status of your patient's skin, you can check the flow sheet to identify the nursing assistant who administered that day's bed bath.

Despite their usefulness, flow sheets can create a legal tangle if you don't avoid two common mistakes.

The first mistake many nurses make is to treat flow sheets casually. For instance, some nurses will routinely check off whatever the previous shift checked off on the flow sheet, regardless of the actual care given, and then carefully chart the actual care in the nurses' notes. Obviously, as part of the legal medical record, the flow sheet must accurately reflect the care given.

A second common mistake is to depend too heavily on the flow sheet. Flow sheets can help you document, quickly and accurately, what care was given and who gave it. But don't neglect to record the *patient's response to care* in your nurses' notes. Like any other chart form, retain it as part of the permanent chart so that you have a progressive picture of the patient's status and a record of your care.

The basis of good documentation

The rules governing documentation come from four sources:

• federal regulations
• state and provincial (Canada) laws
• professional standards
• hospital policies.

Many federal regulations, such as those regarding Medicare and Medicaid, stipulate the form and content of the medical record. Although these regulations don't have the authority of law, most hospitals conform to the regulations to ensure their eligibility for federal funds.

State and provincial laws vary, but all states and provinces require hospitals to keep records documenting a patient's care.

In some states, you'll find more specific guidelines in the nurse practice act; and in Canada, in the public hospital acts. On the whole, however, the states leave the specific requirements to professional organizations.

Two professional organizations have set more stringent standards for documentation than what's required by state law.

The American Nurses' Association (ANA) has included standards for documentation in its *Standards of Nursing Practice*. According to these ANA standards, documentation must be "systematic and continuous..., accessible, communicated, recorded," and readily available to all members of the health-care team.

The Joint Commission on Accreditation of Hospitals' standards require documentation of all phases of the nursing process for each hospitalized patient from admission through discharge.

In all likelihood, your hospital has integrated the regulations, laws, and standards into its own policy manual. Your best assurance that you're following the law is to follow the policy manual. It will tell you who's responsible for keeping each part of a patient's chart and which charting techniques should be used.

A good policy to follow

Hospital policy isn't law, of course, but the law tends to support the policy when documentation questions enter the courtroom. The following case, *Stack v. Wapner* (1976), illustrates this point.

Mrs. Stack was admitted to the hospital to give birth to her fourth child. At 2:45 a.m., according to her chart, intravenous oxytocin was started to induce labor by causing uterine contractions. Accepted medical practice requires constant monitoring of a patient receiving oxytocin. Otherwise, the drug may cause excessive uterine contractions, which may endanger the fetus or rupture the woman's uterus. But Mrs. Stack's labor-room charts didn't document any check on her condition until 5:15 a.m.

After the baby was born, the mother developed heavy uterine bleeding. Unable to stop the bleeding, the doctor performed a total hysterectomy. Later, the patient sued, claiming that inappropriate administration and monitoring of the oxytocin caused the complications that made a hysterectomy necessary.

Both attending doctors testified that they had monitored the administration of the drug. But they had no defense against the evidence that hospital policy required them to document all information on a patient's chart that justified a diagnosis and treatment—and all information relevant to the results. The patient was awarded damages.

Conclusion

The advice "Write it down" can't be overemphasized. (See *When in Doubt, Chart Everything.*) If you've evaluated a patient, given a treatment, checked vital signs, or performed any other task that's essential to your patient's welfare, write it down in the medical record.

You may think documenting is something you do *after* you do your professional job. But—as this review of laws, standards, policies, and court judgments demonstrates—documenting *is* your professional job.

Pitfalls of documentation

The information you document about a patient gives other nurses the knowledge to continue that patient's care where you left off. If you leave something out or make a mistake in the chart, they may give inadequate care. If the patient is injured and sues, your charting omission or error will assume major importance.

Legal importance of good charting

In court, your nurses' notes can be used as evidence of the quality of nursing care that you provide. If a patient is injured, the completeness, consistency, and even legibility of your notes may determine the outcome of the lawsuit. If you find that hard to believe, read these three cases. In each, the nurses' own charts provided evidence against them.

Oza Mae Rogers died of brain damage 7 days after she was admitted to the hospital for injuries suffered in an accident. In the lawsuit that followed, *Rogers v. Kasdan* (1981), the Supreme Court of Kentucky ruled against the doctor and the hospital. The court based its ruling on the patient's medical record: the emergency room records were incomplete, the fluid input/output record was incorrectly tallied, different records contained discrepancies, and several records were illegible and contained incomplete notations.

Patricia Maslonka hemorrhaged and died 3 hours after giving birth to her fourth

When in Doubt, Chart Everything

Have you ever wondered what information you should chart besides your nursing care interventions and patient observations? To be on the safe side, chart as much factual information as you can about your patient's care. This includes:
- incidents
- omitted treatments
- safety precautions
- attempts to reach the doctor.

Omitting any of this information may invite misunderstanding and jeopardize the quality of your patient's care. For example, consider this fictional situation: The doctor's order read, "Out of bed for 20 minutes, three times daily as tolerated." Mr. Cauthen's nurse, Phyllis McKay, helped Mr. Cauthen out of bed after explaining to him that the doctor wanted him to get out of bed and exercise. But as soon as she helped him stand up, he dropped to his knees. Mr. Cauthen was apparently unhurt but *certainly* angry. He complained bitterly that he fell because she made him get out of bed.

Phyllis got him back in bed, checked to be sure his vital signs were normal, and got him to stop complaining long enough for him to agree that he wasn't hurt. Then, feeling that some things are better left unsaid, Phyllis went off to care for another patient without charting the incident, notifying the doctor, or completing an incident report.

Two hours later, nurse Alice Perkins read Mr. Cauthen's chart and assumed he hadn't been out of bed for his exercise. She got about as far as Phyllis did. As soon as Mr. Cauthen tried to stand, he collapsed. And this time, he fractured his hip.

Later, Mr. Cauthen complained to his doctor about his *two* falls. The doctor immediately notified Phyllis' supervisor about the uncharted incident. And Phyllis ended up on probation—all for a "minor" charting omission. Had Mr. Cauthen decided to sue the hospital, Phyllis could also have been charged with malpractice.

---

child. In the lawsuit that resulted, *Maslonka v. Hermann* (1980), the patient's medical record was again the determining factor in the court's decision. According to the court's interpretation of the record, two nurses and four doctors had been negligent. The nurses had poorly monitored the patient's vital signs and had failed to communicate the patient's condition.

Finally, *St. Paul Fire and Marine Insurance Co. v. Prothro* (1979) involved a lawsuit brought by a patient named Prothro. After a total hip replacement, Mr. Prothro was injured while being lowered into a Hubbard bath by an orderly. The metal basket holding him collapsed, struck his hip, and reopened his wound. The orderly stopped the bleeding and took Mr. Prothro to his room, where a staff nurse reclosed the wound with surgical tape. But no one documented the incident.

Several days later, the wound became infected. Subsequently, the doctor had to remove the hip prosthesis, leaving Mr. Prothro with a permanent limp. Mr. Prothro sued the hospital.

The court ruled in his favor and said the determining factor was the absence of crucial information on Mr. Prothro's medical chart, which would have helped the doctor and other health-care professionals provide more appropriate care.

Nine common pitfalls of documentation

As the court cases indicate, charting errors and omissions can undermine the credibility of your nursing care in court. To protect yourself from unforeseen legal and professional consequences, try to chart clearly, accurately, and completely, no matter how tired or busy you are. And, especially when you're tired or busy, remind yourself to watch out for these nine common charting errors.
- *Omissions.* Include all the facts other nurses need to assess your patient's needs.

In a lawsuit, the court may assume that you failed to perform any task you didn't record and may suspect that you omitted information with the intention to cover up incriminating evidence.

• *Personal opinions.* Record what you saw, heard, and did. If your patient says he's mad, record it. If you think he's mad because he's quiet, record only that he's quiet. Otherwise, your personal opinions might influence other nurses' attitudes toward your patient, which could adversely affect the care they provide.

• *Generalizations.* Be specific. Don't use meaningless phrases like, "Had a good day." Instead, describe *why* your patient's day was good. For example: "Patient ate 100% of regular diet; did not complain of pain."

• *Late charting.* Record patient information promptly. The longer you wait, the more likely you are to forget important facts. When you're unable to chart immediately because of patient needs, jot down key information on a note pad to help you recall important information later.

• *Improper abbreviations.* Use commonly accepted abbreviations only, and use them correctly. Ask your supervisor to post a list of acceptable abbreviations where you do your charting, so you don't have to rely on your memory. The wrong abbreviation may endanger your patient's health. For example, suppose you write "O.D." after a medication order instead of "o.d." The significance: O.D. means right eye; o.d. means once daily. The nurse who carries out the order could irreversibly damage the patient's eye. (See *Using Abbreviations,* pages 192 to 195.)

• *Illegibility.* Write clearly and neatly. If others can't read your writing, print. If a court is unable to decipher your notes, it may doubt your credibility.

• *Incorrect spelling.* Be precise. Misspellings lead to confusion. Use a dictionary when you're unsure of spelling or usage. Use common words and expressions to make sure you convey your meaning.

• *Improperly correcting charting errors.* Draw a line through any error, label it *charting error,* and initial it. Never erase, cover over, or scratch out an error. (For a complete discussion on correcting errors, see "The altered medical record," page 187.)

• *Improperly signing your notes.* Sign all your notes with your first initial, full last name, and title. Put your signature on the right side of the page as proof that you entered all the information between the previous nurse's signature and yours. If another nurse on your unit has the same first initial, last name, and title, include a middle initial in your legal signature.

If the last entry is unsigned, immediately contact the nurse who made the entry and have her sign it. If you can't reach her, make a notation to distinguish your entry from hers. (See *Signing Your Nursing Notes,* page 196.)

Common pitfalls in noting doctors' orders

The courts look at all aspects of documentation during a malpractice trial, so be prepared to defend your handling of medical orders, too.

When you take a doctor's order off a patient's medical chart, don't forget to make a check mark in ink on each line of the order. Draw lines through any space between the last written order and the doctor's signature to prevent a later addition to the order. Below the doctor's signature, sign your name, the date, and the time.

Take verbal and telephone orders only in an emergency when the doctor can't immediately attend to the patient. If time and circumstances allow, have another nurse read the order back to the doctor. Record the order on the doctor's order sheet as soon as possible. Note the date, then record the order verbatim. On the following line, write *v.o.* for verbal order or *t.o.* for telephone order. Then write the doctor's name and the name of the nurse who read the order back to the doctor. Sign your name and write the time. Draw lines through any spaces between the order and your verification of the order.

Be sure the doctor countersigns the order within the time specified by hospital policy. Without the countersignature, you can be held liable for practicing medicine without a license.

Countersigning: Some Important Guidelines

As an RN, have you ever worried about the legality of countersigning notes made by LPNs, LVNs, or aides when you haven't supervised their actions?

To ease your worries, find out what your hospital's policy says. Does the hospital interpret countersigning to mean that the LPN/LVN or aide performed her nursing actions *in your presence*? If so, don't countersign unless she did.

If your hospital accepts the fact that you don't always have the time to witness your co-workers' actions, then your countersignature implies that:

● the notes describe care that the LPN/LVN or aide had the authority and competence to perform.
● you have verified that all required patient-care procedures were performed.

What should you do if another nurse asks you to document her care or sign her notes? In a word, "Don't." Unless your hospital policy authorizes—or requires—you to witness someone else's notes, your signature will make you responsible for anything you put in the notes.

Avoiding pitfalls in keeping narcotic records

The legal consequences of improper charting also apply to narcotics records. Be sure you're familiar with local and state regulations as well as hospital policy when you dispense narcotics. These regulations may be more stringent than Title II of the Comprehensive Drug Abuse Prevention and Control Act of 1970, also known as the Controlled Substances Act. As you know, this act holds you accountable for storing all narcotics and barbiturates on your unit and for keeping a record of each distributed dose.

For proper, accurate documentation of narcotics, use the special narcotics records—the control sheet and check sheet—provided by your hospital pharmacy, and follow this procedure:

Before you give a narcotic:
● Verify the count in the narcotics drawer.
● Sign the narcotic control sheet to indicate you removed the drug.
● Get another nurse to sign the control sheet if you waste or discard all or part of a dose.

At the end of your shift:
● Record the amount of each narcotic on the narcotic check sheet while the nurse

beginning her shift counts the narcotics out loud.
● Sign the narcotic check sheet *only* if the count is correct. Have the other nurse countersign.
● Identify and correct any discrepancies before any nurse leaves the unit.

Conclusion
Because you're human, you'll inevitably make errors in documenting patient care. But as a professional you have to strive to minimize the errors that all too frequently turn up on a patient's medical record. Being alert to commonly made errors and identifying ways to avoid them are the first steps you can take toward improving the quality of your patient charting.

The altered medical record

Suppose you're charting Mrs. Smith's vital signs at 10:00 a.m., and you discover you didn't chart them at 8:00 a.m. Or suppose you finish charting your assessment of Mrs. Stanton, and then notice that you've written it on Mr. Williams' chart. Would you

Charting Consistently: The Best Legal Protection

Keeping charts current

Under our hospital's charting policy, a nurse may simply sign her name if she has nothing significant to write on a patient's chart. Hospital policy doesn't state how much time may pass before a note must be written, and I've seen charts with no nurses' notes for as many as 5 days. Don't we need a better policy?—RN, Ariz.

If nothing significant happens to a patient for 5 days, he either doesn't need hospitalization or isn't getting proper care. In that length of time, a patient must be either responding or not responding to treatment—and that alone should be noted.

Anyone reviewing the chart—a new doctor, a hospital utilization committee, a member of an accreditation committee, or a prosecutor investigating malpractice charges—would certainly want to know what happened during those 5 days. And, obviously, a chart with only signatures wouldn't protect you or the hospital from a patient's malpractice claim.

You and the other nurses should start protecting yourselves by charting each patient's condition at least once each shift.

You should also ask for a committee of nurses, hospital lawyers, and administrators to design a new charting policy that will meet legal and accreditation requirements for your kind of institution.

Charting exact times

On the 30-bed pediatric unit where I'm the medication nurse, I've always charted routine medication as given when ordered. For instance, if a doctor orders acetaminophen (Tylenol) three times a day, I write on the medication sheet: Tylenol, t.i.d., 8 a.m.—12 noon—6 p.m. Then, after I give the medication, I put my initials next to the appropriate time. Of course, with 30 patients to care for, I'm sometimes 15 to 30 minutes late with a medication.

My nursing supervisor says I should chart the exact times. I do this for stat and p.r.n. medications, but is it really necessary to be so specific with routinely prescribed drugs?—RN, Ill.

Yes. A patient's chart is a legal document, so you must accurately record everything you do for a patient. This means if a drug is ordered for 8 a.m., but you don't give it until 8:30 a.m., you have to write "8:30" on the patient's medication sheet. You should also record the exact time on the medication cardex.

The most important reason for such accurate charting is to make sure a patient's medication maintains the desired therapeutic level—no drug highs or lows. If you give Mr. Smith's 8 a.m. dosage at 8:15 a.m., write "8:15." Then, be sure he gets his next dosage at 12:15 p.m., not 12 noon, especially if the drug is an antihypertensive or antibiotic, whose effectiveness depends on steady blood levels.

Charting exact times will also protect you if you're ever questioned by a doctor or an attorney. As it is, you'd have a hard time explaining how you gave 30 patients their 8 a.m. medication at the same time.

know how to correct these errors properly? If you do it improperly—and the chart ends up in court—your motives as well as your nursing care may come into question.

If the court uncovers alterations during the course of a trial, it may discount the medical record's value. That's what happened to the nurse involved in a Canadian case, *Joseph Brant Memorial Hospital v. Koziol* (1978). The nurse failed to chart her observations for 7 hours on a postoperative patient who died during that pe-

Secondhand charting

I'm an LPN in a hospital where aides and orderlies aren't allowed to chart the routine patient care they give. Sometimes, I'm sent to a busy unit to help with their charting.

I'm always uneasy about charting for a patient I've never seen, and I'm especially uneasy when the information is obviously inadequate. For some patients, the only information the aide gives me to chart for the whole 8-hour shift is an ambulation order.

This can't be safe for the patients, and I'm afraid it isn't safe for me. Suppose I don't chart that a patient hasn't voided or has had bloody stools. Could omitting such information make me liable for malpractice, even though I wasn't aware of it?

I've tried to cover myself by signing both names to the chart: "E. Lyons, NA/ S. Bradley, LPN." Is there anything else I can do to protect the patients and myself?—LPN, Fla.

You're right to be concerned, because your failure to report a change in a patient's condition could be considered malpractice for two reasons: first, because you failed to fulfill your legal responsibility to the patient, and second, because you failed to meet the acceptable standard of care. If a patient suffered harm because you failed to chart something, both you and your hospital could be considered liable.

Request a new hospital policy requiring nurses with personal knowledge of the patient to chart. Such a request is in the patients' best interests, as well as your own.

In the meantime, you're on the right track when you sign both your name and the aide's name to each chart. One other suggestion: Always add a statement that you haven't personally observed the patient and can't certify the truth of what you've written since your information is secondhand.

Charting the facts

Some nurses on our unit have been writing on the patients' charts, "Primary nursing care could not be given because nurse:patient ratio was 1:20."

To me, charting that primary nursing care wasn't done implies that no nursing care was given. The other nurses point out that they chart the care that's given. They just want the record to show that they're giving what care they can despite an unsafe nurse:patient ratio.

Does such negative "nursing" information belong on the patients' charts?—RN, Utah

Staffing information does *not* belong on a patient's chart. A note, "primary care not given," could be used against the nurse who writes it as evidence in a malpractice suit. The nurses should avoid general statements and chart *exactly* what care they could and did give.

These letters were taken from the files of *Nursing* and *NursingLife* magazines.

---

riod. Later, the patient's family sued the hospital, charging the nurse with malpractice. The nurse insisted that she *had* observed the patient, and, on the instruction of the assistant director of nursing, added the nursing observations to the patient's medical record. The court wasn't convinced. Suspicious of the altered record, it ruled that the nurse's failure to chart her observations at the proper time supported the claim that she'd made no such observations.

In *Thor v. Boska* (1974), the court considered a rewritten copy of a patient's record to be as suspicious as an altered record. The lawsuit was brought by a woman who had seen her doctor several times because of a lump on her breast. Each time, the doctor examined her and made a record of her visit. After 2 years, the woman sought a second opinion and learned she had breast cancer. She sued the first doctor. Instead of producing his records in court, he brought *copies*. He said he'd copied the originals, so they'd be legible. The court inferred that he was withholding incriminating evidence.

State laws regulate alterations

Some state laws specify penalties for tampering with medical records. Improperly adding or changing information in a chart can bring charges of fraudulent concealment or obstruction of justice. Under the California Penal Code, for example, altering a record with fraudulent intent is a misdemeanor.

How to correct your charting errors

Clearly, correcting mistakes is a serious business. But—just as clearly—mistakes occur that *need* to be corrected. Here's how to do it properly, legally, and without charges of attempted cover-up.

To avoid legal problems, use these techniques for *changing* information on a chart. First, draw one line through any incorrect information, *without obscuring it*. Write the date and time, and sign your name. Then, depending on the type of error, do the following:

• If you've used the *wrong chart*—recording your assessment of Mrs. Stanton on Mr. Williams' chart, for example—write "wrong chart" to explain why you've drawn a line through the entry.

• If you've written the *wrong information*, add the correct information. If the incorrect and the correct information are legible, you won't have to write the reason for your change.

• If you've *misspelled* a word, spell it correctly. If you discover the misspelling immediately, you can correct it without adding the date and time and your initials.

If, however, you've *omitted* information, chart it when you remember it. If you

discover at 10 a.m., for example, that you forgot to chart Mrs. Smith's 8 a.m. vital signs, add them after your 10 o'clock entry. Simply write "10 a.m.," then "vital signs for 8/17/83, 8 a.m.." After you record the vital signs, mark the addition "late entry." Always use this method; *never* try to squeeze additional information into the original entry.

If you go home, then realize you've made an error or omitted information, decide whether anyone will need the correct information before your next shift. Call anyone who will need it. When you return, make the appropriate change on the chart.

If the nurse on the previous shift has omitted information, call her at home and tell her. If the information isn't needed before she returns, ask her to correct the record when she does return. If it is needed before then, chart it yourself. Then write, "Charted by [your name] for [her name]." Be sure she countersigns the chart when she returns.

If she's left blank spaces, draw lines through them so no one can insert any information.

If she's made an error, tell her so she—not you—can correct it.

If she's forgotten to sign her name, begin your entry with the date, time, and the statement, "My notations begin at [specify the time]." Then, sign your name to separate your notes from hers.

When not to tamper with charting errors

Suppose you find out a patient is going to sue you or the hospital. You read the medical record to refresh your memory, and you find a charting error. What then? Never make corrections in a situation like that. The plaintiff's attorney may have received a copy of the records before filing the lawsuit. If you change the record after that, the court may interpret it as a cover-up, and you might be charged with tampering.

Leave the record as it is, but make your own record of what the changes should be. Then, you'll have the correct version straight in your mind, and if you're questioned about the error, you'll have something to refer to.

Writing a Discharge Summary

The discharge summary is the final document in each patient's records. Follow your hospital's policy in deciding what format to use and what information to include in the summary. You'll probably need to list significant highlights of your patient's condition, his treatment, and his status at discharge. You may also need to include a home-care instruction sheet, the name of the person accompanying the patient, the patient's discharge address, and his mode of transportation (car, ambulance, taxi).

To make sure you perform this final responsibility, follow these guidelines:
• Before writing your summary, review the patient's problem list, care plan, flow sheets, and progress notes to develop an overall picture of his hospitalization.
• Make a mental list of the highlights of the patient's hospitalization, including any exceptional details or unusual findings.
• Outline all patient teaching, including

what you told him about his diagnosis, diet, medications, activity, special care, follow-up, and referrals. (Also write down this information on a patient instruction sheet in language he can understand so he'll have a record of what you discussed.)

After you write the summary, reread it to be sure it does the following:
• summarizes your patient's care
• provides useful information for further teaching and evaluation, and for readmission
• documents that the patient has the information he needs to care for himself or to get further help
• shows that you've met documentation requirements of the Joint Commission on Accreditation of Hospitals for patient teaching
• helps safeguard you and your employer against malpractice charges.

What if someone asks—or pressures—you to change a record before a case goes to court? The request may seem harmless. For example, someone might note a small disagreement between the progress notes and the nurses' notes over the exact time of an event or the exact size of a wound. No matter how harmless the change seems, you must refuse. For one thing, the court expects and accepts some differences between your records and the doctor's. But more importantly, changing your record would seriously weaken its credibility—and yours. If the pressure continues, report the situation to your supervisor or, if she's doing the pressuring, to *her* supervisor.

Conclusion

Don't compound your error by correcting a charting error improperly. When you correct it, make sure both the incorrect and the correct information are readable and that the reason for the change is obvious. Such clean corrections keep the pa-

tient's record accurate and keep you legally protected.

Computer records: The legal aspects

Like most nurses, you've probably lamented the paperwork involved in keeping your patient's medical records complete. Now modern technology is offering a method to make your record-keeping duties easier: the computerized medical record. Like the manual record system, the computerized medical record provides a documented account of your patient's illness, diagnostic tests, treatments, and medical history. But unlike the manual system, the computerized record stores all your patient's medical data in a single, easily accessible source.

Computerized record keeping also creates problems—problems that mean new

Using Abbreviations

ABBREVIATION	INTENDED MEANING
Apothecary symbols	dram
	minim
	Elixophylline ʒ T ted *TL opium 10 mg*
AU	*auris uterque* (each ear)
	Colymycin gtts iii a uted
Drug names	
MTX	methotrexate
CPZ	Compazine (prochlorperazine)
HCl	hydrochloric acid
DIG	digoxin
MVI	multivitamins *without* fat-soluble vitamins
HCTZ	hydrochlorothiazide
ARA-A	vidarabine
µg	microgram
	Vit B₁₂ 1 µg IM Now
o.d.	once daily
	KCl 15 mEq OD
OJ	orange juice
	Lugol's sol'n ʒ Hs x̄ m OJ

Abbreviations are a safe way to save time when you document *if* you use abbreviations whose meanings are unmistakably clear.

The abbreviations listed below *aren't* clear. Study this list, and avoid using any of the abbreviations it contains.

MISINTERPRETATIONS	CORRECTION
Frequently misinterpreted or not understood.	Use the metric system.
Frequently misinterpreted as OU (*oculus uterque*—each eye).	Write it out.
Frequently misinterpreted as: Mustargen (mechlorethamine HCl) chlorpromazine potassium chloride (The "H" is misinterpreted as "K.") digitoxin multivitamins *with* fat-soluble vitamins hydrocortisone (HCT) cytarabine (ARA-C)	Use the complete spelling for drug names.
When handwritten, frequently misinterpreted as "mg."	Use mcg.
Frequently misinterpreted as "right eye" (OD—*oculus dexter*).	Don't abbreviate "daily." Write it out.
Frequently misinterpreted as "OD" (*oculus dexter*—right eye) or "OS" (*oculus sinister*—left eye). Medications that were meant to be diluted in orange juice and given orally have been given in a patient's right or left eye.	Write it out.

(continued)

Using Abbreviations (continued)

ABBREVIATION	INTENDED MEANING
$\dot{T}$/D $\quad \dot{T}$/D	once daily
	Diabinese 250mg T/d
per os	orally
	Lugol's sol'n gtts x̄ per os
q.d.	every day
	Digoxin 0.25g q.d.
qn	nightly or at bedtime
	Librium 10 mg qh
q.o.d.	every other day
	digoxin 0.25 mg q.i.d.
sub q	subcutaneous
	Heparin 5000 units sub q 2 hrs before surgery
U or u	unit
	NPH 6U Now SC
	NPH 4u Now SC

MISINTERPRETATIONS	CORRECTION
Misinterpreted as "t.i.d."	Write it out.
The "os" is frequently misinterpreted as "left eye."	Use "P.O." or "by mouth" or "orally."
The period after the "q" has sometimes been misinterpreted as "i," and the drug has been given q.i.d. rather than daily.	Write it out.
Misinterpreted as "every hour" when poorly written.	Use "hs" or "nightly."
Misinterpreted as "daily" or "q.i.d." if the "o" is poorly written.	Use "q other day" or "every other day."
The "q" has been misinterpreted as "every." In the example, a prophylactic heparin dose meant to be given 2 hours before surgery was given *every* 2 hours before surgery.	Use "subcut." or write out "subcutaneous."
Misinterpreted as a zero or a four (4), causing a tenfold or greater overdose.	Write it out.

Signing Your Nursing Notes

To discourage nurses from adding information to your nursing notes, draw a line through any blank spaces and sign your name on the far right side of the column.

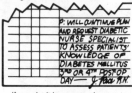

If you don't have enough room to sign your name after the last word of your entry, draw a line from the last word to the end of the line. Then, drop down to the next line, draw a line from the left margin almost to the right margin, and sign your name on the far right side.

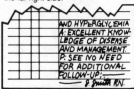

If you have a lot of information to record and you anticipate running out of room on a page, leave room on the right side of the page for your signature. Sign the page, then continue your notes on the next page, and then sign that page as usual.

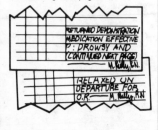

burdens for you. As computers become more common in patient record keeping, you'll need to understand how these burdens affect your practice legally.

Computers enter clinical nursing

Most hospitals and other health-care facilities have been using computers for payrolls and patient billings since the 1960s. A few computers have also made inroads in nursing care—mostly in specialized patient-care departments, such as the intensive care unit and the cardiac care unit. But experts believe the biggest effect computers will have on nursing is in patient charting.

The components of a computerized system

Computerized systems are expensive, and computerized record programs must be extraordinarily large to include the variables needed to chart accurately. For example, your observations of a patient's skin might include variables such as scaly, clammy, cold, dry, inflamed, and purpuric. A computer program must be large enough to offer all these choices.

A few hospitals in the United States and Canada are already using computerized record-keeping systems. Typically, a system consists of a large, centralized computer, to store information, and a much smaller terminal in each work area. These terminals—linked to the main computer by electric cable—look like small television screens with typewriter keyboards.

To use the system, a nurse "signs in" by typing on the keyboard her signature code, a series of numbers and letters that gives a person access to a patient's record. The computer recognizes by her signature code that she has authorized access to the information stored in its memory. When she types her patient's code number, the computer displays the patient's records on the screen. By typing another key, she can order a printed copy of all or part of the patient's record.

Computers can save you time

The computerized medical record can save you the time you now spend filing, searching for, and retrieving information about your patient. It will even save you the time

Charting on Progress Notes?

My hospital recently changed its charting system: everyone now charts on the progress notes. We've already had some problems with the new system.

For one thing, many doctors leave blank lines between their notes and a nurse's note. Isn't this dangerous?

Second, some nurses don't chart anything if the doctor has already written a note adequately covering the patient's condition and care. Is this good nursing practice?—RN, Ore.

First things first. Leaving blank lines between entries on a patient's chart is inviting legal trouble. If someone inserted an entry out of chronological order or padded the notes, an attorney could zero

in on these as suspicious entries when the notes are used as evidence in court. Therefore, ask your hospital administrator to establish a protocol that clearly states that *no one* can leave blank lines.

Your second problem is just as serious. A nurse isn't relieved of her responsibilities in charting when a doctor writes a note, even if his note describes the patient's condition and care. The nurse must still document her *own* observations, interactions with the patient, and nursing care provided. In court, the rule of thumb is—documentation means *done,* and no documentation means *not done.*

This letter was taken from the files of *Nursing* magazine.

---

of calling the laboratory to track down test results that never made it up to the unit. The technicians who record these results will have "called up" the patient's record on their terminal and added the information directly.

Besides saving you time, computers offer you other important advantages. For one thing, computers reduce the risk of misinterpretation by improving legibility—no more problems with a doctor's indecipherable handwriting when you're reading his typed orders on a screen.

Computers also reduce misinterpretation by fostering standardized formats for your assessment reports, flow charts, and care plans. And by time-stamping each entry, computers decrease the chance of scheduling mistakes.

Legal concerns with computerized records

Computerized medical records are such a new development that their legal implications are still being debated. The Joint Commission on the Accreditation of Hospitals has informally recognized them as

legitimate substitutes for manual records. But some state laws require health facilities with computerized records to retain the written records as well.

Until uniform rules are adopted, the computerized record will invite questions that could raise legal risks for you.

By far, the most pressing legal question about the computerized medical record is its threat to your patient's privacy.

With traditional records, you can limit access to information simply by keeping it on the unit. An unauthorized person wouldn't get very far into the charts before you challenged him. But with a computerized system, your patients' records can be called up at any of the terminals. Despite the use of signature codes, many more people have easier access to the computerized record than they do to manual records. That means a much greater chance exists for exposure of your patient's highly personal, private medical information.

Various laws protect the privacy of a patient's medical records. The Federal Privacy Act of 1974 protects confidential

Compounding the Error

The legal office at my hospital insists that we simply line out, then cover, any errors on a patient's chart with white, gummed labels. The long list of errors includes stamping the chart with the wrong patient's plate, making mistakes on the temperature, pulse, and respiration graph, writing notes on the wrong patient's chart, and so on.

I've refused to cover up mistakes because it contradicts everything I've learned in nursing. I still think what I was taught is right: Draw a single line through the error, initial it, and write in the correction. I'm always warning my colleagues about the legal problems they could face if they "gum up" mistakes, and I've complained to my supervisor about the cover-up procedure. But I feel like I'm beating my head against a wall.

Although the legal staff can't prove that the labeling practice is legal, they say I have to prove it's illegal before the situation can be changed. Please help—I don't want to leave this job.

By the way, this is a military hospital.

Does that change the situation?—RN, Calif.

Your hospital's charting strategy is a mess. Gumming over the faulty entries will cripple any legal defense for the hospital or its personnel in a court action. In fact, the charts with labels may not even be legally admissible. Your best plan is to mark an error as soon as you discover it, then refer the reader to the recorded correction.

By the way, the rules are different in a military setting. A military hospital, because of the doctrine of sovereign immunity, can't be sued without its consent. You'd be wise to visit the hospital's legal office again. Get more information about your liability and the hospital's under the Federal Torts Claims Act.

Making an effort to change your hospital's poor charting practices now may save you and your hospital from trouble later.

This letter was taken from the files of *Nursing* magazine.

---

medical information of patients in Veterans' Administration hospitals, and some of the state practice acts impose an ethical duty to guard patients' privacy. However, no one can guarantee that unauthorized persons won't gain access to computerized records.

In 1977, a patient in New York charged that a computerized record system was an invasion of his privacy. In *Whalen v. Roe,* he challenged the constitutionality of a state law that required a patient buying certain drug prescriptions to list his name, address, age, the drug, dosage, and prescribing doctor's name. The state then fed all the information into a computer.

The U.S. Supreme Court upheld the law, but it acknowledged the threat to privacy implicit in a centralized data system. Said Justice William Brennan: "The central storage and easy accessibility of computerized data vastly increase the potential for abuse of that information...."

Health-care professionals and computer programmers have devised some safeguards to protect patients' privacy. The main safeguard is the signature code. By developing a series of access codes, programmers can limit access to the records. For example, your code would allow you to see a patient's entire record, but a technician's code would allow her to see only part of the record.

Using Computers: The Pros and Cons

Computerized records are a mixed blessing for the health-care field. Your institution will undoubtedly be using computers more and more—especially in nursing services. So you need to understand how computers can help and hinder health care. Here's how the pros and cons stack up:

PROs	CONs
• Computers compile valuable data on patient populations.	• Computers sometimes scramble patient information.
• Computers make information retrieval easier.	• Computers threaten patients' rights to privacy and confidentiality.
• Computers make patient information more legible.	• Computers may be used as tools for unauthorized biomedical research.
• Computers allow for efficient and constant updating of patient information.	• Computers break down, making information unavailable for unpredictable periods of time.
• Computers link diverse sources of patient information.	• Computers can perpetuate inaccurate information.
• Computers save time—travel time (delivering slips and information) and time spent making phone calls. A nurse can send request slips and patient information from one data terminal to another quickly and efficiently.	• Computers impose an impersonal distance between you and your patients.

The computer's other disadvantages

In addition to the legal concern of privacy invasion, computers have other disadvantages. Computers threaten the doctor-patient relationship. Doctors fear that patients will be less truthful in providing medical histories and details about illnesses. Why? Because patients worry that computers will be used to improperly divulge their medical information.

Another disadvantage of a computerized medical record system is the need for a backup system. Like all electronic devices, computers occasionally break down, making information unavailable for indeterminate periods. This is why a backup system is required to ensure completeness and continuity in charting.

Computers also sometimes scramble patient information because of mechanical or human error. When this happens, and you discover the mistake, you can't tell how many other health-team members have copies of the record containing the mistake.

Finally, some critics simply think computers are just another piece of equipment that distances you from your patient, making your practice less personal.

Verification helps ensure accuracy

Verification is one way of reducing the chance for error in the computerized record. With verification, you check the accuracy of a doctor's order. It serves the same purpose for the computerized record that signing off a doctor's order serves for the manual record. In a computerized record system, the unit secretary enters a doctor's order into the computer. The order is held in a "suspense file" until a nurse reviews the entry and checks to be sure the unit secretary interpreted and entered the order correctly. After the nurse verifies the order, it's added to the active record file.

Minimizing your legal risks

When you work with the computerized medical record, your liabilities are the same as when you're working with the manual system: you're liable for any patient injuries associated with your charting errors.

Here's how to minimize your legal risks:

- Always double-check all patient information you enter.
- Never tell anyone your signature code.
- Tell your supervisor if you suspect someone is using your code.
- Indicate that the doctor's order is written, verbal (in person), or verbal (by telephone) when you enter it.
- Know your institution's rules and regulations affecting patient privacy.

Conclusion

As a provider of care, you should be ready to learn to use technology that promises to improve patient care. Many experts are convinced that computer technology will do that by freeing you to spend more time meeting your patient's needs.

Selected References

American Hospital Association. *Patient's Bill of Rights.* Chicago: American Hospital Association, 1973.

American Nurses' Association. *Standards of Practice.* Kansas City, Mo.: American Nurses' Association, 1973.

Annas, George J., et al. *The Rights of Doctors, Nurses, and Allied Health Professionals.* Cambridge, Mass.: Ballinger Publishing Co., 1983.

Bennett, H.M. "The Legal Liabilities of Critical Care," *Critical Care Nurse* 2:22, January/February 1982.

Bernzweig, Eli. *The Nurse's Liability for Malpractice: A Programmed Course,* 3rd ed. New York: McGraw-Hill Book Co., 1981.

Blake, M.B. "Computerized Medical Records," *Legal Aspects of Medical Practice* 10:3, 1982.

Broccolo, Bernadette Muller. "The Importance of Proper Medical Record Entries," *Topics in Health Record Management, Legal Issues, Part 2* 2(1):67-74, September 1981.

Cazalas, Mary W. *Nursing and the Law,* 3rd ed. Rockville, Md.: Aspen Systems Corp., 1979.

Creighton, Helen. *Law Every Nurse Should Know,* 4th ed. Philadelphia: W.B. Saunders Co., 1981.

Du Gas, Beverly W. *Introduction to Patient Care: A Comprehensive Approach to Nursing,* 4th ed. Philadelphia: W.B. Saunders Co., 1983.

Fiesta, Janine. *The Law and Liability: A Guide for Nurses.* New York: John Wiley & Sons, 1983.

Hemelt, M., and Mackert, M. *Dynamics of Law in Nursing and Health Care,* 2nd ed. Reston, Va.: Reston Publishing Co., 1982.

Huffman, Edna K. *Medical Record Management.* Berwyn, Ill.: Physicians' Record Co., 1981.

Joint Commission on Accreditation of Hospitals. *Accreditation Manual for Hospitals: 1983 Ed.* Chicago: Joint Commission on Accreditation of Hospitals, 1982.

Regan, William A., ed. "Charting Deficiencies and R.N. Liability," *Regan Report on Nursing Law* 21(8), January 1981.

Regan, William A., ed. "Charting: 'The Truth, The Whole Truth...'," *Regan Report on Nursing Law* 23(1), June 1982.

Regan, William A., ed. "Nurses and Medical Records: Legalities," *Regan Report on Nursing Law* 21(12), May 1981.

Regan, William A., ed. "Postop Infection: Poor Nursing Records," *Regan Report on Nursing Law* 21(6), November 1980.

Rocereto, LaVerne, and Maleski, Cynthia. *The Legal Dimensions of Nursing Practice: A Practical Guide.* New York: Springer Publishing Co., 1982.

Springer, Eric W. "The Medical Record in Today's World," *Topics in Health Record Management, Legal Issues, Part 1* 1(4), June 1981.

Watson, B.L. "Disclosure of Computerized Health Care Information: Provider Privacy Rights Under Supply Side Competition," *American Journal of Law and Medicine* 7:265, 1981.

Weed, Lawrence. "Medical Records That Guide and Teach," *New England Journal of Medicine* 278:593-600, March 1968.

6

Malpractice: Understand It, Avoid It

Since the 1970s, the number of malpractice lawsuits filed against nurses has risen dramatically. The major reason seems to be that patients are increasingly aware of their right to receive quality health care—and increasingly willing to fight for it. When a patient feels his right has been violated or that the care he's received falls below acceptable standards, he may seek compensation through the courts.

You can protect yourself from malpractice lawsuits and help head off the upward trend of malpractice litigation in several ways. The most obvious way is to give your patients the best possible nursing care, according to the highest professional standards. This is your main strength and protection. Happily, it coincides with your constant main concern—the health and welfare of your patients. But you also need a sound knowledge of patients' rights, and you must do your best to respect them. And your own rights—what about them? You need to know what they are and how to safeguard them.

Malpractice—the concept and the laws

Our legal system's view of malpractice evolved from negligence law and the premise, basic to all law, that everyone is responsible for the consequences of his own acts. Over the years, malpractice law developed special doctrines, or theories, to apply to cases involving subordinate-superior relationships. The law books call one such doctrine the doctrine of respondeat superior (let the master answer). It's also called the theory of vicarious liability.

Simply put, this doctrine or theory holds that when a subordinate acting according to his superior's direction (servant to master, employee to employer) is found to have been negligent, he shouldn't have to bear the brunt of damages that may result from faithfully doing as directed. To the extent that a nurse was merely the hospital's functionary, she could claim protection under this theory. This doctrine is discussed many times in Nurse's Legal Handbook.

A concept related to respondeat superior is the borrowed-servant doctrine, which is still applied in malpractice lawsuits, but not as often as it used to be. It could apply in a situation in which you, a hospital employee, commit a negligent act while under the direction or control of someone other than your hospital supervisor, such as a doctor in the operating room. Because the doctor is an independent contractor and you're responsible to him during surgery, you're considered his borrowed servant at the time. If you're sued for malpractice, his liability is vicarious, meaning that even though the doctor didn't direct you negligently, he's responsible because he was in control.

By taking on more responsibility for your patients' welfare, you've stepped out of the doctor's shadow into a personal-liability limelight of your own. Paradoxically, the increased risk you've incurred has come about because patient care is far better than it used to be—thanks to your efforts. Because you've been willing to do more, the educated consumer has come to expect more. And he looks to the courts for relief when he thinks he's gotten less than your best.

Where you and the law are concerned, you need to know how to avoid being named as a defendant in a malpractice lawsuit—how to walk that tightrope between what you perceive as your patient's needs and what your position as a nurse lets you provide. You want informed opinion about what the law says is—and isn't— appropriate nursing care. Obviously, training, background, and experience all play a part. For instance, what the law expects from an RN is sometimes different from what it expects from an LPN or LVN. You also need to know what legal and professional limits your hospital and state board of nursing put on your practice, what rules accrediting agencies have set for your professional conduct, and what guidelines apply when your hospital says one thing and your professional organizations say another.

That's where this chapter can help. It contains the latest information on:
• malpractice
• the rule of res ipsa loquitur
• professional liability insurance—the quality and quantity you need
• statutes of limitations
• what to do if you're sued for malpractice
• how you should conduct yourself if you're testifying as a defendant or an expert witness.

You won't find a more compelling reason to read this chapter than *State of New Jersey v. Winter* (1982). In this criminal negligence case, a nurse was charged with administering blood of an incompatible type to a patient undergoing surgery. The state alleged that when she discovered her error, she attempted to cover up her negligence instead of correcting her error. In the prosecution that resulted, the jury found her actions "reckless and wanton negligence... Show[ing] an utter disregard for the safety of others under circumstances likely to cause death." Although her conviction was later overturned upon appeal, the jury found that the nurse's negligence constituted manslaughter, and the trial court sentenced her to five years in prison.

Malpractice pitfalls

Nursing has changed. No one expects you to *blindly* follow doctors' orders. You're a professional in your own right. And you make your own professional decisions. Of course, you're always legally responsible for those decisions. But this needn't worry you if you consistently practice nursing according to the laws and professional standards of care that govern your practice.

You know that nursing is a much more complicated job than it used to be. Making moment-to-moment decisions about patient care is harder than ever. Under such conditions, your chances of making mistakes have increased—along with your chances of being sued for malpractice.

Remember, negligence is by far the largest category of suits filed against nurses. This is because negligence is *unintentional*. Nurses found liable for negligence didn't set out deliberately to commit negligent acts. They were trying to do their best for their patients, just like you, but most of them met with malpractice pitfalls.

What are malpractice pitfalls? They're liability-producing behaviors that nurses can avoid by using caution, common sense, and heightened awareness of how the law affects nurses. Some common malpractice pitfalls are described below. (See *Tort Claims,* page 203.) Avoid them, and your chances of avoiding malpractice suits will improve.

Discussion and documentation

Avoid being rude or disrespectful to patients or their families. Always remain calm when a patient or his family becomes difficult. Trial attorneys have a saying: "If you don't want to be sued, don't be rude."

Don't offer your opinion when a patient asks you what you think is the matter with him. If you do, you could be accused of making a medical diagnosis—practicing medicine without a license. Don't volunteer information about possible treatments for the patient's condition, or possible choices of doctors, either.

Be careful not to discuss a patient's care or personal business with anyone except

Tort Claims

Like all health-care professionals, you're vulnerable to lawsuits. If a patient feels your nursing care is inappropriate, he might well file a lawsuit claiming one of six torts. The law classifies each of those six torts as either an intentional tort—a direct invasion of someone's legal right—or an unintentional tort—a civil wrong from the defendant's negligence. This chart shows you both intentional and unintentional torts and some examples of improper nursing actions that could lead a patient to use each claim in a lawsuit.

TORT CLAIMS	IMPROPER NURSING ACTION
UNINTENTIONAL TORT	
Negligence	• Leaving foreign objects inside a patient following surgery • Failing to observe an ICU patient as the doctor ordered • Failing to ensure a patient's informed consent • Failing to report a change in a patient's vital signs or status • Failing to report a staff member's negligence that you witnessed
INTENTIONAL TORTS	
Assault	• Threatening a patient
Battery	• Forcing a patient to ambulate against his wishes • Forcing a patient to submit to injections • Striking a patient
False imprisonment	• Confining a patient in a psychiatric unit without a doctor's order • Refusing to let a patient return home
Invasion of privacy	• Releasing private information about a patient to third parties • Allowing unauthorized persons to read a patient's medical records • Allowing unauthorized persons to observe a procedure • Taking pictures of the patient without his consent
Slander	• Making false statements about a patient in front of newspaper reporters

when doing so is consistent with proper nursing care.

Document every verbal order thoroughly, and obtain a corresponding signed order from the doctor as soon as possible.

Never sign your name as a witness without fully understanding what you're signing *and* the legal significance of your signature.

Don't ever correct or revise a patient's medical record after he's filed a lawsuit. The case of *Carr v. St. Paul Fire and Marine Insurance Company* (1974) illustrates the liability a hospital may have when nurses or other employees alter or destroy patient records. The patient in this case was a man who came to the hospital emergency department (ED) suffering severe pain. One of the nurses on duty refused to call a doctor for the patient, so he returned home—and died a short time later. The nurses who'd been on duty in the ED that night testified they'd taken the patient's vital signs—but this couldn't be proved or disproved, because the patient's records had been destroyed. In instructing the jury, the judge indicated that they could find the hospital negligent.

Doctors' orders

Never treat any patient without orders from his doctor (except in an emergency, of course). And don't dispense any medication. Only doctors and pharmacists may legally perform these functions. Don't carry out any order from a doctor, *particularly a medication order,* if you have any doubt about its accuracy or appropriateness. Don't carry out *any* order you don't fully understand (see *Always Questioning These Orders,* page 205).

In *Norton v. Argonaut Insurance Company* (1962), a hospital's assistant director of nursing services temporarily covered a pediatric unit when the charge nurse's help was needed in an emergency. She did question a seemingly high dosage of injectable digoxin ordered for a 3-month-old infant, but she accepted two attending doctors' mistaken endorsements of the order. (They thought she was referring to an *oral* dosage.) In fact, the dosage ordered was an overdose for injectable digoxin. The nurse administered the medication as ordered and the child died. The nurse, the doctor who originally ordered the medication, and the hospital were found liable.

Patient precautions

Don't participate in a surgical procedure unless you're satisfied the patient has given proper informed consent. Never force a patient to accept treatment he's expressly refused. And of course, if you're an operating-room nurse, *always* check and double-check that no surgical equipment such as sponges or instruments (foreign objects) are unaccounted for after an operation is completed. (See *Negligence: Who's Responsible?,* pages 206 and 207.)

Don't use any patient-care equipment you're not familiar with, not trained to use, or which seems to be functioning improperly.

Take every precaution to prevent patient falls. This is a very common area of nursing liability. Patients who are elderly, infirm, sedated, or mentally incapacitated are the most likely to fall.

The case of *Stevenson v. Alta Bates* (1937) involved a patient who'd had a stroke and was learning to walk again. As two nurses, each holding one of the patient's arms, assisted her into the hospital's sunroom, one of the nurses let go of the patient and stepped forward to get a chair for her. The patient fell and sustained a fracture. The nurse was found negligent: the court stated she should have anticipated the patient's need for a chair and made the appropriate arrangements *before* bringing the patient into the sun-room.

Conclusion

Here's a malpractice pitfall that can make any of the others much worse: failure to carry adequate professional liability insurance. This is the Ultimate Pitfall. Remember, if you're ever sued and found liable for damages, your insurance may be all that stands between you and serious financial hardship. This is because your employer may successfully argue that he should not be held vicariously liable for your improper action (or inaction).

Of course, your constant objective as a nurse is to provide the best possible patient care. Worrying about possible malpractice lawsuits won't help you do this. Instead, use your knowledge of malpractice pitfalls constructively. How? By giving your nursing care with conscious intent to avoid malpractice pitfalls. Doing this will help ensure that your care always meets legal and professional standards.

The res ipsa loquitur rule

The Latin phrase *res ipsa loquitur* literally means, "The thing speaks for itself." Res ipsa loquitur is a rule of evidence designed

Always Question These Orders

Do you always assume the doctor is right, and follow his orders even if they seem vague or medically inappropriate? If you do, you could be jeopardizing your nursing career. Your responsibility as a nurse is to question *any* dubious order you receive. Some types of orders may actually be detrimental to your patient's health—and legally dangerous for you.

Here are four types of orders you must always question:

AMBIGUOUS ORDERS

Follow your hospital's policy for clarifying ambiguous orders—orders that are vague or have more than one possible interpretation—and document your actions. If your hospital doesn't have a policy covering this situation, contact the prescribing doctor and (as always) document your actions (see "Telephone Orders"). Then ask your nursing administration for a step-by-step policy to follow in this situation.

INAPPROPRIATE ORDERS

A change in your patient's condition may mean that a standing order is no longer appropriate. When this occurs, delay the treatment until you've contacted the doctor and clarified the situation. Follow your hospital's policy for clarifying the order.

Note: If you're an inexperienced nurse, you should take steps to clarify all standing orders. Contact the prescribing doctor for guidance. Or tell your supervisor you're uncertain about following the order, and let her decide whether to delegate the responsibility to a more experienced nurse.

If, after you carry out the order, the treatment is affecting the patient adversely, discontinue it. Then report all the unfavorable signs and symptoms to the patient's doctor. *Resume treatment only after you've discussed the situation with the doctor and clarified his orders.*

ANY ORDER A PATIENT QUESTIONS

A doctor can change his orders at any time, including while you're off duty. So a patient may know something about his prescribed care that no one has told *you*. If a patient protests a procedure, medication dosage, or medication route—saying that it's different from "the usual," or that it's been changed—give him the benefit of the doubt. Question the doctor's orders, following your hospital's policy if one exists.

TELEPHONE ORDERS

Whenever a doctor gives you an order by telephone, be sure to document all the details. Follow your hospital's policy to the letter. If your hospital has no formal policy, document your conversation and subsequent actions using the following guidelines:

● Write down the time of the call, the date, and the doctor's name; describe the patient's condition and other circumstances that prompted the call.
● Review the patient's condition in detail with the doctor.
● Write down his orders as you listen.
● Read the orders back to him to be sure you've recorded them accurately.
● Document that you've read the orders back and that the doctor confirmed them.

to equalize the plaintiff's and the defendant's positions in court, when otherwise the plaintiff could be at a disadvantage in proving his case—a disadvantage not of his own making. (Res ipsa loquitur *doesn't* apply when a plaintiff simply fails to prove his case.) Essentially, the rule of res ipsa loquitur allows a plaintiff to prove negli-

Negligence: Who's Responsible?

Here's a test. Read these three cases. Decide for yourself who's negligent—the nurse or the doctor. Then check our answers to see how well you did.

NEGLECTING TO SEARCH

In *Piehl v. Dallas General Hospital* (1977), Willi Piehl entered the hospital with stomach ulcers and almost left with a 14-square-inch laparotomy sponge packed around his colon. An X-ray revealed the sponge, which had to be removed through a second operation. Later, Piehl sued the doctor and the hospital—as the employer of the surgeon, the scrub nurse, and the circulating nurse assigned to his case.

Why hadn't the surgeon seen the sponge and removed it? "We take all the sponges we can see or feel," the surgeon testified. "After a pyloroplasty, we don't like to dig around and spread the infection around. If the sponge count is correct, we have no reason to believe a sponge is inside the abdominal cavity or in the wound."

Laparotomy sponges come in packages of five, witnesses at the trial testified. And the smaller 4″ x 4″ sponges come in packages of 10. Before surgery, the nurses count the sponges when they prepare the operating room. During surgery, the nurses routinely lay the used sponges out and count them, together with the unused sponges, in units of 5 for the laparotomy sponges and in units of 10 for the 4″ x 4″ sponges. They do this twice—before and after the patient's abdomen is closed.

Piehl's nurses said the count checked out and they noted this in the medical record. Still, a sponge showed up on Piehl's X-ray.

Who was responsible?

ANSWER
The court concluded that apparently the nurses had miscounted the sponges, but it found the surgeon and his employer, the hospital, guilty. Its reasoning? "Even a summary poking around for all the sponges, in the exercise of ordinary care, would have resulted in the discovery of something the size of a laparotomy sponge. And no emergency made time a critical factor."

NO-SHOW DOCTOR

In *Taylor v. Baptist Medical Center, Inc.* (1981), Robin Taylor was 26 weeks pregnant when she told her obstetrician that labor pains had started. He told her to go to the hospital. The time was 3 a.m.

At the hospital, two experienced obstetric nurses attended Mrs. Taylor. They called the obstetrician several times during the next 8 hours, and each time he said he'd be right over. At 11:30 a.m.,

---

gence by circumstantial evidence, when the defendant has the primary—sometimes the only—knowledge of what happened to cause the plaintiff's injury.

The res ipsa loquitur rule derives from a 19th-century English case, *Byrne v.* *Boodle* (1863). In this case, the injured person had been struck by a flour barrel that fell from a second-floor window of a warehouse. In the ensuing lawsuit, the plaintiff wasn't able to show which warehouse employee had been negligent in al-

Mrs. Taylor gave birth to a stillborn premature infant—10 minutes before the obstetrician arrived.

Mrs. Taylor sued the hospital for failing to provide another doctor or a competent medical attendant, and she sued her obstetrician for failing to care for her during labor and delivery.

Were both the hospital and doctor negligent?

ANSWER
The court found the hospital innocent. The nurses had fulfilled their duty by keeping the obstetrician informed, the court said, and they had no reason to doubt his assurance that he'd "be right over." Furthermore, the two nurses who'd attended Mrs. Taylor were well qualified and provided Mrs. Taylor with skillful and diligent care.

But the court found the doctor negligent. His failure to attend his patient constituted a breach of contract, and Mrs. Taylor had a right to recover damages.

FAILURE TO REPORT

The case of *Kolakowski v. Voris* (1979) involved Edward Kolakowski, who'd undergone a diskectomy. Several hours later, he told his nurses that he couldn't bend his left leg and that his right side was weak and numb. They noted the complaints. And noted them again 1 hour later, 2 hours later, and 4 hours later. One of the nurses called the neurosurgeon but couldn't locate him.

Kolakowski's neurosurgeon saw him the next day and attributed his poor movement and sensation to spinal cord edema. Two days later, a myelogram showed spinal cord compression, and Kolakowski was taken back to the operating room, where the surgeon removed extruded bits of disk and performed a laminectomy. The operation left Kolakowski a quadriplegic.

Kolakowski sued the doctor and the hospital. Hospital attorneys pointed out that Kolakowski's doctor didn't act immediately, even after a day's delay, so the nurses and their employer—the hospital—were not negligent despite the nurses' delay in contacting the doctor. The attorneys asked the courts to drop the lawsuit against the hospital.

Were the hospital attorneys right?

ANSWER
Refusing to drop the hospital from the lawsuit, the court held that Kolakowski's nurses should have known his signs and symptoms were unusual and demanded immediate attention. Thus, they had a duty to relate those signs and symptoms to a doctor immediately. *When* the doctor decided to treat the signs and symptoms had no bearing on the nurses' responsibility, the court ruled.

lowing the barrel to fall. The court applied the concept of res ipsa loquitur to the warehouse owners, who were found liable in the absence of proof that the employees *weren't* responsible for the plaintiff's injury.

What does this rule mean to you, as a nurse?

Res ipsa loquitur is applied in a minority of malpractice cases involving alleged negligence. In most medical malpractice cases, the plaintiff has the responsibility for proving every element of his case against the defendant; until he does, the court presumes that the defendant met the applicable standard of care. But when a court applies the res ipsa loquitur rule, the burden of proof shifts from the plaintiff to the defendant, who must attempt to prove that the plaintiff's injury was caused by something other than his, the defendant's, negligence.

However, this unusual legal situation must be applicable only in special circumstances. Here are some examples:

Suppose you're a defendant in a typical malpractice lawsuit. The plaintiff-patient, through his attorney, alleges that you were professionally negligent. Ordinarily his attorney has the responsibility of proving, by a preponderance of the evidence, that you failed to meet an applicable standard of care. But if the plaintiff-patient's attorney can show that three key elements are present, he can ask the court to invoke the rule of res ipsa loquitur. If the court grants this request, the practical effect is that you and your attorney must prove you *weren't* negligent.

The three key elements are:
• The act that caused the plaintiff's injury was exclusively in your control.
• The injury wouldn't have happened in the absence of your negligence.
• No negligence on the plaintiff's part contributed to his injury.

The following case, *Sanchez v. Bay General Hospital* (1981), illustrates the extent to which courts invoke the res ipsa loquitur rule.

In February, 1975, Mrs. Sanchez entered Bay General Hospital for elective surgery—a laminectomy. Following the surgery, the surgeon implanted an atrial catheter to minimize the chance that an air embolism would form in her heart.

When Mrs. Sanchez was transferred to the postoperative ward, her condition began to deteriorate. In addition, Mrs. Sanchez was still unconscious and unable to contribute to her injury in any manner. Her care was totally under the control of the nurses in the postoperative ward. The nurses there made several initial errors:
• They didn't examine the patient's chart, so they weren't aware that the catheter had been put in place.

• They neglected to check the patient's neurologic status.
• They didn't notify a doctor of her deteriorating vital signs.

Eventually, Mrs. Sanchez went into cardiac arrest, and an emergency department doctor ordered immediate administration of medication. The nurses then made the error that sealed Mrs. Sanchez's fate and caused res ipsa loquitur to apply: They administered medication through the atrial catheter, mistaking it for an I.V. line. But for this act, the patient probably would not have died. The medication went directly to Mrs. Sanchez's heart, causing brain death a few hours later. The children of Mrs. Sanchez later sued the hospital for the wrongful death of their mother.

The court, invoking the res ipsa loquitur rule, granted a directed verdict to the children of Mrs. Sanchez. The court indicated that the hospital had the burden of proving that Mrs. Sanchez's death was caused by something other than the staff's negligence—or, alternatively, that she died even though the staff had given due care to prevent her death. The hospital was unable to refute the court's presumption of negligence. The hospital appealed the directed verdict, but the appellate court sustained the trial court's judgment in favor of Mrs. Sanchez's children.

Courts apply the res ipsa loquitur rule in cases where the defendant was the only one in a position to know what caused the injury, and when the patient knew nothing. Courts *won't* apply the rule when the evidence offered by the defendant satisfactorily explains the facts which appeared to constitute blatant negligence.

Perhaps the most common incident associated with the res ipsa loquitur rule is the so-called foreign-object case. In such a case, a foreign object—for example, a sponge, a needle, or a pin—is left inside the patient after surgery.

Courts have also been willing to invoke the res ipsa loquitur rule because of injuries to plaintiffs involving body parts completely unrelated to the plaintiffs' surgery.

Take the Wisconsin malpractice case, *Beaudoin v. Watertown Memorial Hospital* (1966). A patient suffered second-degree burns on the buttocks during vaginal surgery. She brought suit, claiming negligence. The court applied the res ipsa loquitur rule on the basis that injury to an area unrelated to surgery automatically results from failure to exercise due care.

Critics and defenders of the res ipsa loquitur rule

Critics of the rule feel the courts have been too free in letting plaintiffs use it. They call it "the rule of sympathy" and contend that, by invoking it, the plaintiff can quickly catch the sympathetic ears of judge and jury. Health-care professionals particularly contend that the rule puts them at an unfair disadvantage as defendants. They feel that, by giving the burden of proof, the court singles them out for more negligence liability than other types of defendants. Also, invoking the rule usually eliminates the plaintiff's responsibility to introduce expert testimony. Defenders of the rule feel its value lies in drawing attention to the fact that a plaintiff's unusual or rare injury is itself sufficient to cause suspicion that the defendant was negligent.

How courts in different states apply the rule

In some states, courts cannot apply the res ipsa loquitur rule. Most states, however, do allow courts to apply some form of it. For example, neither Michigan nor South Carolina uses the rule by name but each does permit circumstantial evidence of negligence, which is, in effect, the same concept. Until recently, Pennsylvania rejected the rule outright. But in *Gilbert v. Korvette, Inc.* (1974), it adopted the Restatement of Torts, the evidentiary rule of res ipsa loquitur.

How courts in Canada apply the rule

The Canadian courts formerly applied the rule of res ipsa loquitur infrequently in medical malpractice cases. In most such cases, the courts based their decisions on the "ordinary medical experience of mankind."

Then, in *Holt v. Nesbitt* (1953) and again in *Cardin v. City of Montreal* (1961), the Supreme Court of Canada clearly stated that the rule of res ipsa loquitur applied in malpractice cases. In *Holt v.*

Choosing Liability Insurance

As you probably know, all professional liability insurance policies aren't the same. To find one with the liability coverage that fits your needs, compare the features each policy offers. Does the policy cover claims made *before* the policy expires (claims-made coverage), or does the policy cover negligent acts committed during the policy period, regardless of when the claim is made (occurrence coverage)?

Also, check for these options:

● coverage when nurses under your supervision are negligent

● coverage for misuse of equipment

● coverage for errors in reporting or recording care

● coverage for failure to properly teach patients

● coverage for errors in administering medication

● coverage in case the hospital sues you

● coverage for professional services you perform in an emergency outside your employment setting.

Nesbitt, the plaintiff was a patient of the defendant, an oral surgeon. While the plaintiff was under general anesthesia, a sponge lodged in his windpipe, causing death by suffocation. The court decided that failure to apply the res ipsa loquitur rule would give the health-care practitioner unfair—and therefore unwarranted—protection in a malpractice lawsuit. In effect, the court put the patient's protection from bad medical practice above the health-care practitioner's protection from a difficult malpractice lawsuit.

The Canadian courts progress slowly in mediating malpractice lawsuits. That's because differences in expert opinion are the rule, not the exception, and because many lawsuits present issues not previously resolved. The Canadian courts do, however, seem to want to make sure that the rule doesn't place too heavy a burden on the defendant.

Conclusion
Many states are expanding their applications of the res ipsa loquitur rule, so stay informed about the status of the rule in your state. Your professional nursing organizations and the nursing literature should help keep you posted.

Professional liability insurance

Consider this scenario: You're an operating room nurse responsible for the instrument count in an operating room. During a major surgical procedure on a grossly overweight patient, you hand over various instruments to the surgeon, including an Ochsner clamp (a 9″-long hemostat). After the last suture, you sign off your instrument count list, verifying that all the instruments are present and accounted for. But that Ochsner clamp—it wasn't withdrawn; it remains in the patient's abdominal cavity for 11 months before anyone discovers it. During that time it has rusted, perforated the patient's colon, and caused adhesions.

The patient sues the hospital for malpractice and names you as a defendant for making an incorrect instrument count.

You claim that the surgeon—as "captain of the ship"—had ultimate responsibility; he counters that he's only as competent as those who work with him.

What do you do? Your career and all of the tangible benefits you've worked a lifetime for are now in jeopardy. And the situation could get worse. Consider this: The jury awards the plaintiff a million dollars in damages. Cases like this are becoming more common. Nurses are being named in malpractice lawsuits more and more frequently. Someday it could happen to you.

Because you're vulnerable, you need professional liability insurance. Insurance for nurses isn't new. What is new is that your expanded health-care role makes having insurance crucial. All nurses in any work setting are at risk for malpractice suits. However, the risk increases if you work in a specialized setting, such as an intensive care unit.

Unfortunately, some nurses are skeptical; they believe that purchasing professional liability insurance makes them a more attractive target for compensation claims and increases their chances of being sued. This is dangerous thinking. Given the legal risks you face on the job, you simply can't afford to be without insurance.

Buying financial protection
What do you get when you buy professional liability insurance? You get protection under contract for a designated period from the financial consequences of certain professional errors. The type of insurance policy you buy defines the amount that the insurance company will pay if the judgment goes against you in a malpractice lawsuit.

You can buy a policy designated as "single limits" or "double limits." In a single-limits policy, you buy protection in set dollar increments, for example, $100,000, $300,000, or $1,000,000. The stipulated amount will shield you if a judgment, arising out of a single nursing malpractice occurrence, goes against you.

In the less common double-limits policy, you buy protection in a combination package, such as $100,000/$300,000, $300,000/$500,000, or $1,000,000/$3,000,000. In a double-limits policy, the smaller sum is what your insurance company will make available to protect you from any one injury arising out of a single nursing malpractice occurrence. The larger sum is the amount available if more than one patient sues you for the same alleged error. This happens, for instance, when a nurse administers the wrong medication to several patients. While the single-limits policy will also protect you against injuries to more than one patient, the double-limits policy makes considerably more money available to protect you when you're involved in multiple lawsuits.

What if a judgment against you exceeds the policy limits? This is called an *excess judgment* for which you're personally responsible. Depending on the laws in your

Ensuring Protection after Your Policy Expires

I'm afraid I'm in hot water. I had malpractice insurance for the 5 years I was practicing nursing full time. When I took a year's maternity leave, I let my policy lapse, thinking I'd renew it when I returned to work. During my leave, I found out that a patient I'd cared for 2 years before was threatening to sue the hospital and me for negligent care.

I immediately called my insurance agent. He told me that he couldn't help me because I had a "claims-made" policy. This means that even though I was covered by the policy when I cared for the patient, I'm not covered now—because the claim was made after the policy expired.

My insurance policy had always been my security blanket. Now, I'm scared. What can I do?—RN, Mich.

First of all, the patient is only threatening to sue. He may not actually file a lawsuit. And even if he does, the hospital attorneys may be able to make a settlement with him before the case goes to court. (About 80% of all malpractice cases are settled before a trial.)

If the case does go to court and the patient wins, the hospital's insurance coverage may be sufficient to settle the claim.

You're right to be concerned, though. If you lose the case and, under the *respondeat superior* doctrine the hospital insurance carrier makes a settlement with the patient, the hospital can turn around and sue you for the amount of the settlement. (Providing, of course, that it wasn't actually found liable.) If you have no money, the hospital can deduct from your paycheck. The prospect of years of indebtedness to your employer is frightening indeed, although this seems unlikely from the details you've described.

By all means, when you renew your insurance policy, make sure it's an "occurrence" policy. An "occurrence" policy provides the broadest protection available—it ensures coverage anytime in the future as long as the policy was in force when the incident occurred. Without a doubt, this would be your best security blanket.

This letter was taken from the files of *Nursing* magazine.

---

state, almost everything you own, except for a limited portion of your equity in your home and the clothes on your back, can be taken, if necessary, to satisfy the uninsured portion of a judgment.

Contrast the uninsured nurse with the nurse who had the foresight to protect herself with adequate professional liability coverage. If the insured nurse has a policy limit of $1 million, her own assets probably will never be at risk.

But how can a nurse afford $1 million worth of insurance? You'll be relieved to know that premiums for insurance coverage of, say, $1 million are not much greater than they are for insurance with a

relatively small limit. That's because a substantial part of the premium pays for the insurance company's assumption of any part of the risk in the first place; higher limits don't increase the premium disproportionately. You may be surprised at how reasonably a medical-surgical nurse can buy professional liability insurance at group rates. Even for critical care nurses, the American Association of Critical Care Nurses has generous and reasonably priced coverage. (*See Choosing Liability Insurance, page 209.*)

Types of professional liability insurance protection

Professional liability insurance may cover either the time the malpractice occurred (occurrence policy) or when a lawsuit for damages is filed (claims-made policy).

An occurrence policy protects you against an error of omission occurring during a policy period, regardless of when, after the policy ends, that the patient makes a claim against you.

The claims-made policy protects you only against claims made against you during the policy period. A claims-made policy is cheaper than an occurrence policy because the insurance company is at risk only for the duration of the policy. However, you can purchase an extended-reporting endorsement, or tail coverage, which in effect turns your claims-made policy into an occurrence policy.

What does the insurer owe you?

Professional liability insurance supplies you with more than just financial protection. The insurance company also owes you a legal defense and must provide attorneys to represent you for the entire course of litigation. Since insurance companies aren't in business to lose money, they retain highly experienced attorneys with considerable experience in defending malpractice lawsuits.

When they prepare your defense, they'll investigate the subject of the lawsuit; obtain expert witnesses; handle motions throughout the case; and prepare medical models, transparencies, photographs, and other court exhibits, if necessary. Your insurance company will pay for preparing such a defense.

During litigation—and indeed even before a lawsuit is actually filed in court—your insurance company actively strives for a settlement with the patient's attorneys to save time and money. This may not be in your best interests, however. In the United States, if you believe your professional reputation is at stake, you may be able to refuse to agree to an out-of-court settlement. If your policy contains a threshold limit—a stated amount of money—your insurer can't settle a case out of court without your permission. Without a threshold limit, your insurer has total control over out-of-court settlements.

If the lawsuit against you goes to court, the insurer has the right to control how the defense is conducted. The insurer's attorney makes all the decisions regarding the case's legal tactics and strategy.

Of course, you have a right to be kept advised of every step of the case. Most insurers will keep you informed because the insurer knows that:

• A successful defense depends in part on the defendant's cooperation.

• You can sue the insurer if it fails to provide a competent defense.

If you lose a malpractice lawsuit, the insurance company will cover you for jury-awarded general and special damages. In the United States, juries award *general damages* to compensate for:

• pain and suffering
• worsening change in life-style.

Juries award *special damages* to relieve:

• present and future medical expenses
• past and future loss of earnings
• decreased earning capacity.

In Canada, juries award damages similarly, except that decreased earning capacity is considered part of general, not special, damages.

Whether you practice in the United States or in Canada, your insurance company won't cover you for punitive damages. These damages, awarded in civil cases (usually involving malicious or grossly negligent conduct), are meant to punish the defendant without sending him to prison.

Many states are taking steps to decrease malpractice litigation. One widely accepted way is by imposing a statute of limitations, which limits the amount of time a person has to file a lawsuit. Some states have imposed a maximum limit on how much a jury can award in general damages. This restriction, however, is legally questionable and has been challenged as being unconstitutional. Medical associations and insurance companies are also trying to limit malpractice lawsuits in other ways: by forcing them into arbitration—thus removing them from the province of lay juries—and by requiring that they be screened by a medical malpractice screening panel. If the panel decides the plaintiff's

Respondeat Superior

If a nurse commits a negligent act and a patient sues her, she's not the only one in legal hot water. The patient may also sue the nurse's employer. According to the doctrine of respondeat superior, the employer—hospital, agency, institution, or doctor—is also liable for the nurse's negligence. Why? Because as long as the nurse is considered an employee, her employer is responsible for her actions.

Take, for example, *Crowe v. Provost* (1963): A mother returned with her child to her pediatrician's office one afternoon after having been there earlier that morning. The mother was frantic. She said her child was convulsing. The doctor was out at lunch, so the office nurse briefly examined the child. Then she called the doctor to report the child's condition. She told the doctor that she didn't feel the child's condition had changed since he had examined her and that he didn't need to rush back. The nurse then left the office while the mother and child waited for the doctor to return.

Shortly after the nurse left, the child vomited violently, stopped breathing, and died before the receptionist could contact the doctor. The mother filed negligence charges against the nurse. At the trial, the court found the nurse's negligence was indeed the proximate cause of the child's death. However, the doctor was also liable, according to the doctrine of respondeat superior, since the nurse was working as the doctor's employee.

claim isn't valid, the plaintiff can't file suit unless he posts a bond to cover his defense costs in advance. More than half the states have set up screening panels, although the panels have been criticized by consumer groups and plaintiffs' attorneys and challenged in court as being unconstitutional.

Indemnification: Who gets it and why

If several insurance companies are representing different parties in a malpractice lawsuit, they'll typically file counteractions against the other parties; what they're seeking, of course, is compensation, that is, indemnification, for all or part of any damages the jury awards. Such cross-suits are common. Let's return to the example cited at the start of this entry. The patient would have sued these parties: the hospital, the surgeon, the assisting surgeon, the anesthesiologist, and any nurse who assisted at the actual operation. Many states now permit damages to be apportioned among multiple defendants, the extent of liability depending on the jury's determination of each defendant's relative contribution to the harm done. For example, suppose you were the nurse responsible for the instrument count and the

court found you to be 75% responsible. Your insurance company would pay 75% of the total award. The other insurance companies would be held liable for the remaining 25%, in proportion to the percentage of harm attributed to each remaining defendant. However, if one of the codefendants, say the surgeon, decided that he'd been judged negligent only because of your negligence, he could instruct his insurance attorneys to file a new, separate lawsuit in his name against you.

Suppose you had more than one insurance policy that applied to this patient's claim. For example, you might have malpractice coverage through the hospital where you work and a professional organization you belong to, as well as your own insurance policy. All three insurance companies might well be involved. Who pays how much? That depends on several issues too complex to discuss here. What's important is that you make sure you promptly notify *every* insurance company you have a policy with that you're the target of a malpractice lawsuit. This will prevent any of the companies from using the "policy defense" of lack of notice or late notice. Such policy defenses frequently enable the insurance company success-

Statutes of Limitations

STATE	TIME FROM OCCURRENCE	TIME FROM DISCOVERY
Alabama	2 years	6 months
Alaska	2 years	Applicable only to minors
Arizona	3 years	3 years
Arkansas	2 years	1 year
California	3 years	1 year
Colorado	Not applicable	2 years
Connecticut	2 years	2 years
Delaware	2 years	2 years
District of Columbia	Not applicable	3 years
Florida	2 years	2 years
Georgia	2 years	2 years
Hawaii	Not applicable	2 years
Idaho	2 years	1 year (foreign object lawsuits only)
Illinois	Not applicable	2 years
Indiana	2 years	Not applicable
Iowa	Not applicable	2 years
Kansas	2 years	2 years
Kentucky	Not applicable	1 year
Louisiana	1 year	1 year
Maine	2 years	Not applicable
Maryland	5 years	3 years
Massachusetts	3 years	3 years
Michigan	2 years (for doctors) 3 years (for nurses)	2 years (for doctors) 3 years (for nurses)
Minnesota	2 years	2 years
Mississippi	Not applicable	2 years
Missouri	2 years	2 years

Your state laws specify the length of time within which a person may file a medical malpractice suit. This chart will provide you with current information on the time limits in all 50 states and the District of Columbia. However, due to continuing pressures of special-interest groups, this information is subject to change.

STATE	TIME FROM OCCURRENCE	TIME FROM DISCOVERY
Montana	3 years	3 years
Nebraska	2 years	2 years
Nevada	4 years	2 years
New Hampshire	2 years	Uncertain
New Jersey	Not applicable	2 years
New Mexico	3 years	Not applicable
New York	30 months	30 months
North Carolina	3 years	1 year
North Dakota	Not applicable	2 years
Ohio	Not applicable	1 year
Oklahoma	Not applicable	2 years
Oregon	Not applicable	2 years
Pennsylvania	Not applicable	2 years
Rhode Island	3 years	1 year
South Carolina	3 years	3 years
South Dakota	2 years	Not applicable
Tennessee	1 year	1 year
Texas	2 years	2 years (limited circumstances only)
Utah	Not applicable	2 years
Vermont	3 years	2 years
Virginia	2 years	Not applicable
Washington	3 years	1 year
West Virginia	2 years	2 years
Wisconsin	3 years	1 year
Wyoming	2 years	6 months

fully to avoid responsibility for covering you. (See "What to do if you're sued," page 223.)

Obtaining malpractice insurance

Insurance companies are numerous and offer many kinds of insurance policies. If possible, choose an agent who has experience handling professional liability insurance. If you don't know how to find one, call your local nursing organization. Someone there should be able to give you leads on qualified insurance representatives.

In applying for professional liability insurance, you have to be meticulous in describing your practice. You can secure insurance protection for virtually every aspect of nursing, so the more precise you are about your responsibilities, the more your policy will be tailor-made to your needs. You can get a policy that covers you in specific areas to supplement a general policy that your hospital or clinic has already provided for you. Or you can get a policy that covers you over and above the coverage you already have, such as a group policy offered by a professional organization.

Such organizations offer group plans at attractive premiums. You'll still want to review the extent of that coverage with *your* insurance agent to make sure it's adequate for your needs. This way you'll avoid duplicating insurance protection and be able to fill any gaps in the protection you already have.

Conclusion

What do your insurance policy dollars buy you? In a few words, "relative peace of mind."

At present, most states don't require you to carry professional liability insurance. But someday all states may do just that. Don't wait until it becomes the law in your state; you need professional liability insurance now.

Does employer insurance protect you?

If a patient sues you, will your employer's professional liability insurance protect your professional and financial interests? You have a critical stake in knowing the answer to that question, because you can't afford not to have professional liability protection. Of course, most health-care analysts believe you should have your own professional liability insurance as well. (See "Professional liability insurance," page 210.) But you can't wisely assess your own insurance needs until you determine how much coverage your employer's insurance gives you.

Insurance for health-care institutions

Health-care institutions such as hospitals aren't required to have malpractice insurance, but virtually all of them do. Why? Because an institution is usually liable for an employee's mistakes. And liability imposes the obligation of paying financial damages to injured patients. Without professional liability insurance, your employer would have to pay damages awarded to a patient out of the institution's funds. This, of course, could bankrupt the institution.

What makes your employer liable for your actions? A legal principle called respondeat superior (translated as, "let the master answer"). The principle means that when you negligently cause injury to a patient while acting within the course and scope of your job, your employer is liable for the damages. The principle applies to all professions, not just to health care. For example, a utility company is liable for injuries that result if one of its on-duty truck drivers negligently hits a pedestrian. (See *Respondeat Superior*, page 213.)

Insurance companies that provide professional liability coverage for hospitals and other health-care institutions reduce the risk they assume with that coverage in several ways. One way is by always stipulating a precise coverage period, typically one year. Another way is by carefully defining the type of coverage

When Courts Extend Limits

Answer true or false:
A patient can sue you for malpractice a decade after you've treated him.
The answer:
True, because a court can lengthen the statute of limitations in malpractice lawsuits.

In the following case, *Lopez v. Swyer* (1971), the court lengthened the statute of limitations by nearly a decade because a patient's doctors concealed information from her. New Jersey housewife and mother Mary Lopez, age 32, discovered a lump in her right breast. She underwent a radical mastectomy, and several doctors prescribed postsurgical radiation treatments. Mrs. Lopez's family doctor referred her to a radiologist for the treatments.

Mrs. Lopez had radiation treatments six times a week for more than a month. As a result of this excessive treatment, she suffered extremely painful radiation burns over most of her body. When she asked

why the complications were so severe, her doctors assured her the complications weren't unusual. They never told her that the treatments could have been too numerous and too strong.

Mrs. Lopez's condition worsened. Over the next several years, she was hospitalized 15 times, including twice for reconstructive surgery made necessary because of the radiation treatment. She didn't file a malpractice lawsuit until she heard a consulting doctor tell other doctors, gathered near her hospital bed, that she'd been a victim of negligence.

A lower court dismissed her suit because the 2-year statute of limitations for filing malpractice lawsuits had expired. But an appeals court ruled that the statute of limitations didn't start until Mrs. Lopez found out that her doctors had concealed the truth about her radiation treatments. That ruling let Mrs. Lopez bring the facts in her case before a jury.

---

they'll provide—whether, for example, it's an occurrence or claims-made policy. A third way is by putting exclusions in malpractice policies. These exclusions vary considerably from policy to policy, but all list specific acts, situations, or personnel that the insurance doesn't cover. For example, most policies don't cover court-ordered punitive damages—money a defendant must pay as punishment for injuring a patient. (Don't confuse this with compensatory damages—the amount the jury decides actually covers the loss or harm—which the policy *will* cover.)

How an insurer can deny coverage

Besides exclusions, insurers can use other circumstances to deny coverage to you or your employer, such as:
• The insurance policy lapses because your employer failed to pay the premiums.

• Your employer refuses to cooperate with the insurance company, for whatever reason.
• The insurer discovers that your employer made misstatements on the insurance application.

In some malpractice situations, an insurer could agree to provide you with a defense but refuse to pay damages awarded to a patient. The insurer agrees to defend you in this situation because he doesn't want to be accused of breach of contract. But he must notify you of his intention not to pay damages in a reservation-of-rights letter. This letter informs you and your employer that the insurer believes the case falls outside what's covered by the insurance policy. When your employer and the insurer disagree about whether insurance coverage exists, the dispute may have to be resolved through separate legal action in court. Similarly, you have the right to bring such action against your employer's insurance company if it refuses to cover you.

Assessing the limits of a policy

Each professional liability insurance policy has a maximum dollar coverage limit. Your employer can purchase coverage that exceeds the basic limit, and many hospitals do so for extra protection.

Most hospitals also have a deductible provision that makes the employer responsible for damages under a certain figure. The higher the deductible limit, the lower the premium charged by the insurer.

You should pay careful attention to the deductible limit because your employer can settle a claim against you under that figure without ever consulting you or the insurer. Because you won't have a chance to defend yourself and because many people interpret a settlement as an admission of guilt, such an action could tarnish your professional reputation. A tarnished reputation in turn could jeopardize your ability to get your own professional liability insurance or to get a new job. To minimize this problem, maintain close contact with your employer's legal staff if you're sued, and insist on being informed about each step in the case.

Why hospitals want a threshold limit

Most health-care institutions demand having control over when an insurer can settle a case. To gain this control, the employer normally sets a threshold limit—usually $3,000. The insurer can settle a case below the threshold without the employer's permission. But to settle a case above the threshold, the insurer must get the employer's permission. Why does the employer want the threshold? To protect its reputation for safety and quality care—the same reason you have for not wanting your insurance provider to settle a lawsuit against you without informing you. If an insurer were allowed to settle cases behind an employer's back, the employer could become more prone to malpractice lawsuits as its reputation deteriorates.

How your employer provides for your defense

If you're sued and your employer's insurance covers you, what protection will you get? The insurer has a duty to provide a complete defense, including assigning an attorney to handle the entire case. The insurer will pay the attorney fees as well as any investigation costs and expert witness fees.

The attorney will provide you with an opportunity to confer with him and give your side of the story. If your employer grants written consent to settle the case, the insurer may do so, or it may decide to try the case in court if its legal advisors overrule the employer.

If the plaintiff wins the lawsuit, the insurer is obliged to pay damages awarded to the patient up to the insurance policy's coverage limit.

How indemnity works

Can a hospital or another nurse who's been sued claim, in turn, that you're partly or wholly responsible for the patient's injury? Yes. The numbers of such cross-action suits—called indemnification suits—are rising dramatically. Your own hospital, a fellow nurse, or a lab technician—as long as each has individual professional liability insurance—can file an indemnification suit against you even though you're all covered by the same hospital insurance policy. This possibility strengthens the argument for having your own professional liability insurance.

Conclusion

Never assume you're adequately protected if you're covered under your employer's professional liability insurance policy. You have a right to know exactly how your employer's insurance covers you. To find out, get a copy of the insurance policy from your employer and let your professional liability insurance agent review it. Your agent—usually without a fee—will welcome the chance to determine the extent, limits, and exclusions of your employer's insurance coverage for you. Taking the time to find out how well your employer's insurance protects you could be one of the most legally astute moves you make.

Statutes of limitations

Suppose a patient sues you for malpractice 5 years after he left your care. Ordinarily, his lawsuit won't be valid, because all states have statutes of limitations that specify a shorter period of time a patient may sue for malpractice. So you don't have to worry? Yes, you do—because the patient's attorney knows about the statute of limitations, and he's filing suit anyway. This means he believes the court may set aside the statute for his client. Under certain specific conditions, the court can interpret the statute of limitations to give a plaintiff-patient more time to seek damages.

As you're probably aware, a statute of limitations is a law that specifies a particular number of years within which one person can sue another. For medical malpractice, the statute of limitations is specified in each state's medical malpractice law. (See *Statutes of Limitations,* pages 214 and 215.) Nurses, however, usually aren't expressly covered under these statutes of limitations. This means that when a nurse's defense alleges a patient's malpractice claim is invalid because he didn't file suit until after the statute of limitations had expired, the court must determine which applies: the statute of limitations for state medical malpractice law or the statute of limitations for general personal-injury lawsuits. (The malpractice law's statute of limitations is usually shorter.) The court bases its decision on the two following considerations:

• *how much statute-of-limitations protection the court believes the defendant-nurse's job warrants.* For example, if her job forces her to make many independent patient-care judgments, the court will apply a strict—or short—statute of limitations. A short time limit offers more protection, because the patient has less time to seek damages.

• *the type of negligent act the plaintiff-patient claims the nurse committed.* For example, an injured patient may sue a nurse for any one or for several of the charges that constitute malpractice—such as negligence or breach of contract. The

How to Find an Attorney

Suppose a patient sues you and you don't have an attorney. If you work for a hospital and the patient sues the hospital as well as you, then the hospital's insurance company will handle the case, supplying an attorney to defend you as the hospital's employee.

But what if the patient sues you alone? First, see your professional liability agent; most often your insurance company will appoint an attorney to defend you. But what if you don't have insurance, or you're not satisfied with the attorney the insurance company provides, or the company uses a policy defense and doesn't cover you? Under these circumstances, how do you find an attorney who's experienced in nursing malpractice cases?

How do you know when you've found an attorney who's right for you? Ask other health-care professionals if they've heard of the attorney you're using, and go by his reputation.

• If you work in a hospital with a legal services department, find out if the hospital will provide you with an attorney or refer you to one.

• If you have a relative or friend who is an attorney or a judge, ask him for a referral.

• If you are a member of a professional association, it may be able to refer you to an attorney.

• If none of these situations applies to you, contact your local bar association, listed in the Yellow Pages, for a referral. Try to find an attorney who's experienced in medical malpractice cases.

patient's attorney, of course, determines which charge has the best chance of winning the most damages for his client and structures his case accordingly. Then, if a statute of limitations is used as part of the nurse's defense, the court will decide which statute of limitations to apply in relation to the patient's charges.

How statutes of limitations developed

Why are statutes of limitations necessary? Because as time passes, evidence vanishes, witnesses' memories fail, and witnesses die. A time limit for bringing a lawsuit ensures that enough relevant evidence exists for a judge or jury to decide a case fairly.

To define that limit, state legislatures established statutes of limitations for general negligence that usually give a person 3 years to sue another for damages. These are the laws that plaintiffs invoke in general personal-injury lawsuits. Then, in response to pressure from medical and insurance groups, some states went a step further. They established shorter statutes of limitations for professions that require independent and risk-taking judgments. The statutes of limitations of medical malpractice laws, for example, usually give the patient 2 years or less to sue for damages.

You should know, however, that in some states, only doctors are subject to medical malpractice statutes of limitations—not nurses. Why? Because these states view the nurse as someone basically carrying out orders and not making independent, risk-taking judgments. In a Michigan case, *Kambas v. St. Joseph's Mercy Hospital of Detroit* (1973), for example, a heart attack patient lost full use of his arms after receiving anticoagulant drug injections. Because the patient brought the suit over 2 years after the incident, the defendant-nurse's attorneys tried to invoke Michigan's 2-year medical malpractice statute of limitations. The plaintiff-patient's attorney argued that the state's 3-year general negligence statute should apply. The state supreme court ruled for the patient, concluding that because nurses don't exercise independent judgment, as doctors do, they

aren't entitled to the protection of the medical malpractice statute of limitations.

When does a statute of limitations begin to run?

As we have already said, a statute of limitations sets a limit for filing a malpractice lawsuit, but a patient may be allowed to file suit after the time limit expires. In fact, determining when the applicable statute actually begins to run has become the pivotal question whenever a defense attorney invokes a statute of limitations as a defense in a malpractice case. Normally, the statute begins to run on the date the plaintiff's injury occurred. But what if the plaintiff doesn't *know* he was injured or doesn't find out he has grounds for a suit until after the normal limitations period has expired? Legislatures and the courts—which are continually struggling with this question—have devised a series of rules to help courts decide, in individual malpractice cases, when a statute should properly begin to run. A court can apply these rules, when a plaintiff-patient's attorney requests that it do so, to extend the applicable statute of limitations beyond the limit written in the law. This means that the defendant-nurse's use of a statute of limitations as a defense is invalidated, and the plaintiff-patient's right to sue is affirmed.

The occurrence rule

When legislatures began writing statutes of limitations, many of them decided that short time limits best served the ideal of fairness. So, they passed statutes of limitations that begin to run on the day a patient's injury occurs. Attorneys call this the *occurrence rule;* it generally leads to the shortest time limit. In several states, the courts have interpreted the occurrence rule strictly, so that even badly injured patients have been prevented from bringing suit after the applicable statute of limitations had expired.

The termination-of-treatment rule

When a patient's injury results from a series of treatments extended over time—rather than from a single incident—a court may apply the *termination-of-treatment rule.* This rule says that a statute of limitations begins from the date of the last treatment. In devising this rule, the courts reasoned that for the patient, a series of treatments could obscure just how and when the injury occurred. The U.S. Court of Appeals applied this rule in *Morgan v. Schlanger* (1967). In a lawsuit filed some years after extensive radiation treatment, a cancer patient claimed she suffered radiation-treatment burns. The defendant-doctors argued that the applicable statute of limitations had elapsed. But the court ruled that the statute didn't begin to run until the treatment ended, so the patient's lawsuit was valid.

The termination-of-treatment rule may apply even after the patient leaves a nurse's or a doctor's care. For example, suppose a patient you cared for is injured later, in someone else's care, and sues. If the subsequent health-care providers relied on decisions you made earlier in caring for the patient, the court can find you liable. This rule—called the *constructive continuing treatment rule*—gives the court another way to extend the statute of limitations in malpractice cases.

The discovery rule

Another rule a court can use in determining when a statute of limitations properly begins is based on when a patient discovers the injury. (This may take place many years after the injury occurred *and* after the applicable statute of limitations has formally run out.) This rule—called *the discovery rule*—considerably extends the time a patient has to file a malpractice lawsuit.

Two types of cases where the discovery rule is often applied are cases involving foreign objects left inside patients after surgery (so-called foreign-object cases) and cases involving sterilization. When a nurse or a surgeon leaves a foreign object—such as a scalpel, sponge, or clamp—inside a patient, the patient might not discover the error until long after his surgery. Under the discovery rule, the applicable statute of limitations wouldn't begin to run until the patient found out about the error. A court's decision to apply the discovery rule depends on whether it is satisfied that the patient couldn't have discovered the error earlier. If evidence indicates the pa-

tient should have recognized that something was wrong (for example, if he had chronic pain for months after the surgery but didn't take legal action until long afterward), the court could apply the termination-of-treatment rule instead.

Time limits for applying the discovery rule in foreign-object cases vary from state to state. Missouri allows a patient to file a foreign-object suit up to 10 years after the negligence occurs, the longest period any state allows. California allows the shortest period, 1 year from discovery of injury.

In some lawsuits involving incidents of tubal ligation and vasectomy, the courts have allowed the discovery rule to apply when a subsequent pregnancy occurs. In these cases, the courts' reasoning is that a patient can't discover the negligence until the procedure proves unsuccessful—no matter how long after the surgery this proof occurs.

Because the discovery rule is so generous to plaintiffs, some states—notably Texas—have restricted its application in malpractice cases. These states prefer to keep statutes of limitations' time limits short. A number of states have adopted separate statutes of limitations, one for readily detected injuries and one for injuries discovered later. In California and Ohio, for example, a patient must file suit within 1 year after he discovers an injury. However, a patient is not allowed to file suit after the occurrence of the injury beyond 3 years in California and 4 years in Ohio. Other states permit statute-of-limitations extensions only in foreign-object cases.

Proof of fraud can extend the statute of limitations

Courts, in most states, will extend the limitations period indefinitely if a plaintiff-patient can prove that a nurse or doctor used fraud or falsehood to conceal from the patient information about his injury or its cause. In most concealment cases, the law says that the concealment must be an overt act, not just the omission of an act. The most flagrant frauds involve concealing facts to prevent an inquiry, elude an investigation, or mislead a patient. Such a case was *Garcia v. Presbyterian Hospital*

What to Expect at the Deposition

When you think of being sued, you probably wonder what happens, and what you'd have to do. One event that occurs early in a lawsuit—after it's filed—is the taking of depositions.

In this legal procedure, the attorney for the person suing you (the plaintiff) questions you in the presence of *your* attorney and a court reporter. As part of the discovery process, the deposition enables both parties to review each other's cases to see if one is stronger than the other. Remember, most malpractice cases are settled out of court, so the deposition is crucial.

Before you appear for the deposition, review all the medical records in the case. They may help you recall important facts. During the deposition, the plaintiff's attorney has the right to inspect and copy any materials you bring to aid your memory. So show them to your attorney before the deposition for his inspection and approval.

Your attorney will probably advise you to respond to all questions with simple answers and not to volunteer or elaborate on any information. If you have any doubts, avoid absolute answers. Memory fades with time and, even with the aid of medical records, you won't be expected to recall details or actual conversations that took place some time ago. Remember, if the case goes to court, you'll be held accountable for the answers you gave at the deposition.

Center (1979). In this case, a patient who sued was operated on for cancer of the prostate gland twice in 1972 and once again in 1973. He'd repeatedly asked his doctor and attending nurses why the third operation was needed, but he hadn't received any explanation. Some time later, he learned that the third operation had resulted from retention of a catheter in his body during the second operation. The court held that the applicable statute of limitations did not prevent the patient from bringing suit.

When the plaintiff-patient is a minor or is mentally incompetent

Generally, state laws give special consideration in injury cases to minors and mentally incompetent patients because they lack the legal capacity to sue. Some states postpone applying the statute of limitations to an injured minor until he reaches the age of majority—age 18 or 21, depending on the state. And some states have specific rules about how statutes of limitations apply to minors.

Cases involving mentally incompetent patients who file after statutes of limitations have expired usually follow the discovery rule or a special law. Most of these special laws say that a statute of limitations doesn't begin until the patient recovers from his mental incompetence.

How long should medical records be kept?

Because, in some instances, a patient can file a malpractice suit years after he claims his injury occurred, accurate medical records should be kept on file for years (see *When Courts Extend Limits,* page 217). The complexity of malpractice cases requires you to recall specific clinical facts and procedures. Complete documentation of your care is usually found only in the records. These records provide your best defense. Without them, you're legally vulnerable.

Exactly how long must medical records be maintained? Few states have laws setting precise time periods, but many legal experts urge hospitals and other healthcare facilities to maintain medical record files long after patients are discharged. New Jersey requires hospitals to keep medical records for 7 years. Some states have adopted the Uniform Business Records Act, which calls for keeping records for no less than 3 years.

Settling Out of Court

Malpractice attorneys estimate that only 10% of malpractice lawsuits that are filed actually go to court—and of those that go to court only 10% actually end with a final judgment. What happens to the rest—the vast majority of cases? They're settled out of court.

If you're involved in a malpractice lawsuit, there's a good chance that with your help your attorney will settle out of court. When you discuss settlement with him, remember these points:

• If you're covered by professional liability insurance, the terms of your policy will determine whether you and your attorney, or the insurance company, can control the settlement. Most policies do not permit the nurse to settle a case without the consent of the insurance company. In fact, many policies (especially those provided by employers) permit the insurance company to settle *without the consent* of the individual nurse involved. Review your policy to determine your settlement rights. If the policy isn't clear on this point, call the insurance administrator of your hospital or the insurance company, and ask for clarification.

• Offer your insurance company's representative and your attorney all the information you can about the case, so they can not only evaluate your liabilities (and the plaintiff's liabilities) but also figure the best settlement with the plaintiff. As an attending nurse, you may be in the best position to provide crucial observations concerning the patient's state of mind—often the basis of a successful settlement.

• Remember, if you settle your case out of court, that doesn't mean that you're admitting any wrongdoing. The law regards settlement as a compromise between two parties to end a lawsuit and avoid further expense. In other words, you may choose to pay a settlement rather than incur possible greater expense (both financial and emotional) in defending your innocence at a trial.

Some states allow microfilm copies of medical records to be admitted as evidence in malpractice cases, but other states insist that only the original records can be used in court.

Using the statute-of-limitations defense

When a defendant-nurse and her attorney use a statute of limitations as a defense, they're making—in legal jargon—an affirmative defense. This means that the defendant raises the issue of a statute of limitations, and the plaintiff must prove that it is still running (such as by asserting an extension rule). If the court decides the statute has elapsed, the plaintiff-patient's case is rendered invalid.

Conclusion

If you're named as a defendant in a malpractice lawsuit, you'll need all the help you can get to defend your professional and financial interests. Statutes of limitations provide you with an affirmative defense your attorney won't overlook: the law recognizes the importance of limiting the time when a patient can claim damages against you.

What to do if you're sued

Imagine you're at the nurse's station, catching up on paperwork, when a stranger approaches and asks for you.

The Legal Process: Step by Step

Being named as a defendant in a malpractice lawsuit can be confusing as well as stressful. The antidote is knowing what to expect.

This chart summarizes the basic legal process from complaint to appeal. If you're ever involved in a lawsuit, your attorney will explain the specific procedures that your case requires.

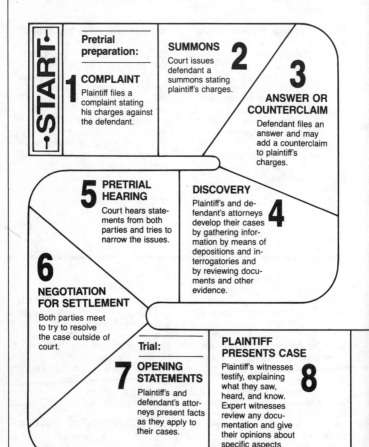

START

Pretrial preparation:

1 COMPLAINT
Plaintiff files a complaint stating his charges against the defendant.

2 SUMMONS
Court issues defendant a summons stating plaintiff's charges.

3 ANSWER OR COUNTERCLAIM
Defendant files an answer and may add a counterclaim to plaintiff's charges.

4 DISCOVERY
Plaintiff's and defendant's attorneys develop their cases by gathering information by means of depositions and interrogatories and by reviewing documents and other evidence.

5 PRETRIAL HEARING
Court hears statements from both parties and tries to narrow the issues.

6 NEGOTIATION FOR SETTLEMENT
Both parties meet to try to resolve the case outside of court.

Trial:

7 OPENING STATEMENTS
Plaintiff's and defendant's attorneys present facts as they apply to their cases.

8 PLAINTIFF PRESENTS CASE
Plaintiff's witnesses testify, explaining what they saw, heard, and know. Expert witnesses review any documentation and give their opinions about specific aspects of the case.

12
CROSS-EXAMINATION
Plaintiff's attorney questions defendant's witnesses.

DEFENDANT CLOSES CASE
Plaintiff's attorney may claim defendant hasn't presented an issue for the jury to decide.

13

14
CLOSING STATEMENTS
Each attorney summarizes his case for the jury.

DEFENDANT PRESENTS CASE
Defendant's witnesses testify, explaining what they saw, heard, and know. Expert witnesses review any documentation and give their opinions about specific aspects of the case.

11

15
JURY INSTRUCTION
Judge instructs the jury in points of law that apply in this particular case.

16
JURY DELIBERATION
Jury reviews facts and votes on verdict.

PLAINTIFF CLOSES CASE
Defendant's attorney may make a motion to dismiss case, claiming plaintiff's evidence is insufficient.

10

17
VERDICT
Jury announces verdict before judge and both parties.

9
CROSS-EXAMINATION
Defendant's attorney questions plaintiff's witnesses.

FINISH

18
APPEAL (OPTIONAL)
Attorneys review transcripts. The party against whom the court ruled may appeal if he feels the judge didn't interpret the law properly, instruct the jury properly, or conduct the trial properly.

Successfully Challenging Malpractice Suits

Suppose a patient in your care is injured and he sues you. If your attorney can establish one of the following defenses, the court will either dismiss the allegations against you or reduce the damages for which you're liable:

DEFENSES	RATIONALE
False allegations	Does the plaintiff have legally sufficient proof that your actions caused his injuries? If he doesn't, the court may rule that the allegations against you are false and dismiss the case.
Contributory negligence	Did the plaintiff, through carelessness, contribute to his injury? If he did, some states permit the court to charge the plaintiff with failing to meet the standards of a reasonably prudent patient, barring him from recovering *any* damages.
Comparative negligence	A few states permit the court to apportion liability— barring the plaintiff from recovering *some*, but not all, of the damages he claims.
Assumption of risk	Did the plaintiff understand the risk involved in the treatment, procedure, or action that allegedly caused his injury? Did he give proper informed consent and so voluntarily expose himself to that risk? If he did, the court may rule that the plaintiff assumed the risk, knowingly disregarding the danger, and so relieved you of liability.
Borrowed servant	Were you working under the direct supervision of a doctor, such as in an operating room? If you were, the court may rule that you *and* the doctor share the liability for your negligence.

When you identify yourself, he thrusts some legal papers into your hands and starts to walk away. Baffled, you manage to ask, "What's this all about?" He replies, "You've just been sued."

As you look over the papers, you realize he's not joking. You recognize the name of a former patient as the suing party (plaintiff), and you see your name listed as the defendant. As you skim through the papers, you learn that you've been accused of "errors and omissions." A nagging worry for most nurses has just be-

come reality for you: you've been sued for nursing malpractice.

What should you do? Failing to respond to the complaint could result in a default judgment against you. Obviously, you must take action. What you should do will depend on whether you have professional liability insurance. Regardless, *you must take action immediately.*

What to do if you're insured

If you're covered by your employer's insurance, immediately contact your legal services administrators at work. They'll tell you how to proceed. (See "Does employer insurance protect you?", page 216.)

If you have your own professional liability insurance, pull out your policy and read the section that tells you what to do when you're sued. Every policy describes whom you should notify and how much time you have to do it. Immediately telephone this representative and tell him you've been sued. *Document the time, his name, and his instructions.* Then, hand-deliver the lawsuit papers to him and get a signed, dated receipt for them. Or send them by certified mail, return receipt requested, so you're assured of a signed receipt.

If you don't contact the appropriate representative within the specified time, the insurance company can refuse to cover you. So to protect yourself, make sure you *act quickly, document your actions,* and *get a receipt.*

Make no mistake: When you notify your insurance company that you've been sued, it will first consider whether it *must* cover you at all. Your company does this by checking for any policy violations you may have committed. For example, your company will check whether you gave late notice of the lawsuit, gave false information on your insurance application, or failed to pay a premium on time. If the company is sure you've committed such a violation, it will use this violation as a *policy defense,* and it can simply refuse to cover you. If the company thinks you've committed such a violation but isn't sure it has evidence to support a policy defense, it will probably send you a letter by certified mail informing you that the company may not have to defend you, but that it will do so while reserving the right to deny coverage later, withdraw from the case, or take other actions. Meanwhile, the company will seek a declaration of its rights from the court. If the court decides the company doesn't have to defend you, the company will withdraw from the case.

Usually, an insurance company takes this action only after careful consideration. Why? Because this action may provide the insured nurse with grounds for suing the company. If you receive such a letter, find your own attorney to defend you in the lawsuit and to advise you in your dealings with the insurance company. If your case against the insurance company is sound, he may suggest that you sue them.

If your insurance company doesn't assert a policy defense, your company representative will select and retain an attorney or a law firm specializing in medical malpractice cases as your *attorney of record* in the lawsuit. Once he's designated as your attorney of record, this attorney is legally bound to do all that's necessary to defend you.

Your employer will almost certainly be named as a codefendant in the lawsuit. But even if this isn't the case, notify your employer that you're being sued. Your insurance company may try to involve your employer as a defendant.

What to do if you're not insured

If you don't have insurance, your own or your employer's, you'll have to find your own attorney. *Don't even consider trying to defend yourself.* You need an attorney who's experienced in medical malpractice, because the case will be complex and the opposition will be composed of experienced attorneys. (See *How to Find an Attorney,* page 219.)

Make appointments with a few attorneys who seem qualified to defend you. (Usually, an attorney won't charge you for this initial meeting.) When you meet with each one, ask how long he thinks the lawsuit will take and how much money he will charge. Also, try to get a feeling for the attorney's understanding of the issues in your case. Then choose one as your attorney of record. Do this as soon as possible.

What your attorney will do

Your attorney will file the appropriate legal documents in response to the papers you were served. Of course, he'll ask you for help in preparing your defense. He should give you a chance to present your position in detail. Remember, all such discussions between you and your attorney are *privileged.* This means that your attorney can't disclose this information without your permission.

The Selection and Use of an Expert Witness

When an attorney looks for an expert witness in a nursing malpractice case, he wants a nurse with two important qualifications: a good educational background and substantial and relevant clinical experience.

Usually an expert witness' credentials have to match or exceed a defendant's. For example, a psychiatric nurse defendant with 2 years' experience may insist that a prospective expert witness have at least comparable experience. Some courts allow an RN to testify about the care an LPN or LVN gives, but not the reverse. Some courts don't allow LPNs/LVNs to testify at all. Others allow an LPN/LVN to testify, but with restrictions.

Before a trial begins, an attorney may call on you, as an expert witness, to review the defendant's file and evaluate the defendant's liability. Then, after the trial begins, the attorney may ask you to testify as an expert witness.

Your attorney will also obtain complete copies of the pertinent medical records and any other documents he or you feel are important in your defense. In addition, he'll use *discovery devices* to uncover every pertinent detail about the case against you. These discovery devices are legal procedures for obtaining information. Some discovery devices your attorney may use include an *interrogatory* (questions written to the other party that require answers under oath), *a deposition* (oral cross-examination of the other party, under oath and before a court reporter), and *a defense medical examination* (a medical examination of the injured party by a doctor selected by your attorney or insurance company).

Of course, the plaintiff-patient's attorney will also use discovery devices, so you may have to answer interrogatories and appear for a deposition as well. Your attorney will carefully prepare you for these procedures. (See *What to Expect at the Deposition,* page 222.)

Your attorney will also prepare you to testify at the trial. He'll tell you how to dress and how to act. Remember, he wants to win the case, too, so do what he tells you. Remember also that your failure to cooperate with an attorney provided by an insurance company can be used as a policy defense.

This doesn't mean you must say or do *anything* he asks. If you feel your attorney is asking you to do or say things that aren't in your best interest, tell him so. You have the right to change attorneys at any time. If you believe an attorney selected by your insurance company is more interested in protecting the company than in protecting you, discuss the problem with a company representative. Then, if you still *feel* that he isn't defending you properly, hire your own attorney. If this happens, you may have grounds for suing the insurance company and the company-appointed attorney.

What to do before your case goes to trial

Study the copies of the medical records. Your attorney will ask you to do this as soon as possible. Examine the complete medical chart, including nurses' notes, laboratory reports, and doctors' orders. On a separate sheet of paper, make appropriate notes on key entries or omissions. But *don't* make any changes on the records. Such an action will destroy your case by undermining your credibility. Remember, you're not the only person with a copy of these records.

Create your own legal file. Ask your attorney to send you copies of all documents and correspondence pertaining to the case. Try to maintain a file that's as complete as your attorney's. Also, make sure you understand all the items in your file. If you receive a document you don't understand, ask your attorney to explain it. Maintaining such a file should keep you up to date on the status of your case and prevent unpleasant surprises in court.

Don't talk about the case. Don't try to placate the person suing you by calling him and discussing the case. Your chances of talking him into dropping his lawsuit are very slim. And every word you say to him can be used against you in court.

In fact, before the trial, don't discuss the lawsuit with *anyone* except your attorney. This will help prevent information leaks that could compromise your case. And to protect your professional reputation, don't even mention to your colleagues that you've been sued.

Protect your property. Ask your attorney about the legal devices you can use to protect your property. Many states have *homestead laws* that permit you to protect a substantial part of the equity in your house, as well as other property, from any judgment against you. Such protection is essential if you don't have insurance or if damages exceed your insurance, and you'll be glad you have it if you lose the case and the damages awarded do exceed your insurance coverage.

Your day in court
Your case may eventually go to trial. While your attorney prepares your defense, he'll also explore the desirability of reaching an out-of-court settlement. If he decides an out-of-court settlement is in your best interest, he'll try to achieve it in the period before your trial date. (See *Settling Out of Court,* page 223.)

If your case does go to trial (see *The Legal Process: Step by Step,* pages 224 and 225), you'll participate in selecting the jury. During this selection process, attorneys for both sides will question prospective jurors, and your attorney will ask your opinion on their suitability. Either attorney may reject a small number of prospective jurors without any reason (this is called a *peremptory challenge*). And you, the plaintiff, or either attorney may reject an unlimited number of jurors for specific reasons. For instance, you may reject

someone who knows the plaintiff or who has any legal interest in the lawsuit. (This is called a *challenge for cause.*)

To help prepare you to testify at the trial, your attorney will ask you to review the complete medical record, your interrogatory answers, and your deposition. In addition, you should review the entire legal file you've been keeping, to make sure you understand all aspects of one.

The trial may last several days—or even several weeks. After all the witnesses have given their testimony, the jury—not the judge—will decide if you're liable. If the jury finds you liable, it will also assess damages against you. In some instances, an arbitration proceeding is utilized instead of a jury trial, but this is the exception and not the rule.

Protecting your professional reputation
During the trial, your professional reputation will be at stake. Project a positive attitude at all times, suggesting you feel confident about the trial's outcome. Never disparage the plaintiff inside or outside the courtroom. Characterizing him as a gold digger, for instance, can only generate bad feelings that may interfere with the settlement. You won't want to speak to him during the trial, but if you do, always be polite and dignified. Remember, you don't want to do anything that suggests you lack confidence in your position or dislike the plaintiff.

As you know, losing a malpractice lawsuit can jeopardize your future. Prospective employers (as well as prospective insurers) will want to know if you've ever lost a nursing malpractice lawsuit or if you've ever been a defendant in one. If you have, you'll probably find job hunting more difficult than it used to be. You'll also pay an increased insurance premium, and you may find that some insurance companies will simply refuse to cover you.

Conclusion
As you continue to expand your nursing expertise and to accept greater patient-care responsibility, you'll also accept greater legal risks. So to help protect yourself, you must keep up with changes in the law that affect your practice. And, of course, you must always practice within

the limits prescribed in your nurse practice act.

If, despite these precautions, a stranger someday thrusts those dreaded legal papers into your hands, follow the recommendations discussed here. They apply no matter where you practice in the United States or Canada. And they'll help you survive a malpractice lawsuit. (See *Successfully Challenging Malpractice Suits,* page 226.)

Testifying in a malpractice lawsuit

When you're called to testify in a malpractice lawsuit, as a defendant or as an expert witness, you can use a number of techniques to help reduce stress and enhance the value of your testimony. In the courtroom, claims, counterclaims, allegations, and contradictory evidence will probably be coming at you hot and heavy at times. Here's how to keep your composure through it all. (For further information, see *The Selection and Use of an Expert Witness,* page 228.)

First, the deposition
Before the trial, you'll be called to give a deposition. (If you've been called to testify as an expert witness, you should be aware that some states don't permit expert witnesses to give pretrial depositions.) Where you give the deposition can vary. It can take place in an attorney's office or in a special room in the courthouse set aside for that purpose. The deposition takes place in a less formal atmosphere than a courtroom provides, but don't forget that a court reporter will be transcribing everything you and the attorneys say. In a way, it's a rehearsal of what will come later, during the actual trial. At the trial, the plaintiff's and the defendant's attorneys have the right to use your testimony to bolster their respective cases.

Under oath: Looking and acting your best
How you come across to the jury from the witness stand is very important. This is when the jury forms its first—and sometimes lasting—impression of your credibility. So dress conservatively, and wear little or no jewelry. You want the jury to concentrate on what you say, not on how you look.

Malpractice lawsuits are notoriously slow-moving. The one you're involved in may seem to be in permanent slow motion. Interruptions may occur in the form of recesses, attorneys' lengthy arguments in judges' chambers, and calling of witnesses out of turn. Be patient no matter what happens. And when you're asked to appear, be prompt. You may not score points by your punctuality, but you'll definitely lose a few if you aren't in court when you're called to testify.

When you testify, the jury doesn't expect you to be letter-perfect or to have instant—or total—recall. If you don't have an answer, say so. Listen closely to questions, and answer only what the questioner has asked. Always answer the questions simply and in lay terms, and *never* elaborate or volunteer information. If you're going to be describing a piece of equipment that's unfamiliar to a layman, get your attorney's approval to bring it to the courtroom and show it to the jury. And above all, be honest. When your testimony must be critical of a colleague or of your hospital's policies, you may be tempted to bend the truth a little. Don't.

The cross-examination: Staying the course
During cross-examination, the opposing attorney will try to discredit your testimony. This may take the form of an attack on your credentials, experience, or education—especially if you're testifying as an expert witness. Another way of discrediting your testimony is by the "hired gun" insinuation. The cross-examining attorney may imply that because you accept payment for your testimony, you're being unethical. Just remember that as an expert witness you have the right to expect compensation for the time you spend on behalf of the case in and out of the courtroom. Say so if the matter comes up.

Another ploy the opposing attorney can use to discredit your testimony is the "hedge." He may try to get you to change

What Makes a Witness "Expert"?

After Cecil Wood died, his wife charged that his nurses had been negligent (*Wood v. Rowland*, 1978).

Mrs. Wood planned to base her case on the expert testimony of a registered nurse named Mrs. Miller. Mrs. Miller had reviewed the pertinent hospital records, and she was prepared to testify that the nurses who cared for Cecil Wood failed to meet a reasonable standard of care in at least four ways:

● One nurse failed to tell the doctor that Cecil Wood had heart disease and was taking medication for it.

● The nurses failed to take Wood's vital signs as ordered by the doctor.

● The nurses failed to take Wood's vital signs before injecting meperidine (Demerol).

● The nurses failed to offer a reasonable standard of care in some tests they performed on Wood.

Mrs. Miller took the witness stand but was never able to give her opinion. The defendant's attorney pointed out that Mrs. Miller had been employed in her work as a nurse by only one hospital. Mrs. Miller had described her qualifications: she'd graduated from a diploma program in 1963 and then had worked at the same hospital for 3 years—until 1966. For the next 2 years, she'd worked as an office nurse. Then she'd been unemployed for 5 years. In May, 1973—one month after Cecil Wood's death—Mrs. Miller had started working again as a float nurse, in the same hospital where she'd worked previously.

Mrs. Miller testified that her education and experience made her familiar with local nursing standards, even though she'd never worked in the hospital where Cecil Wood had been a patient. But the defendant's attorney asked if Mrs. Miller knew the standards of nursing care or procedures in other hospitals. She said no. The defendant's attorney then said that policies may vary from hospital to hospital—that the policies of the hospital where Mrs. Miller worked might have been different from the hospital policies where Mr. Wood died. Finally, he asked the judge to refuse to allow Mrs. Miller to testify as an expert witness and to enter a directed verdict in favor of the hospital. The judge agreed.

Mrs. Wood appealed. If you were the appellate judge, how would you decide?

The appellate judge said the trial judge who refused to accept Mrs. Miller as an expert witness was wrong. According to the appellate judge, Mr. Wood's care didn't concern hospital administrative standards, which *would* require an expert witness familiar with the standards adopted by various hospitals. Instead, the Wood case concerned professional nursing standards—requiring an expert witness in *that* area. Did Mrs. Miller have this expertise? Yes, said the appellate judge; the courts define an expert as someone who has superior knowledge on a subject. Mrs. Miller's education and experience were not common to the average person, so she met this test. The fact that she worked in only one hospital might have affected the weight of her testimony, but it didn't disqualify her from giving it.

or qualify an answer you gave previously on direct examination or at the deposition. He may also try to confuse the issue by asking you a similar—but hypothetical—question with a slightly different—but significant—slant. Just remember that a simple but sincere "I don't know" often reinforces a jury's belief in your honesty and competence. Obviously, your best protection against cross-examination jitters is adequate preparation.

Conclusion

In most states, nurses now are recognized as professionals, uniquely qualified to give testimony about how their profession is—and should be—practiced. (See *What Makes a Witness "Expert"?*, page 231.) For example, a Pennsylvania malpractice lawsuit typified the courts' acceptance of nursing as a distinct profession (*Capan v. Divine Providence Hospital*, 1980). In this case, the court wouldn't let a doctor testify on nursing standards because he couldn't show that he knew his hospital's nursing standards. In a Georgia-based malpractice lawsuit (*McCormick v. Avret*, 1980), a patient developed a permanent injury from a severe infection and sued. The patient alleged that the injury resulted from a doctor's faulty technique in withdrawing blood. The court allowed a nurse to testify on techniques for maintaining equipment sterility (although not on the standard of care for drawing blood).

The measure of professionalism for nurses includes how much integrity they exhibit while testifying in the courtroom as well as in the settings where they practice their profession. If you're ever called to testify during a malpractice lawsuit, do all you can to represent your profession with honesty and dignity.

Selected References

Alton, Walter G., Jr. *Malpractice: A Trial Lawyer's Advice for Physicians.* Boston: Little, Brown & Co., 1977.

Bernzweig, Eli. *The Nurse's Liability for Malpractice: A Programmed Course,* 3rd ed. New York: McGraw-Hill Book Co., 1981.

Cazalas, Mary W. *Nursing and the Law,* 3rd ed. Rockville, Md.: Aspen Systems Corp., 1979.

Creighton, Helen. *Law Every Nurse Should Know,* 4th ed. Philadelphia: W.B. Saunders Co., 1981.

Eccard, Walter T. "A Revolution in White: New Approaches in Treating Nurses as Professionals," *Vanderbilt Law Review* 30:839, 1977.

Hemelt, M., and Mackert, M. *Dynamics of Law in Nursing and Health Care,* 2nd ed. Reston, Va.: Reston Publishing Co., 1982.

James, A. Everette, ed. *Legal Medicine with Special Reference to Diagnostic Imaging.* Baltimore: Urban & Schwarzenberg, 1980.

Kinkela, Gabriella G., and Kinkela, Robert V. "Hospital Nurses and Tort Liability," *Cleveland-Marshall Law Review* 18:53, January 1969.

Kraftds, Melvin D. *Using Experts in Civil Cases,* 2nd ed. New York: Practising Law Institute, 1982.

Mackert, M.E., and Hemelt, M.D. "Prescription for a Witness," *NursingLife,* 2(1):80, January/February 1982.

Medical Malpractice Litigation 1982, Litigation and Administrative Practice Series. New York: Practising Law Institute, 1982.

Murchinson, Irene, et al. *Legal Accountability in the Nursing Process,* 2nd ed. St. Louis: C.V. Mosby Co., 1982.

Pozgar, George D. *Legal Aspects of Health Care Administration,* 2nd ed. Rockville, Md.: Aspen Systems Corp., 1983.

Sheridan, Peter N. "Sindell and Its Sequelae—or How to Manage Multiparty Litigation," *Forum* 17(4):1116-38, Spring 1982.

Walker, Dorothy. "Nursing 1980: New Responsibility, New Liability," *Trial* 16(12): 42-47, December 1980.

Wright, Cecil A., and Linden, Allen M. *Canadian Tort Law: Cases, Notes, and Materials,* 7th ed. Toronto: Butterworth and Co., 1980.

7

Contracts and Collective Bargaining

In recent years, more and more nurses have felt the need to join an employee union. On the theory that strength comes in numbers, these nurses have joined forces to bargain with their employers for improved economic and working conditions. And many such groups have achieved their goals.

But for most nurses, the decision to join a union isn't an easy one. They maintain the traditional view that union activity is unprofessional. For them, negotiating for wages and working conditions impedes, rather than assures, quality patient care. Other nurses are reluctant to depend on an organization for their economic and professional well-being. They prefer to deal with their employer on a one-to-one basis. Still others object to the cost of union dues and the commitment of time and effort that unions demand of their members.

If you're one of the nurses who's still wrestling with these issues, this chapter will help you. You'll become familiar with the pros and cons of union membership, the functions of unions, and the legal mechanisms—collective bargaining, grievance procedures, and arbitration—that unions use to achieve their economic and professional objectives.

At some point in your career, you may have to choose whether or not to join a union. Prepare now, so you can make the right decision when that time arrives.

In conclusion, all nurses are concerned about their economic status and working conditions. Decent wages mean economic security for you and any family members who may depend on you. Optimum work-ing conditions can mean job security, job satisfaction, and the chance to deliver the best possible patient care.

How you ensure that your economic and working conditions meet your personal and professional standards depends on your particular situation. Joining a union may or may not be the best means for you to achieve your goals. To find out, take a close look at the issue of union membership—its advantages, disadvantages, and alternatives. The best decision you can make about whether or not to join a union is an informed one.

Contracts—check before you sign

Did you sign a contract when you began your current job? If so, did you read it carefully before you signed it? Chances are you just glanced at it, then signed your name to it. Even if you took the time to read it, you may not have known what terms to look for or understood all the conditions. For example, was the contract an individual or union contract? Did it contain any implied terms? Did it adequately define your duties, the extent of your authority, and your benefits? Did it explain the procedure for terminating the contract?

These questions are important for you. Why? Because you're likely to work in more than one hospital during your career. And each time you transfer, you'll

Elements of a Legal Contract

A legal contract must contain the following three elements:

Promise(s)
Two or more legally competent parties must promise each other to do or not do something.

Mutual understanding
The parties involved must clearly understand the terms and obligations the contract imposes on them.

Compensation
The parties involved must agree that, to fulfill the contract, only lawful actions will be performed in exchange for something of value.

enter into some type of contractual agreement with your new employer.

Knowing what to look for in a contract will help you decide if a job is really right for you. And being able to interpret contract terms will help you function within the contract's specified limits.

Recognizing various types of contracts

A contract is a legally binding agreement that one or more persons or groups makes with another person or group either to do or not to do something. But unlike a simple agreement, which isn't legally binding, a contract can be enforced in court.

According to U.S. and Canadian law, a contract is legally binding if:
• you've accepted an offer from another person or persons either to do or not to do something
• you and the other person are legally competent—of age and without mental impairment
• you and the other person understand the terms of the agreement
• the terms of the agreement are lawful
• you receive something of value, such as money, from the other person for fulfilling

the agreement.

In general, agreements regarding conscience, morals, and social activities aren't legally binding. For example, if you break a lunch date with a friend, you can't be fined or taken to court for violating your agreement. But if you violate any term in a legally binding contract, you might face such consequences.

The law protects the parties of an expressed contract from fraudulent practices by requiring that these contracts, such as mortgages and deeds, be written.

In most cases, the contract you enter into with your employer will also be a formal, written contract. It may be an individual contract (which you negotiate personally with your employer) or a collective contract (which a labor organization or union negotiates with the employer for the employees). Contract terms may differ between the two. In an *individual contract,* wage increases may be awarded automatically and may not be linked to certain criteria, such as merit or experience; in a *collective* or *union contract,* wage increases may be awarded automatically based on merit and seniority.

Other contracts that you make with patients or co-workers will probably be either expressed or implied contracts. An expressed contract may be written or oral. Suppose that during an interview at a hospital you're offered a position as a staff nurse for a particular shift at a particular salary. If you verbally agree to the offer, you've entered into an oral expressed contract. However, if you verbally agree to it and sign the hospital's written draft of the terms, you've entered into a written expressed contract. If you sign only a *statement* saying you've read and understood the hospital's policies and procedures, this is not an expressed contract, but rather an implied contract. The specificity of the contract's wording determines whether it's expressed or implied.

Contracts, of course, do not have to be written to be legal and binding. Most oral contracts are as legal and binding as written contracts. However, legal problems can arise. To begin with, most state courts don't consider an oral contract valid if its terms cannot be fulfilled within a year. An example is an employment contract, which

The ANA and Collective Bargaining

Since 1946, the American Nurses' Association (ANA) has supported collective bargaining, and most RNs have chosen their state nurses association as their collective bargaining representative. Because state nurses associations are professional associations—not just labor organizations—their role in the collective bargaining process is controversial.

Proponents contend the state nurses associations, with their many professional concerns besides salary and working conditions, are the natural labor representatives for a group of professionals who come to the bargaining table with more than the traditional economic concerns.

Opponents who belong to the associations wonder whether collective bargaining itself is professional, and whether it's an appropriate role for their professional association to play. Members of some state nurses associations say no, and their associations don't engage in collective bargaining.

Employers and other unions challenge the associations' ability to represent staff nurses' interests and needs. These opponents say that so many association members are supervisors and administrators that state nurses associations are management-dominated and, therefore, are inappropriate employee bargaining representatives. Some employers exert pressure on their nursing managers not to participate in their state nurses association because of the association's labor activities.

Once a state nurses association gets involved in collective bargaining, its activities are the same as any other bargaining agent's. The association represents its members in contract negotiations and in resolving grievances.

usually runs indefinitely. In the previous example of an oral expressed contract, the period of employment would determine the contract's validity.

In addition, since the terms and conditions of oral contracts aren't committed to paper (as written contracts are), oral contracts are subject to each party's memory and interpretation. Changes in hospital policy and personnel, and the passage of time, can blur the original interpretation of the contract and cause disagreements between parties about its correct terms and promises.

Most contracts contain implied conditions—elements of the contract that aren't explicitly stated but are assumed part of the contract. For example, your employer will assume that you'll practice nursing in a safe, competent manner, as defined by your nurse practice act and your professional standards, and that you'll maintain the hospital's standards and follow its policies and procedures. At the same time, you'll assume, based on implied conditions, that your employer will staff your unit adequately and with qualified personnel, will ensure a safe working environment, and will provide all necessary supplies and equipment for you to do your job.

If you decide to accept the contract, you can verbally agree to it, sign it, provide a written acceptance of it, or simply report for duty. If you fail to respond in any way to the offer, the employer can't interpret your silence as acceptance. But he may withdraw his offer to you, without penalty, at any time before you accept it. (See *Elements of a Legal Contract,* page 234.)

Breach of contract

When you breach a contract, you've unjustifiably failed to perform all or part of your contractual duty. A substantial breach of contract is never lawful. If you signed a contract which specified that you would work every third weekend and then you refused to do so, you would be breaching your contract. Your employer can either discharge (fire) you or seek an injunction against you. An injunction is a court order that would prevent you from working as a nurse for another employer. However, since an injunction is difficult to obtain and expensive, a hospital rarely seeks one against a nurse. But even if your employer doesn't take action against you, your breach of contract may damage your reputation and make it difficult for you to get a job at another hospital.

Your employer can also be guilty of breach of contract. If, for example, your employer fails to give you the vacation time specified in your contract, he has breached your contract. You can attempt to rectify the situation by first discussing it with your immediate supervisor. Show her your paycheck stubs as proof of the hours you worked and the compensation you received for it, and compare the stubs with your assigned work schedule. Then discuss the terms of your contract with her, and give her an opportunity to explain the error. If she offers you no satisfactory compensation and you've exhausted all channels of appeal, you may need to discuss the problem with an attorney who has contract expertise. Provide the attorney with a written log of your attempts to rectify the situation, including what each person said and the date and time of their statements.

If you work in Canada, instead of seeking out an attorney, you can appeal for help to the provincial government agency that enforces minimum employment standards legislation. They will not charge you a fee.

Terminating a contract
When you terminate a contract, you've either fulfilled all your obligations under the contract or absolved yourself of the obligation to fulfill the contract's terms.

Most contracts don't specify termination dates for your services. You can terminate them at any time, if you follow proper notification procedures. You can terminate other contracts, including those with termination dates, if your employer agrees to it. Follow the procedures outlined in your contract for giving written notice to your employer of your plans to leave. Most contracts require that you give 2 to 4 weeks' notice. If your contract has an automatic termination date, don't renew the contract after it expires.

Your employer can terminate your contract if he determines that you're incompetent or that you've behaved unprofessionally on the job. This includes actions such as yelling at a patient or striking him or a member of his family. Before discharging you, your employer would probably give you several warnings about the quality of your work. Then he might confront you with several examples of your shortcomings from previous written evaluations of your performance. If you don't want to lose your job, you should discuss areas of improvement with him. He might be willing to arrange a probation period for you during which you can work to regain his confidence in you.

If you disagree with your employer's complaints, you can request an evaluation by someone else who supervised your work, or you can request a transfer to another unit where you'd be reevaluated after an agreed-on length of time. However, your employer isn't obligated to agree to either request. If he doesn't, you can seek written support from your co-workers that will refute your employer's complaints. You can also seek support from your employee union, if you have one. It may file a grievance in your behalf.

If you feel you've been unjustly terminated, you should do these things: ask your co-workers to vouch for you in writing; if you belong to a union, seek union support; and if you don't belong to a union, hire an attorney to represent you.

When is a contract invalid?
A contract is considered invalid when the agreement concerns actions that are either illegal or impossible to carry out. A contract is considered illegal or void when: (1) a person lies to an employer about her qualifications as a nurse and signs a contract with him; (2) a person is forced to sign a contract; (3) the agreement involves theft or other unlawful actions; (4) a minor or mentally incompetent person signs the contract.

A contract is considered impossible to carry out when a party to the contract becomes physically or mentally disabled.

Facts about Nurses' Unions

If you're like most nurses, you have many questions about unionization. Here are questions and answers that'll clarify some of the issues:

Q Can I join a labor union?
A Yes. Congress amended the National Labor Relations Act in 1974 to cover private, nonprofit hospitals and health-care institutions. The law covers all private hospitals that provide at least $250,000 worth of health-care services a year and all related facilities that provide services worth at least $100,000. Most hospitals and nursing homes fall in those categories. Before then, the law allowed only nurses in profit-making hospitals and nursing homes to unionize.

Q Can I be forced to join a union?
A If you work under a contract that includes a "union shop," you have to join the union within a specified time to keep your job. If the contract provides for an

"open shop," you can choose not to join the union and still keep your job.

Q Can the hospital where I work fire me for helping to organize a union there?
A Federal regulations strictly forbid an employer from firing you or taking any other reprisal against you for union organizing.

Q What consequences do I face if I refuse to participate in my union's strike?
A As long as you continue to work, your hospital or health-care institution will pay your wages and benefits. No union can force you to strike. But you might face some antagonism—even retaliation—from those colleagues who do strike.

Conclusion
Knowing about contracts won't directly improve the quality of your nursing care. But your ability to recognize the various types of contracts, to know what to look for in them, and to understand their limits can help you protect your rights as an employee and also secure benefits that will increase your satisfaction on the job.

Organizing a union

Since 1974, the number of nurses who've joined unions has increased significantly. Why? In that year, Congress amended the National Labor Relations Act to allow employees of private, nonprofit health-care institutions and agencies to unionize. (The act applies to employees of hospitals and other health-care facilities with an annual

revenue of at least $250,000 and to nursing homes, visiting nurses associations, and related facilities with an annual revenue of at least $100,000.)

So if you work in such a place, you have the protected right to join a union and to help organize a bargaining unit. (Before 1974, only nurses in profit-making hospitals or nursing homes could join unions and get labor-related protection from the law.)

After nurses won the right to unionize, many unions sought to represent them. The American Nurses' Association (ANA) has supported unionization for nurses since 1946. In fact, state ANA affiliates serve as the bargaining agent for most unionized nurses—representing more than 130,000 nurses. All other unions combined represent only about 50,000 nurses. (See *The ANA and Collective Bargaining,* page 235.)

Although the amendment opened the door for widespread efforts to persuade nurses to join union ranks, many nurses are not sure of their rights and limitations.

If you wanted to join a union or help organize one, would you know what legal protections and limitations you'd have? This entry will give you the information you need to understand how a union can become your representative in a health-care institution.

The pros and cons of unionization

Many nurses have joined unions to improve their economic status, their working conditions, and their professional status. But some nurses have ambivalent feelings about unionization. You might share those feelings considering unionization's pros and cons.

Union proponents argue that unionization gives you a strong voice in bread-and-butter issues such as wages, benefits, and pensions. They also point out that unionization assures you fair grievance procedures and more influence in patient-care decisons. And it gives you more control over working conditions, such as scheduling and staffing. With these advantages, unionization equalizes the bargaining power between you and your employer.

But critics of unionization point to some disadvantages. Many critics say unionization tarnishes nursing's image by shifting attention from nurses' traditional focus on meeting patients' needs to concern about their economic status. Some nurses fear the potential disruptiveness of picketing and strikes. Other nurses argue that unionization creates an antagonism between them and their employers that prevents effective cooperation. (See *Facts about Nurses' Unions,* page 237.)

Protecting your right to unionize

Who protects your right to unionize? The regulations governing union organizing among nurses come under the jurisdiction of the National Labor Relations Board (NLRB), the federal agency that enforces the national labor laws. The NLRB will protect you when you want to organize a union or decertify one (vote the union out), protect your right to join a union, or defend you against unfair labor practices. The NLRB will also help an employer by enforcing regulations that control picketing and strikes and by providing remedies for a union's unfair labor practices.

If you want to organize a union, the NLRB will supervise procedures for elections. These procedures encompass rules that both the union and management must follow during an election. In this way, the NLRB hopes to check unfair labor practices that may arise during the election process. (See *Recognizing Unfair Labor Practices,* page 239.)

Following the rules for union elections

If you want to get a union election where you work, the first step involves distributing authorization cards or, sometimes, a petition. Nurses or union representatives may distribute the cards. Nurses who want a chance to vote on the issue (whether they want a union or not) sign an authorization card. In the United States, if at least 30% of the eligible nurses sign the cards, you or the union can ask the NLRB to authorize and supervise an election. (If 50% or more of the eligible nurses sign the cards, the law allows the employer to forego the election process and simply recognize the union. This rarely occurs.) In Canada, 35% to 50% of the nurses must sign the cards to authorize an election. (For more on the election process, see *What Happens When the Union Wants In,* page 240.)

The union and management may disagree about which nurses are eligible to vote. Either side can challenge a nurse's eligibility. The NLRB will settle an eligibility dispute by reviewing the nurse's job description, her actual duties and responsibilities, and her supervisory functions, if any.

If you're voting in a union election, you may find more than one union on the ballot. The reason: After the first petitioning union demonstrates that 30% or more of the eligible nurses want an election, other unions can get on the ballot if they can get a show of interest from 10% of the nurse-employees.

Recognizing Unfair Labor Practices

Like other employees, you have a legal right to participate in union activities. If your employer infringes on that right—through interference, domination, discrimination, or refusal to bargain—you can charge your employer with unfair labor practice. What's an unfair labor practice? Read the following examples to find out.

Interference includes:
• unilaterally improving wages or benefits during a union campaign to influence employees to vote against the union
• making coercive statements about participation in union activities
• threatening to close down the facility if a union is elected
• questioning employees about union activities
• spying on—or implying the possibility of spying on—union meetings.

Domination includes:
• paying a union's expenses
• giving union leaders special compensation or benefits
• taking an active part in organizing a union.

Discrimination includes:
• discharging, disciplining, or threatening an employee for joining a union or for encouraging others to join
• refusing to hire anyone who belongs to a union
• refusing to reinstate or promote an employee because she testified at a National Labor Relations Board hearing
• enforcing rules unequally between employees who are involved in union activities and those who aren't.

Refusal to bargain includes:
• taking unilateral action that affects any employment conditions either covered in an existing contract or included among legally mandated areas of bargaining
• refusing to meet with a union representative
• refusing to negotiate a mandatory issue
• demanding to negotiate a voluntary issue.

Management's limitations and rights

To protect your right to organize and belong to a union, the NLRB requires management to comply with five major limitations:
• Management can't interfere with your organizing activities.
• Management can't discriminate against you for participating in union activities, for testifying against management, or for filing a grievance.
• Management can't dominate a union by gaining undue influence over it, such as by paying union expenses or giving union leaders special benefits.
• Management can't refuse to bargain in good faith.
• Management must assume responsibility for any unfair labor practice committed by a supervisor.

But management also has rights protected by the NLRB. Under the law, management can:
• tell you the disadvantages of belonging to a union
• explain to you your election rights, such as your right to refuse to sign an authorization card
• encourage you to vote in a union election.

Limitations placed on the union

The union must also comply with certain limitations. The NLRB ensures that the union:
• bargains in good faith
• assumes responsibility for any unfair labor practice committed by union officials
• doesn't threaten or force you to support the union

What Happens When the Union Wants In: The Election Process

Suppose you're working in a hospital in the United States (election procedures in Canada vary from province to province) where some of the employees want to unionize. Organizers have distributed leaflets and authorization cards. At least 30% of all the proposed union employees must sign these cards to authorize a union election. (If 50% or more sign authorization cards and the employer chooses to recognize the union, the law doesn't *require* an election.)

After the employees sign the authorization cards, the following steps occur:

● The union organizer notifies the National Labor Relations Board (NLRB), and an NLRB representative steps in as a referee and organizes the election.

● The employer may challenge any employee's eligibility. For example, an employee in a supervisory position may not be considered eligible according to the employer's interpretation of the law.

● The NLRB holds a hearing to decide who's eligible to join the union.

● The NLRB determines the place and election date. Then the employer and the union begin campaigning.

● The employer provides the NLRB with a list of the names and addresses of all eligible employees within 7 days after the NLRB announces the election date and place. The NLRB gives this list to the union.

● On election day, employees vote by secret ballot to accept or reject the union. If more than one union is on the ballot, the nurse can select one of the unions or vote for no representation.

● The NLRB representative tallies the votes. The results depend on *the majority of the ballots cast*, regardless of what proportion of eligible employees actually vote. (If only a minority of eligible employees actually vote, those few employees will decide the question of unionization for all the employees.)

● If a majority of the voting employees choose the union, that union is legally required to represent *all* eligible employees, even those who didn't vote. The NLRB will certify the union as the employees' collective bargaining representative.

● If a majority of the voting employees reject the union, the law prohibits another election involving any union for one year.

● doesn't demand that your employer do business only with companies—such as suppliers—that have unions.

Neither management nor the union can interfere with your individual rights assured by other laws, such as the Fair Labor Standards Act, the Civil Rights Act, the Age Discrimination in Employment Act, or equal rights amendments in states where those laws exist.

The unionization process

Nurses may start efforts to organize by asking a union for assistance. The union will assign one of its experienced workers to help in the organizing process. Often this person is a former hospital employee who has worked in a union organizing campaign. (See *Protecting Your Right to Organize a Union,* page 243.)

The union can support the effort to unionize by supplying encouragement, stationery, printing, legal advice, organizational guidance, and other services. The union can also arrange for meeting halls and for publicity. And the union can file the proper election petitions with the NLRB.

The election determines whether the union wins or loses. To win, the union must get votes from a majority of the nurses who voted. If elected, the union will negotiate a contract that will include mutually agreeable wages, benefits, and work rules, devised by the negotiators and ratified by members of the bargaining unit.

Remember that regardless of the election's outcome, everyone will continue to work together. If the union wins, both management and labor will have to adjust to new rules spelled out in the contract. If the union loses, management should correct the problems that led to the organizing campaign, or it will probably face a renewed union effort in the future.

Different bargaining units usually represent different groups of workers in the same hospital. The NLRA empowers the National Labor Relations Board to decide what's an appropriate bargaining unit. In a few instances, RNs and LPNs/LVNs have been put in the same bargaining unit, with the consent of the RNs. In other instances, RNs have won the right to bargain as a separate professional group, while LPNs/LVNs have been placed in a bargaining unit with technicians and health-care assistants.

Be prepared to expend a lot of energy after you commit yourself to helping a unionization drive. A great deal of work is involved.

Don't let your commitment prevent you from maintaining good relations with supervisors and co-workers who oppose the union. When your viewpoints and those of others compete, heated arguments and feelings of resentment can result. Remember that labor and management don't have to be adversaries.

Conclusion

If you believe that organizing a union is necessary to improve the professional or economic status of the nurses who work in your institution, remember: the full force of the law will protect your efforts.

The legalities of collective bargaining

Collective bargaining is a legal process in which employees, acting as an organized unit, negotiate with their employer about working conditions and economic issues such as wages, hours, and fringe benefits. The process is based on the principle that, in a democracy, all groups have the right to organize. However, nurses and other health-care professionals have been explicitly granted that right only since 1974. Since then, nurses have made great strides in the area of collective bargaining. Today, nurses across the country are improving their professional and economic status through active participation in collective bargaining units.

The first milestone for collective bargaining came in 1935 with the passage of the National Labor Relations Act (NLRA). This act required employers to bargain with their employees, and it provided for the formation of a National Labor Relations Board (NLRB) to enforce the provisions of the act.

A second milestone for nurses came in 1946, when the American Nurses' Association (ANA) launched its Economic Security Program to establish national salary guidelines for nurses. Together with the NLRA, the ANA facilitated nurses' right to bargain collectively.

In the years between 1946 and 1974, a number of federal and state laws affecting collective bargaining rights were passed—some of them narrowing previous laws.

In 1947, for example, the National Labor Management Relations Act (NLMRA)—known as the Taft-Hartley Act—said nonprofit organizations, including nonprofit hospitals, didn't have to bargain with their employees.

In 1962, an amendment to the NLMRA gave federal employees, including nurses, the right to bargain collectively.

And in 1974, another amendment explicitly granted employees of nonprofit facilities the right to bargain collectively again. (This amendment, officially named the 1974 Health Care Amendments to the Taft-Hartley Act, is commonly called the Taft-Hartley Amendment.)

In the meantime, several states had passed legislation requiring nonprofit hospitals to bargain with their employees. So nurses who worked for nonprofit hospitals in Connecticut, Idaho, Massachusetts, Michigan, Minnesota, Montana, New Jersey, New York, Oregon, Pennsylvania, and Wisconsin had some bargaining rights all along.

State laws also define the rights of nurses who work for state, county, and municipal health-care institutions. Some states give these government employees the right to organize and bargain, but not the right to strike. Other states assign a specific arm of the state government to negotiate labor concerns or mandate pay scales for state-employed nurses.

The National Labor Relations Board's purpose

Congress, in the NLRA, provided for the formation of the NLRB to administer and enforce the act's provisions. (See *Appealing to the NLRB*, page 244.) (In Canada, the provincial labour relations boards handle local labor issues, and the Canada Labour Relations Board deals with labor issues at the federal level, as in the case of military hospitals.)

The NLRB is specifically responsible for enforcing the NLRA and the NLMRA, determining appropriate bargaining units for employee groups, resolving disputes between labor and management, and conducting elections for employee bargaining representatives. The NLRB will not assert jurisdiction over labor laws for minimum wages, overtime pay, termination, and discrimination unless those issues have been written into the employees' labor contract and the contract doesn't provide for binding arbitration of alleged violations. If arbitration is provided for, the NLRB usually declines its jurisdiction and defers to the arbitrator.

The NLRB recognizes seven bargaining units within health-care facilities. The units, most recently identified in the NLRB case *St. Francis Hospital and Local 474, International Brotherhood of Electrical Workers* (1984), are:
• RNs and working nurses with licenses pending
• doctors, excluding house staff
• all other professionals
• technical workers, including LPNs and LVNs
• service and nonskilled maintenance employees, such as ward clerks, nursing assistants, aides, and orderlies

• skilled maintenance employees, such as plumbers
• business clerical staff. (Such bargaining units don't exist in Canada.)

The NLRB resolves disputes between an employer and any of these bargaining units by interpreting provisions in the NLMRA. For example, according to the law, a hospital *must* bargain with its employees, each party bargaining in good faith, about issues that directly or indirectly affect wages, hours, or working conditions. The NLRB has broadly interpreted the mandatory bargaining issues to include seniority; leaves of absence; work schedules and assignments; time off, including breaks, holidays, and vacation time; benefits; promotion policies; layoff policies; and grievance and discipline procedures. The NLRB also considers employee representation concerns as mandatory bargaining issues. These concerns include arbitration, union dues payroll check-off, and other union security matters. (See *The Perils of Not Bargaining*, page 245.)

Bargaining is only necessary for other issues if both the hospital and the employees voluntarily agree to it. For example, the NLRB considers as voluntary bargaining issues all other possible legal employment issues. Illegal issues such as requiring newly hired employees to join a union in less than 30 days, or prohibiting a person from being hired or from receiving benefits or promotions because of his age, race, sex, or religion are prohibited from being bargaining issues.

Since nurses can't force an employer to bargain over voluntary issues, bargaining for professional concerns usually depends on how committed the nurses are to the issues, how willing they are to bargain for them, and how flexible the employer is.

The NLRB interprets the employer's obligation to bargain in good faith as his responsibility to recognize and accept all validly selected employee representatives. And it views an employer's interference with his employees' organized activity as illegal infringement on the employees' right to organize and bargain collectively.

If a hospital or bargaining unit disagrees with an NLRB decision, either party can appeal that decision in a federal appellate

Protecting Your Right to Organize a Union

Who'll protect you if your hospital punishes you solely because you're involved in unionizing activities? The federal government will—in the form of the National Labor Relations Board (NLRB). The board enforces the National Labor Relations Act. This act explicitly sets forth your rights to form and join a union. The scenario that follows illustrates how the NLRB will protect your unionizing efforts:

Suppose you're working as a hospital pediatrics nurse. You support an effort to unionize the hospital's nurses. When asked by union organizers, you agree to distribute union pamphlets to your colleagues. You begin giving out pamphlets in the nurses' lounge, but a hospital administrator orders you to stop. He tells you the hospital's solicitation policy prohibits anyone from distributing literature inside the hospital. You remind him that the hospital has allowed employees to distribute other information. For example, the hospital let hospital nurses

put a volunteer information booth in the hospital's lobby for the city cancer society. You ignore the administrator's order and resume handing out the pamphlets.

The next day you're called into your nursing supervisor's office and fired. Stunned, you ask for an explanation. The supervisor gives you two reasons: violating the hospital's nonsolicitation policy and disobeying the administrator.

You file an unfair labor practice charge with the NLRB. After a hearing, the board concludes that the hospital can't prevent you from distributing the pamphlets on your own time in a nonwork area. The board also concludes that the hospital was discriminatory in applying the nonsolicitation policy.

In this situation, the board would order the hospital to reinstate you, pay your back wages, and refrain from punishing you or any other nurse who was active in the union drive.

court. In Canada, the courts won't interfere with a professional organization's decision unless that organization has acted outside its jurisdiction or has violated common law through its decision.

The NLRB hears many disputes on determining appropriate bargaining units (cases include *Mercy Hospitals of Sacramento, Inc.,* 1975; and *St. Francis Hospital and Local 474, International Brotherhood of Electrical Workers,* 1984). In the latter case, it was determined that a "disparity of interest" test should be used for determining appropriate bargaining units in the health-care industry. The new standard will require that "sharper than usual differences" be demonstrated in employee wages, hours, and working conditions before a separate unit in a health-care institution will be granted.

The NLRB also hears cases on defining the supervisor's role and protecting the

employee's right to picket and solicit (cases include *NLRB v. Baptist Hospital,* 1979; and *Los Angeles New Hospital,* 1981). For example, in *NLRB v. Baptist Hospital,* the NLRB reaffirmed its prohibition of solicitation in upper-floor hospital corridors and sitting rooms that adjoined patient rooms and treatment rooms. However, the board upheld the employees' right of solicitation in first floor lobbies, the gift shop, and the cafeteria, unless the hospital could prove that patients frequented those areas.

The decision to strike

Collective bargaining doesn't guarantee that the bargaining parties will ultimately reach an agreement. If the parties arrive at a stalemate in which neither party is willing to compromise, employees may decide to strike in hopes of forcing the employer to make concessions. A strike decision is an extreme measure, so labor

Appealing to the NLRB

Employees, as well as employers, can appeal to the National Labor Relations Board (NLRB) about unfair labor practices. What can you do if you're organizing a union and you feel management is engaging in unfair labor practices? First, tell your union organizer. If she feels your charges are valid, either you or the union can report the charges to the NLRB. The board will ask you for a sworn statement concerning the dates and times of the alleged events, the names and positions of management staff involved, and the names and addresses of other employee witnesses. Your statement will serve as a legal affidavit and will supply the board with the information it needs to carry out an investigation.

Suppose the board finds through its investigation that your charges are valid—that management is engaging in unfair labor practices. Then, it'll issue a formal complaint against the employer.

The employer may appeal the board's finding. However, if the court upholds the board's determination, the employer must comply with the board's penalty—usually reinstating employees, issuing back pay, or restoring other benefits.

Consider this fictional example: While nurses at Good Faith Hospital were organizing a union campaign, supervisors asked them for the names of nurses who attended the meetings sponsored by the organizers. Also, one supervisor suggested to her staff that if a nurses' union were organized, the union might try to force management to increase wages—which, because of the hospital's precarious financial position, could cause layoffs. Several nurses complained about the supervisor's remarks at a subsequent union meeting. The union organizers agreed that management was interfering with union organization—an unfair labor practice—and consequently filed a charge with the board.

laws have established provisions that require any curtailment of services to be orderly, thus protecting the employer and the public.

Some Canadian provinces prohibit health-care employees from striking. In these provinces, compulsory arbitration is imposed when employees and employer fail to reach an agreement. The arbitrator can then draft and impose contract terms.

In the United States, negotiating parties must follow this timetable—and series of steps—before a strike can be called:
• The side wanting to modify or terminate the contract must notify the other side 90 days before the contract expires (or labor or management proposes that changes take place).
• If, 30 days later, the two sides don't agree, they must notify the Federal Mediation and Conciliation Service (FMCS), and the corresponding state agency, of the dispute.

• Within 30 days, the FMCS will appoint a mediator and, if necessary, an inquiry board.
• Within 15 days, the inquiry board will give both sides its recommendations.
• If, after 15 more days, the parties don't agree, the employees may plan to strike. If the union didn't have employees vote earlier, it will hold a strike vote at this point.
• If a majority of employees vote to strike, the union must send management a notice at least 10 days before the scheduled strike, specifying the exact date, time, and place of the strike. The strike cannot be scheduled before the contract expires.

Employees who ignore the strike provisions and engage in illegal strikes lose the protection of the NLRA. They may be discharged by their employer. Unions that sanction or encourage illegal strikes may have their certification revoked by the NLRB.

The Perils of Not Bargaining

Can a hospital avoid collective bargaining by refusing to recognize its staff's union? Of course not. The law—strengthened by court-case decisions—requires a hospital to bargain in good faith with duly elected unions. Here's a key court case, *Eastern Maine Medical Center v. NLRB* (1981), that illustrates this principle:

Nurses at Eastern Maine Medical Center voted 114 to 110 to be represented by the Maine State Nurses' Association, the state's largest nurses' union. In response, the hospital administration adopted a strong anti-union stand, refusing to meet with the nurses for collective bargaining talks. Moreover, the administration gave substantial wage-and-benefit increases to nonunion employees and withheld the increases from the union nurses.

The administration's policy of not bargaining with the union made the union nurses bitter and frustrated. And the union filed unfair labor practice charges against the hospital administration.

The National Labor Relations Board (NLRB) concluded that the hospital had violated the National Labor Relations Act by refusing to bargain in good faith and had discriminated against the union nurses. The board directed the hospital administration to negotiate with the union and to pay the wage-and-benefit increases withheld from the union nurses.

In upholding the board's actions, an appeals court ruled that the hospital's refusal to negotiate violated the nurses' collective bargaining rights.

What's involved in delaying a strike

Employees may delay a strike for up to 72 hours if they feel the extra time would enable them to come to terms with management.

To delay the strike, they must give management written notice at least 12 hours before the strike was scheduled to start.

If the initial strike date passes during the negotiations, the union must issue another 10-day strike notice.

If the contract expires during the negotiations, the employer and employees remain bound by the contract.

Conclusion

Collective bargaining is relatively well established among nurses in the United States and Canada. But it remains a controversial and often emotional topic. Many nurses who recognize the benefits of a collective voice still wonder whether organized union activity is consistent with their professional philosophies. Unfortunately, no single answer exists, because each nurse's professional and economic situation is unique.

To help assess your particular situation and to make an informed decision about participating in collective bargaining, ask yourself these questions: Will collective bargaining help my professional and economic status? Can I address my professional concerns through collective bargaining? Can I devote the time and effort that such organized activity demands? Can I change my working conditions as an individual, or do I need to organize with other nurses?

Only you can answer these questions. Keep in mind, as you ponder them, that labor laws exist to protect your rights as an employee as well as the rights of your employer.

Grievances and arbitration

As a staff nurse or a nurse manager, you can appreciate the need for procedures to settle labor disputes. You know what happens when an employee's dispute isn't resolved: Tempers quicken, morale declines, and apparent injustices smolder. That's why union and management officials give grievance and arbitration procedures high priority when they negotiate collective bargaining agreements.

As unions become more common in hospitals and other health-care institutions, you need to understand how grievance and arbitration procedures work. Even if your workplace isn't unionized, understanding these procedures can help you create fair work rules and grievance procedures where you work.

Filing a grievance: A method of resolving disputes

When unionized employees and management sign a labor contract, they agree to abide by certain rules and policies during the contract's duration. A contract can't cite every dispute that may arise, so it includes grievance procedures. Grievance procedures establish specific steps that both sides agree to follow in trying to resolve disputes in an orderly fashion.

What's a grievance? That depends on the contract. Some contracts define a grievance as any complaint that reflects dissatisfaction with union or management policies. But most contracts define a grievance as a complaint that involves contract violations.

As a staff nurse, you or your union representative can file a grievance against your employer. Your union can file a grievance against management. Management can file a grievance—usually called a disciplinary action—against any employee. Most grievances are filed against management because of management's decision-making role.

Types of grievances

Most grievances fall into one of two classifications: unfair labor practices and violations of a contract, a precedent, or a past practice. (See *Legitimate Grievances,* page 247.) Unfair labor practices are tactics prohibited by state and federal labor laws. For example, under federal law, an employer who discriminates against you because you're involved in union activities commits an unfair labor practice. Violations of a contract, precedent, or past practice are actions that break mutually accepted work rules. For example, suppose your contract says a supervisor must give you 2 weeks' notice before making you rotate to another shift. If a supervisor assigns you to another shift without giving you notice, you can file a grievance.

The causes of grievances

Grievances can involve an almost infinite number of complaints, but some occur consistently. Management often takes disciplinary action against employees who:
- allow personal problems to interfere with their jobs
- fail to perform their assigned duties
- show poor work habits, such as tardiness or unreliability
- take an antagonistic attitude toward management in labor relations when serving in union positions.

Employees often file grievances against supervisors who:
- dispense discipline inconsistently
- show favoritism
- treat employees unfairly.

Other common sources of grievances include management's selection policies for promotions, favored shift assignments, disciplinary actions, and merit salary raises. Staff nurses sometimes file grievances when they're temporarily assigned head nurse responsibilities without getting commensurate pay.

Many grievances result from unwitting contract violations (such as poorly thought-out work load decisions) by *first-level* or *mid-level managers.* Personnel and labor relations departments can resolve many actions that would otherwise lead to grievances by answering labor questions and offering advice.

Legitimate Grievances

If you're not sure whether you have a legitimate grievance, read these examples of the five types of grievances. If your grievance matches one, it's probably legitimate.

Contract violations

Your employment contract is binding between you *and* your employer. If your employer violates that contract, you have a valid grievance. In the following examples, assume that the contract prohibits the employer action described:

• You're performing the charge nurse's job 2 or 3 days a week but still receiving the same pay as other staff nurses.

• You've had to work undesirable shifts or on Sundays more often than other nurses.

• Your supervisor doesn't post time schedules in advance.

• Your employer discharges you without just cause.

Federal and state law violations

Any action by your employer that violates a federal or state law would be the basis for a grievance, even if your contract permits the action. For example:

• You receive less pay for performing the same work as a male nurse.

• You don't receive overtime pay that you're entitled to.

• Your employer doesn't promote you because of your race.

Past practice violations

A past practice—one that's been accepted by both parties over an extended period but is suddenly discontinued by the employer without notification—may be the basis for a grievance. For example:

• Your employer charges you for breaking equipment when others haven't been charged.

• Your employer revokes parking lot privileges.

• Your employer eliminates a rotation system for float assignments.

A past practice violation often becomes a complicated grievance and can occur even if the past practice isn't specified in the contract. If the practice violates the contract, either party can demand that the contract be enforced. If the practice is unsafe, an arbitrator may simply abolish it.

Health and safety violations

Grievances in this category most often involve working conditions an employer is responsible for even if the contract doesn't cover the specific complaint. For example:

• You're required to hold patients during X-rays.

• You have no hand-washing facilities near patient rooms.

Employer policy violations

Your employer can't violate its own rules without being guilty of a grievance, even though it can change the rules unilaterally. For example:

• You haven't received a performance evaluation in 2 years, although your employee handbook states that such evaluations will be done annually.

• Your employer assigns you a vacation period without your consent, contrary to personnel policies.

Grievances follow step-by-step patterns
The elements of a grievance procedure vary from contract to contract. But the key elements always include reasonable time limits for filing a grievance and making a decision, procedures to appeal a grievance to higher union-management levels

if the grievance isn't resolved, assigning priority to crucial grievances (such as worker suspensions or dismissals), and an opportunity for both sides to investigate the complaint.

The first step is usually an informal discussion between nurse and supervisor.

She may then submit her complaint in writing. If the supervisor doesn't or can't resolve the grievance, the nurse can ask for a union representative, or steward, to assist her. The representative will meet with the supervisor to discuss the grievance's merits. If the supervisor stands firm, the nurse can then file a written complaint within a contract-specified time period. Subsequent hearings move to higher levels of management. The number of steps in a grievance procedure varies with each contract's provisions.

Gripe or grievance: Making the distinction

Smooth labor relations require both sides to honor the contract's terms and to show good will when using the grievance procedures. Participants from both sides need to consider when to compromise or retreat on a disputed issue. For instance, union representatives must often defuse complaints before they become formal grievances. And an effective union representative must distinguish between a grievance and a gripe. What's the difference? A grievance is a substantive complaint that involves a contract violation. A gripe is a personal problem unrelated to the contract.

Sometimes union or management representatives pursue a groundless grievance for political or harassment purposes. A nurse's self-interest or her resentment of authority can lead to a groundless grievance. So can a supervisor's poor decision making or misuse of her authority. And sometimes neither side can work out a settlement on a substantive issue.

Whatever the reason, sometimes the grievance procedure fails to resolve the dispute. That's when arbitration enters the picture.

The process of arbitration

Arbitration is a process that settles a labor dispute by presenting evidence to a neutral labor relations expert, usually an employee of a private or government agency. Unions and management aren't legally required to include arbitration clauses in their contracts, so arbitration isn't automatic. One side must seek it after the grievance procedure fails to resolve the dispute. The side requesting arbitration gives a written notice to the other side that arbitration has been called for. Then the requesting side contacts one of several national agencies that supply arbitrators, such as the Federal Mediation and Conciliation Service or the American Arbitration Association. Sometimes the labor contract specifies which agency to use. Both sides must agree on a specific arbitrator and the date, time, and place for the arbitration hearing.

The arbitration hearing closely follows a courtroom proceeding, although it's not as formal. The side that requests the arbitration has the burden of proof and must present evidence that the contract has been violated. (However, when a nurse challenges disciplinary action, management must prove its case first by presenting supporting evidence.) In any arbitration hearing, both sides may call and cross-examine witnesses. The requesting side makes a closing summary, followed by one from the opposing side. Each side can submit written briefs instead of making summary statements.

The arbitrator usually renders a written decision weeks or even months after the hearing. But if both sides request an immediate response, the arbitrator can issue an oral decision and withhold a written explanation of the decision unless requested by both sides.

Both sides prefer arbitration to a lengthy court fight because arbitration is speedier and less expensive, and it doesn't require attorneys. But when a dispute goes to arbitration, both sides lose control of the outcome because, in the United States, the arbitrator's decision is binding. The other side can challenge the decision in court, but the court rarely overturns an arbitrator's decision. In Canada, the court may supervise arbitration itself but will never overturn an arbitrator's decision.

Resolving complaints due to unfair labor practices

Most grievances arising from contract violations follow contract-stipulated grievance and arbitration procedures. But allegations of unfair labor practices go to the National Labor Relations Board (NLRB), the federal agency that prosecutes unfair labor practices. The NLRB will conduct a hearing to review evidence and then issue a decision. Either side can challenge an NLRB decision in court.

If a nurse has a complaint involving discrimination on the basis of race, religion, national origin, age, or sex, she can file a charge of discrimination with the federal Equal Employment Opportunity Commission (EEOC) or a comparable state agency in addition to filing a grievance. The EEOC handles violations of laws such as:

• the Equal Pay Act of 1963, which forbids wage discrimination based on an employee's sex

• the Civil Rights Act of 1964, which forbids job and wage discrimination based on an employee's religion, race, sex, or ethnic background

• the Age Discrimination in Employment Act of 1967, which forbids discrimination based on an employee's age.

The EEOC will also prosecute disputes involving sexual harassment. Employees don't have to be union members to file a complaint with the EEOC.

Conclusion

Grievance and arbitration procedures exist to ensure that you have recourse when a contract is violated or when disciplinary actions are unfair. Remember, at any time during your nursing career—in a staff or supervisory position—you could become involved in a labor dispute. You might be an employee filing a grievance, a witness in an arbitration hearing, or a supervisor accused of treating an employee unfairly. Your best help *then* will be the knowledge of grievance and arbitration procedures you can start getting *now*.

Selected References

American Nurses' Association. *Guidelines for the Individual Nurse Contract.* Kansas City, Mo.: American Nurses' Association, 1974.

Bernzweig, Eli P. *The Nurse's Liability for Malpractice: A Programmed Course,* 3rd ed. New York: McGraw-Hill Book Co., 1981.

Cazalas, Mary. *Nursing and the Law,* 3rd ed. Rockville, Md.: Aspen Systems Corp., 1979.

Creighton, Helen. *Law Every Nurse Should Know,* 4th ed. Philadelphia: W.B. Saunders Co., 1981.

Fenner, Kathleen M. *Ethics and Law in Nursing.* New York: Van Nostrand Reinhold Co., 1980.

The Guide to Basic Law and Procedures under the National Labor Relations Act. Washington, D.C.: U.S. Government Printing Office, 1978.

Hemelt, Mary, and Mackert, Mary. *Dynamics of Law in Nursing and Health Care,* 2nd ed. Reston, Va.: Reston Publishing Co., 1982.

Klaus, Robert C. "The Ins and Outs of Collective Bargaining," *Journal of Nursing Administration* 10(9):18-21, September 1980.

8

Ethical Problems

How do you fulfill your professional obligation to provide adequate care and treatment when a patient exercises his right to decline life-supporting measures?

How do you meet your ethical and legal responsibilities when you suspect a colleague of professional incompetence?

These are the kinds of ethical questions you face. Modern technology has given you the ability to maintain life with artificial means. But modern society has given the consumer-patient the right to refuse such treatment. Modern professional standards have given you the responsibility to make independent ethical decisions. But modern laws are vague and confusing.

In deciding how to handle the ethical questions you face so often, you'll draw on your own experience and moral principles, of course.

But you'll also need to know how society views such questions, and how those views have shaped professional standards (such as the American Nurses' Association Code of Ethics), laws, and court decisions. (See *Is the ANA Code Legal?*.)

The University of Colorado Medical Center offers a course in medical ethics that suggests you use a nine-step procedure for making ethical decisions. Here's what you should do:

• Identify the health problem.
• Identify the ethical problem.
• State who's involved in making the decision (such as the nurse, the doctor, the patient, the patient's family).
• Identify your role. (Quite possibly, your role may not require a decision.)
• Consider as many possible alternative decisions as you can.

• Consider the long- and short-range consequences of each alternative decision.
• Weigh all of these considerations, and make your decision.
• Consider how this decision fits in with your general philosophy of patient care.
• Follow the situation until you can see the actual results of your decision. Use that information to help you make future decisions.

Conclusion

A study of the ethical issues in this chapter offers several benefits. It will increase your effectiveness as a care giver and decision maker by helping you understand the value systems and legal standards that operate in clinical situations. It will help you recognize situations with a potential for conflict, enabling you to work through them before a conflict develops.

Above all, this chapter will help you understand your own moral code—and how it serves as a basis for your nursing actions and decisions.

Life support for dying patients

When you help resuscitate terminally ill patients or provide care to replace or sustain their vital functions (such as lung or kidney function) with machines, are you prolonging life—or prolonging dying?

This question isn't just an exercise in semantics. It's a question that goes to the very heart of your professional ethics. It's really asking: What are the proper roles of medicine and nursing in caring for the dying?

The technology that prompts these questions is only a few decades old. Until then, little could be done to prolong a dying patient's life. Today, death can often be significantly delayed. But should it be?

Holding death at bay requires a great deal of skill on your part. Not only do you have to develop technologic expertise and the confidence to apply it quickly, but you also have to deliver that expertise in a way that makes prolonged life bearable for your patient and his family.

And holding death at bay takes time. Dying patients receiving extraordinary life support—such as artificial respirators, resuscitators for cardiopulmonary arrests, and dialysis—require extraordinary amounts of your time, keeping you away from other patients.

Meanwhile, the ethical questions keep nagging at you. Should you ignore the needs of patients whose conditions are improving but who will soon deteriorate no matter what you do? Should you do all you can to keep a comatose patient alive without knowing what he'd *want* you to do? Should you abide by a family's plea to "do all you can" when the whole situation is so remote from their daily lives that they can barely understand what you're doing or why?

You've seen the same confusion in your co-workers' attitudes toward maintaining or withdrawing life support, so you can't even look to them for guidance.

In fact, the confusion exists in all levels of our society—among professionals and lay people, in our legislatures, and in the institutions we've traditionally depended on to give us ethical and legal guidance: our churches and our courts.

Society's view of life-support measures
Extraordinary life-support measures themselves are generally accepted. Most people in our society favor using these measures when a patient has a temporary or reversible threat to his life. Ongoing debate, however, centers on the uses of extraordinary life-support measures with the dying.

Some people propose that such measures are appropriate only when they will

Is the ANA Code Legal?

Does the American Nurses' Association (ANA) Code for Nurses carry any legal weight? Could I lose my nursing license if I violated that code?—RN, Mo.

No. You won't lose your license if you violate the 11-point ANA code. Membership in the ANA is voluntary, so you can't be bound by the ANA code. Keep in mind, however, that the code sets *ethical* standards of conduct and practice for the nursing profession. And it can be cited as a guideline for professional conduct and your relationships in a malpractice lawsuit. So you should be aware of the code's provisions and how they apply.

Of course, you can lose your license for violating your state's nurse practice act, which sets *legal* practice standards for nurses in your state.

This letter was taken from the files of *Nursing* magazine.

improve the quality of a person's life. But they can't agree on a definition of quality. Does improving the quality mean diminishing the suffering? Or does it mean increasing the patient's cognitive awareness, mental competence, productivity, or social worth?

Before allowing for extraordinary measures—such as transplants—to be used, medical ethics boards add two more considerations: Will the patient be able to cope with the results? And will society have the resources to support them?

People generally favor extending life in some situations and letting it end in others.

You may have found that your own beliefs vary with different situations. For example, you may believe in withdrawing or withholding intervention to let death occur naturally, in theory. But you may favor extraordinary measures for patients who request them—because you don't think you have a right to try to influence patients' decisions.

Religious beliefs also play into the debate. Some religious groups, such as Christian Scientists, emphasize their reliance on God, not medical intervention. Others accept most forms of medical intervention but seek to define their limits. The Jehovah's Witnesses define limits on *specific kinds* of intervention, forbidding blood transfusions even in life-threatening emergencies. The Roman Catholic church, on the other hand, defines limits on *specific situations* in which intervention is used. For example, in 1980, the Catholic Church upheld the patient's right to refuse extraordinary treatment to protect "both the dignity of the human person and the Christian concept of life against a technological attitude that threatens to become an abuse."

In the midst of this debate, you must contribute and carry out decisions regarding terminally ill patients—when to provide life support and when not to; when to switch on mechanical equipment, and when to turn it off; when to resuscitate, and when not to. Inevitably, many of these decisions have legal as well as ethical dimensions. So you must protect yourself and your patients by finding out how the legislatures and the courts have viewed such decisions in the past.

U.S. and Canadian laws on treatment of the terminally ill
Unfortunately, current state and provincial laws governing treatment of the terminally ill vary—in large part because no one can define a satisfactory point where a terminal illness becomes terminal.

The Canadian Criminal Code, for example, says that doctors and nurses have a legal duty to perform an act if the omission of that act is or may be dangerous to life. Does this mean that health-care professionals have a duty to use all extraordinary means available to keep all patients alive? Well, the answer depends on your definitions of "alive" and "dead."

The traditional definition of death—cessation of cardiopulmonary functions—has been outdated by technology. With mechanical support, cardiopulmonary functions can be artificially maintained for long periods of time. This obviously creates a double-bind situation: we have to keep treating the patient until he dies, but he can't die as long as we keep treating him.

One response to this dilemma was a more sophisticated definition of death, based on the concept of brain death. Although a few states have adopted laws defining brain death, most states haven't, evidently accepting the American Medical Association's position that "death shall be determined by the clinical judgment of the physician using the necessary, available, and currently accepted criteria."

But some states have supported the belief that patients themselves should play a major role in deciding whether—and when—extraordinary measures are appropriate.

Right-to-die laws
In 22 states and the District of Columbia, the responsibility for deciding whether to provide or continue life support is shared by the patient. These states are the states that have right-to-die or living-will laws. (See *Living-Will Laws,* pages 148 to 155.)

According to the earliest of these, the 1977 California Natural Death Act, a patient with a terminal illness may sign a "directive" asking his doctor not to use life-prolonging measures. The patient must sign the directive while he's emotionally and mentally competent. He must have two witnesses—and neither witness can be involved in his care. And he must wait for 14 days after the diagnosis of his terminal illness to make such a directive. Once made, however, it's legally binding on the health-care team, unless the patient revokes it.

Similar provisions are found in the right-to-die laws of 21 other states and the District of Columbia. All emphasize the voluntary aspect of the patient's decision, and all permit only the withholding or withdrawing of treatment.

Worth noting, too, is the legal status of living wills. Even in states without right-to-die laws, the wills provide a record of the patient's wishes at a time when he was competent, and they may serve as a basis for later court decisions about terminating treatment.

Because patients have the right to refuse treatment, no legal problem arises when a mentally competent adult refuses lifesaving or life-support treatments (see *Withdrawing Life Support*).

But what if the patient later becomes incompetent? For example, suppose a competent patient refuses dialysis. Eventually, because of increasing uremia, he becomes obtunded and unable to make decisions. If he then develops pneumonia and needs ventilatory support, should the doctor prescribe it?

Each situation would have to be judged on its own merits. Generally, however, courts have ruled that—when no reasonable chance of recovery exists—extraordinary medical care may be withheld from terminally ill and incompetent patients who have previously, "clearly and convincingly," expressed opposition to the use of extraordinary life-support measures. Thus, a living will—a prior directive—would "clearly and convincingly" express his wishes, and should be followed.

The rights of incompetent patients
The question of a patient's right to refuse treatment is more complicated, of course, if the patient is incompetent.

Generally, however, the courts have relied on substitute judgment when they decide this question for incompetent adults. That is, they try to decide what the patient would have decided if he'd been legally competent. The courts attempt to balance such diverse factors as discomfort and pain, possible side effects of treatment, and prospective benefits.

Only rarely, out of a conviction that treatment would permit the patient to live a useful life, do the courts overrule the patient's decision or wishes. Sometimes, if the patient's death would leave his children orphaned, the court might use this as a basis to overrule his decision.

Withdrawing Life Support

Who has the legal right to decide whether to withdraw life-support treatment? Usually, the patient alone.

The terminally ill adult who's legally competent has the right to refuse any treatment, including life-sustaining treatment.

If a patient becomes unconscious or incompetent but his wishes are certain, your hospital may withdraw or withhold life support without applying to the courts for a ruling. A patient's wishes are considered certain if he's previously expressed his views or his desires on the matter of life support in a living will or less formally to his family.

Even if the patient has been judged incompetent and no one knows what his wishes were when competent, life-support treatment can be withheld once it is determined that the burden of treatment greatly outweighs the benefit to the patient.

If the patient is a minor or if he's never been competent, life support treatment can't be withheld without a court order. And, except in states with natural death acts, a court order is needed to withdraw life-support treatment once it's been initiated.

Four court cases
Among court cases involving incompetent patients, four deserve mention here:
• *In re Quinlan* (1976)
• *Superintendent of Belchertown State School v. Saikewicz* (1977)
• *Eichner v. Dillon* (1980)
• *In re Storar* (1981).

In both the Quinlan (New Jersey) and Saikewicz (Massachusetts) cases, the courts emphasized that a patient's right to refuse treatment is not forfeited by incompetence. In the Quinlan case, the court allowed treatment to be withdrawn; in the

Saikewicz case, the court allowed treatment to be withheld. Both rulings were based on what the patient would presumably have decided if he'd been able to make the decision personally (substitute judgment).

The New Jersey court gave Ms. Quinlan's "guardian and family" the right to withdraw Ms. Quinlan's life support in the face of conflicting prognoses. Her parents were thus granted the authority to make a decision on her behalf. The guardian can exercise this authority if the family and the doctor concur that "no reasonable possibility" exists that the patient will return to a "cognitive, sapient state," and if a hospital ethics committee agrees.

In the Saikewicz case, the Massachusetts court allowed withholding of cancer chemotherapy from a developmentally disabled man because prolonging his life for a few months wasn't in his best interest. The Saikewicz case involved substitute judgment to withhold treatment for a patient who could never have made a competent decision himself. The court upheld the decision to withhold treatment because of the likelihood of adverse side effects, the small chance of remission, and the certainty that treatment would cause the patient further suffering.

In the Eichner case, the New York State appeals court accepted a patient's earlier wishes as sufficient reason not to maintain his life by "extraordinary means." The patient, a priest, had discussed Karen Quinlan's situation with other priests and indicated that if he were ever in the same situation, he would want the respirator disconnected.

These three cases seem to show the role of substitute judgment clearly. The *In re Storar* case, however, muddies the water. In this case, the New York State appeals court ruled that Storar's transfusions should be continued despite a prognosis of only 6 months to live. Because Storar had never been competent and could never have made his own decision, the court said it had no way of knowing what the patient would have wanted. Although some doctors and attorneys disagree with the decision, further clarification must await another court challenge.

In reviewing these four decisions, several points clearly emerge. First, the courts are most concerned with protecting the patient's right of self-determination. Second, the courts are ready to leave medical decisions, specifically diagnoses and prognoses, in the doctors' hands. And third, when making decisions on behalf of incompetent patients, the courts look closely at the patients' previous wishes, medical prognoses, potential suffering, and quality of continued life.

Deciding what action to take

As a nurse who cares for terminally ill patients, you don't have the luxury of waiting until all the ethical and legal arguments are settled. You will often be forced to implement a medical regimen, whether you agree with it or not. To handle this difficult situation, remember these guidelines.

You can contribute to the medical decision-making process in several ways. You can observe and report a patient's physical and emotional status. And you can support your patient's decisions and make sure his doctor and other members of the health-care team hear about them.

In addition, you can volunteer for hospital committees charged with developing policies on life support, resuscitation, no-code, and critical care unit admissions. Be sure all new policies both spell out criteria to be applied in specific situations and require written documentation of any clinical decisions and discussions with patients and families.

If you work with patients receiving extended life support, someday someone (most likely a doctor) will order you to "pull the plug" or to stop further treatment. When this happens, protect yourself—and the patient—by observing these precautions:

• Ask your hospital's legal department about the legality of the decision to discontinue treatment.

• Insist that the order be put in writing, with the doctor's signature, before you carry it out.

• Check the patient's medical record to make sure it either clearly states that the patient is brain dead or indicates why treatment is being discontinued. For ex-

Your Role in Withholding or Withdrawing Life Support

Suppose the terminally ill patient you're caring for refuses life-support treatment. You've been trained to provide, not withhold, health care. What's your role now?

Your frequent contact with the patient puts you in an opportune position to support his decision. This includes letting the patient express his feelings about his situation and assisting him in getting answers to questions about his prognosis, treatments, side effects, and so on.

If the patient is unconscious and the family participates in making the decision to withhold life-support measures, they'll need your help. Family members will probably experience ambivalent feelings. In part, these feelings stem from confusion over prognosis. Family members may be torn between a belief that "where there's life, there's hope" and a desire to end the loved one's suffering. They'll also feel grief, which may be disrupted by the slowness of the dying process and by confusion over the meaning of slight changes in the patient's condition. Some family members feel guilt; many feel anger; and others feel both.

With family dynamics disrupted as different members deal with their grief at a different pace, the family will need you to help prepare them for the crisis and to assist them through it. Encourage them to express their feelings. Reassure them concerning their participation in making the decision. Answer all their questions about alternatives. Help them cope by encouraging them to use supportive resources. If members experience spiritual distress, you may refer them to the chaplain, if appropriate. In some hospitals, life support can be withdrawn over a period of hours, instead of abruptly. This method can help the family cope because it facilitates a peaceful, more natural dying process.

Whenever you're caring for the terminally ill patient on life support, you should know your state law regarding the definition of death and the binding nature of living wills. Also, keep accurate and complete documentation of events surrounding life-support termination and the patient's death. The legal importance of your records can't be overestimated.

---

ample, the record might show that a court decision was obtained. Or it might elaborate on the patient's prognosis and summarize discussions with the patient and family regarding continued treatment.

• Review hospital documentation policies to verify that the record is complete.

• Make sure the person making the decision to discontinue treatment is authorized to do so. In some hospitals, the attending doctor may write the order; in others, a doctor's department head may need to concur in the order. If an organ will be removed for transplantation, the doctors involved with either the transplantation or the organ retrieval program cannot make the decision.

• Keep your nurses' notes current. Make sure they supply a complete record of continuing care and indicate exactly when you reduced or terminated each treatment. If brain death is the basis for withdrawing treatment, the pronouncement of death should precede the discontinuation of life support. (For further discussion see Your Role in Withholding or Withdrawing Life Support.)

Conclusion

Apart from all legalities, your job is to make sure the patient's last hours are as comfortable as possible. And pay special attention to his family's needs; even though they've agreed to the patient's death, this is a difficult time for them. In short, be a nurse in the fullest sense of the word—a professional who's caring and compassionate.

Patients who want to die

Who should decide whether to give or withhold lifesaving treatment? In the two situations that follow, the patients have made decisions about how their lives should end. How would you respond?

Mrs. Keeley, an 85-year-old widow, has lived at the Shady Valley Nursing Home for nearly 4 years. You've always considered her a bright, cheerful person—one who loves to mix with the other residents.

But she's also a practical person. "When my time comes," she's often told you and other nurses, "I want you to let me go naturally. After all, I've had a full life, my children are all busy raising large families of their own, and my money won't last forever. Besides, my husband Jack is waiting for me to join him in heaven."

This morning, while making your rounds, you find Mrs. Keeley slumped over in her bed. You speak to her, but she doesn't answer. When you check her pulse, you find it weak and irregular.

The question: What do you do now?

Mr. Perillo, a carpenter in his early fifties, has spent the past 4 days on your surgical unit, where you're working the night shift. His problem is lung cancer, which is causing severe pain and a frightening shortness of breath. Even worse, his doctor told him earlier today that the cancer will no longer respond to medical therapy.

At about 3 a.m., Mr. Perillo complains of pain, so you bring him an as-needed medication. While you sit with him, he tells you his health insurance benefits are about to run out. He mentions that he and his wife have drifted apart during the past several years. Despite this, she's agreed to continue working to support the family, which includes two teenage children.

"Look," he suddenly tells you, "I want to die. It'll spare me a lot of pain, free my wife, and provide insurance money so my kids can go to college. Please, help me get some pills so I can end it all right away."

The question: What do you do now?

These two stories are fictional. Still, they represent situations you may face if you work with dying patients.

At any given time, a million Americans are living with a terminal prognosis. And each year, 2 million Americans die—80% of them in hospitals or other institutions where nurses have direct-line responsibility. Obviously, the more you know about the ethical and legal dimensions of caring for the dying, the better you'll be able to handle situations such as the ones just described.

The ethics of withholding care

Given America's cultural and religious diversity, you would expect viewpoints about elective death to vary widely. For some Americans, the thought of withholding life support is abhorrent. This view probably comes from our society's preoccupation with youth and health and a perception of death as something apart from life—a stark tragedy to be avoided at all costs.

For other Americans, letting a patient die a natural death is not only a mark of clear thinking but also of love and concern for a suffering patient.

This group views mercy as a moral obligation, and compassion as the motivating force behind any decision to let a patient die. Accordingly, death isn't the worst thing that can befall an individual. Thus, acts of omission (not instituting life-support measures) as well as acts of commission (withdrawing already instituted life-support measures) are moral when the result and the intent are in the patient's best interest.

In regard to a patient like Mrs. Keeley—who told you many times to let her die a natural death—this group would urge you not to try to prolong her life. They would tell you that your patient's integrity as a human being demands that she be given the right to choose, and that protecting her choice is more important than continuing her biological functions.

Most religious groups agree that health professionals aren't obligated to preserve life in all terminal cases. The religious position is also based on the proposition that human life is more than biologic function—it must also evidence certain qual-

The Patient's Right to Choose: ANA Viewpoints

The American Nurses' Association (ANA) has emphasized the right of competent patients to participate in making decisions about their health and in evaluating the health care they receive. It has supported this right in two important documents, the ANA Code of Ethics (1976) and the Social Policy Statement about Nursing (1980).

The ANA Code of Ethics says each patient—including a terminally ill or dying patient—has these rights:
• to decide what treatments he will refuse or accept
• to receive the information he needs to make an informed decision
• to be warned of the possible side effects of different treatments.

The code also states that nurses must respect each patient as an individual, regardless of his health problems.

The Social Policy Statement says that nurses must respect each patient's right to self-determination and independence, and that nurses must recognize their patients' dignity as they carry out their nursing duties.

---

ities of self-awareness and cognition to merit the name "human life." Thus today's religious thinkers agree with their ancient counterparts who asserted that the essence of human character lies in a person's rational faculties.

Applying general principles

But theory sometimes falls apart in practice. Even those Americans who support the general principle that a patient has a right to choose a natural death may feel differently when the general principle is applied to a specific patient, especially someone they know.

Mrs. Keeley's children, for example, may suddenly reverse their previous support for their mother's right to die in the emotionally charged hours when you have to implement her decision to "do nothing." Because of guilt, fear, anger, or an overwhelming feeling of loss, they may insist on continuing life support regardless of her wishes.

Your dilemma may also be complicated by pressure from doctors and other nurses who urge the use of new or experimental techniques that may help others in the future.

And, finally, you may face the stress of your own contradictory impulses. You may recognize all patients' rights to be spared heroic yet futile procedures. Yet you may feel that actually withholding those procedures from a particular patient conflicts with your professional (and, usually, legal) commitment to do everything possible.

Look for guidelines

Before you find yourself in a situation where you're forced to make crucial decisions between life and death and ordinary and extraordinary measures, try to clarify your professional and legal obligations.

Read your institution's policy on withholding care. If your hospital doesn't have one, volunteer to develop one.

Read your state or provincial nurse practice act, and examine the standards and codes of ethics of professional societies (see The Patient's Right To Choose: ANA Viewpoints).

Find out which laws your state has passed protecting patients' right to die natural deaths. The most common laws protecting this right are called right-to-die laws or Living-Will Laws (see pages 148 to 155). But your state may have other laws relating to death and the care of the dying, such as laws covering brain death, resuscitation, defibrillation, and medication administration.

And, finally, keep up with nursing literature that tells you how current court decisions reflect and shape the ethics of letting a patient die.

Court decisions on the right to die

The courts have generally upheld the right of competent patients to make life-or-death medical choices. In this way, courts have supported the ethical view that doctors and nurses are consultants who provide expert advice. But patients are the final arbiters of their own lives.

True, the courts sometimes overrule a patient's right. For example, they may empower doctors to give lifesaving treatment to minors even though the minors' legal guardians seek to withhold treatment. And the courts may empower doctors to give lifesaving treatment to competent adults if failure to give such care could leave orphaned children.

But these exceptions are rare. The decision of *In re Osborne* (1972) is more typical of the courts' attitude toward patients' right to die. This case involved a Jehovah's Witness who refused blood transfusions on religious grounds. Citing the First Amendment, the court supported his right to refuse lifesaving treatment even though he had a young wife and two dependent children.

In the case *In re Quinlan* (1976), the court established the right of patients or their proxies to authorize the withdrawal of life-support mechanisms. And in *Superintendent of Belchertown State School v. Saikewicz* (1977), the court supported the right of incompetent patients to refuse life-prolonging measures, such as chemotherapy. This right-to-die principle was further extended by the New Jersey Supreme Court in January 1985 in the case in re Conroy. The court said that life-sustaining treatment may be withheld or withdrawn from elderly patients who are mentally incompetent and whose life expectancy, even with life-sustaining treatment, is relatively short. Before treatment can be withheld or withdrawn, "best interest" tests must be carried out to learn what the person's views on life support had been while competent and whether the burden of treatment greatly outweighs the benefits to the patient. (See *Withdrawing Life Support,* page 253.)

Implementing your decision

If you can ethically support the decision to let a patient like Mrs. Keeley die, continue to provide nursing support, including comfort and hygiene measures. Also, continue to talk to her and explain what's happening—even if she's comatose.

In short, show the same care and respect you'd show if her recovery were certain. (For other discussion see *Hospice Care: A Growing Alternative,* page 259).

If you can't accept the decision to let a patient die, explain your position to your supervisor and ask to be relieved of your assignment.

Letting someone die versus helping someone die

The ethics involved with a patient like Mr. Perillo—who asks you to give him a fatal overdose of pills—are very different. Although social and legal prohibitions against suicide have been modified, the ancient Western religious injunction against suicide continues to exert a powerful legal and ethical influence. Even those who agree with the idea of letting a disease run its course make a moral distinction between this inaction against death and the direct action of causing death.

One ethical basis for this distinction comes from the biblical injunction "You shall not kill" (Exodus 20:13). Its adherents insist that all killing is wrong, that the body must be respected, and that the sanctity of life, not the quality of life, is the paramount principle.

Clearly, you can't act alone to help a patient like Mr. Perillo die. But that doesn't mean you can't help him at all. When you find yourself in such a situation, try to determine whether the patient is acting out of a firm conviction or expressing a temporary depression. If he seems sincerely committed, ask his permission to contact his doctor to try to find ways to support his wishes.

Depending on your state laws, charting his comments, or the existence of a living will, may lay the groundwork for withholding life-support measures later in his care.

Hospice Care: A Growing Alternative

Hospice care shifts the emphasis of care from the traditional goal of lifesaving at all costs to that of palliative care or assistance with dying. Using a multidisciplinary team, a hospice tries to provide the highest quality care for the remaining life of the terminally ill patient.

By concentrating on pain and symptom control and psychosocial and spiritual support, the hospice staff practices euthanasia in its most literal sense—it aims to provide an easy, painless death.

According to Cicely Saunders, founder of the modern hospice movement, active listening, support, and adequate pain and symptom control decrease patients' yearning for a quick death. With adequate support during the dying process, they'll want to be able to experience all the "good" living time they have left. This assertion, however, has only anecdotal, not statistical, support.

For some patients and their families, hospice care represents a natural, humane, dignified, ethical, and legally uncomplicated approach to death.

For nurses, hospice care theoretically resolves the legal dilemmas about the validity of informed consent, the appropriateness of calling a "no code," and the possible liability for being involved in involuntary euthanasia. In the last decade, the movement has grown rapidly and has been virtually unchallenged in the courts.

Conclusion

For you, as a nurse, an ethical and compassionate response to a patient who wants to die involves listening, accepting, and trying to help him fulfill his wish. You needn't do more—but you should never do less. (For additional information see A "Right-to-Die" Survey, page 260).

Organ donation and transplantation

Jack Bowen, a 20-year-old university student, was driving home for Christmas vacation. Suddenly, his car swerved off the road and crashed head-on into a tree. A passing motorist found Jack unconscious with his head against the steering wheel.

An hour later, Jack was brought into the emergency department of the nearest hospital. He had no spontaneous respirations and no reflex response to painful stimuli. His pupils were nonreactive with no doll's eye movement. After being stabilized on a respirator, Jack was transferred to the intensive care unit.

By the time his parents arrived the next morning, Jack had had two flat EEGs, 24 hours apart. Each showed no brain wave activity. Jack's doctor told the parents that these and other tests met the generally accepted medical criteria for death and the state's legal definition of brain death. He offered his sympathy, answered a few questions, and left.

Jack's nurse stayed with the parents after the doctor left. She listened to their expressions of pain and confusion and tried to comfort and support them. The nurse also got more information for them when they asked about donating some of Jack's organs. As the mother said, "At least it'll make some sense out of this senseless situation."

The next day, Jack was pronounced dead and taken to the operating room, where the organs to be donated were removed. His eyes went to a man who'd been blind for 5 years. And his kidneys went to two people: a mother with two children and a young college student like Jack.

Jack's case is hardly unusual. For example, some 5,000 kidney transplants are performed each year in the United States. In addition, doctors performed 309 heart,

268 liver, 37 lung, and 49 pancreas transplants in a recent sample year.

You may already have cared for a transplant donor or recipient. If you haven't, you probably will. At that point, you'll find yourself facing a number of important medical, ethical, and legal issues.

Medical and ethical issues

Medically speaking, the number of transplants is increasing because of three main developments:
• improved surgical techniques
• more success with medications to suppress immunologic response to transplanted organs
• improved ability to type tissues correctly.

In addition, today's technology allows organs to be preserved for a longer time—and, if necessary, to be flown to recipients all over the world. And organs are welcomed in more and more nations, as both the idea of transplantation and the acceptance of brain-death criteria gain increasing approval.

Ethically, the decision to donate or accept an organ usually rests with the answer to the key question: Dare I make a decision that involves taking organs from one person's body to save or improve the quality of another's life? The answer usually depends on a person's social, cultural, and religious values.

In general, Western society has supported the idea of saving or improving another's life by giving of oneself. But Western society has also considered body mutilation, either before or after death, taboo.

Today, this attitude is slowly changing. One reason is growing public awareness of successful organ transplants. Another is the pro-transplant stand being taken by the major religions.

The Roman Catholic Church, for example, generally views organ transplantation as permissible, provided the organ recipient will benefit and the donor (if not already brain dead) will survive without being deprived of some vital function. Other Christian churches also support organ transplantation. Although they don't consider anyone obliged to donate an organ, they support donation as a gift of

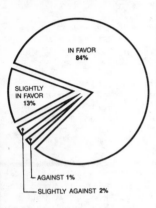

A "Right-to-Die" Survey

Q How do you feel about withholding all life-sustaining treatment from dying patients who don't want it?

IN FAVOR 84%

SLIGHTLY IN FAVOR 13%

AGAINST 1%

SLIGHTLY AGAINST 2%

Q How do you feel about mercy killing or active euthanasia for dying patients who request it?

AGAINST 42%

IN FAVOR 13%

SLIGHTLY AGAINST 14%

SLIGHTLY IN FAVOR 31%

More than 2,000 nurses responded to these questions during the *NursingLife* right-to-die probe.

Answering Questions about Organ Donation

Your dying patient may want to discuss organ donation with you. So that you can help him reach a decision, the National Kidney Foundation has prepared answers to some of the questions you'll probably be asked.

Q Is there a need for organ donors?
A Yes. Thousands of lives every year are lost because donors of kidneys and other organs are so scarce.

Q How can I become a donor?
A Sign a donor card in the presence of two witnesses who also sign. You have several donor options: You can donate any organ or part that is needed; you can restrict the donation to the organs or parts you specify; or you can donate your entire body for anatomical study.

Q Is there an age requirement for donors?
A Yes. Anyone older than age 18 may become a donor. A person age 18 or younger must have his parents' permission.

Q Do I have to register with an agency?
A No. Your signed, witnessed donor card is all that's needed.

Q Do I have to mention the organ donation in my will?
A No. You may mention it in your will if you wish, but your donor card is a kind of pocket will and is all you need. Obviously this makes the card important. Tell your family and your doctor of your wishes to ensure their cooperation.

Q Can I change my mind later?
A Yes. Simply tear up the card. Nothing else is necessary.

Q Can I be sure my gift will be used?
A You can be sure it will be used if possible. Sometimes, of course, an organ can't be used because no compatible recipient can be found or because the organ isn't healthy.

Q When will my gift be used?
A The organ will probably be removed within an hour after death. According to the Uniform Anatomical Gift Act (the model law that governs organ donation issues in each state), the doctor in attendance is responsible for determining that life has ceased and that the donor's wishes may be carried out. The act specifies, however, that the doctor attending the dying person not participate in either the removal or the transplantation. That's the job of the hospital and the transplant team.

Q Does organ donation affect funeral and burial arrangements?
A No. Removal of organs or tissues won't interfere with customary funeral or burial arrangements. These remain the responsibility of relatives or persons in charge of the estate. If you want to will your body to a medical center for anatomical study, you must make arrangements with the medical center.

Adapted with permission from The National Kidney Foundation, Inc.

---

love freely given.

Traditional Jewish ethics have forbidden body mutilation, except to save a life. Orthodox Judaism still adheres to this view; but Conservative and Reform Judaism have broken with this view and impose no

Conflicting Ethical Views

Nurses like you sent in these letters with their responses to nursing ethics surveys. Two of these nurses graphically describe the conflicts they felt when the care ordered for terminally ill patients clashed with their personal nursing ethics.

"Before taking my present position as office nurse for an internist, I worked in a coronary care–intensive care unit for 4 years. I became thoroughly convinced that people should be allowed to die with dignity. To have to resuscitate an 80- or 90-year-old patient when he was tired of living and requesting to die, is cruel. Or to keep a patient on life-sustaining equipment even with a flat EEG, is cruel for the family as well as the patient. A class I recently took on bioethics helped me look closer at my feelings and face some of the ethical questions that we often try to run away from."

"I believe my values have not changed in 25 years of nursing, but that my experience and maturity have helped me to reaffirm them....the dignity of the patient in terminal illness must be maintained. And the patient and his family continue to need education in these matters.

"There are many things worse than death. I would never hesitate to give a respiration-depressing drug to a terminal patient in pain. Yet, I would never intentionally give an overdose.

"The definition of what constitutes life should not be a matter for the courts. Termination of life-support systems should follow consultation between family, physician, and spiritual advisor."

"I was recently involved in a situation that put me in the middle of a family's request and the doctor's order. The patient was a man in his seventies with a past history of severe cardiac disease, CVA [cerebrovascular accident], and now terminal cancer and a recent respiratory arrest, leaving him in our intensive care unit on a respirator and unresponsive. During my shift, the patient arrested again, and our resuscitation efforts

restrictions on organ transplantation.

Despite such changing views, many people still have a strong aversion to mutilation, even after death. Some, for example, can't bring themselves to allow a loved one's body to be autopsied. And others can't tolerate the thought of their own or a family member's body being surgically invaded to obtain a donated organ.

Although mutilation is the basic issue to be resolved, for many people, organ transplants raise other ethical questions, such as, How should society allocate its resources? If an infant and an elderly person both need corneas, for example, or a professor and a prisoner both need a kidney, who should get the organ? And who should decide?

And how should society allocate its limited financial resources? Is an experimental liver transplant for one patient *worth* hundreds of thousands of dollars in public funds? Or should these be spent to meet the needs of a greater number of people?

As a nurse, you may find yourself torn by such conflict when you're counseling patients or families about organ donation or when you're caring for a cadaveric organ donor. (See *Answering Questions about Organ Donation,* page 261.)

Resolving such conflicts requires a willingness to examine your beliefs and identify their sources. Only then will you be able to feel comfortable with providing care.

Legal issues

Whatever your ethical beliefs, you should be aware of certain legal risks and responsibilities in organ donation and organ

were successful once more. His wife and son then came to visit, and when I told his wife about her husband's most recent condition, the wife asked why he was being 'tortured' this way, since she and her son had both expressed their desire to let him die in peace without further 'heroics' after the first time he had been coded. She said the attending physician was aware of her wishes, however we had no legal no-code order at that time. The physician had been notified of the patient's second respiratory arrest and was now on his way to the hospital. I explained the situation to the wife and son, and told them we would all speak with the doctor when he arrived and get the order not to resuscitate. Unfortunately, the patient then had a cardiac arrest before the doctor arrived and one of the other nurses began CPR [cardiopulmonary resuscitation]. While we worked on the patient, his son came into the room and very calmly, but adamantly, told us, "No! No more—stop and let him die." The son then left the room, leaving us standing there quite stunned. The resident in charge of the code then told us to continue CPR. I immediately refused as did the other two nurses present, telling the resident of the earlier conversation I had with the wife and son. I suggested to the resident that if he wanted CPR resumed, that he should do it, but he also just stood there, unsure of what to do. At that time, the intern and respiratory therapist resumed CPR, until the attending physician arrived about 5 to 10 minutes later. After he asked about the surrounding circumstances, he finally decided to stop the CPR, and our patient died.

"We discussed the whole experience with our nursing supervisor. She agreed it was a 'sticky' situation, but said since we did not have a no-code order, we could not take an order from a family member, as when the son came into the room and told us to stop our efforts—we should have continued CPR. This just left all of us upset and confused. It's a shame that our society is so 'sue-happy' that we have to become so legally aware during a time like this, even when a family's wishes were being so clearly expressed but we had to wait for the physician to 'give the word'."

These letters were sent by nurses during a *NursingLife* ethics probe.

transplant situations.

First, for a donation to be made, the donor's consent is necessary. Getting consent from an adult who wants to donate a kidney is routine, for example—removing one kidney doesn't decrease life expectancy, and the transplant success rate is considerable.

If the donor can't consent, either because he's mentally incompetent or a minor, the courts allow parents or guardians to consent as long as the donor and recipient are related. In *Strunk v. Strunk* (1969), a Kentucky court authorized a transplant from a developmentally disabled 27-year-old to his brother. And in *Masdev v. Harrison* (1957) and *Hart v. Brown* (1972), Massachusetts and Connecticut courts ruled that parents could consent to transplants between minor identical twins.

For cadaveric organ donation, all 50 states have adopted the Uniform Anatomical Gift Act, which provides two ways to donate organs:

• In Canada and the United States, any person 18 or older may indicate his desire to become an organ donor by signing a uniform donor card (or similar document) in the presence of two witnesses. In many states this intent is recorded on the back of a driver's license. Legally, this decision is binding on the person's family after his death. As a practical matter, however, most hospitals will comply with the family's wishes.

• A family member may authorize donation of a decedent's organs by signing an appropriate document. If death occurs within 24 hours of admission to a hospital or results from an accident, homicide, or other unnatural cause, a medical examiner must also consent to the organ donation.

Of course, for any cadaveric donation to occur, death must be legally established first. By 1980, 28 states and several provinces had recognized brain death as a valid definition of death. But even in states and provinces without brain-death laws, medical practice—and court decisions—have upheld the brain-death concept (see "When a Patient Dies," page 88).

Your role
Given these medical, ethical, and legal considerations, what's your role as a nurse assigned to care for a prospective organ donor or recipient?

As in any other medical or surgical procedure, getting consent for organ transplants and donations is a medical responsibility. But you can help by answering questions, or by referring patients and their families to someone who can.

With a prospective donor, your first job is to help the patient or his family decide whether to donate an organ. Tell them that this is a question they'll need to answer; then give them objective information (or find someone who can) so that the patient or his family can make an informed decision.

When your patient is a prospective recipient, outline the advantages and disadvantages of transplant procedures as objectively as possible. Then let the patient (or, if necessary, his family) decide whether or not to consent.

Conclusion
What if you're opposed to the idea of donations and transplantation? If you don't know why you feel this way, try to identify the reasons. Until you understand your feelings better, ask to be excused from caring for prospective donors or recipients.

If you're opposed to the procedure for a specific donor or recipient, share your concerns with the medical team. If you still feel uncomfortable, share your concerns with the hospital administration.

Abortion

Mention the word "abortion" to a group of nurses, doctors, or other health-care workers, and the debate begins. Some are for it, some against it, and some aren't sure.

As an individual, you have a right to your opinion about abortion. But as a nurse, you must try not to let your personal opinion interfere with your care of patients exercising their legal right to abortions. To meet that duty, you need to be familiar with abortion's current legal status.

Changing laws on abortion
Abortion's been practiced since the dawn of recorded history. In the United States, however, before the 1960s, state laws severely limited or outlawed abortions. Women faced with unwanted pregnancies were caught between the laws against abortion and society's intolerance of out-of-wedlock pregnancies and illegitimate births.

In the 1960s, some states passed less restrictive abortion laws. But in *Roe v. Wade* (1973), the U.S. Supreme Court took the question out of the states' hands. The Court ruled that abortion was a right derived from the constitutional right to privacy. Although the Constitution nowhere specifically declares such a right, the Court found it in the framers' intent and in the Fourteenth Amendment, which, the Court said, precludes government intrusion into the personal matter of "whether to beget and bear a child." According to the Court, a woman and her doctor could jointly decide whether to abort a fetus during the first two trimesters. During the second trimester the abortion procedure may be regulated by law, but only to reasonably preserve and protect maternal health. Thus, most of the decision-making power was taken away from state legislators and given to those directly involved in the question. (In Canada, abortion is legal only with the approval of a hospital's committee on therapeutic abortion.)

The ruling didn't shut the states out entirely, however. It said that a state's interest began when the fetus became viable. That, of course, prompted increased debate on when life begins.

When does life begin?

A biologist might say life begins at conception. A theologian might back up the moment into eternity, or he might move it ahead to "when the woman feels life" (quickening). But for many centuries, the courts had their own reference point: life, most suggested, began at birth. For example, only persons had rights under common law, and the unborn weren't considered "persons." Neither were the stillborn. Thus, a birth attendant, by reporting either "life" (even a few fleeting breaths) or "no life," had the power to secure or cut off an infant's rights. But gradually, both statutory and common law began to view life as beginning before birth. Among other things, this allowed compensation for prenatal injuries.

In questions of abortion, the emphasis has shifted from "birth" to "viability." The revised (1979) fifth edition of *Black's Law Dictionary* defines abortion as: "the intentional expulsion or removal of an unborn child from the womb other than for the principal purpose of producing a live birth or removing a dead fetus." While this definition suggests that abortion is unlawful, modern common law accepts the definition but considers the conduct lawful. This shift demonstrates the law's capacity to catch up with the issues and the times.

In 1976, the Supreme Court upheld viability as the earliest point at which a state could interfere with a woman's right to have an abortion. Thus, in *Planned Parenthood of Central Missouri v. Danforth* (1976), the Court ruled unconstitutional a Missouri law that required health-care workers to protect fetal life *before* viability, under threat of civil and criminal penalties.

The state can place some restrictions on the abortion itself, however. In the *first trimester,* the state can require that the doctor be duly licensed (*Roe v. Wade*, 1973) and that reasonable records be kept (*Planned Parenthood of Central Missouri v. Danforth,* 1976), but not that the abor-

tion take place in a hospital accredited by the Joint Commission on Accreditation of Hospitals (*Doe v. Bolton,* 1973). (Nearly 80% of legal abortions now take place outside hospitals, a decided increase from 50% in 1973.)

In the *second trimester,* the state may impose more stringent regulations to protect the pregnant woman's health and safety. But because the state has no overriding interest in the nonviable fetus, it can't prohibit the use of saline procedure or require the protection of fetal life (*Planned Parenthood of Central Missouri v. Danforth,* 1976).

In the *third trimester,* the state's interest in the viable fetus becomes sufficient to prohibit abortion unless the doctor believes that continuing to carry the fetus poses a danger to the pregnant mother's health.

Who pays for an abortion?

Although the courts have upheld women's right to have abortions, they've been less willing to say that the state must pay for it. In some instances, therefore, a woman's inability to pay for an abortion effectively cancels her right of choice. (In Canada, provincial health plans cover the cost of abortions done in a hospital for health reasons.) Even so, an estimated 1.2 million legal and illegal abortions were performed in the United States in 1980. According to some estimates, 15% of U.S. women of childbearing age (15 to 44) have had at least one abortion.

Compared to other countries, the U.S. abortion rate is near the middle. Canada and western European countries have lower rates. Eastern European countries, the Soviet Union, and Japan have higher rates.

Until 1976, abortions were covered under federal Medicaid programs. But in that year, Congress accepted the Hyde Amendment to the Labor–Health, Education, and Welfare Appropriations Act, effectively removing abortion from federal Medicaid coverage.

In *Harris v. McRae* (1980), the U.S. Supreme Court upheld the constitutionality of the original Hyde Amendment and its later revisions. As a result, state Medicaid programs may subsidize childbirth

Codes for Nurses

American Nurses' Association Code for Nurses

The Code for Nurses is based upon belief about the nature of individuals, nursing, health, and society. Recipients and providers of nursing services are viewed as individuals and groups who possess basic rights and responsibilities, and whose values and circumstances command respect at all times. Nursing encompasses the promotion and restoration of health, the prevention of illness, and the alleviation of suffering. *The statements of the Code and their interpretation provide guidance for conduct and relationships in carrying out nursing responsibilities consistent with the ethical obligations of the profession and quality in nursing care.*

● The nurse provides services with respect for human dignity and the uniqueness of the client unrestricted by considerations of social or economic status, personal attributes, or the nature of health problems.

● The nurse safeguards the client's right to privacy by judiciously protecting information of a confidential nature.

● The nurse acts to safeguard the client and the public when health care and safety are affected by the incompetent, unethical, or illegal practice of any person.

● The nurse assumes responsibility and accountability for individual nursing judgments and actions.

● The nurse maintains competence in nursing.

● The nurse exercises informed judgment and uses individual competence and qualifications as criteria in seeking consultation, accepting responsibilities, and delegating nursing activities to others.

● The nurse participates in activities that contribute to the ongoing development of the profession's body of knowledge.

● The nurse participates in the profession's efforts to implement and improve standards of nursing.

● The nurse participates in the profession's efforts to establish and maintain conditions of employment conducive to high-quality nursing care.

● The nurse participates in the profession's effort to protect the public from misinformation and misrepresentation and to maintain the integrity of nursing.

● The nurse collaborates with members of the health professions and other citizens in promoting community and national efforts to meet the health needs of the public.

Reprinted with permission of the American Nurses' Association

Code of Ethics for the Licensed Practical Nurse

● The licensed practical nurse shall practice her profession with integrity.

● The licensed practical nurse shall be loyal—to the physician, to the patient, and to her employer.

● The licensed practical nurse strives to know her limitations and to stay within the bounds of these limitations.

● The licensed practical nurse is sincere in the performance of her duties and generous in rendering service.

● The licensed practical nurse considers no duty too menial if it contributes to the welfare and comfort of her patient.

● The licensed practical nurse accepts only that monetary compensation which is provided for in the contract under which she is employed, and she does not solicit gifts.

● The licensed practical nurse holds in confidence all information entrusted to her.

● The licensed practical nurse shall be a good citizen.

● The licensed practical nurse participates in and shares responsibility for meeting health needs.

● The licensed practical nurse faithfully carries out the orders of the physician or

registered nurse under whom she serves.
• The licensed practical nurse refrains from entering into conversation with the patient about personal experiences, personal problems, and personal ailments.
• The licensed practical nurse abstains from administering self-medication, and in event of personal illness, takes only those medications prescribed by a licensed physician.
• The licensed practical nurse respects the dignity of the uniform by never wearing it in a public place.
• The licensed practical nurse respects the religious beliefs of all patients.
• The licensed practical nurse abides by the Golden Rule in her daily relationship with people in all walks of life.
• The licensed practical nurse is a member of The National Federation of Licensed Practical Nurses, Inc., and the state and local membership associations.
• The licensed practical nurse may give credit to a commercial product or service, but does not identify herself with advertising, sales, or, promotion.

Reprinted with permission of The National Federation of Licensed Practical Nurses

International Council of Nurses Code For Nurses

The fundamental responsibility of the nurse is fourfold: to promote health, to prevent illness, to restore health, and to alleviate suffering.

The need for nursing is universal. Inherent in nursing is respect for life, dignity, and rights of man. It is unrestricted by considerations of nationality, race, creed, color, age, sex, politics, or social status.

Nurses render health services to the individual, the family, and the community, and coordinate their services with those of related groups.

NURSES AND PEOPLE
The nurse's primary responsibility is to those people who require nursing care.

The nurse, in providing care, respects the beliefs, values, and customs of the individual.

The nurse holds in confidence personal information and uses judgment in sharing this information.

NURSES AND PRACTICE
The nurse carries personal responsibility for nursing practice and for maintaining competence by continual learning.

The nurse maintains the highest standards of nursing care possible within the reality of a specific situation.

The nurse uses judgment in relation to individual competence when accepting and delegating responsibilities.

The nurse, when acting in a professional capacity, should at all times maintain standards of personal conduct that would reflect credit upon the profession.

NURSES AND SOCIETY
The nurse shares with other citizens the responsibility for initiating and supporting action to meet the health and social needs of the public.

NURSES AND CO-WORKERS
The nurse sustains a cooperative relationship with co-workers in nursing and other fields.

The nurse takes appropriate action to safeguard the individual when his care is endangered by a co-worker or any other person.

NURSES AND THE PROFESSION
The nurse plays the major role in determining and implementing desirable standards of nursing practice and nursing education.

The nurse is active in developing a core of professional knowledge.

The nurse, acting through the professional organization, participates in establishing and maintaining equitable social and economic working conditions in nursing.

Reprinted with permission of the International Council of Nurses

Guidance When Dealing with Colleagues

Danger to patients: The alcoholic nurse

I work with a 40-year-old nurse who had a good employment record until a few weeks ago.

Since then, she's made many medication errors—including giving the wrong preoperative medication to a patient. She's come in late several times, and she's often absent from the floor. I've also smelled alcohol on her breath. Do you have any suggestions on how to handle this?—RN, Mich.

Sounds like your colleague may be suffering from some kind of stress and using alcohol to cope with it. Unchecked, her use of alcohol could turn into a more serious problem than the stress.

Since your colleague's problems are endangering her patients, talk to her or tell her supervisor what you've observed. The supervisor should sit down with her, tell her the behavior problems that have interfered with her work, and ask her what's causing the problems.

If the nurse admits she's abusing alcohol, the supervisor must first make abso-

lutely clear that reporting for duty under the influence of alcohol will not be tolerated. Then the supervisor should help her identify some alternate coping mechanisms and, if possible, some solutions to her stress.

In the meantime, if the nurse's behavior continues to endanger her patients, the supervisor must take the steps necessary to protect them—either by limiting the nurse's contact with patients or by relieving her of her duties until she's learned to cope effectively with her stress.

Either way, once you've talked to the supervisor, you can best help your colleague by keeping her problem confidential.

Reporting an abusive colleague

I saw a nurse in my pediatric unit slap and shake a 2-year-old recently when he refused to take his medication.

I was horrified that she might be abusing children. So far, no one else has said or done anything about her behavior.

What's worse, I've only been working here a couple of months, and I don't want

---

but exclude all abortions, even those deemed "medically necessary." However, some state courts (California, New Jersey, and Massachusetts) have held that the *state* constitution requires Medicaid funding for medically necessary abortions if the state also pays the costs of childbirth.

The continuing controversy

Despite the laws and court decisions regulating abortion, the ethical controversy continues. Two organized groups are particularly prominent: the National Right to Life Committee (NRLC) and the National Abortion Rights Action League (NARAL).

The NRLC, a pro-life group, focuses on fetal rights and seeks to restrict or elimi-

nate maternal choice. The group favors a constitutional amendment that would grant the fetus rights at the time of conception. Such an amendment would void the *Roe v. Wade* right-to-privacy ruling.

In contrast, NARAL, a pro-choice group, places maternal rights first and favors abortion as an alternative to unwanted pregnancies. The group contends that women should be free to choose when (and when not) to have a baby, and that abortion is safe.

Your role

You have a personal right to side with either argument, of course. But that right normally shouldn't interfere with your

to rock the boat. I know my colleague is generally a good nurse. She's been on this unit 15 years.

What's my responsibility in this situation? Where can I turn for help?—RN, Ohio

First, tell your supervisor. Isolated or not, the incident could be grounds for legal charges from the child's parents.

If you continue to suspect that your colleague is abusing children, insist that your supervisor talk to her. If she refuses, talk with your director of nursing.

Why do you have to get involved? The safety and well-being of your young patients is the first priority, of course. But consider this, too: At least one court decided that health-care professionals who didn't report suspected child abuse were liable for further injuries the child sustained.

Protection for reporting negligence

When a nurse asks what to do about poor patient care, attorneys and ethicists advise her to compile records, then talk with her supervisor. Doesn't the nurse run the risk of being fired or having to resign? Or is there some legal protection for nurses who report poor practices?—RN, N.Y.

Some states do offer protection to encourage nurses and other health-care professionals to report poor practices. Two new additions to New York's Public Health Law grant immunity from civil problems that interfere with nursing practice. In exchange, however, the laws make reports of patient abuse and professional misconduct mandatory for doctors in residential health-care facilities. Failure to report such actions is unprofessional conduct.

Other states have mandated peer accountability in the rules and regulations that accompany their nurse practice acts. Check with your state nurses associations for the latest news on your legal responsibilities and protection in such situations.

These letters were taken from the files of *Nursing* and *NursingLife* magazines.

professional duty.

Some states have laws giving nurses a "conscience" right to refuse to participate in abortions because of moral or ethical reasons. In states without such laws, you could be subject to an employer's disciplinary action for refusing to participate in an abortion. However, as a practical matter, most institutions can and do adjust staffing patterns and schedules to accommodate objections, when possible.

You may provide abortion counseling, though getting the patient's informed consent, as you know, is the doctor's province. Many patients are uncertain about the procedures and risks involved in abortion—and about possible alternatives. As a counselor, you can help patients consider available options, resolve their conflicts, and make their decisions.

One caution, though. If you have conflicts about abortion, discuss them with a competent supervisor or counselor—not with the patient. If you can't resolve the conflicts, you may need to transfer to another unit.

First- and second-trimester care

Technical procedures during a first-trimester abortion are relatively simple, not unlike those used for dilation and curettage. Follow prescribed protocol before and during the operation. Postoperatively, monitor appropriate physical parameters, such as vital signs, the amount of bleeding, and urine output, and be alert for signs and symptoms of possible complications.

The patient's emotional needs, however, may be the major complications you face. For example, a freckle-faced, adopted 16-year-old was admitted to a hospital for a first-trimester aspiration. Although her parents had approved the abortion, they were angry that she needed one. The patient tearfully told the nurses about her parents' accusations. "You're just like your real mother when she had you," they'd said. The implication obviously was, "You're no good, either." To help improve her self-image, her nurses spent extra time listening attentively to her feelings. They tried to show her, "You're good." When she was discharged, she said, "You know, I expected this to be a horrible day, but you made it bearable. Thanks for being so good to me."

A second-trimester abortion poses technical difficulties, so you'll need to give more support. When the exact expulsion time can't be predicted (as in the saline solution procedure), monitor the patient's contractions and coach her. Delivering a fetus unattended can be very frightening for the patient.

Your own role in dealing with an aborted fetus can also be frightening and upsetting, especially if the fetus shows any signs of life. In this situation, follow prescribed procedures or standing orders.

Following expulsion of the fetus, give care similar to immediate postpartum care, watching vital signs, bleeding, and cleanliness.

The patient who undergoes a second-trimester abortion may also need more emotional support. Most of these patients have experienced more conflict, more barriers, and more hassles. And some, particularly those undergoing the abortion of a wanted pregnancy (after amniocentesis, for example), may feel an extra-acute sense of loss.

Conclusion

You can alter a patient's perception of abortion by kindness and consideration. A quality nurse-patient relationship will also improve the patient's self-image and promote a quick recovery. In addition,

such a relationship will help the patient respect her reproductive potential—and to make responsible choices that will eliminate the need for another abortion.

No-code and slow-code: The legalities

As a nurse, you've undoubtedly struggled from time to time with conflict between your ethical concerns for patients and the certainty of what the law requires of you. This conflict can be acute when you're the first to arrive at the bedside of a terminally ill patient in cardiac or respiratory arrest. His life depends on whether or not you call a code and initiate resuscitation efforts.

This entry discusses the legal status of no-code and so-called slow-code orders and provides realistic guidelines for managing the difficult ethical conflicts that can arise.

No-code orders

When a patient's terminally ill, and his imminent death is expected, his doctor and family (and sometimes the patient, too) will often agree that a no-code order is appropriate to end his suffering. The doctor writes it, and the staff carries it out when the patient goes into cardiac or respiratory arrest. This is a legal order, and you'll incur no liability when you don't attempt to resuscitate such a patient and he subsequently dies. But it must be a written order. *Any unwritten or undocumented no-code order is a so-called slow-code order—an illegal order.* So if the doctor gives you a verbal no-code order as he's rushing off to attend another patient, or gives you such an order over the telephone, or instructs you not to write down his verbal no-code order, remember—only a *written no-code order is legally defensible. You must document the verbal order in your nurses' notes and insist that the doctor sign off on it—and you must refuse a no-code order he gives you over the telephone.*

The seriousness of this situation can't be underestimated. If a patient you didn't try to resuscitate dies, and no written no-code order exists, you can be charged with *murder or manslaughter*. This isn't the typical nursing malpractice situation, which usually involves a patient who's still alive, though injured. This patient's injuries, and the damages a court may exact from a defendant-nurse who's found liable, obviously can't compare in severity with the situation of a dead slow-coded patient and a nurse charged with murder. With so profound a risk of liability, you need to be secure in your knowledge of legally correct nursing practice in no-code situations.

But even a written no-code order can pose problems for you. Suppose you think a doctor's order may be premature, because your nursing assessment and nursing diagnosis indicate the patient's death may not be imminent. If you've any doubt about the timing of a doctor's written no-code order, you have a legal and professional obligation to question the order. This is because you have the duty, as your patient's advocate, to exercise independent professional judgment in caring for him.

In this situation, you can delay carrying out the order until the doctor confirms or corrects it to your satisfaction. Here's how to proceed:

• Before you speak with the patient's doctor, document your nursing assessment and nursing diagnosis, which caused you to question the no-code order, in the patient's chart.

• Next, discuss your concerns with the doctor. Ask him to clarify his reasons for no-coding the patient. If his explanation removes your doubts, you'll probably decide to withdraw your objection and carry out the no-code order. If his explanation isn't satisfactory, or if he refuses to discuss the matter with you, request an administrative opinion on how you should proceed. Begin with your head nurse, but be prepared to go through your institution's entire chain of command if necessary. (Of course, if your institution has a written policy for how to assess no-code orders, you should follow it.) You may also want to talk with the medical chief of staff.

Until you're satisfied that the no-code order is appropriate, you can delay carrying it out. This means you'll call a code, and attempt resuscitation, if the patient goes into cardiac or respiratory arrest.

• Document your request for clarification of the no-code order, and the doctor's satisfactory or unsatisfactory explanation (or refusal to give one), on the patient's chart.

In some instances, you know that challenging a doctor's order can be very unpleasant. But it couldn't be more unpleasant than the consequences—a patient's premature death and a possible lawsuit—if you're right about the timing of the order but carry it out anyway.

The ethical issues involved in no-code orders center on the dying patient's rights to care, comfort, dignity, and self-determination. (See *Conflicting Ethical Views*, pages 262 and 263.) The nursing staff—especially those in critical-care areas—must often accept no-code orders for patients they've become close to. But keeping your emotions in check during a personally painful no-code situation isn't easy. What can you do? Try to accept a patient's imminent death, and to work through your feelings, *before* the crisis occurs.

One way to do this is by consciously recalling the grief you felt when someone you loved died. This is a painful process, but preparing yourself this way will help you make unclouded nursing decisions when the no-coded patient goes into cardiac or respiratory arrest. If you *don't* work out some of your feelings about a patient's death beforehand, you (and other staff members) may become caught up in unrealistic rescue fantasies that impede clearheaded responses to the no-code order. To best serve the patient's interests, you must put your personal feelings aside. You can also prepare yourself for no-coded patients' deaths by regularly assessing your reactions to death and dying, and by keeping up with studies in this area.

Sometimes, because of your attachment to a patient, you may feel angry at his doctor, his family, or both for their decision to issue a no-code order. Remember, this decision is a very painful one for everyone involved, not just for you. Don't make the situation worse by standing in judgment of the patient's family or by publicly criticizing their decision.

Taking Hospital Supplies: Where Do You Draw the Line?

Attitudes and norms about taking hospital supplies for personal use vary considerably from place to place. That's what a recent *NursingLife* magazine ethics probe discovered.

What's considered theft by staff persons in one hospital might be a fringe benefit in another. Taking ends of gauze rolls that would be thrown out anyway, for example, wouldn't be considered wrong in many places. As one nurse respondent wrote, "We look on it as conserving and reusing items that would've ended up in a wastebasket."

Despite a certain amount of accepted practice, however, hospital theft is an increasingly serious problem that certainly contributes to escalating health-care costs. A U.S. Department of Commerce report, *Crime in the Service Industry,* estimated typical losses for hospitals at about $1,000 per bed per year.

When asked whether *other* nurses take supplies for personal use, 12% of those who responded to the probe said yes, commonly, and 21% said most nurses do sometimes. That's *one third* reporting a rather prevalent condition. Close to half said a few do sometimes, and the rest said they'd heard of it but had no first-hand knowledge.

Still, the incidence of stealing seems lower today than in 1974. *Nursing74,* in a similar poll, found that about 20%—8% more nurses than in the recent survey—thought stealing was common.

Yet how much of the stealing does anyone see? For each hospital employee who's caught stealing, there are probably 10 or more who aren't, estimated Steve M. Rhodes, LPN, RCST, in a 1981 article for *Hospital Topics* magazine. As central service director at Lutheran Hospital in Fort Wayne, Indiana, he's seen various methods for sneaking supplies out—such as stuffing linens and towels into knitting sacks, or taping instruments inside empty cartons.

Taking supplies like these raises the cost of health care, but stealing medications is potentially more serious. Although aspirin and antacids top the list, 3% of the probe respondents said they had stolen narcotics, and 18% had stolen other

---

Slow-code order? Refuse it, document it

Any unwritten, documented but unsigned, or unstated but "understood" no-code order is an illegal slow-code order. If you carry out such an order, and the patient dies because you didn't make an effort to resuscitate him, you can be liable for wrongful death (and for practicing medicine without a license).

Strictly speaking, the existence of such a serious and clear-cut legal risk should mean that so-called slow-codes are never agreed to, or carried out, by health-team members. But, as you probably know, slow-codes *do* happen. Maybe you've even been involved.

If so, why?

- Maybe you weren't aware of how serious the legal consequences could be for you.
- Maybe you lacked the confidence to speak up and ask the doctor to put the slow-code order in writing as a no-code order.
- Maybe you thought that documenting the order in your nurses' notes, without the doctor's countersignature, was sufficient to make the order valid.
- Maybe you and the other members of the health care team, including the doctor, had a strong personal attachment to a terminally ill patient that made writing a no-code order emotionally difficult. So no one discussed or wrote it, but everyone silently agreed to it.

prescription drugs. Over a third said that medications other than aspirin and antacids were at least occasionally stolen from the hospital. Recent statistics on nurses stealing such medications for their own use, when compared with statistics from *Nursing74* magazine's poll, show some decrease over the years.

Many respondents felt justified in stealing a medication they needed to keep on working. As one nurse supervisor wrote, "Usually it's for headache, nausea, diarrhea, or sometimes asthma or sinus problems. We're so short-staffed that it's almost impossible to let nurses go home. We often work when we're less than well because we know there's nobody to replace us."

Such a situation in itself may make nurses want to take drugs. Psychologist John W. Jones has correlated nurses' theft of drugs with their degree of burnout. As reported in the November 1981 issue of *Nursing Management* magazine, burned-out employees tend to steal more hospital supplies and drugs than those who *don't* suffer from frustration, interpersonal tension, work pressures, and anger toward patients, co-workers, and supervisors. And sometimes burned-out employees steal, not because they really want the items but because they want to commit an aggressive act against their employer.

A Canadian nurse who responded to the probe wrote that she'd taken narcotics and other drugs to cope with burnout and depression. She confessed, "I took Valium, Dalmane, chloral hydrate, and Librium to help me to sleep and to cope with an uncaring and demanding administration. I worked in a place where we were encouraged to 'tell' on our fellow employees; where hostility between nurse and nurse's aide was actively promoted... where mistakes we admitted won us a day's suspension from duty without pay, even for a first offense."

Adapted with permission from a *NursingLife* ethics probe, "Stealing—Where Do You Draw The Line," *NursingLife,* January/February 1983.

Only one way exists to avoid a slow-code order's dire legal consequences: *Every no-coded patient must have a written order.* Unless the doctor has written a no-code order or signed off on documentation of his verbal order, always initiate resuscitation efforts for a terminally ill patient in cardiac or respiratory arrest.

Never forget that your primary legal and professional responsibility to every patient, including terminally ill patients, is to give care that meets applicable standards—care that a reasonably prudent nurse with equivalent education, training, and experience would give in the same circumstances. *Preservation of life* is the overriding duty of nursing and medical staff; you can never relinquish this duty

except when a doctor writes a no-code order for your patient.

Remember, too, that if a lawsuit results from your involvement in a patient's death because of slow-coding, you'll have no written evidence that the doctor gave the verbal no-code order. (Without evidence, juries usually find that a claimed event did not occur.) Don't forget that doctors commonly have an edge when lawsuits come to trial: until nurses attain a fully professional image, most juries will give a doctor's testimony more weight than a nurse's.

Another way to provide evidence that a doctor gave a verbal, unsigned no-code order is to keep a personal journal in which you document unusual events, including slow-codes, that occur on the unit. Of course, if you've refused to take part in the illegal order, you won't need any other defense.

The ethical considerations of a slow-code situation pale beside the legal ones. Consider this: If you fail to meet a personal ethical requirement on the job, you may have trouble facing yourself in the mirror for awhile. But if you fail to meet a legal requirement, you may have trouble that won't go away, and you'll wind up facing a jury.

Of course, you feel pity and grief for a terminally ill patient whose suffering must continue for lack of a no-code order. In this situation, the patient's best helped by your efforts to *get* a written order—not by ambivalence and equivocation on the part of the health team. In effect, a staff that permits an illegal slow-code response to end a patient's life is inviting a jury to decide whether the failure to call a code was reasonable under the circumstances.

When the patient's wish to die is challenged

This is a truly difficult dilemma for you—and for the doctor, who may want to no-code the patient but, to avoid any legal repercussions, yields to the family's pressure. At stake here is every competent adult's right to participate in the formulation of his treatment plan, to choose among alternative treatment modalities, and to *refuse treatment. If a terminally ill patient has expressed his wish not to be coded, and you call a code when he goes into cardiac or respiratory arrest, you're violating his right to refuse treatment. But if you don't* call a code (in the absence of a written no-code order), you're practicing medicine without a license, and you're liable for his death if he dies.

In a double-bind situation like this, one way to proceed is as follows:
• If a terminally ill patient tells you he doesn't want to be resuscitated in the event of a crisis, document his statement (in his own words) and chart his apparent degree of awareness and orientation.
• If the doctor knows of the patient's wish and still refuses to write a no-code order, document this in your notes. The doctor has the same conflict with the patient's right to refuse treatment that you have,

and he may be liable if he doesn't comply with the patient's request.

Without a written no-code order, should you attempt resuscitation on a patient who's said he doesn't want it? In the final analysis, the answer's "yes." Your best course, though, is to try to get the doctor to write the no-code order *before* a crisis occurs. This may prove difficult in the face of a family's denial of the patient's imminent death, or a doctor's concern about a possible lawsuit. But it's your duty to your patient, if your nursing assessment and nursing diagnosis corroborate the patient's belief that his death will occur soon. (Of course, if his status is such that recovery still seems possible, defer asking for the no-code order—and resuscitate if needed.)
• If your terminally ill patient has prepared a living will, make sure his doctor has seen it. It may or may not be legally binding in your state (see "Your responsibility for a patient's living will," page 147). The doctor, perhaps in conjunction with a hospital administrator, will decide what action to take concerning it.

Conclusion

No doubt about it—no-code/slow-code situations are tough for nurses. They're painful ethically, and they're fraught with legal peril in which the unsigned verbal no-code order (the so-called slow-code) figures prominently.

If a doctor gives you a slow-code order, you'll need courage and self-confidence to insist that he countersign your documentation of the order. You'll need these qualities if he *doesn't* sign, too. Why? Because you'll have to resuscitate the patient as needed, in spite of the doctor's order and, possibly, in spite of your ethical feelings about the situation.

If your institution doesn't have a written policy for assessing and carrying out no-code orders, work to get one. (The American Heart Association's guidelines can help you get started.) Ask your head nurse and your nursing colleagues to help you put a proposal together and get administrative approval of it. Then, when a doctor gives you a questionable no-code order, that policy will lend weight to your request that he follow legally correct no-code procedures.

Nurse Addicts: Precautions to Take

What precautions can you take when you suspect that a nurse in your department has a drug or alcohol addiction problem? Your hospital's policy should tell you. If it doesn't, suggest that your hospital institute these precautions:
- Two nurses must sign for all lost or damaged medications.
- A medication count is required at the beginning and end of each shift.
- Narcotics administration sheets will be occasionally audited.

Even without a hospital policy, you can protect your patients by following these do's and don'ts.

DO's

- Ask your patients occasionally if they received the medication charted by nurses on other shifts. Note the medication's effectiveness. Be suspicious if a medication suddenly—or unexpectedly—is ineffective. This might indicate that the patient is not receiving full dosage.
- Watch for—and be suspicious of—a nurse's dramatic change in behavior.
- Report any evidence of a nurse's drug or alcohol abuse to your nursing supervisor.

DON'Ts

- Don't search a suspected nurse's possessions or private property.
- Don't make assumptions—stick only to the facts.
- Don't allow your opinions or biases to cloud your judgment.

When a colleague is incompetent

The American Nurses' Association (ANA) Code for Nurses says you have a professional responsibility to "safeguard the client and the public when health care and safety are affected by the incompetent, unethical, or illegal practice of any person." (See *Codes for Nurses*, pages 266 to 267).

The International Council of Nurses Code of Nursing Ethics, adopted by the Canadian Nurses Association, has a similar provision: "[Nurses should take] appropriate action to safeguard the individual when his care is endangered by a co-worker or any other person." But how do you know when a colleague's behavior should be reported? Or how to go about it?

When should you report a colleague?

Before reporting a colleague or other health-care professional for incompetent, unethical, or illegal conduct, assess the situation carefully. Make sure you have a solid case by asking yourself questions such as these:
- Is the conduct truly a matter of incompetence, poor ethics, or illegality, or is it simply conduct with which you disagree?
- Would the conduct be acceptable if the outcome had been different? If so, are you judging the results rather than the conduct?
- Has the conduct harmed a patient, or does this possibility exist?

You may not always know the answers, especially in situations where the conduct is mediocre but not necessarily incompetent. In these situations, you'll have to weigh the consequences of either waiting or taking immediate action. Obviously, the more likely patient injury seems, the more pressure you'll feel to take action. (See *Guidance When Dealing With Colleagues*,

---

Steps to Follow When You Report Unsafe Practices

Consider this scenario: The night medication nurse on your unit keeps an accurate narcotics count, but you continually see evidence of poor pain control on her shift. You're suspicious, but you know she's one of the most conscientious workers on your understaffed unit. She's also the sole supporter of two young children. What should you do?

Blowing the whistle is never easy. But because you're committed to patient health and safety, it's a responsibility you can't shirk. To give information about a co-worker's unethical or incompetent conduct, follow these guidelines:

• Go through channels. Follow your institution's procedures for dealing with complaints of unethical or improper conduct. If the person you're reporting to is part of the problem, go to that person's supervisor.

• Be clear. Describe in writing the questionable or dangerous conduct and its consequences.

• Be accurate. Describe the facts of the situation that you know to be true. Describe why you're not sure of certain things (for example, because a medical record is locked in the hospital administrator's office).

• Be consistent. Get the story right the first time, and stick with it.

• Be discreet. Don't gossip about the situation with co-workers, and don't contribute to rumors about it.

• Be candid. If you try to hide aspects of the situation, your credibility will be damaged.

• Get support. Get the support of co-workers you know and trust. Encourage them to contribute written statements corroborating your report.

• Be persistent. If the situation is a sensitive one, you may be pressured to forget it. Remember that the issue is an important one: you owe it to your profession and your patients to pursue it.

---

pages 268 to 269.)

When you're reasonably sure of your ground, what next? The ANA code suggests that you first approach your colleague directly. Share your concern that her conduct is hurting patient care. The exchange may have one of several outcomes. The colleague may convince you that what she's doing is indeed acceptable. Or you may convince her she's wrong; she may agree to change her ways. These outcomes don't present any problem. But what do you do if she agrees she's wrong and asks you to cover up?

When a colleague asks you to cover up

You may be tempted to say yes when a colleague asks you to cover up her mistakes, incompetence, or unethical conduct.

Maybe she's a close friend who you feel needs a little more time to cope with the alcohol problem or whatever problem you've uncovered. Even if she isn't a friend, maybe you've been taught not to sit in judgment of others, or you just don't like to tattle. Besides, maybe you'll be the one making the mistake next time, and you'll want your colleagues' support. Or maybe you simply feel your life has enough stress, and the last thing you need is more stress from the notoriety that often accompanies whistle blowing.

Before you give in to these very human considerations, think about the likely consequences if you *do* cover up:

• In some states and provinces, failing to report a colleague's unacceptable conduct may be considered unprofessional conduct and grounds for disciplinary action by the licensing agency.

• The cover-up might harm patients, bringing legal as well as moral and ethical consequences.

• You might lose your job.

• You might be named in a malpractice lawsuit if you were aware of your colleague's negligence.

• You might be subject to criminal penalties if the cover-up involves narcotics.

• The cover-up might harm the person you're trying to help. If your colleague has a drug problem, for example, she may delay getting treatment. (See *Nurse Addicts: Precautions to Take,* page 275.)

• If discovered and publicized, cover-ups damage the relationship between the nursing profession and the public. A public that knows nurses hide each other's incompetence is unlikely to trust or respect nurses.

Then what should you do when a colleague asks you to cover up her incompetent or unethical conduct or if she simply refuses to change and, in effect, tells you to get lost? If this happens, tell her you can't agree to cover up or remain silent. If her patients are endangered, take appropriate action to protect them. Then, follow your employer's established procedures for reporting incompetent, unethical, or illegal conduct. (By the way, if your employer doesn't have a clear statement of such procedures, urge that one be developed now—before you need to use it.)

You may want to draw on help from unbiased sources, such as clergymen or ombudsmen. They may be able to provide valuable guidance—and minimize your risk of reprisal. (See *Steps To Follow When You Report Unsafe Practices,* page 276.)

If your employer fails to act, your next step is to report the conduct to the appropriate state or provincial licensing agency. Reports to such agencies may be protected from reprisal by statutory law or administrative rule. If not, consider sending an anonymous complaint. To learn about current requirements and protections, contact your state or provincial board of nursing.

Conclusion

Reporting a colleague is difficult—personally and professionally. But one of the marks of any profession's maturity is its members' willingness to police themselves. Through your willingness to share in that often unpleasant task, you'll help nursing maintain its integrity and justify the public's trust.

Selected References

American Nurses' Association. *Code For Nurses With Interpretive Statements.* Kansas City, Mo.: American Nurses' Association, 1976.

American Nurses' Association. *Nursing: A Social Policy Statement.* Kansas City, Mo.: American Nurses' Association, 1980.

Annas, George J., et al. *The Rights of Doctors, Nurses and Allied Health Professionals.* Cambridge, Mass.: Ballinger Publishing Co., 1983.

Aroskar, M.A. "Anatomy of an Ethical Dilemma: the Theory...the Practice," *American Journal of Nursing* 80:658-63, April 1980.

Binkin, N., et al. "Illegal Abortion Deaths in the United States: Why Are They Still Occurring?" *Family Planning Perspectives* 14:163-67, May/June 1982.

Cazalas, Mary W. *Nursing and the Law,* 3rd ed. Rockville, Md.: Aspen Systems Corp., 1979.

Creighton, Helen. *Law Every Nurse Should Know,* 4th ed. Philadelpia: W.B. Saunders Co., 1981.

Curtin, Leah, and Flaherty, M. Josephine. *Nursing Ethics: Theories and Pragmatics.* Bowie, Md.: Robert J. Brady Co., 1981.

Davis, P.S. "Medico-Legal Considerations and the Quality of Life," *Topics in Clinical Nursing* 3:79-85, October 1981.

Hemelt, M., and Mackert, M. *Dynamics of Law, Nursing and Health Care,* 2nd ed. Reston, Va.: Reston Publishing Co., 1982.

Kalish, Richard A. *Death, Grief and Caring Relationships.* Monterey, Calif.: Brooks/Cole Publishing Co., 1981.

Olson, Janice. "To Treat or to Allow to Die: An Ethical Dilemma in Gerontological Nursing," *Journal of Gerontological Nursing* 7:141, March 1981.

Saunders, Cicely. "The Care of the Dying Patient and His Family," in *Ethics in Medicine: Historical Perspectives and Contemporary Concerns.* Edited by Reiser, Stanley J., and Dyck, Arthur J. Cambridge, Mass.: MIT Press, 1977.

Thompson, Joyce B., and Thompson, Henry O. *Ethics in Nursing.* New York: Macmillan Publishing Co., 1981.

Veatch, Robert M. *Case Studies in Medical Ethics.* Cambridge, Mass.: Harvard University Press, 1977.

Walker, A. Earl. *Cerebral Death,* 2nd ed. Baltimore: Urban & Schwarzenberg, 1981.

Appendices and Glossary

A: Basic Human Rights

The Bill of Rights and Amendment XIV of the Constitution of the United States define the basic human rights that all persons under all circumstances, including hospitalization, are entitled to. These rights are as follows:

The Bill of Rights

ARTICLE I

Congress shall make no law respecting an establishment of religion, or prohibiting the free exercise thereof; or abridging the freedom of speech, or of the press; or the right of the people peaceably to assemble, and to petition the Government for a redress of grievances.

ARTICLE II

A well regulated Militia, being necessary to the security of a free State, the right of the people to keep and bear Arms, shall not be infringed.

ARTICLE III

No Soldier shall, in time of peace be quartered in any house, without the consent of the Owner, nor in time of war, but in a manner to be prescribed by law.

ARTICLE IV

The right of the people to be secure in their persons, houses, papers, and effects, against unreasonable searches and seizures, shall not be violated, and no Warrants shall issue, but upon probable cause, supported by Oath or affirmation, and particularly describing the place to be searched, and the persons or things to be seized.

ARTICLE V

No person shall be held to answer for a capital, or otherwise infamous crime, unless on a presentment or indictment of a Grand Jury, except in cases arising in the land or naval forces, or in the Militia, when in actual service in time of War or public danger; nor shall any person be subject for the same offence to be twice put in jeopardy of life or limb; nor shall be compelled in any criminal case to be a witness against himself, nor be deprived of life, liberty, or property, without due process of law; nor shall private property be taken for public use, without just compensation.

ARTICLE VI

In all criminal prosecutions, the accused shall enjoy the right to a speedy and public trial, by an impartial jury of the State and district wherein the crime shall have been committed, which district shall have been previously ascertained by law, and to be informed of the nature and cause of the accusation; to be confronted with the witnesses against him; to have compulsory process for obtaining witnesses in his favor, and to have the Assistance of Counsel for his defence.

ARTICLE VII

In Suits at common law, where the value in controversy shall exceed twenty dollars, the right of trial by jury shall be preserved, and no fact tried by a jury shall be otherwise re-examined in any Court of the United States, than according to the rules of the common law.

ARTICLE VIII

Excessive bail shall not be required, nor excessive fines imposed, nor cruel and unusual punishments inflicted.

ARTICLE IX

The enumeration in the Constitution, of certain rights, shall not be construed to deny or disparage others retained by the people.

ARTICLE X

The powers not delegated to the United States by the Constitution, nor prohibited by it to the States, are reserved to the States respectively, or to the people.

ARTICLE (Amendment) XIV

Section I. All persons born or naturalized in the United States, and subject to the jurisdiction thereof, are citizens of the United States and of the State wherein they reside. No State shall make or enforce any law which shall abridge the privileges or immunities of citizens of the United States; nor shall any State deprive any person of life, liberty, or property, without due process of law; nor deny to any person within its jurisdiction the equal protection of the laws.

B: Federal and State Court Systems

SUPREME COURT OF THE UNITED STATES
Hears lawsuits between states, appeals from U.S. Court of Appeals, and appeals from state supreme courts if cases involve federal law or constitutional rights.

U.S. COURT OF CLAIMS
Hears lawsuits against the federal government that involve a constitutional right, federal laws or regulations, or government contracts.

U.S. COURT OF APPEALS
Hears appeals from U.S. district courts and the U.S. Tax Court.

U.S. COURT OF CUSTOMS AND PATENT APPEALS
Hears appeals from the U.S. Customs Court.

U.S. DISTRICT COURTS
Hear federal, criminal, and civil lawsuits.

U.S. TAX COURT
Hears lawsuits involving tax disputes.

U.S. CUSTOMS COURT
Hears lawsuits involving the U.S. Patent and Trade offices, and other federal agencies.

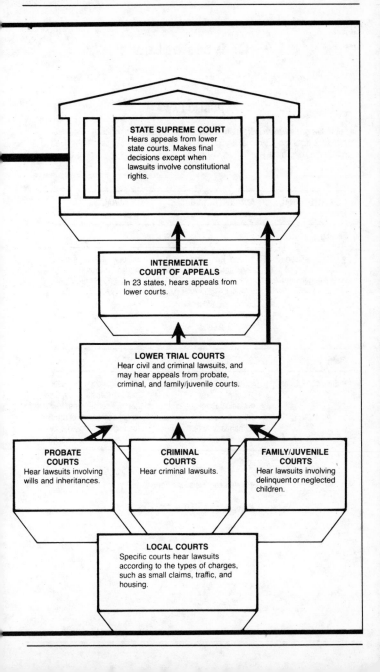

STATE SUPREME COURT
Hears appeals from lower state courts. Makes final decisions except when lawsuits involve constitutional rights.

INTERMEDIATE COURT OF APPEALS
In 23 states, hears appeals from lower courts.

LOWER TRIAL COURTS
Hear civil and criminal lawsuits, and may hear appeals from probate, criminal, and family/juvenile courts.

PROBATE COURTS
Hear lawsuits involving wills and inheritances.

CRIMINAL COURTS
Hear criminal lawsuits.

FAMILY/JUVENILE COURTS
Hear lawsuits involving delinquent or neglected children.

LOCAL COURTS
Specific courts hear lawsuits according to the types of charges, such as small claims, traffic, and housing.

C: Types of Law

PUBLIC LAW

Public law deals with an individual's relationship to the state. As the chart below indicates, the legal aspects of that relationship may concern matters of constitutional, administrative, or criminal law.

CONSTITUTIONAL LAW	ADMINISTRATIVE LAW	CRIMINAL LAW
Federal		
• U.S. Constitution • Civil Rights Act	• Food, Drug, and Cosmetic Act • Social Security Act (Medicare/Medicaid) • National Labor Relations Act	• Comprehensive Drug Abuse Prevention and Control Act (Controlled Substance Acts) • Kidnapping
State		
• State constitution	• Nurse Practice Act • Medical Practice Act • Pharmacy Act • Workmen's compensation laws • State Labor Relations Act • Employment Security Act	• Criminal code that defines murder, manslaughter, criminal negligence, rape, fraud, illegal possession of drugs (and other controlled substances), theft, assault, battery

PRIVATE (CIVIL) LAW

Private law deals with the relationships between individuals. As the chart below indicates, the legal aspect of these relationships divides into matters that concern contract law, torts, or protective/reporting law. Note that protective/reporting laws are sometimes considered criminal law, depending on how the state has classified them.

CONTRACT LAWS	TORTS	PROTECTIVE/ REPORTING LAWS
Federal		
● None	● Federal Torts Claims Act (to allow claims against the state)	● Child Abuse Prevention and Treatment Act
		● Privacy Act of 1974
State		
● Employment contracts	● State Torts Claims Act (to allow claims against the state)	● Age of consent statutes for medical treatment, drugs, sexually transmitted disease
● Business contracts with clients	● Negligence (common law claim)	● Privileged communications statute
● Contracts with allied groups	● Malpractice statute (professional liability)	● Abortion statute
● Uniform Commercial Code	● Assault	● Good Samaritan Act
	● Battery	● Child abuse/neglect statute
	● False imprisonment	● Elderly abuse statute
	● Invasion of privacy	● Domestic violence statute
	● Libel	● Involuntary hospitalization statute
		● Living will legislation

D: How to Interpret Legal Citations

How do you look up a law (statute or regulation) or court case? First, go to your county courthouse law library or local law school library with your legal citation in hand. If you're looking for an overview or summary of a law or court case, look up your citation in a standard legal reference, such as a legal encyclopedia *(Corpus Juris Secundum)* or a legal text *(Restatements of Law)*.

If you want to locate a complete text of the law or case, you must first have a full citation, such as the ones shown here.

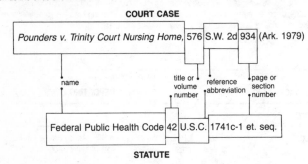

A full citation includes the name of the law or court case and a series of identifying numbers and letters. If you're missing some or all of the identifying numbers and letters, you'll need to look up the law or case name in the index of one of the legal references listed at right.

Once you get the full citation, you'll need to know how to interpret it. The letters in the series of identifying numbers and letters are an abbreviation for the legal reference that contains the law or case. For example, "L.W." stands for *United States Law Week.* (To find out what the abbreviation in your citation stands for, see the list of common legal references at right.)

The number that precedes the abbreviation indicates either a volume number or title classification within the legal reference. A title classification is a body of laws or cases on a particular subject, such as malpractice. A title can be one book or many books, depending on the amount of cases that bear on the titles.

If you're dealing with a law, one set of numbers follows the abbreviation. They indicate the section within the reference volume or title in which you'll find the law.

If you're dealing with a court case, two sets of numbers follow the abbreviation. The first set indicates the page where you'll find the case. The second set, in parentheses, indicates the year of the decision.

Sometimes, a court case on the state level will have two complete series of identifying numbers. The first series is the *official citation,* indicating where the case can be found in that state's set of court case decisions. The second series is the *unofficial citation,* indicating where the case can be found in a commercially published set of court case decisions grouped by region. These regional sets are explained in the listing at right. Interpreting this second series of numbers and letters works exactly the same way that interpreting the first series works. If the case citation only quotes the regional (commercial) listing, then the state court that heard the case, such as the Pennsylvania Commonwealth Court, is included in the parentheses with the date of the case.

TYPE OF LAW/CASE	LEGAL REFERENCE	ABBREVIATION
Federal court decisions	*United States Law Week* (contains recently issued unofficial Supreme Court decisions)	L.W.
	United States Reports (contains official federal court decisions)	U.S.
	Supreme Court Reporter (contains official Supreme Court decisions)	S. Ct.
	Lawyers Edition, United States Supreme Court (contains official Supreme Court decisions)	L. Ed.
	Federal Reporter (contains court of appeals decisions)	F.
	Federal Supplement Series (contains Federal District Court of Appeals decisions)	F. Supp.
State court decisions	About two thirds of the states publish state court decisions in official state sets	Standard state abbreviations
	All states are included in the commercially published National Reporter System, which groups state court decisions by region: *North Eastern Reporter* *Atlantic Reporter* *South Eastern Reporter* *Southern Reporter* *North Western Reporter* *South Western Reporter* *Pacific Reporter*	N.E. A. S.E. So. N.W. S.W. P.
Federal statutes	*United States Law Week* (contains chronologic list of recently enacted statutes)	L.W.
	United States Statutes at Large (contains chronologic lists of all statutes enacted during a single legislative session)	STAT. or STAT. AT L.
	United States Code (contains all statutes arranged by title)	U.S.C.
State statutes	All states publish state statutes in official state sets	Standard state abbreviations
Federal regulations	*Code of Federal Regulations* (contains federal regulations arranged by title)	C.F.R.
	The Federal Register (contains updates to the C.F.R.)	F.R.
State regulations	All states publish state regulations in official state sets	Standard state abbreviations

E: Canadian Nurse Practice Acts: Province-by-Province Review

Unlike the nurse practice acts in the United States, most Canadian provincial nurse practice acts don't define registered nursing practice; they just describe qualifications for becoming a registered nurse (RN) and grounds for RN license denial, revocation, or suspension. Two provinces, Newfoundland and Prince Edward Island, *do* define the

	Alberta Chapter R-12	British Columbia Chapter 302	
Qualifications for RN licensure			
Graduation from high school or equivalent	●		
Enrollment in an approved nursing program		●	
Graduation from an approved nursing program	●	●	
Proper academic qualifications	●		
Prescribed amount of clinical experience	●		
Passing the registered nurse examination	●	●	
Paying registration fee	●	●	
Good character	●	●	
Fluency in English or French			
Age 21 or older			
Grounds for RN license denial, revocation, or suspension			
Dishonesty			
Professional misconduct		●	
Professional incompetence		●	
Physical or mental incompetence		●	
Addiction to drugs or alcohol		●	
Breaching the nurse practice act		●	
Indictment for, or conviction of, a criminal act		●	
Failure to pay registration fee			
Fraud or misrepresentation in obtaining license		●	
Fraudulent use of the initials or title "RN"	●		
Penalty for fraudulent use of the initials or title "RN" — Fine	$50	$2,000	
Penalty for fraudulent use of the initials or title "RN" — Imprisonment	30 days		

"registered nurse" as "any person who is possessed of the qualifications required by this Act, and who is authorized to offer service for the care of the sick and to give care intended for the prevention of disease and to receive remuneration therefor, and who is a member in good standing of the [provincial] association."

The Yukon Territory has no RN licensing body. To practice there, an RN must be registered with one of the 10 provincial nurses associations or with the Northwest Territories' nurses association. All these associations require annual licensure renewal.

	Manitoba Chapter R/40	New Brunswick Chapter 82	Newfoundland Chapter 268	Northwest Terr. Chapter 6	Nova Scotia Chapter R-10	Ontario Chapter 196 Part IV	Prince Edward Is. Chapter N-3	Quebec Chapter I-8	Saskatchewan Chapter R-12.1	Yukon Terr.
		●			●					
		●								
		●	●		●	●	●	●	●	
	LEFT TO THE ASSOCIATION'S DISCRETION; SUBJECT TO CHANGE			●						NO LICENSING BODY
				●						
		●	●		●	●	●	●	●	
		●	●		●	●				
		●		●					●	
						●	●			
		●								
	●		●		●					
	●		●	●	●	●	●		●	
	●		●	●		●			●	
	●		●	●					●	NO LICENSING BODY
	●		●	●	●					
							●			
				●				LEFT TO THE ASSOCIATION'S DISCRETION; SUBJECT TO CHANGE		
	●		●		●				●	
	●		●		●					
	●	●	●	●			●	●	●	
	$100	$100	$50	$500	$100	$2,000	$100		$200	
			30 days	30 days		6 mos	14 days		6 mos	

(continued)

Canadian Nurse Practice Acts:
Province-by-Province Review *(continued)*

Of the provinces that recognize registered nursing assistants, only one, Saskatchewan, actually defines the term in its nurse practice act. It says a nursing assistant is "a person who is trained to care for convalescent, subacutely ill and chronically ill patients, and to assist nurses in the care of acutely ill patients, and who is certified as a nursing assistant..."

	Alberta Chapter N-13 RNA	British Columbia Chapter 300 LPN	
Qualifications for NA or LPN licensure			
Graduation from approved NA or LPN program	●		
Prescribed amount of clinical experience			
Passing NA or LPN examination			
Paying registration fee	●	●	
Good character	●		
Fluency in English or French			
Age 21 or older			
Grounds for NA or LPN license denial, revocation, or suspension			
Dishonesty			
Professional misconduct			
Professional incompetence			
Physical or mental incompetence			
Addiction to drugs or alcohol			
Conviction for a criminal act			
Failure to pay registration fee	●		
Fraud or misrepresentation in obtaining license			
Fraudulent use of the initials or title "NA " or "LPN"	●	●	
Penalty for fraudulent use of the initials or title "NA" or "LPN" — Fine	$500	$100	
Penalty for fraudulent use of the initials or title "NA" or "LPN" — Imprisonment			

Newfoundland, the Northwest Territories, and the Yukon Territory have no licensing bodies for nursing assistants or practical nurses. To practice there, an NA or LPN must be registered with one of the associations in the provinces that do have NA or LPN licensing boards. All such associations require annual licensure renewal (as specified in the provincial nurse practice acts).

	Manitoba Chapter P100 LPN	Manitoba Chapter P100 RNA	New Brunswick Chapter 60	Newfoundland	Northwest Terr.	Nova Scotia Chapter R-10 RNA	Ontario Chapter 196 Part IV RNA	Prince Edward Is. RNA	Quebec RNA	Saskatchewan Chapter R-12.1 CNA	Yukon Terr.
	●	●		NO LICENSING BODY	NO LICENSING BODY	LEFT TO THE ASSOCIATION'S DISCRETION; SUBJECT TO CHANGE	●	LEFT TO THE ASSOCIATION'S DISCRETION; SUBJECT TO CHANGE	LEFT TO THE ASSOCIATION'S DISCRETION; SUBJECT TO CHANGE	●	NO LICENSING BODY
	●										
	●						●			●	
	●						●				
		●								●	
							●				
	●										
	●			NO LICENSING BODY	NO LICENSING BODY			LEFT TO THE ASSOCIATION'S DISCRETION; SUBJECT TO CHANGE	LEFT TO THE ASSOCIATION'S DISCRETION; SUBJECT TO CHANGE		NO LICENSING BODY
	●						●			●	
	●						●			●	
	●										
	●										
	●									●	
	●									●	
	●	●				●	●			●	
	$100	$100				$100	$2,000			$50	
							6 mos			3 mos	

F: Nurse Practice Acts: Misdemeanors Subject to Penalty

			Alabama Titles 12 & 34	Alaska Title 8	
Selling or fraudulently obtaining or furnishing nursing diploma, license renewal, record			●		
Practicing nursing under cover of fraudulent or illegal diploma, license, record			●	●	
Practicing nursing without a license (except in emergency)			●	●	
Using designation with name that falsely implies licensure			●	●	
Practicing nursing when license has lapsed, or has been suspended or revoked			●	●	
Conducting nursing education not approved by board			●	●	
Violating provision of nurse practice act			●		
Employing unlicensed persons to practice nursing				●	
Failing to report employment of unlicensed nurses					

PENALTIES

First offense	**Fine**	min.			■	
		max.	$2,000			
	Imprisonment	min.				
		max.	1 yr			
Subsequent offenses	**Fine**	min.			■	
		max.	$2,000			
	Imprisonment	min.				
		max.	1 yr			

■ = depends on violation   ★ = none stated   **F** = fine only   **M** = misdemeanor

	Arizona Titles 13 & 32	Arkansas Title 72	California Business and Professions Code	Colorado Titles 12 & 18	Connecticut Title 20	Delaware Title 24	District of Columbia Title 2	Florida Chapter 469
	●	●	●	●	●	●	●	
	●	●	●			●	●	
	●	●	●	●	●	●	●	●F
	●	●	●	●		●	●	●M/F
	●	●	●	●		●	●	●F
	●	●	●			●		
	●	●	●		●	●	●	
								●F
		$25	$20					
	$500	$500	$1,000	$500	$500	$1,000	$200 or $300	■
			10 days					
	30 days		1 yr	90 days	6 mos	1 yr	60 or 90 days	
		$25	$20					
	$500	$500	$1,000	■	$500	$1,000	$200 or $300	■
			10 days	1 yr				
	30 days	30 days	1 yr	2 yrs	6 mos	1 yr	60 or 90 days	

(continued)

Nurse Practice Acts:
Misdemeanors Subject to Penalty *(continued)*

	Georgia Titles 16 & 43	Hawaii Title 25	
Selling or fraudulently obtaining or furnishing nursing diploma, license renewal, record	●	●	
Practicing nursing under cover of fraudulent or illegal diploma, license, record	●	●	
Practicing nursing without a license (except in emergency)	●	●	
Using designation with name that falsely implies licensure	●	●	
Practicing nursing when license has lapsed, or has been suspended or revoked	●	●	
Conducting nursing education not approved by board	●	●	
Violating provision of nurse practice act	●	●	
Employing unlicensed persons to practice nursing	●		
Failing to report employment of unlicensed nurses			

PENALTIES

			Georgia Titles 16 & 43	Hawaii Title 25	
First offense	Fine	min.	★		
		max.		$500	
	Imprisonment	min.			
		max.			
Subsequent offenses	Fine	min.	★		
		max.		$1,000	
	Imprisonment	min.			
		max.		1 yr	

■ = depends on violation   ★ = none stated   F = fine only   M = misdemeanor

	Idaho Title 54	Illinois Chapter 111	Indiana Titles 25 & 35	Iowa Titles 8 & 36	Kansas Title 65	Kentucky Title 26	Louisiana Title 37	Maine Title 32
	●	●	●	●	●	●	●	●
	●	●	●				●	●
	●	●	●	●	●		●	●
	●	●	●	●	●		●	●
	●	●	●		●		●	●
	●	●	●		●		●	
	●	●	●		●	●	●	●
							$10	
	$50	■	$1,000	$1,000	■	■	$100	$100
			180 days	1 yr			30 days	10 days
							$100	
	$100	■	$1,000	$1,000	■	■	$300	$200
								10 days
	6 mos		180 days	1 yr			60 days	30 days

(continued)

Nurse Practice Acts:
Misdemeanors Subject to Penalty *(continued)*

	Maryland Health Occupations	Massachusetts Chapter 112	
Selling or fraudulently obtaining or furnishing nursing diploma, license renewal, record	●		
Practicing nursing under cover of fraudulent or illegal diploma, license, record	●		
Practicing nursing without a license (except in emergency)	●	●	
Using designation with name that falsely implies licensure	●	●	
Practicing nursing when license has lapsed, or has been suspended or revoked	●		
Conducting nursing education not approved by board			
Violating provision of nurse practice act	●		
Employing unlicensed persons to practice nursing			
Failing to report employment of unlicensed nurses	●		

PENALTIES

First offense	Fine	min.			■	
		max.	$100			
	Imprisonment	min.				
		max.				
Subsequent offenses	Fine	min.			■	
		max.	$500			
	Imprisonment	min.				
		max.	6 mos			

■ = depends on violation   ★ = none stated   F = fine only   M = misdemeanor

	Michigan Chapter 333	Minnesota Chapters 148 & 609	Mississippi Title 73	Missouri Title 22	Montana Title 37	Nebraska Title 71	Nevada Title 54	New Hampshire Title 30
		●	●	●	●	●	●	●
	●F	●	●	●	●	●		
	●F	●	●	●	●	●	●	●
	●M	●	●	●	●	●		●
	●F	●	●	●	●	●		●
		●	●	●	●	●	●	●
					●	●	●	●
			●	●				
			$100		$100			
	■	$700	$1,000	■		■	$1,000	■
			1 yr					
		90 days					6 mos	
			$100					
	■	$700	$1,000	■	$300	■	$1,000	■
			1 yr					
		90 days			6 mos		6 mos	

(continued)

Nurse Practice Acts:
Misdemeanors Subject to Penalty *(continued)*

	New Jersey Title 45	New Mexico Chapter 61	
Selling or fraudulently obtaining or furnishing nursing diploma, license renewal, record	●	●	
Practicing nursing under cover of fraudulent or illegal diploma, license, record			
Practicing nursing without a license (except in emergency)	●	●	
Using designation with name that falsely implies licensure	●	●	
Practicing nursing when license has lapsed, or has been suspended or revoked	●	●	
Conducting nursing education not approved by board	●	●	
Violating provision of nurse practice act	●	●	
Employing unlicensed persons to practice nursing		●	
Failing to report employment of unlicensed nurses			

PENALTIES

			New Jersey Title 45	New Mexico Chapter 61	
First offense	Fine	min.			
		max.	$200	$1,000	
	Imprisonment	min.			
		max.		1 yr	
Subsequent offenses	Fine	min.			
		max.	$500 per violation	$1,000	
	Imprisonment	min.			
		max.		1 yr	

■ = depends on violation   ★ = none stated   F = fine only   M = misdemeanor

	New York Education Law & Penal Law	North Carolina Chapter 90	North Dakota Title 43	Ohio Title 47	Oklahoma Title 59	Oregon Titles 16 & 52	Pennsylvania Title 63	Rhode Island Chapter 5
	●F	●	●	●	●	●	●	●
		●	●	●		●	●	●
	●F	●	●	●		●	●	●
				●		●	●	●
	●F			●		●	●	●
		●	●			●	●	●
					●	●	●	●
		●				●		

	New York Education Law & Penal Law	North Carolina Chapter 90	North Dakota Title 43	Ohio Title 47	Oklahoma Title 59	Oregon Titles 16 & 52	Pennsylvania Title 63	Rhode Island Chapter 5
		■		$100	$50			$300
			$500	$500	$100	$500	■	
	4 yrs		30 days	90 days		30 days		
	■	■		$100	$100 per violation		■	$500
			$500	$500		$500		
			30 days	90 days		30 days		1 yr

(continued)

Nurse Practice Acts:
Misdemeanors Subject to Penalty *(continued)*

	South Carolina Title 40	South Dakota Titles 22 & 36	
Selling or fraudulently obtaining or furnishing nursing diploma, license renewal, record		●	
Practicing nursing under cover of fraudulent or illegal diploma, license, record		●	
Practicing nursing without a license (except in emergency)	●	●	
Using designation with name that falsely implies licensure	●	●	
Practicing nursing when license has lapsed, or has been suspended or revoked		●	
Conducting nursing education not approved by board			
Violating provision of nurse practice act	●	●	
Employing unlicensed persons to practice nursing			
Failing to report employment of unlicensed nurses			

PENALTIES

				South Carolina Title 40	South Dakota Titles 22 & 36	
First offense	Fine	min.		$100		
		max.		$500	$100	
	Imprisonment	min.		30 days		
		max.		90 days	30 days	
Subsequent offenses	Fine	min.		$100		
		max.		$500	$100	
	Imprisonment	min.		30 days		
		max.		90 days	30 days	

■ = depends on violation ★ = none stated F = fine only M = misdemeanor

Tennessee Section 63	Texas Title 71 (Health)	Utah Title 58	Vermont Title 26	Virginia Titles 18.2 & 54	Washington Chapters 9 & 18	West Virginia Chapter 30	Wisconsin Title 40A	Wyoming Title 33
●	●	●	●	●	●	●		
●	●	●	●	●	●	●		
●	●	●	●	●	●	●	●	●
●	●	●	●	●	●	●		●
●	●	●	●	●	●	●		
●		●	●	●		●		
●		●	●	●	●	●	●	●
			●				●	

$100	$50					$25		
$400	$500	■	$1,000	$1,000	$5,000	$250	$250	$100
11 mos 29 days	30 days		6 mos	1 yr	1 yr		1 yr	6 mos
$100	$50					$25		
$400	$500	■	$1,000	$1,000	$5,000	$250	$250	$100
11 mos 29 days	30 days		6 mos	1 yr	1 yr		1 yr	6 mos

G: Child Abuse Statutes

STATE	CITATION	APPLIES TO
Alabama	Ala. Code Tit. 26, Section 26-14-1 (1975)	Hospitals, clinics, sanitariums, doctors, physicians, surgeons, medical examiners, coroners, dentists, osteopaths, optometrists, chiropractors, podiatrists, nurses, school teachers and officials, peace officers, law enforcement officials, pharmacists, social workers, day-care workers or employees, mental health professionals, any other person called on to render aid or medical assistance to any child, or any person.
Alaska	Alaska Stat. Sections 47.17.010 to 47.17.070 (1971)	Practitioners of healing arts, school teachers, social workers, peace officers and officers of the division of corrections, administrative officers of institutions, licensed day-care providers, licensed foster-care providers, or any other person.
Arizona	Ariz. Rev. Stat. Ann. Section 13-3620 (1976)	Physician, hospital intern or resident, surgeon, dentist, osteopath, chiropractor, podiatrist, medical examiner, nurse, psychologist, school personnel, social worker, peace officer, or any other person responsible for the care of children.
Arkansas	Ark. Stat. Ann. Sections 42.807-42.818 (1975)	Physician, surgeon, coroner, dentist, osteopath, resident, intern, registered nurse, hospital personnel (engaged in admission, examination, care, or treatment), teacher, school official, social service worker, day-care center worker, or any other child or foster-care worker, mental health professional, peace officer, law enforcement official, and any other person.
California	Cal. Penal Code Sections 11165-11174	Physician; surgeon; dentist; resident; intern; podiatrist; chiropractor; marriage, family, or child counselor; psychologist; religious practitioner; registered nurse employed by public health agency, school, or school district; superintendent or supervisor of child welfare; certified pupil personnel employee of public or private school system; principal or teacher; licensed day-care worker; administrator of summer day camp or child-care center; social worker; peace officer; probation officer.

The information adapted for this chart is deemed accurate upon recent review. Since state laws may be revised, this information is subject to change. So consult your individual state statute.

AGE LIMIT	REPORT TO	IMMUNITY PROVISION	PHYSICIAN-PATIENT PRIVILEGE ELIMINATED	NATURE OF OFFENSE FOR NOT REPORTING
18	Duly constituted authority—chief of police, sheriff, Department of Pensions and Security or its designee, but not an agency involved in the acts or omissions of reported child abuse or neglect.	Yes	Yes	Misdemeanor
16	Department of Health and Welfare, peace officer.	Yes	Yes	Class B misdemeanor
18	Municipal or county peace officer or protective services of state Department of Economic Security.	Yes	Yes	Class 2 misdemeanor
18	Person in charge of institution or his designated agent who shall report. District or state Social Services Division of the Department of Social and Rehabilitative Services.	Yes	Yes	Misdemeanor; civil liability for damages proximately caused by failure to report
18	Local police authority, juvenile probation department, county welfare department, county health department.	Yes	Yes	None

(continued)

Child Abuse Statutes *(continued)*

STATE	CITATION	APPLIES TO
Colorado	Colo. Rev. Stat. Ann. Sections 19-10-101 through 19-10-115 (1975)	Physician, child health associate, medical examiner, dentist, osteopath, optometrist, chiropractor, podiatrist, registered or licensed practical nurse, hospital personnel engaged in admission, care, or treatment, Christian Science practitioner, school official or employee, social worker, worker in a family-care home or child-care center, mental health professional, any other person.
Connecticut	Conn. Gen. Stat. Rev. Section 17-38a (1973)	Physician, nurse, medical examiner, dentist, psychologist, school teacher, principal, guidance counselor, social worker, police officer, clergyman, coroner, osteopath, optometrist, chiropractor, podiatrist, any person paid to care for children, or mental health professional.
Delaware	Del. Code Ann. Tit. 16 Sections 901-909 Rev. (1974)	Physician; any person in healing arts, medicine, osteopathy, or dentistry; intern; resident; nurse; school employee; social worker; psychologist; medical examiner, or any other person.
Florida	Fla. Stat. Ann. Sections 827.01 to 827.09 (1977)	Physician, dentist, podiatrist, optometrist, intern, resident, nurse, teacher, social worker, employee of a public or private facility serving children.
Georgia	Ga. Code Ann. Sections 74-109 to 74-111 (1977)	Social workers, teachers, school administrators, child-care personnel, day-care personnel, law enforcement personnel, any physician, intern, resident osteopath, podiatrist, public health nurse, or any other person.
Hawaii	Hawaii Rev. Stat. Sections 350-1 to 350-5 (1968) as amended (Supp. 7)	Doctor of medicine, osteopathy, dentistry, or any of the other healing arts; registered nurse; school teacher; social worker; medical examiner; and any other person.
Idaho	Idaho Code Sections 16-1619 through 16-1629 (1976)	Physician, resident, intern, nurse, coroner, school teacher, day-care personnel, social worker, any other person.

AGE LIMIT	REPORT TO	IMMUNITY PROVISION	PHYSICIAN-PATIENT PRIVILEGE ELIMINATED	NATURE OF OFFENSE FOR NOT REPORTING
"Child"	City department or local law enforcement agency or the county or district department of social services. Receiving agency is to report to central registry.	Yes	Yes	Class 4 misdemeanor; civil liability for damages proximately caused by failure to report
18	Commissioner of Children and Youth Services or local police department.	Yes	Yes	Misdemeanor
18	Division of Child Protective Services, Department of Services for Children and Youth and Their Families.	Yes	Yes	Fined not more than $100 or imprisoned not more than 15 days
18	Person in charge of institution, Department of Health and Rehabilitative Services.	Yes	Yes	Misdemeanor of 2nd degree
18	Person in charge of institution, county health officer, child welfare agency designated by Department of Human Resources, and police authority.	Yes	No	Misdemeanor
18	Person in charge of medical facility, Department of Social Services and Housing.	Yes	Yes	Petty misdemeanor
18	Law enforcement agency, person in charge of institution or designee. Law enforcement officials report to Department of Health and Welfare.	Yes	Yes	None

(continued)

Child Abuse Statutes *(continued)*

STATE	CITATION	APPLIES TO
Illinois	Ill. Ann. Stat. Ch. 23 Sections 2051-2061 (1975)	Physician, hospital, surgeon, dentist, osteopath, chiropractor, podiatrist, Christian Science practitioner, coroner, school teacher, school administrator, truant officer, social worker, social services administrator, registered nurse, licensed practical nurse, director or staff assistant of a nursery school or a child day-care center, law enforcement officer, or personnel of the Illinois Department of Public Aid.
Indiana	Ind. Ann. Stat. Sections 31-6-11-1 to 31-6-11-22 (1973)	Any person.
Iowa	Iowa Code Ann. Sections 235A.1 to 235A.24	Health practitioner, social worker, certified psychologist, certified school employee, employee of a licensed day-care facility, member of the staff of a mental health center, peace officer, any other person.
Kansas	Kan. Stat. Ann. 38-716 to 38-756	Persons licensed to practice healing arts, dentistry, optometrist, engaged in postgraduate training programs approved by the state board of healing arts, certified psychologists, Christian Science practitioners, licensed social workers, every licensed professional nurse or licensed practical nurse, teacher, school administrator or other employee of a school, chief administrative officer of a medical-care facility, every person licensed by the secretary of health and environment to provide child-care services or employees of the person so licensed at the place where the child-care services are being provided to the child, or any law enforcement officer.
Kentucky	Ky. Rev. Stat. Ann. Sec. 199.335 (1964) as amended 1970, 1972, 1974	Physician, osteopathic physician, nurse, teacher, school administrator, social worker, coroner, medical examiner, and any other person.

AGE LIMIT	REPORT TO	IMMUNITY PROVISION	PHYSICIAN-PATIENT PRIVILEGE ELIMINATED	NATURE OF OFFENSE FOR NOT REPORTING
18	Department of Child and Family Services, local law enforcement agency.	Yes	Yes	None
18	Local Child Protection Service, law enforcement agency.	Yes	Yes	Class B misdemeanor
18	Department of Social Services, law enforcement agency.	Yes	Yes	None
"Child"	District court of county in which such examination or attendance is made, treatment is given, school is located, or such abuse or neglect is extant; or the Department of Social and Rehabilitation Services.	Yes		Misdemeanor
18	Person in charge of institution, Department of Human Resources.	Yes	Yes	None

(continued)

Child Abuse Statutes *(continued)*

STATE	CITATION	APPLIES TO
Louisiana	La. R.S. 14:403 (1964) as amended 1970, 1974, 1975, and 1977	Any person, physicians, interns, residents, nurses, hospital staff members, teachers, social workers, other persons or agencies having responsibility for care of children.
Maine	Me. Rev. Stat. Ann. Tit. 22 Sections 4011-4017 (1975) as amended 1977	Any medical physician, resident, intern, medical examiner, dentist, osteopathic physician, chiropractor, podiatrist, registered or licensed practical nurse, Christian Science practitioner, teacher, school official, social worker, homemaker, home health aide, medical or social service worker for families and children, psychologist, child-care personnel, mental health professional, or law enforcement official.
Maryland	Family Law Section 5-901-912 (1984)	Every health practitioner, educator, social worker, or law enforcement officer who contacts, examines, attends, or treats a child.
Massachusetts	Mass. Ann. c. 119 Section 51A (1973) as amended 1984	Physician, medical intern, medical examiner, dentist, nurse (public or private), school teacher, educational administrator, guidance or family counselor, probation officer, social worker or policeman. Any other person may report.
Michigan	Mich. Statutes Ann. Section 25.248 (1)-(Mich. Comp. Law Section 722.621) (1975)	Physician, coroner, dentist, medical examiner, nurse, audiologist, certified social worker, social worker, technician, school administrator, counselor or teacher, law enforcement officer, duly regulated child-care provider.
Minnesota	Minn. Stat. Ann. Section 626.556 (1975)	Professional or his delegate engaged in practice of the healing arts, social services, hospital administration, psychological or psychiatric treatment, child care, education, or law enforcement. Any person may report.
Mississippi	Miss. Code Ann. Sections 43-21-353 to 43-21-355, and 93-21-1 to 93-21-29 (1983)	Attorney, physician, dentist, intern, resident, nurse, psychologist, teacher, social worker, school principal, child-care giver, minister, any law enforcement officer, and all other persons.

AGE LIMIT	REPORT TO	IMMUNITY PROVISION	PHYSICIAN-PATIENT PRIVILEGE ELIMINATED	NATURE OF OFFENSE FOR NOT REPORTING
18	Parish child welfare unit, parish agency responsible for protection of juveniles, local or state law enforcement agency.	Yes	Yes	Misdemeanor
18	Person in charge of institution, Department of Health and Welfare.	Yes	Yes	None specified
18	Local department of social services, appropriate law enforcement agency.	Yes	Yes	None
18	Person in charge of institution, Department of Public Welfare, attorney for county, and medical examiner if death occurs.	Yes	Yes	Punished by fine not greater than $1,000
18	Department of Social Services, person in charge of institution.	Yes	Yes	Misdemeanor
"Child"	Local welfare agency, police department; deaths to medical examiner or coroner who will notify the local welfare agency or police department.	Yes	Yes	Misdemeanor
18	State welfare department which will thereafter make a referral to the person designated by the judge of the county youth court or family court.	Yes	Yes	None

(continued)

Child Abuse Statutes *(continued)*

STATE	CITATION	APPLIES TO
Missouri	Mo. Ann. Stat. Sections 210.110 to 210.165 (1975)	Physician, coroner, dentist, chiropractor, optometrist, podiatrist, resident, intern, nurse, hospital and clinic personnel, psychologist, mental health professional, social worker, day-care center worker, juvenile officer, probation or parole officer, teacher, principal or any school official, minister, Christian Science practitioner, peace officer, law enforcement official, other person with responsibility for child care and any other person may report.
Montana	Title 41 Chapter 3 as amended (1983)	Physician, nurse, teacher, social worker, attorney, law enforcement officer, Christian Science practitioner and other religious healers, osteopaths, podiatrists, any other person.
Nebraska	Neb. Rev. Stat. Supp. Sections 28-1501 to 28-1508 (1975)	Physician, medical institution, nurse, school employee, social worker, any other person.
Nevada	Nevada Rev. Stat. Sections 200.501 through 200.508	Physician, dentist, chiropractor, optometrist, resident or intern; superintendent, manager, or other person in charge of a hospital or similar institution; professional or practical nurse, physician assistant, psychologist, emergency medical technician, or ambulance attendant; attorney, social worker, school authority, or teacher; every person who maintains or is employed by a licensed child-care facility or children's camp.
New Hampshire	New Hampshire Rev. Stat. Ann. Sections 169.37 to 169.45 (1975) as amended 1975	Physician, county medical referee, psychiatrist, resident, intern, dentist, osteopath, optometrist, chiropractor, psychologist, therapist, registered nurse, hospital personnel, Christian Science practitioner, teacher, school official, school counselor, social worker, day-care worker, any other child- or foster-care worker, law enforcement official, priest, minister, or rabbi, or any other person.
New Jersey	New Jersey Rev. Stat. Ann. Sections 9:6-8.1 to 9:6-8.7 (1974)	Any person.

AGE LIMIT	REPORT TO	IMMUNITY PROVISION	PHYSICIAN-PATIENT PRIVILEGE ELIMINATED	NATURE OF OFFENSE FOR NOT REPORTING
18	Person in charge of institution, Missouri Division of Family Service; deaths to medical examiner or coroner who will report to the police, peace officer, prosecuting juvenile officer, Missouri Division of Family Services.	Yes	Yes	Misdemeanor
18	Department of Social and Rehabilitation Services, local affiliate, county attorney where child resides.	Yes	Yes	Civil liability for damages
*	Department of Public Welfare, police department, town marshal, office of sheriff.	Yes	Yes	Misdemeanor and fined $100
18	Local office of Welfare Division of Department of Human Resources, any county agency authorized by juvenile courts to receive reports, any police department or sheriff's office.	Yes	Yes	Gross misdemeanor (could interpret to cover failure to report)
18	Bureau of Child and Family Services, Division of Welfare, Department of Health and Welfare.	Yes	Yes	Misdemeanor
18	Bureau of Child and Family Services, Division of Welfare, Department of Health and Welfare.	Yes	Yes	Misdemeanor

(continued)

*18, or incompetent or disabled persons, or age 6 or younger left unattended in a motor vehicle

Child Abuse Statutes *(continued)*

STATE	CITATION	APPLIES TO
New Mexico	N.M. Stat. Ann. Sections 32-1-15 et. seq. (1983)	Physician, resident, intern, law enforcement officer, registered nurse, visiting nurse, school teacher, social worker, any other person.
New York	N.Y. Soc. Service Law Sections 411 to 428 (1973)	Physician, surgeon, medical examiner, coroner, dentist, osteopath, optometrist, resident, intern, registered nurse, Christian Science practitioner, hospital personnel, social services worker, school official, day-care center director, peace officer, mental health professional, and any other person.
North Carolina	N.C. Cent. Stat. Sections 7A-542 to 7A-552 (1980)	Any person.
North Dakota	N.D. Cent. Code Sections 50-25.1-01 to 50-25.1-14 (1975) as amended, 1982	Physician, nurse, dentist, optometrist, medical examiner or coroner, any other medical or mental health professional, school teacher or administrator, school counselor, social worker, day-care center or any other child-care worker, police, law enforcement officer, and any other person.
Ohio	Ohio Rev. Code Ann. Section 2151.421 (1977)	Attorney; physician, intern, resident, dentist, podiatrist, or practitioner of a limited branch of medicine or surgery as defined in section 4731.15 of the revised code; registered or licensed practical nurse, visiting nurse, or other health-care professional; licensed psychologist, speech pathologist, or audiologist; coroner; administrator or employee of a child day-care center; administrator or employee of a certified child-care agency or other public or private child services agency; school teacher or school authority; social worker; or person rendering spiritual treatment through prayer in accordance with the tenets of a well-recognized religion.

AGE LIMIT	REPORT TO	IMMUNITY PROVISION	PHYSICIAN-PATIENT PRIVILEGE ELIMINATED	NATURE OF OFFENSE FOR NOT REPORTING
18	County social services office of the Health and Social Services Department in the county of child's residence or probation services office in judicial district of child's residence, D.A.'s office.	No	Yes	Misdemeanor
18	Statewide Central Register of Child Abuse and Maltreatment, local child protective service, person in charge of institution.	Yes		Class A misdemeanor; civil liability for damages proximately caused by failure to report
18	Director of social services of county where child resides, parents, other caretakers.	Yes	Yes	None
18	Division of Community Services of the Social Service Board of North Dakota.	Yes	Yes	Class B misdemeanor
18, or any handicapped person under age 21	Person in charge of institution, Children Services Board or county department of welfare exercising the children services function, or municipal or county police officer in county of child's residence or where abuse or neglect occurred.	Yes	Yes	None specified

(continued)

Child Abuse Statutes *(continued)*

STATE	CITATION	APPLIES TO
Oklahoma	Okla. Stat. Ann. Tit. 21 Sections 845-848 (1965), as amended 1984-5	Physicians, surgeons, dentists, osteopathic physicians, residents, interns, every other person.
Oregon	Ore. Rev. Stat. Sections 418.740 to 418.775 (1975)	Public or private official, physician, intern, resident, or dentist; school employee; licensed practical or registered nurse; employee of department of human resources, county health department, community mental health program; county juvenile department; licensed child-caring agency; peace officer; psychologist; clergyman; social worker; optometrist; chiropractor; certified provider of day care or foster care; attorney; law enforcement agency; police department; sheriff's office; or county juvenile department.
Pennsylvania	Pa. Stat. Ann. Tit. 11 Sections 2201 to 2224 (1975)	Any person who in the course of their employment, occupation, or practice of their profession contacts children; licensed physician; medical examiner; coroner; dentist; osteopath; optometrist; chiropractor; podiatrist; intern; registered nurse or licensed practical nurse; hospital personnel engaged in the admission, examination, care or treatment of persons; a Christian Science practitioner; school administrator; school teacher; school nurse; social services worker; day-care center worker or any other child-care or foster-care worker; mental health professional; or peace officer or law enforcement official.
Rhode Island	R.I. Gen. Laws Ann. Sections 40-11-1 to 40-11-17 (1976)	Physicians, and any person.

AGE LIMIT	REPORT TO	IMMUNITY PROVISION	PHYSICIAN-PATIENT PRIVILEGE ELIMINATED	NATURE OF OFFENSE FOR NOT REPORTING
18	County office of the Department of Institutions, Social and Rehabilitative Services where injury occurred.	Yes	Yes	
18	Local office of Children's Services Division, law enforcement agency.	Yes	No	Misdemeanor
18	Person in charge of institution or agency, Department of Public Welfare of the Commonwealth of Pennsylvania.	Yes	Yes	First failure to report is a summary offense, subsequent failure to report is a misdemeanor of the 3rd degree
18	Director of Social and Rehabilitative Services, law enforcement agency.	Yes	Yes	Misdemeanor and fined up to $500

(continued)

Child Abuse Statutes *(continued)*

STATE	CITATION	APPLIES TO
South Carolina	S.C. Code Ann. Sections 20-7-480 to 20-7-630 (1962) as amended 1972, 1974, 1976	Any physician, nurse, dentist, optometrist, medical examiner or coroner, or any other medical/mental health professional, Christian Science practitioner, child care worker, police or law enforcement officer, school teacher, social worker, any other person.
South Dakota	S.D. Codified. Laws Ann. Sections 26-10-11, 26-10-15 (1964) as amended 1973, 1976, 1984	Physician, surgeon, dentist, doctor of osteopathy, chiropractor, optometrist, podiatrist, psychologist, social worker, hospital intern or resident, law enforcement officer, teacher, school counselor, school official, nurse, or coroner.
Tennessee	Tenn. Code Ann. Sections 37-1-401 to 37-1-412 (1973) as amended 1975	Any person.
Texas	Tex. Family Code Ann. Sections 34.01 to 34.06 (1975)	Any person.
Utah	Utah Code Ann. Section 78-3b-1 et. seq. (1983)	Any person.
Vermont	Vt. Stat. Ann. T.33 Sections 681-689 (1974) as amended 1975, 1976 and 1977	Physician, surgeon, osteopath, chiropractor, or physician assistant licensed or registered; resident physician, intern, or any hospital administrator; psychologist, school teacher, day-care worker, school principal or school guidance counselor; mental health professional, social worker, probation officer, clergyman, or any other person.

AGE LIMIT	REPORT TO	IMMUNITY PROVISION	PHYSICIAN-PATIENT PRIVILEGE ELIMINATED	NATURE OF OFFENSE FOR NOT REPORTING
18	State or local child protective services agency.	Yes	Yes	Misdemeanor
18	State's attorney of county where child resides, Department of Social Services, County Sheriff, or City Police.	Yes	Yes	Class I misdemeanor
*	Judge with juvenile jurisdiction, Tennessee Department of Human Resources, office of sheriff, law enforcement official where child resides, person in charge of institution.	Yes	Yes	Misdemeanor and fined not more than $50 or imprisoned 3 months, or both
**	State Department of Public Welfare, agency designated by court to protect children, local or state law enforcement agency.	Yes	Yes	Class B misdemeanor
18	Local city police, county sheriff's office, office of the Division of Family Services, person in charge of institution.	Yes	Yes	Class B misdemeanor
†	Commissioner of Social and Rehabilitative Services.	Yes	No	Fined not more than $500

*18, reasonably presumed to be under 18
**18 who has not been married
†Under age of majority

(continued)

Child Abuse Statutes (continued)

STATE	CITATION	APPLIES TO
Virginia	Va. Code Ann. Sections 63.1-248.1 to 63.1-248.17 (1975)	Persons licensed to practice healing arts; residents; interns; nurses; social workers; probation officers; teachers; persons employed in a public or private school, kindergarten, or nursery; persons providing child care for pay on a regular basis; Christian Science practitioner; mental health professional or law enforcement officer. Any person may report.
Washington	Wash. Rev. Code Ann. Sections 26.44.010 to 26.44.900 (1975)	Practitioner, professional school personnel, nurse, social worker, psychologist, pharmacist, employee of social or health services. Any person may report.
Wisconsin	Wis. Stat. Ann. Section 48.981 (1984-85)	Physician, coroner, surgeon, nurse, hospital administrator, dentist, social worker, school administrator, child care worker.
West Virginia	West Va. Code Ann. Sections 49-6A. 1 to 49-6A-10 (1977)	Medical, dental, mental health professional; Christian Science practitioner; religious healer; school teacher or other school personnel; social service worker; child-care or foster-care worker; peace officer, or law enforcement official. Any other person may report.
Wyoming	Wyo. Stat. Ann. Sections 14-3-101 to 14-3-215 (1977)	Any person.
District of Columbia	D.C. Code Ann. Sections 22-901 to 22-902 (1981)	Not specified.

AGE LIMIT	REPORT TO	IMMUNITY PROVISION	PHYSICIAN-PATIENT PRIVILEGE ELIMINATED	NATURE OF OFFENSE FOR NOT REPORTING
18	Person in charge of institution or department, Department of Welfare of the county or city where child resides or abuse or neglect occurred; juvenile and domestic relations district court if an employee of the Department of Welfare is the one suspected of abusing the child.	Yes	Yes	Fined not more than $500 for first failure and for any subsequent, not less than $100 or not more than $1000
*	Law enforcement agency, Department of Social and Health Services.	Yes	Yes	Gross misdemeanor
18	County child welfare agency, sheriff, city police department.	Yes	**	Not fined more than $1,000 or imprisoned not more than 6 mos.
18	Local state department of child protective services agency; report deaths to medical examiner or coroner.	Yes	Yes	Misdemeanor
19	Person in charge of institution, Department of Health and Social Services, Division of Public Assistance and Social Services.	Yes	Yes	None
18, or any child in custody under age 14	Person in charge of institution, Metropolitan Police Department of the District of Columbia, Child Protective Services Division of the Department of Human Resources.	Yes	Not specified	Not specified

*18, any mentally retarded person
**See Section 325.21

Glossary

A

abuse of process • A civil action for damages in which it is alleged that the legal process has been used in a manner not contemplated by law. This action might be brought by a health practitioner attempting to countersue a patient or by a psychiatric patient attempting to demonstrate wrongful confinement.

administrator • Overseer of the general effectiveness and efficiency of an agency, who is concerned with organization, planning, development, growth, change, operations, budgets, and evaluation.

admissible • Authentic, relevant, reliable information presented during a trial, which may be used to reach a decision; nurses' notes are usually admissible if the information in them hasn't been altered.

adult • **1.** One who is fully developed and matured and who has attained the intellectual capacity and the emotional and psychological stability characteristic of a mature person. **2.** A person who has reached full legal age.

adverse drug effect • A harmful, unintended reaction to a drug administered at normal dosage.

affidavit • A written statement sworn to before a notary public or an officer of the court.

affirmative defense • A denial of guilt or wrongdoing based on new evidence rather than on simple denial of a charge, as a plea of immunity according to a good samaritan law. The defendant bears the burden of proof in an affirmative defense.

agency • A relationship between two parties in which the first party authorizes the second to act as agent on behalf of the first. It usually implies a contractual arrangement between two parties managed by a third party, the agent.

agent • A party authorized to act on behalf of another and to give the other an account of such actions.

age of majority • 18 or 21 years, depending on the state or Canadian provincial laws.

Alcoholics Anonymous (AA) • An international nonprofit organization, founded in 1935, consisting of abstinent alcoholics whose purpose is to help alcoholics stop drinking and maintain sobriety through group support, shared experiences, and faith in a power greater than themselves.

alcoholism • The extreme dependence on excessive amounts of alcohol, associated with a cumulative pattern of deviant behaviors. Alcoholism is a chronic illness with a slow, insidious onset, which may occur at any age. The etiology is unknown, but cultural and psychosocial factors are suspect, and families of alcoholics have a higher incidence of alcoholism. Frequent intoxication has cumulative destructive effects on an individual's family and social life, working life, and physical health. The most frequent medical consequences of alcoholism are central nervous system depression and cirrhosis of the liver. The severity of each of these is increased in the absence of food intake. Alcoholic patients also may suffer from alcoholic gastritis, peripheral neuropathies, auditory hallucinations, and cardiac problems. Abrupt withdrawal of alcohol in addiction causes weakness, sweating, and hyperreflexia. The severe form of alcohol withdrawal is called delirium tremens. Extreme caution should be used in administering drugs to the alcoholic patient because of the possibility of additive central nervous system depression. The treatment of alcoholism consists of psychotherapy (especially group therapy by organizations like Alcoholics Anonymous), electroshock treatments, or drugs that cause an aversion to alcohol.

AMA • Against medical advice; refers to when a patient decides to leave a health-care facility against his doctor's advice.

American Medical Association (AMA) • A professional association whose membership is made up of approximately half of the total licensed physicians in the United States, including practitioners in all recognized medical specialties as well as general primary care physicians. The AMA is governed by a Board of Trustees and House of Delegates. Trustees and delegates represent various state and local medical associations as well as such government agencies as the Public Health Service and medical departments of the Army, Navy, and Air Force.

American Nurses' Association (ANA) • The national professional association of registered nurses in the United States. It was founded in 1896 to improve standards of health and the availability of health care given in order to foster high standards for nursing, to promote the professional development of nurses, and to advance the economic and general welfare of nurses. The ANA is made up of 53 constituent associations from 50 states, the District of Columbia, Guam, and the Virgin Islands, representing more than 900 district associations. Members may join one or more of the five Divisions on Nursing Practice: Community Health; Gerontological; Maternal and Child Health; Medical-Surgical; and Psychiatric and Mental Health Nursing. These Divisions are coordinated by the Congress for Nursing Practice. The Congress evaluates changes in the scope of practice, monitors scientific and educational developments, encourages research, and develops statements that describe ANA policies regarding legislation affecting nursing practice. Other commissions within the Association include the Commission on Nursing Education, the Commission on Nursing Services, the Commission on Nursing Research, and the Economic and General Welfare Commission.

American Red Cross • One of more than 120 national organizations that seek to reduce human suffering through various health, safety, and disaster relief programs in affiliation with the International Committee of the Red Cross. The Committee and all Red Cross organizations evolved from the Geneva Convention of 1864, following the example and urging of Swiss humanitarian Jean Henri Dunant, who aided wounded French and Austrian soldiers at the Battle of Solferino in 1859. The American Red Cross has more than 130 million members in about 3,100 chapters throughout the United States. Volunteers constitute the entire staffs of about 1,700 chapters. Other chapters maintain small paid staffs and some professionals but depend largely on volunteers.

answer • The response of a defendant to the complaint of a plaintiff. The answer contains a denial of the plaintiff's allegations and may also contain an affirmative defense or a counterclaim. It is the principal pleading on the part of the defense and is prepared in writing, usually by the defense attorney, and submitted to the court.

appellate court • A court of law that has the power to review the decision of a lower court. It does not make a new determination of the facts of the case; it reviews only the way in which the law was applied in the case.

appellee • A party in an appeal that won the case in a lower court. The appellee argues that the decision of the lower court should not be modified by the appellate court.

arbitrator • An impartial person appointed to resolve a dispute between parties. The arbitrator listens to the evidence as presented by the parties in an informal hearing and attempts to arrive at a resolution acceptable to both parties.

assault • An attempt or threat by a person to physically injure another person.

associate degree in nursing • An academic degree after satisfactory completion of a 2-year course of study, usually at a community or junior college. The recipient is eligible to take the national licensing examination to become a registered nurse. An associate degree in nursing is not available in Canada.

attending physician • The physician who is responsible for a particular, usually private, patient. In a university setting, an attending physician often also has teaching responsibilities and holds a faculty appointment. Also called attending (informal).

attorney of record • The attorney whose name appears on the legal records for a specific case, as the agent of a specific client.

audit • A methodical examination; to examine with intent to verify. Nursing audits examine standards of nursing care.

authorization cards • Cards employees sign to authorize a union election.

autopsy • A postmortem examination of a body to determine the cause of death.

B

bachelor of science in nursing (BSN) • An academic degree awarded upon satisfactory completion of a 4-year course of study in an institution of higher learning. The recipient is eligible to take the national licensing examination to become a registered nurse. A BSN degree is prerequisite to advancement in most systems and institutions that employ nurses. Compare **associate degree in nursing.**

bargaining agent • A person or group selected by members of a bargaining unit to represent them in negotiations.

bargaining unit • A group of employees who participate in collective bargaining as representatives of all employees.

BASIC • *abbr* Beginners' All-purpose Symbolic Instruction Code, a programming language widely used on personal computers and small business systems.

battered woman syndrome (BWS) • Repeated episodes of physical assault on a woman by the man with whom she lives, often resulting in serious physical and psychological damage to the woman. Such violence tends to follow a predictable pattern. The first phase is characterized by the man acting increasingly irritable, edgy, and tense. Verbal abuse, insults, and criticism increase, and shoves or slaps begin. The second phase is the time of the acute, violent activity. As the tension mounts, the woman becomes unable to placate the man, and she may argue or defend herself. The man uses this as the jus-

tification for his anger and assaults her, often saying that he is "teaching her a lesson." The third stage is characterized by apology and remorse on the part of the man, with promises of change. The calm continues until tension builds again. The battered woman syndrome occurs at all socioeconomic levels, and one half to three quarters of female assault victims are the victims of an attack by a lover or husband. It is estimated that between one and two million women a year are beaten by their husbands. Men who grew up in homes in which the father abused the mother are more likely to beat their wives than are men who lived in nonviolent homes. Personal and cultural attitudes also affect the incidence of wife battering.

battery • The unauthorized touching of a person by another person, such as when a health-care professional treats a patient beyond what the patient consented to.

benefits • Nonsalary forms of compensation an employer provides for employees—for example, medical and dental insurance.

block charting • A method of charting in which you detail, in paragraph form, procedures you carried out during a block of time.

board of health • An administrative body acting on a municipal, county, state, provincial, or national level. The functions, powers, and responsibilities of boards of health vary with the locales. Each board is generally concerned with the recognition of the health needs of the people and the coordination of projects and resources to meet and identify these needs. Among the tasks of most boards of health are prevention of disease, health education, and implementation of laws pertaining to health.

borrowed-servant doctrine • A legal doctrine that courts may apply in cases when an employer "lends" his employee's services to another employer who, under this doctrine, becomes liable for the employee's wrongful conduct.

brain death • Generally, the cessation of brain wave activity. The legal definition of this condition varies from state to state. (See "When a patient dies," page 88.)

breach of contract • Failing to perform all or part of the contracted duty without justification.

breach of duty • The neglect or failure to fulfill in a proper manner the duties of an office, job, or position.

British Medical Association (BMA) • A national professional organization of physicians in the United Kingdom.

BSN • *abbr* **bachelor of science in nursing.**

C

Canadian Association of University Schools of Nursing (CAUSN) • A national Canadian organization of nursing schools affiliated with institutions of higher learning.

Canadian Nurses Association (CNA) • The official national organization for the professional registered nurses of Canada who are members of one of the 10 provincial nurses' associations and the Northwest Territories' association. The CNA, a federation of these 11 associations, is supported by contributions of the 140,000 members of the regional associations. The chief objective of the CNA is to promote conditions conducive to the good health of the people and to good patient care.

"captain of the ship" doctrine • A legal doctrine that considers a surgeon responsible for the actions of his assistants when those assistants are under the surgeon's supervision. This doctrine is similar to the borrowed-servant doctrine.

causa mortis • A state of mind in a person approaching death.

Centers for Disease Control (CDC) • A federal agency of the United States government that provides facilities and services for the investigation, identification, prevention, and control of disease. It is concerned with all aspects of the epidemiology and the laboratory diagnosis of disease. Immunization programs, quarantine regulations and programs, laboratory standards, and community surveillance for disease are among the activities of the CDC.

central processing unit (CPU) • In data processing: the group of physical components of a computer system containing the logical, arithmetical, and control circuits for the system. Also called hardware.

certification • Recognition that a nurse is specially qualified, based on predetermined standards, to provide nursing care in a particular area of nursing practice.

chain of custody • evidentiary rule requiring that each individual having custody of a piece of evidence be identified and that the transfer of evidence from one custodian to another be documented so that all evidence is accounted for. Also referred to as chain of evidence.

child abuse • The physical, sexual, or emotional maltreatment of a child. It may be overt or covert and often results in permanent physical or psychiatric injury, mental impairment, or, sometimes, death. Child abuse occurs predominantly to children less than age 3 and is the result of complex factors involving both parents and child, compounded by various stressful environmental circumstances, such as poor socioeconomic conditions, inadequate physical and emotional support within the family, and any major life change or crisis, especially those crises arising from marital strife. Parents at high risk for abuse are characterized as having unsatisfied needs, difficulty in forming adequate interpersonal relationships, unrealistic expectations of the child, and a lack of nurturing experience, often involving neglect or abuse in their own childhoods. Predisposing factors among children include the temperament, personality, and activity level of the child; birth order; sensitivity to parental needs; and a need for special physical or emotional care resulting from illness, premature birth, or congenital or genetic abnormalities. Also called battered child syndrome. Compare **child neglect.**

child neglect • The failure by parents or guardians to provide the basic needs of a child by physical or emotional deprivation that interferes with normal growth and development or that places the child in jeopardy. Compare **child abuse.**

child welfare • Any service sponsored by the community or special organizations that provides for the physical, social, or psychological care of children in need of it.

chronic care • A pattern of medical and nursing care that focuses on long-term care of people with chronic diseases or conditions, either at home or in a medical facility. It includes care specific to the problem, as well as other measures to encourage self-care, to promote health, and to prevent loss of function.

circumstantial evidence • Testimony based on inference or hearsay rather than actual personal knowledge or observation of the facts in question.

civil defense laws • That body of statutory law that is invoked when the jurisdiction is under attack, as in a state of war.

claims-made policy • A professional liability insurance policy that covers the holder for the period in which a claim of malpractice is made. The alleged act of malpractice may have occurred at some previous time, but the policy insures the holder when the claim is made.

clinical nurse specialist (CNS) • A registered nurse who holds a master of science degree in nursing (MSN) and who has acquired advanced knowledge and clinical skills in a specific area of nursing and health care.

CNA • *abbr* **Canadian Nurses' Association.**

CNF • *abbr* Canadian Nurses' Foundation.

CNM • *abbr* certified nurse-midwife.

CNS • *abbr* clinical nurse specialist.

code • **1.** A published body of statutes, as a civil code. **2.** A collection of standards and rules of behavior, as a dress code. **3.** A symbolic means of representing information for communication or transfer, as a genetic code. **4. Informal.** A discreet signal used to summon a special team to resuscitate a patient without alarming patients or visitors. See also **no-code order.**

codes • **1.** A system of assigned terms designed by a medical institution for quick and accurate communication during emergencies or for patient identification. **2.** Short values of data used to feed commands to a computerized hospital information system.

collective bargaining • A legal process in which representatives for organized employees negotiate with their employer about such matters as wages, hours, and working conditions.

commitment • **1.** The placement or confinement of an individual in a specialized hospital or other institutional facility. **2.** The legal procedure of admitting a mentally ill person to an institution for psychiatric treatment. The process varies from state to state but usually involves judicial or court action based on medical evidence certifying that the person is mentally ill. **3.** A pledge or contract to fulfill some obligation or agreement, used especially in some forms of psychotherapy or marriage counseling.

common law • Law derived from previous court decisions, not from statutes. Also called case law.

comparative negligence doctrine • A doctrine by which a court assigns partial responsibility for the defendant's alleged negligence to the plaintiff in the case.

compensation • All forms of payment from an employer to an employee, including salary and benefits.

complaint • **1.** A pleading by a plaintiff made under oath to initiate a suit. It is a statement of the formal charge and the cause for action against the defendant. For a minor offense, the defendant is tried on the basis of the complaint. A more serious felony prosecution requires an indictment with evidence presented by a state's attorney. **2. Informal.** Any ailment, problem, or symptom identified by the client, patient, member of the person's family, or other knowledgeable person. The chief complaint is often the reason that the person has sought health care.

computerized record system • A system that stores medical records in the memory bank of a computer.

confidentiality • A professional responsibility to keep all privileged information private.

consent form • A document, prepared for a patient's signature, that discloses his proposed treatment in general terms.

contract duties • Duties defined in an employment contract.

contract violations • Actions that break mutually accepted employment rules.

convalescent home • See **extended-care facility.**

cooperation strategy • A plan for bringing about change in which the initiator influences others to adapt to the change, using open communication and interpersonal skills.

coronary care unit (CCU) • A specially equipped hospital area designed for the treatment of patients with sudden, life-threatening cardiac conditions. Such units contain resuscitation and monitoring equipment and are staffed by personnel specially trained and skilled in recognizing and immediately responding to cardiac emergencies with cardiopulmonary resuscitation techniques, the administration of antiarrhythmic drugs, and other appropriate therapeutic measures.

coroner • A public official who investigates the causes and circumstances of a death occurring within a specific legal jurisdiction or territory, especially a death that may have resulted from unnatural causes. Also called medical examiner.

corporate liability • A judicial process by which the court will disregard the usual liability immunity of corporations and corporate officers.

counterclaim • A claim made by a defendant establishing a cause for action in his favor against the plaintiff. The purpose of a counterclaim is to oppose or detract from the plaintiff's claim or complaint.

countersignature • The signature you must obtain from another health professional to verify information, or your signature that verifies another health-care provider's information.

criminal abortion • The intentional termination of pregnancy under any condition prohibited by law.

CRNA • *abbr* certified registered nurse anesthetist. See **nurse anesthetist.**

cross-examination • The questioning of a witness by the attorney for the opposing party.

CRT • *abbr* cathode-ray tube, or the display screen on a computer terminal or heart monitor similar to a television screen.

custodial care • Services and care of a nonmedical nature provided on a long-term basis, usually for convalescent and chronically ill individuals. Kinds of custodial care include board and personal assistance.

D

damages • An amount of money a court orders a defendant to pay the plaintiff, in deciding the case in favor of the plaintiff.

death • **1.** Apparent death: the cessation of life as indicated by the absence of heartbeat or respiration. **2.** Legal death: the total absence of activity in the brain and the central nervous, cardiovascular, and respiratory systems, as observed and declared by a physician.

declared emergency • The situation when a government official formally identifies a state of emergency.

default judgment • A judgment rendered against a defendant because of the defendant's failure to appear in court or to answer the plaintiff's claim within the proper time.

defendant • The party that is named in a plaintiff's complaint and against whom the plaintiff's allegations are made. The defendant must respond to the allegations.

defense of impossibility • A legal defense that says a violation of a contract was literally impossible to avoid.

delinquency • **1.** Negligence or failure to fulfill a duty or obligation. **2.** An offense, fault, misdemeanor, or misdeed; a tendency to commit such acts.

delinquent • **1.** Characterized by neglect of duty or violation of law. **2.** One whose behavior is characterized by persistent antisocial, illegal, violent, or criminal acts; a juvenile delinquent.

dependent nursing function • A function the nurse performs, with another professional's written order, on the basis of that professional's assessment and judgment, for which that professional is accountable.

deposition • A sworn pretrial testimony given by a witness in response to oral or written questions and cross-examination. The deposition is transcribed and may be used for further pretrial investigation. It may also be presented at the trial if the witness cannot be present. Compare **discovery, interrogatories.**

direct access • The right of a health-care provider and a patient to interact on a professional basis without interference.

direct examination • The first examination of a witness called to the stand by the attorney for the party the witness is representing.

direct patient care • Care of a patient provided in person by a member of the staff. Direct patient care may involve any aspects of the health care of a patient, including treatments, counseling, self-care, patient education, and administration of medication.

disaster • A sudden event that creates a number of victims with extensive injuries.

discovery • A pretrial procedure that allows the plaintiff's and defendant's attorneys to examine relevant materials and interrogate all parties to the case.

dismiss • To discharge or dispose of an action, suit, or motion trial.

Doctor of Medicine (MD) • See **physician.**

Doctor of Osteopathy (DO) • See **physician.**

doctrine of parens patriae • A doctrine that appoints the state as legal guardian of a child or incompetent adult when an individual hasn't been appointed as guardian.

documentation • The preparing or assembling of written records.

drug • **1.** Any substance taken by mouth; injected into a muscle, the skin, a blood vessel, or a cavity of the body; or applied topically to treat or prevent a disease or condition. Also called medicine. **2. Informal.** A narcotic substance.

drug abuse • The use of a drug for a nontherapeutic effect, especially one for which it was not prescribed or intended. Some of the most commonly abused substances are alcohol, amphetamines, barbiturates, and methaqualone. Drug abuse may lead to organ damage, addiction, and disturbed patterns of behavior. Some illicit drugs, such as lysergic acid diethylamide and phencyclidine hydrochloride, have no recognized therapeutic effect. Use of these drugs often incurs criminal penalty in addition to the potential for physical, social, and psychological harm. See also **drug addiction.**

drug addiction • A condition characterized by an overwhelming desire to continue taking a drug to which one has become habituated through repeated consumption because it produces a particular effect, usually an alteration of mental activity, attitude, or outlook. Addiction is usually accompanied by a compulsion to obtain the drug, a tendency to increase the dose, a psychological or physical dependence, and detrimental consequences for the individual and society. Common addictive drugs are barbiturates, ethanol, and morphine and other narcotics, especially heroin, which has slightly greater euphorigenic properties than other opium derivatives. See also **alcoholism, drug abuse.**

Drug Enforcement Administration (DEA) • An agency of the federal government empowered to enforce regulations regarding the import or export of narcotic drugs and certain other substances or the traffic of these substances across state lines.

duty • A legal obligation owed by one party to another. Duty may be established by statute or other legal process, as by contract or oath supported by statute, or it may be voluntarily undertaken. Every person has a duty of care to all other people to avoid causing harm or injury by negligence.

E

emancipated minor • A minor who's legally considered an adult, free from parental care, and completely responsible for his own affairs.

Emergency Medical Service (EMS) • A network of services coordinated to provide aid and medical assistance from primary response to definitive care, involving personnel trained in the rescue, stabilization, transportation, and advanced treatment of trauma or medical emergency patients. Linked by a communications system that operates on both a local and regional level, EMS is usually initiated by a citizen calling an emergency number. Stages include the first medical response; involvement of ambulance personnel, medium and heavy rescue equipment, and paramedic units, if necessary; and continued care in the hospital with emergency room nurses, emergency room doctors, specialists, and critical-care nurses and physicians.

emergency nursing • Nursing care provided to prevent imminent severe damage or death or to avert serious injury. Activities that exemplify emergency nursing care include basic life support, cardiopulmonary resuscitation, control of hemorrhage, and burn care.

euthanasia • Deliberately bringing about the death of a person who's suffering from an incurable disease or condition, either actively—by administering a lethal drug—or passively—by withholding treatment.

executing a will • Carrying out a person's wishes as expressed in his will.

expert witness • A person who has special knowledge of a subject about which a court requests testimony. Special knowledge may be acquired by experience, education, observation, or study but is not possessed by the average person. An expert witness gives expert testimony or expert evidence. This evidence often serves to educate the court and the jury in the subject under consideration.

expressed contract • A verbal or written agreement between two or more people to do, or not do, something.

extended-care facility • An institution devoted to providing medical, nursing, or custodial care for an individual over a prolonged period of time, as during the course of a chronic disease or during the rehabilitation phase after an acute illness. Kinds of extended-care facilities are intermediate-care facilities and skilled nursing facilities. Also called **convalescent home, nursing home.**

extraordinary life-support measures • Resuscitative efforts and therapies done to replace a patient's natural vital functions.

F

false imprisonment • The act of confining or restraining a person without his consent for no clinical or legal reason.

family nurse practitioner (FNP) • A nurse practitioner possessing skills necessary for the detection and management of acute self-limiting conditions and management of chronic stable conditions. An FNP provides primary, ambulatory care for families, in collaboration with primary-care physicians.

FDA • *abbr* **Food and Drug Administration.**

fee-for-service • **1.** A charge made for a professional activity, as for a physical examination. **2.** A system for the payment of professional services in which the practitioner is paid for the particular service rendered, rather than receiving a salary for providing professional services as needed during scheduled hours of work or time on call.

fiduciary relationship • A legal relationship of confidentiality that exists whenever one person trusts or relies on another—such as a doctor-patient relationship.

first aid • The immediate care given to an injured or ill person. It includes self-help and home-care measures if medical assistance isn't readily available. Attention is directed first to the most critical problems: evaluation of the patency of the airway, the presence of bleeding, and the adequacy of cardiac function. The patient is kept warm and as comfortable as possible.

five-step nursing process • A nursing process comprising five broad categories of nursing behaviors: assessment, nursing diagnosis, planning, intervention, and evaluation. The nurse gathers information about the patient, formulates nursing diagnoses, develops a plan of care with the patient, implements the plan of care, and evaluates the effects of the intervention. The nurse involves the patient and the patient's family to the greatest extent possible. Implicit in the nursing process is a therapeutic and personal relationship between the nurse, the patient, and the patient's family.

flexible staffing patterns • Work schedules that vary—for example, 10- and 12-hour shifts, shorter workweeks, and special weekend schedules.

flextime, flexitime • A system of staffing that allows flexible work schedules. A person working 7 hours daily might choose to work from 7 to 3, 10 to 5, or other hours. Use of the system tends to improve morale and decrease turnover.

FNP • *abbr* **family nurse practitioner.**

Food and Drug Administration (FDA) • A federal agency responsible for the enforcement of federal regulations regarding the manufacture and distribution of food, drugs, and cosmetics.

forensic medicine • A branch of medicine that deals with the legal aspects of health care.

G

gerontologic nursing • A type of nursing care, in which a nurse may specialize, that provides specifically for the physical, intellectual, and emotional needs of the elderly.

grandfather clause • A waiver that allows a person to continue to practice as a nurse after new qualifications are enacted into law. It further protects the property right of her license but does not confer the equivalent of a bachelor's degree.

grievance • A substantial complaint that involves working conditions or contract violations.

grievance procedure • Steps employees and employer agree to follow to settle disputes.

gross negligence • The flagrant and inexcusable failure to perform a legal duty in reckless disregard of the consequences.

ground rules • Rules governing a particular situation that describe legitimate behavior.

guardian ad litem • A person appointed by the court to safeguard a minor's legal interest during certain kinds of litigation.

H

health-care consumer • Any actual or potential recipient of health care, as a patient in a hospital, a client in a community mental health center, or a member of a prepaid health maintenance organization.

health-care industry • The complex of preventive, remedial, and therapeutic services provided by hospitals and other institutions, nurses, doctors, dentists, government agencies, voluntary agencies, noninstitutional care facilities, pharmaceutical and medical equipment manufacturers, and health insurance companies.

health professional • Any person who has completed a course of study in a field of health, as a registered nurse. The person is usually licensed by a governmental agency or

health provider • Any individual who provides health services to health-care consumers.

hospice • A system of family-centered care designed to assist the chronically ill person to be comfortable and to maintain a satisfactory life-style through the terminal phases of dying. Hospice care is multidisciplinary and includes home visits, professional medical help available on call, teaching and emotional support of the family, and physical care of the client. Some hospice programs provide care in a center as well as in the home.

hospital information system (HIS) • A computer-based information system with multi-access units to collect, organize, store, and make available data for problem solving and decision making.

hospital quality assurance program • A program developed by a hospital committee that monitors the quality of the hospital's diagnostic, therapeutic, prognostic, and other health-care activities.

human investigations committee • A committee established in a hospital, school, or university to review applications for research involving human subjects in order to protect the rights of the people to be studied. Also called **human subjects investigation committee.**

human subjects investigation committee • See **human investigations committee.**

I

ICCU • *abbr* intensive coronary-care unit.

ICU • *abbr* **intensive care unit.**

illegal (criminal) abortion • Induced termination of a pregnancy under certain circumstances, or at a gestational time, prohibited by law. In Canada, an abortion not approved by a hospital therapeutic abortion committee. Many illegal abortions are performed under medically unsafe conditions.

immunity from liability • Exemption of a person or institution, by law, from a legally imposed penalty.

immunity from suit • Exemption of a person or institution, by law, from being sued.

implementation • **1.** A deliberate action performed to achieve a goal, as carrying out a plan in caring for a patient. **2.** In five-step nursing process: a category of nursing behavior in which the actions necessary for accomplishing the health-care plan are initiated and completed.

implied contract • A verbal or written agreement—inferred rather than expressed—between two or more people to do, or not do, something.

independent contractor • A self-employed person who renders services to clients and independently determines how the work will be done.

independent practice • The practice of certain aspects of professional nursing that are encompassed by applicable licensure and law and require no supervision or direction from others. Nurses in independent practice may have an office in which they see patients and charge fees for service. In all nursing settings, state practice acts define aspects of nursing practice that are independent and may define those to be done only under supervision or direction of another individual, usually a doctor.

informed consent • Permission obtained from a patient to perform a specific test or procedure after the patient has been fully informed about the test or procedure.

injunction • A court order restraining a person from committing a specific act.

in loco parentis • Latin phrase meaning "in the place of the parent." The assumption by a person or institution of the parental obligations of caring for a child without adoption.

inpatient • **1.** A patient who has been admitted to a hospital or other health-care facility for at least an overnight stay. **2.** Pertaining to the treatment of such a patient or to a health-care facility to which a patient may be admitted for 24-hour care.

institutional licensure • A proposed procedure in which licensure for almost all health professions would be abandoned and the responsibility for assessing professional competence would fall to the health-care facility where the health professional is employed. Proponents maintain that health needs would be better and more flexibly served. Opponents maintain that knowledge, judgment, and competence are the products of a good basic education in the profession and that educators cannot teach the profession without a set of standardized expectations, as are now provided by government-controlled licensing procedures and certifying examinations.

intensive care • Constant, complex, detailed health care as provided in various acute, life-threatening conditions. Special training is necessary to provide intensive care. Also called critical care.

intensive care unit (ICU) • A hospital unit in which patients requiring close monitoring and intensive care are housed for as long as needed. An ICU contains highly technical and sophisticated monitoring devices and equipment, and the staff in the unit is educated to give critical care as needed by the patients.

intermediate care • A level of medical care for certain chronically ill or disabled individuals in which room and board are provided but skilled nursing care is not.

International Red Cross Society • An international philanthropic organization, based in Geneva, concerned primarily with the humane treatment and welfare of the victims of war and calamity and with the neutrality of hospitals and medical personnel in times of war. See also **American Red Cross.**

Interrogatories • A series of written questions submitted to a witness or other person having information of interest to the court. The answers are transcribed and are sworn to under oath. Compare **discovery, deposition.**

intervention • **1.** Any act performed to prevent harm from occurring to a client or to improve the mental, emotional, or physical function of a client. A physiologic process may be monitored or enhanced, or a pathologic process may be arrested or controlled.

2. The fourth step of the nursing process. This step includes nursing actions taken to meet patient needs as determined by nursing assessment and diagnosis.

invalid contract • Any contract concerning illegal or impossible actions; no legal obligation exists.

J

JCAH • *abbr* **Joint Commission on Accreditation of Hospitals.**

job description • A written statement describing responsibilities of a specific job and the qualifications an applicant for that job should have.

Joint Commission on Accreditation of Hospitals (JCAH) • A private, nongovernmental agency that establishes guidelines for the operation of hospitals and other health-care facilities, conducts accreditation programs and surveys, and encourages the attainment of high standards of institutional medical care. Members include representatives from the American Medical Association, American College of Physicians, and American College of Surgeons.

joint practice • **1.** The (usually private) practice of a doctor and a nurse practitioner who work as a team, sharing responsibility for a group of patients. **2.** In inpatient nursing, the practice of making joint decisions about patient care by committees of the doctors and nurses working on a division.

L

law • **1.** In a field of study: a rule, standard, or principle that states a fact or a relationship between factors, as Dalton's law regarding partial pressures of gas or Koch's law regarding the specificity of a pathogen. **2. a.** A rule, principle, or regulation established and promulgated by a government to protect or to restrict the people affected. **b.** The field of study concerned with such laws. **c.** The collected body of the laws of a people, derived from custom and from legislation.

legal abortion • Induced termination of pregnancy by a doctor before the fetus has developed sufficiently to live outside the uterus. The procedure is performed under medically safe conditions prescribed by law.

legal death • See **death.**

liability • Legal responsibility for failure to act, and so causing harm to another person, or for actions that fail to meet standards of care, so causing another person harm.

liaison • A nurse who acts as an agent between a patient, the hospital, and the patient's family, and who speaks for the entire health-care team.

licensed practical nurse (LPN) • A person trained in basic nursing techniques and direct patient care who practices under the supervision of a registered nurse. The course of training usually lasts 1 year. In Canada an LPN is called a nursing assistant. Also called **licensed vocational nurse** *(U.S.).*

licensed vocational nurse (LVN) • See **licensed practical nurse.**

licensure • The granting of permission by a competent authority (usually a governmental agency) to an organization or individual to engage in a practice or activity that would otherwise be illegal. Kinds of licensure include the issuing of licenses for general hospitals or nursing homes; for health professionals, such as physicians; and for the production or distribution of biological products. Licensure is usually granted on the basis of education and examination rather than performance. It is usually permanent, but a periodic fee, demonstration of competence, or continuing education may be required. Licensure may be revoked by the granting agency for incompetence, criminal acts, or other reasons stipulated in the rules governing the specific area of licensure.

lie detector • An electronic device or instrument used to detect lying or anxiety in regard to specific questions. A commonly used lie detector is the polygraph recorder, which senses and records pulse, respiratory rate, blood pressure, and perspiration. Some experts hold that certain patterns indicate the presence of anxiety, guilt, or fear, emotions that are likely to occur when the subject is lying.

litigant • A party to a lawsuit. See also **defendant, plaintiff.**

litigate • To carry on a suit or to contest.

living will • A witnessed document indicating a patient's desire to be allowed to die a natural death, rather than be kept alive by heroic, life-sustaining measures.

locality rule • Allowance made, when considering evidence in a trial, for the type of community, and its standards, in which the defendant practices his profession.

LPN • *abbr* **licensed practical nurse.**

LVN • *abbr* **licensed vocational nurse.** See **licensed practical nurse.**

M

malfeasance • Performance of an unlawful, wrongful act. Compare **misfeasance, nonfeasance.**

malpractice • A professional person's wrongful conduct, improper discharge of professional duties, or failure to meet standards of care, which results in harm to another person.

mandatory bargaining issues • Issues such as wages and working conditions that an employer must address during collective bargaining.

master's degree program in nursing • A postgraduate program in a school of nursing, based in a university setting, that grants the degree Master of Science in Nursing (MSN) to successful candidates. Nurses with this degree often work in leadership roles in clinical nursing, as consultants in various settings, and in faculty positions in schools of nursing. Some programs also prepare the nurse to function as a nurse-practitioner in a specific specialty.

MD • *abbr* **Doctor of Medicine.** See **physician.**

Medicaid • A federally funded, state-operated program of medical assistance to people with low incomes; authorized by the Social Security Act.

medical record • A written, legal record of every aspect of the patient's care.

medical release form • The form an institution asks a patient to sign when he refuses a particular medical treatment. The form protects both the institution and the health-care professional from liability if the patient's condition worsens because of his refusal.

medical staff • All doctors, nurses, and health professionals responsible for providing health care in a hospital or other health-care facility. Medical staff personnel may be full-time or part-time, employed by the facility, or simply affiliated—that is, not employees.

Medicare • Federally funded national health insurance authorized by the Social Security Act for certain persons age 65 or older.

medicolegal • Of or pertaining to both medicine and law. Medicolegal considerations are a significant part of the process of making many patient-care decisions and in determining definitions and policies regarding the treatment of mentally incompetent people and minors, the performance of sterilization or therapeutic abortion, and the care of terminally ill patients. Medicolegal considerations, decisions, definitions, and policies provide the framework for informed consent, professional liability, and many other aspects of health-care practice.

mental status examination • A diagnostic procedure for determining the mental status of a person. The trained interviewer poses certain questions in a carefully standardized manner and evaluates the verbal responses and behavioral reactions.

midwife • **1.** In traditional use: a person who assists women in childbirth. **2.** According to the International Confederation of Midwives, World Health Organization, and Federation of International Gynecologists and Obstetricians,

"a person who, having been regularly admitted to a midwifery educational program fully recognized in the country in which it is located, has successfully completed the prescribed course of studies in midwifery and has acquired the requisite qualifications to be registered and/or legally licensed to practice midwifery." Among the responsibilities of the midwife are supervision of pregnancy, labor, delivery, and puerperium. The midwife conducts the delivery independently, cares for the newborn, procures medical assistance when necessary, executes emergency measures as required, and may practice in a hospital, clinic, maternity home, or in a woman's home. **3.** A lay-midwife. **4.** A nurse-midwife or Certified Nurse-Midwife.

minor • A person not of legal age; beneath the age of majority. Minors usually cannot consent to their own medical treatment unless they are substantially independent from their parents, are married, support themselves, or satisfy other requirements as provided by statute.

misdemeanor • An offense that is considered less serious than a felony and carries with it a lesser penalty, usually a fine or imprisonment for less than 1 year.

misfeasance • An improper performance of a lawful act, especially in a way that might cause damage or injury. Compare **malfeasance.**

MSN • *abbr* **Master of Science in Nursing.** See **master's degree program in nursing.**

N

National League for Nursing (NLN) • An organization concerned with the improvement of nursing education, nursing service, and the delivery of health care in the United States. Among its many activities are accreditation of nursing programs at all levels, preadmission and achievement tests for nursing students, and compilation of statistical data on nursing manpower and on trends in health-care delivery. It acts as the testing service for the State Board Test Pool Examinations for registered and practical nurse licensure.

negligence • failure to act as an ordinary prudent person; conduct contrary to that of a reasonable person under similar circumstances.

negligent nondisclosure • The failure to completely inform a patient about his treatment.

negotiation • A meeting where an employer and employees confer, discuss, and bargain to reach an agreement.

NLN • *abbr* **National League for Nursing.**

no-code order • A note, written in the patient record and signed by a doctor, instructing staff not to attempt to resuscitate a terminally ill patient if he suffers cardiac or respiratory failure.

nonfeasance • A failure to perform a task, duty, or undertaking that one has agreed to perform or that one had a legal duty to perform. Compare **malfeasance, misfeasance.**

nurse • **1.** A person educated and licensed in the practice of nursing. The practice of the nurse includes data collection, diagnosis, planning, treatment, and evaluation within the framework of the nurse's singular concern with the person's response to the problem, rather than to the problem itself. The nurse acts to promote, maintain, or restore the health of the person; wellness is the goal. The nurse may be a generalist or a specialist and, as a professional, is ethically and legally accountable for the nursing activities performed and for the actions of others to whom the nurse has delegated responsibility. **2.** To provide nursing care. See also **five-step nursing process, nursing, registered nurse. 3.** To breast-feed an infant.

nurse anesthetist • A registered nurse qualified by advanced training in an accredited program in the specialty of nurse anesthetist to manage the anesthetic care of the patient in certain surgical situations.

nurse clinician • A nurse who is prepared to identify and diagnose problems of clients by using the expanded knowledge and skills gained by advanced study in a specific area

of nursing practice. The specialist may function independently within standing orders or protocols and collaborates with associates to implement a plan of care that is focused on the client.

nurse practice act • A law enacted by a state's legislature outlining the legal scope of nursing practice within that state.

nurse practitioner • A nurse who, by advanced training and clinical experience in a branch of nursing (as in a master's degree program in nursing) has acquired expert knowledge in a specialized branch of practice.

nurse's aide • A person who is employed to carry out basic nonspecialized tasks in the care of a patient, such as bathing and feeding, making beds, and transporting patients.

nurses' notes • A means of documenting the care the nurse provides and the patient's response to that care; a legal document that can be submitted as admissible evidence in a court of law.

nurse's registry • An employment agency or listing service for nurses who wish to work in a specific area of nursing, usually for a short period of time or on a per diem basis.

nursing • **1.** The professional practice of a nurse. **2.** The process of acting as a nurse, of providing care that encourages and promotes the health of the person being served. **3.** Breast-feeding an infant. See also **nurse.**

nursing administrator • A nurse who's responsible for overseeing the efficient management of nursing services.

nursing assessment • The first step of the nursing process, which involves the systematic collection of information about the patient from multiple sources, including the history, physical examination, and laboratory findings. This information is analyzed and the nurse formulates inferences or impressions about the patient's needs or problems.

nursing assistant • Canada. A person trained in basic nursing techniques and direct patient care who practices under the supervision of a registered nurse.

nursing audit • A thorough investigation designed to identify, examine, or verify the performance of certain specified aspects of nursing care using established criteria. A concurrent nursing audit is performed during ongoing nursing care. A retrospective nursing audit is performed after discharge from the care facility, using the patient's record. Often, a nursing audit and a medical audit are performed collaboratively, resulting in a joint audit.

nursing-care plan • A plan that is based on a nursing assessment and a nursing diagnosis, devised by a nurse. It has four essential components: the identification of the nursing-care problems and a statement of the nursing approach to solve those problems; the statement of the expected benefit to the patient; the statement of the specific actions taken by the nurse that reflect the nursing approach and the achievement of the goals specified; and the evaluation of the patient's response to nursing care and the readjustment of that care as required. See also **nursing assessment.**

nursing diagnosis • Descriptive interpretations—accepted by the National Group on the Classification of Nursing Diagnosis—of collected and categorized information indicating the problems or needs of a patient that nursing care can affect.

nursing home • See **extended-care facility.**

nursing process • An organizational framework for nursing practice, encompassing all the major steps a nurse takes when caring for a patient. These steps are assessment, planning, implementation, and evaluation.

nursing skills • The cognitive, affective, and psychomotor abilities a nurse uses in delivering nursing care.

nursing specialty • A nurse's particular professional field of practice, such as surgical, pediatric, obstetric, or psychiatric nursing. Compare **subspecialty.**

O

ombudsman • A person who investigates complaints, reports findings, and helps to achieve equitable settlements.

open shop • A place of employment where employees may choose whether or not to join a union.

ordinary negligence • The inadvertent omission of that care which a reasonably prudent nurse would ordinarily provide under similar circumstances.

P

patient • 1. A health-care recipient who is ill or hospitalized. **2.** A client in a health-care service.

patient classification systems • Ways of grouping patients so that the size of the staff needed to care for them can be estimated accurately.

patient overload/staffing shortage • The situation that occurs when the number of patients exceeds an institution's medical, nursing, and support-staff resources to care for them properly.

patient record • A collection of documents that provides a record of each time a person visited or sought treatment and received care or a referral for care from a health-care facility. This confidential record is usually held by the facility, and the information in it is released only to the person or with the person's written permission. It contains the initial assessment, health history, laboratory reports, and notes by nurses, physicians, and consultants, as well as order sheets, medication sheets, admission records, discharge summaries, and other pertinent data. A problem-oriented medical record also contains a master problem list. The patient record is often a collection of papers held in a folder, but, increasingly, hospitals are computerizing the records after every discharge, making the past record available on visual display terminals. Also called chart (informal).

patient's bill of rights • A list of patients' rights. The American Hospital Association, health-care institutions, and various medical, nursing, and consumer organizations have prepared such lists, which, in some states, have become law.

pediatric nurse practitioner (PNP) • A nurse practitioner who, by advanced study and clinical practice, has gained expert knowledge in the nursing care of infants and children.

physician • **1.** A health professional who has earned a degree of Doctor of Medicine (MD) after completion of an approved course of study at an approved medical school and satisfactory completion of National Board Examinations. **2.** A health professional who has earned a degree of Doctor of Osteopathy (DO) by satisfactorily completing a course of education in an approved college of osteopathy.

physician's assistant (PA) • A person trained in certain aspects of the practice of medicine to provide assistance to a physician. A physician's assistant is trained by physicians and practices under the direction and supervision and within the legal license of a physician. Training programs vary in length from a few months to 2 years. Health-care experience or academic preparation may be a prerequisite to admission to some programs. Most physician's assistants are prepared for the practice of primary care, but some practice subspecialties, including surgical assisting, dialysis, or radiology. National certification is available to qualified graduates of approved training programs. The national organization is the American Association of Physician's Assistants (AAPA). Also called **physician's associate.**

physician's associate • See **physician's assistant.**

plaintiff • A person who files a civil lawsuit initiating a legal action. In criminal actions, the prosecution is the plaintiff, acting in behalf of the people of the jurisdiction.

PNP • *abbr* **pediatric nurse practitioner.**

policy defense • Reasons given by professional liability insurance carriers to deny coverage when a client submits a claim. Reasons for denial may include failure to pay a premium on time and failure to renew the policy.

practicing medicine without a license • Practicing activities defined under state law in the medical practice act without physician supervision, direction, or control.

practitioner • A person qualified to practice in a special professional field, such as a nurse practitioner.

privileged communication • A conversation in which the speaker intends the information he's giving to remain private between himself and the listener.

privilege doctrine • A doctrine that protects the privacy of persons within a fiduciary relationship, such as a husband and wife, a doctor and patient, or a nurse and patient. During legal proceedings, a court can't force either party to reveal communication that occurred between them unless the party who'd benefit from the protection agrees to it.

problem-oriented medical record • A record-keeping system in which all members of the health-care team combine their information in a special format that goes by the acronym SOAP. Each note combines Subjective data, Objective data, Assessment and Plan. Also, the patient's active and inactive problems are documented on a master problem list.

problem patient • A label sometimes applied to a patient on the basis of his inadequate coping capabilities, which lead to inappropriate behaviors that his nurses find irritating and frustrating.

pro-choice • The philosophy that a woman has the right to choose either to continue or to terminate her pregnancy.

professional corporation (PC) • A corporation formed according to the law of a particular state for the purpose of delivering a professional service.

professional liability • A legal concept describing the obligation of a professional person to pay a patient or client for damages caused by the professional's act of omission, commission, or negligence. Professional liability better describes the responsibility of all professionals to their clients than does the concept of malpractice, but the idea of professional liability is central to malpractice.

professional liability insurance • A type of liability insurance that protects professional persons against malpractice claims made against them.

professional nursing • That level of nursing practice which, according to the American Nurses' Association's entry-level requirement proposal, would require a bachelor's degree.

professional organization • An organization created to deal with issues of concern to its members, who share a professional status.

pro-life • The philosophy that the unborn fetus has the right to develop to term and to be born.

proprietary hospital • A hospital operated as a profit-making organization. Many are owned and operated by physicians primarily for their own patients, but they also accept patients from other physicians. Others are owned by investor groups or large corporations.

Provincial Territorial Nurses' Association (PTNA) • An association of nurses organized at the provincial or territorial level. The Canadian Nurses' Association is a federation of the 11 PTNAs.

proximate cause • A legal concept of cause and effect, which says a sequence of natural and continuous events produces an injury that wouldn't have otherwise occurred.

psychiatric nurse practitioner • A nurse practitioner who, by advanced study and clinical practice, has gained expert knowledge in the care and prevention of mental disorders.

Q

qualified privilege • A conditional right or immunity granted to the defendant because of the circumstances of a legal case.

quality of life • A legal and ethical standard that's determined by relative suffering or pain, not by the degree of disability.

R

RCP • *abbr* Royal College of Physicians.

RCPSC • *abbr* Royal College of Physicians and Surgeons of Canada.

RCS • *abbr* Royal College of Surgeons.

reasonably prudent nurse • The standard a court uses to judge whether another nurse would have acted similarly to the defendant under similar circumstances.

Red Cross • 1. See **International Red Cross Society. 2.** See **American Red Cross.**

registered nurse (RN) • 1. United States A professional nurse who has completed a course of study at a school of nursing accredited by the National League for Nursing and who has taken and passed the State Board Test Pool Examination. A registered nurse may use the initials RN following her signature. RNs are licensed to practice by individual states. **2. Canada** A professional nurse who has completed a course of study at an approved school of nursing and who has taken and passed an examination administered by the Canadian Nurses' Association Testing Service. See also **nurse, nursing.**

registry • 1. An office or agency in which lists of nurses and records pertaining to nurses seeking employment are maintained. **2.** In epidemiology: a listing service for incidence data pertaining to the occurrence of specific diseases or disorders, as a tumor registry.

res ipsa loquitur • "The thing speaks for itself." A legal doctrine that applies when the defendant was solely and exclusively in control at the time the plaintiff's injury occurred, so that the injury would not have occurred if the defendant had exercised due care. When a court applies this doctrine to a case, the defendant bears the burden of proving that he wasn't negligent.

respondeat superior • "Let the master answer." A legal doctrine that makes an employer liable for the consequences of his employee's wrongful conduct while the employee is acting within the scope of his employment.

resuscitative life-support measures • Actions taken to reverse an immediate, life-threatening situation (for example, cardiopulmonary resuscitation).

review committee • A group of individuals delegated to inspect and report on the quality of health care in a given institution.

right-of-conscience laws • A legal equivalent to freedom of thought or of religion.

right-to-access laws • Laws that grant a patient the right to see his medical records.

right-to-die law • A law that upholds a patient's right to choose death by refusing extraordinary treatment when the patient has no hope of recovery. Also referred to as a natural death law or living-will law.

RN • *abbr* **registered nurse.**

Royal College of Physicians (RCP) • A professional organization of physicians in the United Kingdom.

Royal College of Physicians and Surgeons of Canada (RCPSC) • A national Canadian organization that recognizes and confers membership on certain qualified physicians and surgeons.

Royal College of Surgeons (RCS) • A professional organization of surgeons in the United Kingdom.

S

School Nurse Practitioner (SNP) • A registered nurse qualified by postgraduate study to act as a nurse practitioner in a school.

scope of practice • In nursing, the professional nursing activities defined under state or provincial law in each state's (or Canadian province's) nurse practice act.

service of process • The delivery of a writ, summons, or complaint to a defendant. The original of the document is shown; a copy is served. Service of process gives reasonable notice to allow the person to appear, testify, and be heard in court.

settlement • An agreement made between parties to a suit before a judgment is rendered by a court.

signature code • A code of letters and/or numbers that are entered into the computer to identify the user.

skilled nursing facility (SNF) • An institution or part of an institution that meets criteria for accreditation established by the sections of the Social Security Act that determine the basis for Medicaid and Medicare reimbursement for skilled nursing care, including rehabilitation and various medical and nursing procedures.

slow-code order • A verbal or implicit order from a doctor instructing staff to refrain from resuscitating a terminally ill patient after apparent death, until a point is reached when CPR is unlikely to be successful. An illegal order.

SNF • *abbr* **skilled nursing facility.**

SOAP • An acronym for the format used in problem-oriented record keeping; it represents: Subjective data, Objective data, Assessment data, and Plans.

socialized medicine • A system for the delivery of health care in which the expense of care is borne by the government.

source-oriented records • A record-keeping system in which each professional group within the health-care team keeps separate information on the patient.

specialization • Concentration in a specific branch of nursing, or in a particular clinical area, through focused work experience or formal education, or both.

staff • **1.** The people who work toward a common goal and are employed or supervised by someone of higher rank, as the nurses in a hospital. **2.** A designation by which a staff nurse is distinguished from a head nurse or other nurse. **3.** In nursing education: the non-professional employees of the institution, as librarians, technicians, secretaries, and clerks. **4.** In nursing service administration: the units of the organization that provide service to the 'line,' or administratively defined hierarchy, as the personnel office is 'staff' to the director of nursing and the nursing service administration.

staffing pattern • In hospital or nursing administration: the number and kinds of staff assigned to the particular units and departments of a hospital. Staffing patterns vary with the unit, department, and shift.

standard • **1.** A criterion that serves as a basis for comparison for evaluating similar phenomena or substances, as a standard for the practice of a profession. **2.** A pharmaceutical preparation or a chemical substance of known quantity, ingredients, and strength that is used to determine the constituents or the strength of another preparation. **3.** Of known value, strength, quality, or ingredients.

standard death certificate • A form for a death certificate commonly used throughout the United States. It is the preferred form of the United States Census Bureau.

standards of care • In a malpractice lawsuit, those acts performed or omitted that an ordinary, prudent person, in the defendant's position, would have done or not done; a measure by which the defendant's alleged wrongful conduct is compared.

standing orders • A written document containing rules, policies, procedures, regulations, and orders for the conduct of patient care in various stipulated clinical situations. The standing orders are usually formulated collectively by the professional members of a department in a hospital or other health-care facility.

State Board Test Pool Examination • An examination prepared by the National Council of State Boards of Nursing for testing the competency of a person to perform as a newly licensed registered nurse. Each jurisdiction within the United States and its territories reg-ulates entry into the nursing practice; each requires the candidate to pass the examination. The content is planned to test the candidate's knowledge of the nursing process as applied to the broad areas of nursing practice, including maternal and child health, medical and surgical nursing, and psychiatric nursing. The process includes five steps: assessing, analyzing, planning, implementing, and evaluating. Knowledge, comprehension, application, and analysis of the nursing process are tested as they apply to decision-making situations.

state of emergency • A widespread need for immediate action to counter a threat to the community.

statutes of limitations • Laws that specify the length of time within which a person may file specific types of lawsuits.

statutory law • A law passed by a federal or state legislature.

statutory rape • Sexual intercourse with a female below the age of consent, which varies from state to state.

steward • A union representative.

subspecialty • A professional and highly specialized field of practice, as nursing in dialysis, or neurology. Compare **specialization.**

substantive laws • Laws that define and regulate a person's rights.

substitute consent • Permission obtained from a parent or legal guardian of a patient who's a minor or who has been declared incompetent by the court.

substitute judgment • A legal term indicating the court's substitution of its own judgment for that of a person the court considers unable to make an informed decision, such as an incompetent adult.

summary judgment • A judgment requested by any party to a civil action to end the action when it is believed that there is no genuine issue or material fact in dispute.

summons • A document issued by a clerk of the court upon the filing of a complaint. A sheriff, marshal, or other appointed person serves the summons, notifying a person that an action has been begun against him. See also **service of process.**

support group • People whom a person confides in and draws on for support, either as individuals or in a group setting.

T

terminate • To fulfill all contractual obligations or to absolve oneself of the obligation to fulfill them.

termination process • The procedure an employer follows to fire an employee.

testamentary • Any document, such as a will, which doesn't take effect until after the death of the person who wrote it.

therapeutic abortion • Induced termination of pregnancy to preserve the health, safety, or life of the woman.

therapeutic privilege • A legal doctrine that permits a doctor, in an emergency situation, to withhold information from the patient if he can prove that disclosing it would adversely affect the patient's health.

third-party reimbursement • Reimbursement for services rendered to a person in which an entity other than the giver or receiver of the service is responsible for the payment. Third-party reimbursement for the cost of a subscriber's health care is commonly paid by insurance plans.

time charting • A method of charting in which you detail at regular time intervals—for example, every ½ hour—the care administered to a patient at that particular time.

tort • A private or civil wrong outside of a contractual relationship.

traditional staffing patterns • Work schedules that follow 8-hour shifts, 7 days a week, including evening and night shifts.

U

unfair labor practices • Tactics used by the employer or union that are prohibited by state and federal labor laws.

Uniform Anatomical Gift Act • A law, in all 50 states, that allows anyone over age 18 to sign a donor card, willing some or all of his organs after death.

union shop • A place of employment where employees must join a union.

United States Public Health Service (USPHS) • An agency of the federal government responsible for the control of the arrival from abroad of any people, goods, or substances that may affect the health of U.S. citizens. The agency sets standards for the domestic handling and processing of food and the manufacture of serums, vaccines, cosmetics, and drugs. It supports and performs research, aids localities in times of disaster and epidemics, and provides medical care for certain groups of Americans.

V

verbal order • An order given directly and in person by a doctor to a nurse.

voluntary bargaining issues • Issues such as noneconomic fringe benefits that an employer or union may or may not address during collective bargaining.

W

workmen's compensation • Insurance that reimburses an employer for damages he's required to pay when an employee is injured on the job.

writ of habeas corpus • A constitutional right to a court hearing that any person has when imprisoned or detained for allegedly breaking the law.

wrongful death statute • A statute existing in all states that provides that the death of a person can give rise to a cause of legal action brought by the person's beneficiaries in a civil suit against the person whose willful or negligent acts caused the death. Prior to the existence of these statutes, a suit could be brought only if the injured person survived the injury.

wrongful life action • A civil suit usually brought against a physician or health facility on the basis of negligence that resulted in the wrongful birth or life of an infant. The parents of the unwanted child seek to obtain payment from the defendant for the medical expenses of pregnancy and delivery, for pain and suffering, and for the education and upbringing of the child. Wrongful life actions have been brought and won in several situations, including malpracticed tubal ligations, vasectomies, and abortions. Failure to diagnose pregnancy in time for abortion and incorrect medical advice leading to the birth of a defective child have also led to malpractice suits for a wrongful life.

Indexes

Court-Case Citation Index

Horton v. Niagara Falls Memorial Center, 380 N.Y.S. 2d 116 (App. Div. 1976), pp. 50, 100

Hunt v. Palm Springs General Hospital, 352 So. 2d 582 (Fla. Dist. Ct. App. 1977), pp. 96, 110

Hunter v. Hunter, 65 O.L.R. 586 (1930), p. 91

J

Jefferson v. Griffin Spalding County Hospital Authority, 247 Ga. 86; 247 S.E. 2d 457 (1981), p. 79

Johnston v. Black Co., 33 Cal. App. 2d 363; 91 P. 2d (1939), p. 54

Jones v. Hawkes Hospital, 175 Ohio St. 503; 196 N.E. 2d 592 (1964), p. 20

Joseph Brant Memorial Hospital v. Koziol, 2 CCLT 170 (S.C.C. 1978), pp. 188-189

K

Kambas v. St. Joseph's Mercy Hospital, 189 N.W. 2d 879 (1971); rev'd, 205 N.W. 2d 431 (Mich. 1973), p. 220

Kansas State Board of Nursing v. Burkman, 531 P. 2d 122 (Kan. 1975), p. 23

Katz v. United States, 389 U.S. 347 (1967), p. 78

Kinikin v. Heupel, 305 N.W. 2d 589 (Minn. 1981), p. 65

Kolakowski v. Voris, 395 N.E. 2d 6 (Ill. App. Ct. 1979), p. 207

Kyslinger v. United States, 406 F. Supp. 800 (W.D. Pa. 1975), p. 124

L

Laidlaw v. Lions Gate Hospital, [1969] 70 W.W.R. 727 (B.C. 1969), pp. 110-111

LaMade v. Wilson, 512 F. 2d 1348 (D.C. Cir. 1975), p. 120

Lane v. Candura, 376 N.E. 2d 1232 (Mass. App. Ct. 1978), pp. 76, 146-147

Larrimore v. Homeopathic Hospital Association, 176 A. 2d 362; aff'd, 181 A. 2d 573 (Del. 1962), p. 21

Leib v. Board of Examiners for Nursing, 411 A. 2d 42 (Conn. 1979), p. 28

Lopez v. Swyer, 279 A. 2d 116 (N.J. Super. Ct. App. Div. 1971), p. 217

Los Angeles New Hospital, 244 N.L.R.B. 960 (1979); enforced, 640 F. 2d 1017 (9th Cir. 1981), p. 243

Lott v. State, 225 N.Y.S. 2d 434 (1962), p. 90

Lovato v. Colorado, 601 P. 2d 1072 (1979), pp. 89-90

M

Mapp v. Ohio, 367 U.S. 643 (1961), p. 144

Marcus v. Frankford Hospital, 445 Pa. 206; 283 A. 2d 69 (1971), p. 173

Masdev v. Harrison, Mass. Sup. Ct. Equity No. 6851, June 12, 1957, p. 263

Maslonka v. Hermann, 414 A. 2d 1350 (N.J. Super. Ct. App. Div 1980), pp. 184-185

May v. Broun, 492 P. 2d 776 (Or. 1972), p. 117

McCarl v. State Board of Nurse Examiners, 396 A. 2d 866 (Pa. Commw. 1979), p. 13

McCormick v. Avret, 154 Ga. App. 178; 267 S.E. 2d 759 (1980), p. 232

McCutchon v. Mutual of Omaha Insurance Co., 354 So. 2d 759 (La. Ct. App. 1978), p. 59

McIntosh v. Milano, 168 N.J. Super. 466 (1979), p. 82

McKinney v. Tromly, 386 S.W. 2d 564 (Tex. Civ. App. 1964), p. 41

In re Melideo, 88 Misc. 2d 974; 390 N.Y.S. 2d 523 (Sup. Ct. 1976), p. 79

Melville v. Sabbatino, 30 Conn. Supp. 320 (1973), p. 133

Mercy Hospitals of Sacramento, Inc., 217 N.L.R.B. 765 (1975), p. 243

Methodist Hospital v. Ball, 50 Tenn. App. 460; 362 S.W. 2d 475 (1961), p. 111

Misericordia Hospital Medical Center v. N.L.R.B., 623 F. 2d 808 (2nd. Cir. 1980), pp. 102-103

Mohr v. Jenkins, 393 So. 2d 245 (La. Ct. App. 1980), p. 40

Mohr v. Williams, 95 Minn. 261; 104 N.W. 12 (1905), p. 65

Moore v. Guthrie Hospital, 403 F. 2d 366 (4th Cir. 1968), p. 119

Morgan v. Schlanger, 374 F. 2d 235 (4th Cir. 1967), p. 221

Re Mount Sinai Hospital and Ontario Nurses Association, 17 L.A.C. (2d) 242 (1978), pp. 101-102

N

Natanson v. Kline, 350 P. 2d 1093 (Kan. 1960), p. 65

N.L.R.B. v. Baptist Hospital, 442 U.S. 773 (1979), p. 243

Norton v. Argonaut Insurance Co., 144 So. 2d 249 (La. Ct. App. 1962), pp. 21, 100, 119, 204

N.Y.C. Health and Hospitals Corporation v. Sulsona, 367 N.Y.S. 2d 686 (1975), p. 89

N.Y. State Association for Retarded Children, Inc. v. Carey, 438 F. Supp. 440 (E.D. N.Y. 1977), pp. 142, 143

O

O'Connor v. Donaldson, 422 U.S. 563 (1975), pp. 140, 142

Oliff v. Florida State Board of Nursing, 374 So. 2d 1054 (Fla. Dist. Ct. App. 1979), p. 23

O'Neill v. Montefiore Hospital, 11 A.D. 2d 132; 202 N.Y.S. 2d 436 (1960), p. 95

In re Osborne, 294 A. 2d 372 (D.C. 1972), pp. 74, 258

P

Parham v. J.R., 442 U.S. 584 (1979), p. 133

People v. Doe, 96 Misc. 2d 975; 410 N.Y.S. 2d 233 (1978), p. 80

People v. Kraft, 3 Cal. App. 3rd 890 (1970), p. 145

Piehl v. Dallas General Hospital, 571 P. 2d 149 (Or. 1977), p. 206

Pisel v. Stamford Community Hospital, 180 Conn. 314 (1980), p. 20

Planned Parenthood of Central Missouri v. Danforth, 428 U.S. 52 (1976), pp. 79, 132, 265

Pounders v. Trinity Court Nursing Home, 576 S.W. 2d 934 (Ark. 1979), pp. 87-88

Powell v. Columbian Presbyterian Medical Center, 49 Misc. 2d 215; 267 N.Y.S. 2d 450 (Sup. Ct. 1965), pp. 75-76

Q

In re Quinlan, 137 N.J. Super. 227; 348 A. 2d 801 (Ch. Div. 1975); modified, 70 N.J. 10; 355 A. 2d 647 (1976), pp. 74, 253, 254, 258

R

Ramos v. Lamm, 639 F. 2d 559 (10th Cir. 1980), p. 146

Randal v. California State Board of Pharmacy, 49 Cal. Rptr. 485 (1966), p. 118

Richardson v. Brunelle, 398 A. 2d 383 (N.H. 1979), pp. 5, 24

Rochin v. California, 342 U.S. 165 (1952), p. 145

Roe v. Wade, 410 U.S. 113 (1973), pp. 78, 79, 264, 265, 268

General Index

353

LPNs/LVNs, 122; elements of, 4-5, 12-14; exemptions for emergency care, 177; and health-care advice, 172; interpretation, problems of, 12-14; and license denial, revocation, or suspension, grounds for, *32-39;* licensure qualifications and, 5, *6-11;* misdemeanors listed in, 292-301; and nurse practitioner role, 44; origin, 1-2, *2,* 5; state boards of nursing and, 4-5; violations, 25; and work in special-care units, 106-107, 111

Nurse practitioner, 41-47; certification requirements, 44; financial concerns of, 46-47; forms of protection for, 45; and hospital privileges, obtaining, 47; job opportunities for, 47; as independent contractor, 46, *46,* 47; legal scope of practice of, 41, 44-45; liability of, in different practice settings, 44-45; medical diagnosis by, 20, 41, 44; professional concerns of, 47; role of, development of, 43-44

Nurse registration acts, 1-2

Nurses' notes: documenting service as witness, 105-106; signing, 186, *196*

Nursing department manual, elements of, 93

Nursing diagnosis: definition, 12; legal status of, 2; vs. medical diagnosis, 5, 12, 20

Nursing law: history, 1-2; landmarks, *2;* permissive vs. mandatory, 1-2

Nursing practice: in alternative (nonhospital) settings, 53-56; boundaries of, defining, *31;* in Canada, 4, 110-111; legal risks in, 92-158, and licensing laws, 21-23; vs. medical practice, 30-31, 40-41, *42-43;* in special-care units, 111; standards, 3

O

Occupational health nurse, *57*

Occurrence rule, in statute of limitations, 220

Off-duty nursing actions, legal risks in, 160-178

Organ donation and transplantation, 259-264; legal issues, 262-264; medical and ethical issues of, 260-262; nurse's role in, 264

Organ donor, and definition of death, 89

P

Parens patriae doctrine, 139
Parents Anonymous, 138

Patient(s): "against medical advice," nurse's responsibility for, 86-88; deceased, nurse's responsibility for, 88-91; lawful detention of, 88; who wants to die, 256-259. *See also specific type of patient.*

Patient care: in geriatric facilities, 49-50, 51-52; standards, 2-3

Patient overload, coping with, 101-102

Patient safety, 111-117; establishing liability for, 116-117; hospital's responsibility for, 115-116; special concerns, 113; in special-care units, *112-113;* standards of care, 112-113

Patient's rights, 61-91; from birth to adulthood, changes in, *75;* after death, 88; for developmentally disabled, 138-144; in geriatric facility, 50, 52; to health-care information, 124-125; to information about case, 61-62, 63, 64, 66, 70, 124; interpretation of, 63-64; to leave hospital, 86-88 (*see also* Patient(s), "against medical advice"); legislation, 2, 62; for mentally ill patient, 70, 138-144; nurse's responsibilities in, 64; to privacy, 78-83, 141, 144 (*see also* Confidentiality of patient information); public support for, 61, 62; to refuse information about case, 70-71; to refuse treatment, 64, 67, 74-78, *79,* 87; of suspected criminal, 144-145, 146; to view medical records, 83-84, 86; to writ of habeas corpus, 141-142. *See also* Bill of rights, patient's.

Patient teaching: benefits, 125; nurse's responsibility for, 122-126; process of, 122; role of LPN in, 125; team approach to, 125-126

Pharmacy practice acts, 118

Physician's assistant, nurse's responsibility to take orders from, 13

Prisoner, detention of, in hospital, 88

Prison hospital nursing, 146-147

Privacy. *See* Patient's rights, to privacy.

Private-duty nurse, 47-49; advantages, 47; financial concerns of, 48; and hospital privileges, obtaining, 48-49; hospital's liability for, 48; as independent contractor, 47, 48; legal risks of, 48-49; referral list, 47-48; responsibilities of, 48; staff nurse working with, 49

Privilege: doctrine, 80, 82, 83; therapeutic, 67

Problem-oriented records, 181

Professional liability insurance, 210-213, 216; applying for, 216; choosing, *209;* company's role in defending nurse charged with malpractice, 212-213; cost of, 211;

Nursing85 Books™

CLINICAL POCKET MANUAL™ SERIES
Diagnostic Tests
Emergency Care
Fluids and Electrolytes
Signs and Symptoms
Cardiovascular Care
Respiratory Care
Critical Care
Neurologic Care
Surgical Care
Medications and I.V.s
Ob/Gyn Care
Pediatric Care

NURSING NOW™ SERIES
Shock
Hypertension
Drug Interactions
Cardiac Crises
Respiratory Emergencies
Pain

NURSE'S CLINICAL LIBRARY™
Cardiovascular Disorders
Respiratory Disorders
Endocrine Disorders
Neurologic Disorders
Renal and Urologic Disorders
Gastrointestinal Disorders
Neoplastic Disorders
Immune Disorders

NURSING PHOTOBOOK™ SERIES
Providing Respiratory Care
Managing I.V. Therapy
Dealing with Emergencies
Giving Medications
Assessing Your Patients
Using Monitors
Providing Early Mobility
Giving Cardiac Care
Performing GI Procedures
Implementing Urologic Procedures
Controlling Infection
Ensuring Intensive Care
Coping with Neurologic Disorders
Caring for Surgical Patients
Working with Orthopedic Patients
Nursing Pediatric Patients
Helping Geriatric Patients
Attending Ob/Gyn Patients
Aiding Ambulatory Patients
Carrying Out Special Procedures

NURSE'S REFERENCE LIBRARY®
Diseases
Diagnostics
Drugs
Assessment
Procedures
Definitions
Practices
Emergencies
Signs and Symptoms

NURSE REVIEW™ SERIES
Cardiac Problems

Nursing85 DRUG HANDBOOK™

PROFESSIONAL TRADE BOOKS
Health Assessment Handbook
MediQuik Cards™
Nurse's Legal Handbook
Cardiovascular Care Handbook
Emergency Care Handbook